INTERNATIONAL NOIR

Traditions in World Cinema

General Editors
Linda Badley (Middle Tennessee State University)
R. Barton Palmer (Clemson University)

Founding Editor
Steven Jay Schneider (New York University)

Titles in the series include:

Traditions in World Cinema
by Linda Badley, R. Barton Palmer and Steven Jay Schneider (eds)

Japanese Horror Cinema
by Jay McRoy (ed.)

New Punk Cinema
by Nicholas Rombes (ed.)

African Filmmaking: North and South of the Sahara
by Roy Armes

Palestinian Cinema: Landscape, Trauma and Memory
by Nurith Gertz

Chinese Martial Arts Cinema: The Wuxia Tradition
by Stephen Teo

Czech and Slovak Cinema: Theme and Tradition
by Peter Hames

The New Neapolitan Cinema
by Alex Marlow-Mann

The International Film Musical
by Corey K. Creekmur and Linda Y. Mokdad (eds)

American Smart Cinema
by Claire Perkins

Italian Neorealist Cinema
by Torunn Haaland

Magic Realist Cinema in East Central Europe
by Aga Skrodzka

Italian Post-neorealist Cinema
by Luca Barattoni

The Spanish Horror Film
by Antonio Lázaro-Reboll

Post-beur Cinema
by Will Higbee

New Taiwanese Cinema in Focus
by Flannery Wilson

Forthcoming titles include:

Films on Ice
by Scott Mackenzie and Anna Westerståhl Stenport

New Romanian Cinema
by Christina Stojanova and Dana Duma

Contemporary Japanese Cinema Since Hana-Bi
by Adam Bingham

Australian International Pictures (1946–75)
by Adrian Danks and Constantine Verevis

Slow Cinema
by Tiago de Luca and Nuno Barradas Jorge

Contemporary Latin American Cinema: New Transnationalisms
by Dolores Tierney

Nordic Genre Film
by Tommy Gustafsson and Pietari Kääpä

The Italian Sword-and-Sandal Film
by Frank Burke

www.euppublishing.com/series/tiwc

INTERNATIONAL NOIR

Edited by Homer B. Pettey and R. Barton Palmer

EDINBURGH
University Press

To Jennifer Jenkins, as always

Edinburgh University Press is one of the leading university presses in the UK. We publish academic books and journals in our selected subject areas across the humanities and social sciences, combining cutting-edge scholarship with high editorial and production values to produce academic works of lasting importance. For more information visit our website: www.edinburghuniversitypress.com

© editorial matter and organisation Homer B. Pettey and R. Barton Palmer, 2014, 2016
© the chapters their several authors, 2014, 2016

Edinburgh University Press Ltd
The Tun – Holyrood Road
12 (2f) Jackson's Entry
Edinburgh EH8 8PJ

First published in hardback by Edinburgh University Press 2014

Typeset in 10/12.5pt Sabon by
Servis Filmsetting Ltd, Stockport, Cheshire

A CIP record for this book is available from the British Library

ISBN 978 0 7486 9110 4 (hardback)
ISBN 978 1 4744 1306 0 (paperback)
ISBN 978 0 7486 9111 1 (webready PDF)
ISBN 978 0 7486 9112 8 (epub)

The right of the contributors to be identified as authors of this work has been asserted in accordance with the Copyright, Designs and Patents Act 1988 and the Copyright and Related Rights Regulations 2003 (SI No. 2498).

CONTENTS

	List of Illustrations	vii
	Acknowledgements	ix
	Notes on the Contributors	xi
	Introduction: The Noir Impulse *Homer B. Pettey*	1
1.	British Noir *Jim Leach*	14
2.	French Noir 1947–79: From Grunge-noir to Noir-hilism *Susan Hayward*	36
3.	French Neo-noir: An Aesthetic for the *Policier* *Maureen Turim*	61
4.	Early Japanese Noir *Homer B. Pettey*	85
5.	The Gunman and the Gun: Japanese Film Noir since the Late 1950s *David Desser*	112
6.	Darker than Dark: Film Noir in its Asian Contexts *Stephen Teo*	136

7.	Nordic Noir and Neo-noir: The Human Criminal *Andrew Nestingen*	155
8.	Indian Film Noir *Corey K. Creekmur*	182
9.	The New Sincerity of Neo-noir *R. Barton Palmer*	193
10.	Post-noir: Getting Back to Business *Mark Bould*	220

Selected Bibliography of International Film Noir	241
Selected Filmography of International Film Noir	246
Index	258

LIST OF ILLUSTRATIONS

Figure I.1	Grace Chang in *The Wild, Wild Rose* (1960)	5
Figure I.2	Rita Hayworth in *Gilda* (1946)	6
Figure I.3	Entrapment within the sewer in *Kanal*	8
Figure 1.1	Diana Dors in *Yield to the Night*	21
Figure 1.2	Dirk Bogarde as a young thug in *The Blue Lamp*	26
Figure 1.3	Information gathering in *The Long Good Friday*	29
Figure 2.1	Paul Meurisse in *Les Diaboliques*	45
Figure 2.2	Charles Aznavour in a Bogartesque trenchcoat in *Le Pianiste*	53
Figure 3.1	Montmartre, with Sacré Cœur silhouetted in the background, above Pigalle from *Bob le flambeur*	63
Figure 3.2	Dancing girls at Santi's in *Le Cercle rouge*	71
Figure 3.3	Nathalie Baye as Nicole handling the cops in *La Balance*	76
Figure 4.1	*Dragnet Girl*	93
Figure 4.2	Mifune's death in *Drunken Angel*	105
Figure 4.3	Conclusion image from *Black River*	108
Figure 5.1	Theatre front in *The Most Terrible Time in My Life*	121
Figure 5.2	Alienated figures of *Rainy Dog*	124
Figure 5.3	Stray Cat from *Pistol Opera*	131
Figure 6.1	Mirroring of black and white forces in *Drug War*	149
Figure 6.2	Rural police, innocent suspect and cultural violence in *Memories of Murder*	151
Figure 7.1	Eva Henning in *Girl with Hyacinths*	161

Figure 7.2	Swedish-style neo-noir, *Easy Money*	170
Figure 7.3	Finnish-style neo-noir, *Lights in the Dusk*	174
Figure 8.1	Dev Anand listens to Geeta Bali play in *Baazi*	186
Figure 9.1	Barber shop in *The Man Who Wasn't There*	206
Figure 9.2	Kathleen Turner	215
Figure 9.3	Marilyn Chambers	216
Figure 10.1	Clive Owen in the Guggenheim Museum in *The International*	229
Figure 10.2	Dark prelude to homicide in *Blind Shaft*	234

ACKNOWLEDGEMENTS

First thanks should always go to the contributors. James Leach undertook the daunting task of conveying the breadth of British noir and produced an exceptional chapter that will long be cited by film scholars. With a joyful and adventurous spirit, Susan Hayward worked out the most thoughtful and substantial conceptual approaches to French noir that certainly benefit all film scholars. Moreover, Susan re-evaluated her initial assumptions and took a decidedly different approach, all the while explaining the complexity of her trenchant analysis, of which I am in awe. Moreover, her new categorisation for French noir will serve as a model for film historians. Maureen Turim opened up new critical insights into the landscape of contemporary French noir and provided this volume with a fascinating thought-piece on those films. Scholars of Japanese noir will always be referring to David Desser's insights on the transformation of contemporary versions of the genre. He has a command of Japanese film that rivals Earl Miner's with Classical Japanese poetics, which constitutes my highest praise. Few critics of international noir have possessed or do possess Stephen Teo's comprehensive overview of the essential elements and complexities of Asian noir. Professor Teo also kindly reviewed the list of Hong Kong and Korean noirs and made significant suggestions and corrections, for which a debt is now owed. Including Nordic noir in this volume was due to Andrew Nestingen's amazing critical work in this burgeoning field; a debt of gratitude must be extended for his provocative discussion of that element of the genre. Professor Nestingen's fine list of Nordic noirs was included in its entirety in the Selected Filmography section, for which gratitude is also given. Corey

Creekmur provided a intriguing interpretation of Indian noir that worked through both global and local variants for the genre and style, while maintaining that Indian noir substantially differs from American and European noirs in terms of narrative of gender relationships and the role of choreography and song as foundational to its national cinema. Mark Bould put all scholars back to work with his exceptionally fine assessment of what constitutes the current and clearly the future extension of noir in the postmodern world. Looking back on this very important collection of essays, my highest praise for the acumen, rigorous scholarship and service to future scholars seems somehow not quite sufficient. As I read their chapters again, I am struck by the elegance of their critical and conceptual approaches. Again, to them, I owe so much, but I do offer my friendship.

Special thanks goes to my co-editor R. Barton Palmer, whose work on neo-noirs will be a ready source for scholars and historians in the field. His open acceptance for the variety of critical approaches to *International Noir* was crucial for allowing these scholars to explore their various viewpoints. Moreover, Barton's sensitivity to editorial issues and his knowledge of film noir have made this project possible. In my estimation, he may well be the last truly Renaissance man in the humanities. His breadth and depth are astonishing and enviable.

As I mentioned in the *Film Noir: Classical Traditions* volume for Edinburgh University Press, close friends outside the academy often contribute more to one's development than they realise or would be willing to admit in a civil suit in court. For remaining partners willing to commit numerous crimes, as well as for providing me with decades of enjoyable camaraderie, I would like to express my sincere thanks, love and admiration to Chip Johannessen and Carter Burwell, both of whom possess a kind of genius that always astonishes us. For years of fruitful, often hilarious discussions about foreign films, I owe a considerable debt to William Johnsen. I will remain fortunate for knowing all of them. For providing me with a venue for my first publications and for commencing life-long friendships, my fondest regards go to the *Harvard Lampoon*, still one of the great American institutions.

Finally, this work could not have been completed without the advice, sound commentary and critiques, and especially the love of Jennifer Jenkins, who reminds me daily that the life of the mind requires a good, sincere heart.

Homer B. Pettey
Tucson, Arizona

NOTES ON THE CONTRIBUTORS

Mark Bould is Reader in Film and Literature at the University of the West of England, and co-editor of *Science Fiction Film and Television*. He is the author of *Film Noir: From Berlin to Sin City* (2005), *The Cinema of John Sayles: Lone Star* (2009) and *Science Fiction* (2012), co-author of *The Routledge Concise History of Science Fiction* (2011), editor of *Africa SF* (2013) and co-editor of *Parietal Games* (2005), *The Routledge Companion to Science Fiction* (2009), *Fifty Key Figures in Science Fiction* (2009), *Red Planets* (2009) and *Neo-Noir* (2009).

Corey K. Creekmur is Associate Professor of English, Film Studies and Gender, Women's and Sexuality Studies at the University of Iowa. He has co-edited three volumes, *Out in Culture: Gay, Lesbian, and Queer Essays on Popular Culture* (1995), *Cinema, Law, and the State in Asia* (2007) and *The International Film Musical* (2012), and has published essays on American cinema, Hindi cinema and comics. He is also General Editor of the Comics Culture series for Rutgers University Press. His forthcoming work includes a study of gender and sexuality in the Western genre, and a volume on the contemporary Hindi historical film.

David Desser is Professor Emeritus of Cinema Studies at the University of Illinois. He is the author of *The Samurai Films of Akira Kurosawa* and *Eros Plus Massacre: An Introduction to the Japanese New Wave Cinema*, the editor of *Ozu's Tokyo Story* and co-editor of *The Cinema of Hong Kong: History, Arts, Identity*; *Reframing Japanese Cinema: Authorship, Genre, History*; and *Cinematic Landscapes: Observations on the Visual Arts of China and Japan*.

He did DVD commentary for the Criterion Edition of *Tokyo Story* and *Seven Samurai*. He is a former editor of *Cinema Journal* and of *The Journal of Japanese and Korean Cinema*.

Susan Hayward is Emeritus Professor at the University of Exeter. She is the author of several books on French cinema (*French National Cinema*; *Luc Besson*; *Simone Signoret: The Star as Cultural Sign*; *Les Diaboliques*; *French Costume Drama of the 1950s: the Fashioning of Politics in Film*) and is also the author of *Cinema Studies: The Key Concepts* (now in its 4th edition). She has written widely on French cinema and her work appears in various anthologies and peer-reviewed journals. Currently she is writing a study of Daniel Gélin and his reception in the French fanzine *Cinémonde*.

Jim Leach is Professor Emeritus at Brock University, Ontario, where he taught in the Department of Communication, Popular Culture and Film. He is the author of books on filmmakers Alain Tanner and Claude Jutra, as well as *British Film* (2004) and *Film in Canada* (2nd edition 2011). He has also published a monograph on *Doctor Who* (2009), co-edited a volume on Canadian documentary films (2003) and developed a Canadian edition of Louis Giannetti's *Understanding Movies* (5th edition 2011).

Andrew Nestingen is professor of Scandinavian Studies and adjunct in cinema studies at the University of Washington, Seattle. His most recent book is *The Cinema of Aki Kaurismäki: Contrarian Stories* (2013). Other books include *Crime and Fantasy in Scandinavia: Fiction, Film, and Social Change* (2008), *Scandinavian Crime Fiction* (2011), co-edited with Paula Arvas, and *Transnational Cinema in a Global North* (2005), co-edited with Trevor Elkington. He is working on a book titled *Violent Fictions: Representations and Rituals*, which deals with Scandinavian and other Euro-American literature and film.

R. Barton Palmer is Calhoun Lemon Professor of Literature at Clemson University, South Carolina, where he also directs the film studies programme. He is the author, editor or co-editor of more than fifty books and a hundred book chapters and journal articles, including two volumes on film noir.

Homer B. Pettey, Associate Professor of Literature and Film, English Department, University of Arizona, has soon-to-be published chapters on Hitchcock's American noirs (Cambridge University Press), Wyatt Earp biopics (State University of New York Press) and violence in noir (Praeger). He has also written essays on Melville and Faulkner, as well as working as a script consultant for several television series.

Stephen Teo is presently Associate Professor in the Wee Kim Wee School of Communication and Information, Nanyang Technological University,

NOTES ON THE CONTRIBUTORS

Singapore. Before joining NTU, he was a research fellow at the Asia Research Institute, National University of Singapore from 2005 to 2008. He is also an adjunct professor of RMIT University, Melbourne, and a senior research fellow of the Asia Research Institute, National University of Singapore. Teo is the author of *Hong Kong Cinema: The Extra Dimensions* (1997), *Wong Kar-wai* (2005), *King Hu's A Touch of Zen* (2007), *Director in Action: Johnnie To and the Hong Kong Action Film* (2007), *Chinese Martial Arts Cinema: The Wuxia Tradition* (2009) and *The Asian Cinema Experience: Styles, Spaces, Theory* (2013).

Maureen Turim is Professor of Film and Media Studies in the Department of English at the University of Florida. She has published three books: *The Films of Oshima Nagisa. Images of a Japanese Iconoclast* (1998); *Flashbacks in Film: Memory and History* (1989); and *Abstraction in Avant-Garde Films* (1985), as well as over ninety essays in journals on theoretical, historical and aesthetic issues in cinema and video, art, cultural studies, feminist and psychoanalyst theory, and comparative literature. *Desire and its Renewal in the Cinema* is the title of her current work.

TRADITIONS IN WORLD CINEMA

General editors: **Linda Badley and R. Barton Palmer**
Founding editor: **Steven Jay Schneider**

Traditions in World Cinema is a series of textbooks and monographs devoted to the analysis of currently popular and previously underexamined or undervalued film movements from around the globe. Also intended for general interest readers, the textbooks in this series offer undergraduate- and graduate-level film students accessible and comprehensive introductions to diverse traditions in world cinema. The monographs open up for advanced academic study more specialised groups of films, including those that require theoretically oriented approaches. Both textbooks and monographs provide thorough examinations of the industrial, cultural and socio-historical conditions of production and reception.

The flagship textbook for the series includes chapters by noted scholars on traditions of acknowledged importance (the French New Wave, German Expressionism), recent and emergent traditions (New Iranian, post-Cinema Novo) and those whose rightful claim to recognition has yet to be established (the Israeli persecution film, global found footage cinema). Other volumes concentrate on individual national, regional or global cinema traditions. As the introductory chapter to each volume makes clear, the films under discussion form a coherent group on the basis of substantive and relatively transparent, if not always obvious, commonalities. These commonalities may be formal, stylistic or thematic, and the groupings may, although they need not, be popularly identified as genres, cycles or movements (Japanese horror, Chinese martial arts cinema, Italian Neorealism). Indeed, in cases in which a group of films is not already commonly identified as a tradition, one purpose of the volume is to establish its claim to importance and make it visible (East Central European Magical Realist cinema, Palestinian cinema).

Textbooks and monographs include:

- An introduction that clarifies the rationale for the grouping of films under examination
- A concise history of the regional, national, or transnational cinema in question
- A summary of previous published work on the tradition
- Contextual analysis of industrial, cultural and socio-historical conditions of production and reception
- Textual analysis of specific and notable films, with clear and judicious application of relevant film theoretical approaches
- One or more bibliographies/filmographies.

Monographs may additionally include:

- Discussion of the dynamics of cross-cultural exchange in light of current research and thinking about cultural imperialism and globalisation, as well as issues of regional/national cinema or political/aesthetic movements (such as new waves, postmodernism or identity politics)
- Interview(s) with key filmmakers working within the tradition.

INTRODUCTION: THE NOIR IMPULSE

Homer B. Pettey

International noir may well be a tautology, since film noir from its inception has always been a culturally diverse genre, style, sensibility and movement. Paul Cooke has argued that Hollywood's global expansion can be explained not only by its 'providing the world with the most appealing film aesthetics and narrative structures', but also more recently by its being 'fiercely protective of its distribution dominance, lobbying for increasing global deregulation during the GATT and subsequent World Trade Organisation talks'.[1] Defining international noir poses similar problems for designation of any type of 'world', 'international' or 'global' cinema. As Rosalind Galt and Karl Schoonover contend for 'art cinema', 'world' suggests 'a fetishistic multiculturalism', while, for them, 'international' tends to be too Eurocentric and too associated with Marxist film history; hence, they choose 'global' as a somewhat problematic alternative.[2] If 'international' noir incites the wrath of peevish theorists, so be it, particularly since noir, in a world and global context, requires an analytic sensitivity to aesthetic and narrative influences migrating across countries and continents. Indigenous cinematic art needs to be acknowledged in its own right, but, as with European and especially American noir, it developed as a result of responses to and absorption and adaptation of other film cultures. International noir invariably entails recategorisation of the history, development and expansion of film noir, as well as investigation of the artistic *impulse* to represent global modernity and its psycho-social anxieties, its political dilemmas and violence, and its challenge to traditional views of gender by means of this pervasive aesthetic.

The late 1950s to the early 1960s were expansive years for international cinema, as can be observed by the example of Wang Tianlin's *The Wild, Wild Rose* (*Yau mooi gwai ji luen*, 1960). This Mandarin Chinese musical film noir concerns a chanteuse seductress (Grace Chang) in Wan Chai, a notorious pleasure district of Hong Kong. As a musical noir, the film already reveals the mixed cultural influences that have created late-twentieth-century global cinema. This admixture of styles, generic formula and cinematic aesthetics, especially in the Cold War era, was certainly due in part to the dominance of Hollywood worldwide. Still, the adaptation of musical styles takes on its own unique Chinese sensibility, and represents a maturing of Hong Kong style from the 1950s. In 1957, Chang created a sensation in *Mambo Girl* (*Man bo nu lang*) with her untamed, unrestrained, obviously liberated 'crazy, crazy, crazy' body rhythms and song styling. Clad in harlequin-patterned cigarette slacks and a tight sweater, Chang's movements are captured in overhead and straight-on shots, granting optimal vantage points for observing her swinging Chinese-style *Mambo*. *Mambo*, in both its expressive song and dance, derives from the Bantu for 'incident, happening, action', as well as 'palaver' and 'story'.[3] Here, *Mambo* is the culmination of released tensions, the narrative of the body in between cultures, as well as geographically in between traditions of mainland China and the new freedom of Hong Kong. While eccentrically teenaged and Westernised, especially in the lengthy concluding dance sequence, *Mambo Girl* still retains themes of Confucian ethics (*lunli*), particularly filial piety, which the narrative of the melodrama finds in the emotional expression of the dance.[4] Significantly, the film and its successor, *The Wild, Wild Rose*, display examples of the modern Chinese woman caught between traditional codes of feminine behaviour and her own desire to express a modern, powerfully unruly sexuality.

The credit sequence opens with Grace Chang in silhouette dancing with a rose between her teeth on a black stage, illuminated by a enormous white rose before a modernist, grey rhomboid backdrop. A spotlight captures her in a strapless sheath as she hurls the rose to the floor, then churns her way down the stage steps, with the title and names appearing in Chinese across each riser. The film narrates the doomed life of the independent, alluring Deng Sijia, a nightclub singer, whose performances mirror her own tempestuous love life. She performs a extraordinary range of enticing musical arrangements, from slow, sultry chanteuse numbers to 1950s jazz to updated, Hong Kong versions of classical opera. Donning a man's cape and hat, she sings '*La donna è mobile*' ('Woman is fickle'), reversing the gender roles from Verdi's *Rigoletto* by taking on the Duke of Mantua's guise. In another number, she dances a spirited, smouldering flamenco in high-contrast lighting; provocatively, the camera captures her *soleà escobillias* tapping pattern in long shots to accentuate her form in tight, high-waisted black matador pants. In a visually obverse number, the camera follows the flouncing Deng Sijia about the chiaroscuro-lit bar as she belts out '*Ja Jambo!*' wearing a tight, light-coloured cocktail dress and shaking maracas with gleeful abandon. Later, smiling, lithely moving about the empty bar in three-four tempo as she sings 'The Merry Widow', Deng Sijia seductively lures Liang Hanhua (Zhang Yang), a classically trained pianist now part of her jazz band, for her own gratification. He wants her to follow a traditional woman's role, but in noir melodramatic fashion, her longing for independence threatens their relationship. Despondent, Hanhua succumbs to alcoholism. Returning to the nightclub scene, Grace Chang auditions dresses in a geisha outfit as *Cio-Cio* for her Mandarin version of '*Un bel di, vedremo*' ('One beautiful day, we will see') from Puccini's *Madama Butterfly*, sung above an oddly compatible Latin jazz accompaniment. The film presents her final numbers as a montage of noir-lit, short sequences of her previous songs and dances. She barely completes her flamenco dance before Hanhua stabs her to death.

All of these scenes from *The Wild, Wild Rose* reveal the emotional, noir impulse to portray sexuality and portending destruction. Still, one moment fully captures the international noir sensibility in its cinematographic energy and experimentation. Those film noir elements accentuate the melodramatic reconfigurations of Bizet's *Carmen* into a sleazy, smoke-filled nightclub, aptly named the *New Ritz*. Deng Sijia provides a soulful, highly sexually suggestive Chinese rendition of the 'Habanera' as she seduces all males with flirtatious, sinuous movements. Backed by a jazz trio of upright bass, bongos and piano, from out of the darkness Deng Sijia begins the number while she plays a metal guitar, which is supported by her fully exposed, black-stockinged leg as she rests her high heel upon a chair. As she strums, she chants the rhyming Chinese phrases that set the tone for her own cynical, *femme fatale* view of romance: '*Ai qing bu guo shi yi zhong pu tong de wan yi yi dian ye bu xi qi / Nan ren bu guo shi yi jian xiao qian de dong xi, you shen mo liao bu qi*' ('Love is just an ordinary thing / that's not special at all / Men are only for fun / Nothing marvellous either'). She moans with obvious sexual anticipation in her refrain before the words 爱 *ai* ('love') and 男人 *nan ren* ('men').

She dances with her legs exposed to the upper thighs, as she sings three times in French '*L'amour*'. Then, in long shots, she moves away from the stage, singing and twirling through the audience, occasionally teasing a male customer. In a medium to close-up sequence, she repeats the opening rhyming phrases, her accent on 'love' and 'men' now becoming a throaty, orgasmic 'ah' as her arms move erotically up her body until she throws them over her head, as though she were sexually climaxing. The number shifts from quasi-operatic to late 1950s style jazz mambo. The 'cha-cha' style of the era was considered exceptionally sexualised and wild. As the camera focuses on her swaying buttocks in her tight dress, she moves in on her next conquest, the already engaged Liang Hanhua. The 'Habanera' concludes with Chang's erotic, powerful feminine silhouette in pure noir lighting.

No fewer than four continents contribute to this exhilarating number: North America with the film noir elements; South America with the 'cha cha' and mambo rhythms; Europe with the stylistic influence of opera and the chanteuse heritage; and Asia itself with its cinematic redefining of noir. Africa can be included among these global influences in terms of the source for Caribbean mambo tempos. Chang's performance recalls the numerous nightclub scenes of American noir, such as the uncredited Chinese dancer in the Coconut Beach Club number from *Murder, My Sweet* (1944) and, most apparently, Rita Hayworth's 'Put the Blame on Mame' in *Gilda* (1946). Hayworth's self-assured dancing style derives from her background with her parents' Spanish troupe, which she adapted into the Latin American style so popular in the 1940s in the United States. Unlike objects of fixation sexualised by the male gaze, Hayworth's dancing celebrates her sexuality as *Gilda* calls into question 'notions of masculinity and normality'.[5] Hayworth's overt sexuality, like Chang's feminine power, is calculated and controlled, not just for the audience in their nightclubs, but also for the camera. As Melvyn Stokes points out, Hayworth's brazen dance, nearly a striptease movement, confirms her ability to mesmerise the audience at least four times:

> But there are four occasions in the sequence when she looks directly into the camera: while she sings 'That brought on the "Frisco quake"' (five seconds), twice while rolling off her glove (three seconds and four seconds) and while she moves towards the camera and back.[6]

Chang has four moments of seduction with the camera as well: when she first moans 'love' and 'men'; in her almost animalistic growl with the second moans before 'love' and 'men', at both times eyeing the nightclub denizens and then the camera; as she approaches Hanhua for her first moment of seduction; and as she concludes with her warning to all 'If I fall in love with you...'. Unlike Hayworth's transformation in *Gilda* from retaliatory bad-girl into Hollywood musical good-girl, Chang's Wild Rose does not find reconciliation, but rather endures the deadly fate of love and affection that she warns against in her 'Habanera'.[7] Where Gilda's dance attempts to bare all, Deng Sijia's performance indicates that she bears all.

Grace Chang even outpaces in energy and eroticism the frenetic Shizuko Kasagi's 'Jungle Boogie' enticement in the *yakuza* dance hall scene from Kurosawa's *Drunken Angel* (1948). Chang's numbers also recall Raymond Bernard's *Faubourg-Montmartre* (1931), with Odette Barencey singing a song about prostitutes along the street:

Et y a des mômes	And there are kids
Comm' des fantômes	Like ghosts

INTRODUCTION: THE NOIR IMPULSE

Qui déambulent sur le trottoir,	Who pace up and down the sidewalk
Au crépuscule,	At twilight,
Cherchant chaqu' soir	Looking each evening for
Un idiot d'homme	An idiot of a man
Offrant un' somme pour s'entendr'	Offering a sum to hear some
dir' des mots d'amour.	Words of love.[8]

Faubourg-Montmartre captures the 'seedy milieu' of pimps and whores with the 'somber influence of German visual design', placing it among early Expressionist experiments.[9] This song becomes, as with most numbers in American noir, part of the urban sonic-scape that defines modernity.[10]

Cultural politics certainly play a role in the noir impulse that conveys the emotional turmoil of the Cold War era. In 1946, Columbia publicised *Gilda* as a film aimed at the political unease about the reconfiguration of the postwar world, by relying upon 'the fantasy and nightmare of a war-related psyche' and the shift from 'wartime espionage to cold war paranoia'; the campaign even included an atomic blast to emphasise the potency of *Gilda*.[11] The Hundred Flowers Campaign, a pogrom by Mao Zedong to crack down on dissenters, began in 1956, and within the year would forge the Anti-Rightist Movement to quell any criticism of the ruling factions of the People's Republic of China, leading to the persecution of over half a million people.[12] In Hong Kong, during the annual celebration of the Republic of China on 10 October 1956, riots broke out in the Kowloon and Tsuen Wan districts and lasted for more than two days, as pro-communist factions faced off against Nationalists. Zhou En-lai attacked the British use of force in the incident and Beijing rhetoric assumed a bellicose posture as though mainland China were threatened by

Figure I.1 Grace Chang in *The Wild, Wild Rose* (1960).

Figure I.2   Rita Hayworth in *Gilda* (1946).

these riots: Kowloon, so close to Canton, would have 'a direct bearing on peace in that area of China'.[13] It is not difficult, then, to read into Hong Kong films, from *Mambo Girl* to *The Wild, Wild Rose*, expressions of the torn cultural politics of the region playing out in noir fashion by means of sexual and gender conflicts.

Much the same can be said for European films adapting noir aesthetics during this period. In 1957, towards the end of the supposed America noir cycle (1940–59), two black-and-white films vied for top honours at Cannes: Andrzej Wajda's *Kanal* (1956) shared the Jury Prize with Ingmar Bergman's *The Seventh Seal* (1957). The year 1957 also witnessed the releases of Bergman's *Wild Strawberries* and Mikhail Kalatozov's *The Cranes are Flying*, which would garner the Palme d'Or in 1958. Nostalgia, war, death and rebellion are themes in these films. While none of these films would find itself listed under film noir, all three do reveal both an aesthetic and narrative impulse that clearly resonates with noir sensibilities.

The Cranes are Flying is a nostalgic, patriotic film of the horrors faced in the Soviet Union by the Nazi invasion in World War II. It concerns the cruel realities that accompany human frailty, betrayal and psyche dissociation during war. Kalatozov's first feature, *Salt for Svanetia* (*Sol' Svanetii*, 1930), literally the struggle of a mountain village waiting to obtain salt as the Bolsheviks construct a road, provided an experimental, proto-noir aesthetic by varying 'high- and low-angle shots, extreme long-shots and extreme close-ups', and exploiting lighting effects, all of which become intensified in *The Cranes are Flying*.[14] Evident noir elements occur when Mark (Alexander Shvorin), the weak, morally corrupt pianist, in the smoke-filled, dimly lit room, plays for a gathering of decadent lost souls. In the famous blackout scene, when Boris (Alexei Batalov) and Veronika (Tatiana Samoilova) dream of the future, cinematographer Sergei Urusevsky again 'used all kinds of broken glass ... to achieve the lighting effects' that convey the countless moods Veronika experiences.[15] For the close-up of Veronika's face, after she has discovered that her family's apartment has been utterly destroyed, Kalatozo and Urusevsky rely upon extreme underlighting to accentuate her ghostly sense of loss and alienation. During the night of the Nazi bombing of the city, shattering panes of glass provide only momentary light, as blackness metaphorically envelops the scene of Mark's rape of Veronika. The noir impulse of Kalatozov's style appropriately displays the intensity of psycho-emotional anxiety that the Russian people have endured during the Nazi blitzkrieg.

Kanal concerns the nihilistic endeavours of the Home Army during the Warsaw Uprising against Nazi occupation in World War II. The Nazi-controlled city overwhelms the Polish forces, who are ordered to retreat into the sewers in order to make their way to the city's central district. Half of the film is devoted to their slogging through the slime, filth and mire of human waste, ultimately to perish without defeating the Nazis. It is a nostalgic tale of human endurance and suffering, as well as a portrait of the real-world resignation to death in war. Wajda chooses noir lighting effects for many of the poignant, all-too-human moments of despair and helplessness in the sewers beneath the city and its Nazi occupiers. Wounded and clinging to Stokrotka (Teresa Izewska) for support and comfort, the ever-weakening Korab (Tadeusz Janczar) desperately tries to negotiate the interminable blackness and endless corridors of the labyrinthine sewer system. Stokrotka knows of a way out but when they reach the outlet to the river, it proves to be another form of entrapment, more desperate because the freedom of the river lies just beyond the impassable ironwork grill:

INTERNATIONAL NOIR

Figure I.3 Entrapment within the sewer in *Kanal*.

> STOKROTKA: *I can see it! I can see a light, Jacek!*
> Some diffused light is apparent further on down the tunnel. Korab and Stokrotka embrace and kiss with a painful passion. Break the embrace smilingly, she looks out. The outlet of the sewer is blocked by an iron grill. Beyond it, in bright daylight, turns a wide river with green meadows on the other side, in the distance. A trickle of foul water runs out of the sewer and into the river.

After Stokrotka discovers that they are still trapped, she tries to maintain her composure and comfort the dying Korab, although she cannot quite believe the terrible condition fate has doomed them to:

> KORAB: *Is it much further?*
> Light reflection from the water flickers over his face. Stokrotka, seen from outside, grasps the bars and stares out hopelessly. She pushes her head between the bars.[16]

All the while, Korab slumps down, near death. This scene reminds one of the sewer chases in Anthony Mann's *He Walked By Night* (1948) and Carol Reed's *The Third Man* (1949). All three films rely upon the allegory of the sewer as the product and place for criminal effluence, but only *Kanal* presents criminality as an imposed fascist politics that besmears cultural heroics with the dark matter of war.

Bergman in the 1950s was certainly creating his own version of film noir, in which the aesthetics reflect ambiguous moral and uncertain metaphysical issues. In *The Seventh Seal*, Death playing chess with medieval Crusader is an overt noir allegory for the intellectual yet martial game of human existence. The war theme is often overlooked in studies of *The Seventh Seal*, even though the knight has returned from his Western conquest campaign, an enforcement of political-moral authority which now seems almost devoid of meaning. The opening sequence sets the noir tone and visual expression for the entire film, as the knight experiences the bleak world before encountering Death, 'a man in black':

> The knight returns to the beach and falls on his knees. With his eyes closed and brow furrowed, he says his morning prayers. His hands are clenched together and his lips form the words silently. His face is sad and bitter. He opens his eyes and stares directly into the morning sun which wallows up from the misty sea like some bloated, dying fish. The sky is gray and immobile, a dome of lead. A cloud hangs mute and dark over the western horizon. High up, barely visible, a sea gull floats on motionless wings. Its cry is weird and restless.[17]

The atmosphere of the natural world turned into a noir expression of disorientation and alienation also occurs at the conclusion of Robert Wise's *Odds Against Tomorrow* (1959), which serves as a 'noir gris', for its mixed palette of almost-white and nearly-black shadings allegorises the racial tensions in American culture. Similarly, *The Seventh Seal*'s contrasting depths for its noir greyscape reflects Bergman's existential, obsessive fear of 'how precarious life was in the wake of the Second World War and in the middle of the Cold War arms race'.[18]

The preceding year, 1956, was relevant to the content of these films, since it was a year of anxious political events. The Hungarian Revolution pitted rebellious students and intellectuals in Budapest against pro-Soviet officials, but on 4 November 1956, Soviet troops invaded and attacked dissenters and civilians alike, resulting in thousands dead or wounded and a mass exodus from the country: nearly 200,000 people escaped Hungary, among whom 38,000 eventually reached the United States for asylum.[19] The Suez Crisis, in late October, combined British, French and Israeli forces in a plan to control the Suez Canal, the Sinai Peninsula and Egypt. Britain's position in the incident became increasingly untenable in the eyes of the world. Pierson Dixon, Great Britain's Permanent Representative to the United Nations, warned the Foreign Office on 5 November 1956 that the Eden government was being perceived 'in the same low category as the Russians in their bombing of Budapest'.[20] That was just one day after Soviet forces entered Hungary. Not surprisingly, no Nobel Peace Prize was awarded in either 1955 or 1956. The next year, the 1957 Nobel Peace Prize was awarded to Lester Pearson for resolving the Suez Crisis by drafting a United Nations resolution that created an emergency international

UN forces (UNEF), which then entered the region and soon brought the crisis to an end.[21]

H-8..., a Yugoslavian film from 1958, opens with credits superimposed over stark contrast lighting of a single window wiper, heavy rain on a windscreen and oncoming lights, nearly recreating the conditions of a horrific highway accident of April 1957, and yet its newscast-like voiceover narrative reminds the viewer 'but any similarity with those involved is coincidental'. The orchestra, although having a storming sound quality, also relies upon kettledrums for syncopated, militaristic rhythm. The film, as the voiceover explains, is 'dedicated to the unknown driver who would not stop after causing a crash. All we know is that the number plate began with H-8'. The crash involves the Zagreb 6.15 pm bus, with twenty-two passengers, including six women and three children, and a truck that is hauling sheet metal heading to Zagreb. These initial shot sequences are filmed in extreme high-contrast light, with illumination primarily provided by the dim crepuscular sky and oncoming vehicle headlights. Interior shots of the bus utilise rear-as-front projection for the ever-elapsing highway before the bus's headlights.

As a minor point at first, the voiceover informs us that the truck driver's son, born in 1944, 'passed the fifth grade after retaking history'. The remedial history of the son underscores the film's allegorical import. Of course, 1944 marked the failure of the Belgrade Offensive, during which the Nazis were forced from the city and its environs.[22] The film begins on 14 April 1957 which marked, of course, the very month from which would continue for more than a decade the long, independent struggle by Tito against the Soviet Union's head-on conflict with Yugoslavian socio-political mobility, and which would produce the most profound rupture in Eastern European communist hegemony. Within the first nine minutes, we learn the plot line of the entire film, at least in terms of the bare-bones outline of the tragic accident, its aftermath, and the anonymous car driving away hurriedly, although no one is chasing it. Then, the film proper begins with a narrative of the various passengers on the bus and those in the truck, all captured in exceptional noir camera angles, chiaroscuro lighting and urban, alienating details. The film's human comedy represents the internal psychological problems afflicting modern culture, and the external conflicts of disruption to unification of couples, marriage and harmony among citizens. *H-8...* is not a heavy-handed mimetic correspondence to Yugoslavian society; it is a filmic expression of the necessity for a noir impulse to convey the dissonance, dissatisfaction and dissociation of modernity within a culture striving merely to exist as human beings, with all their foibles and problems. The crash, which we know about from the outset, represents an inevitable human tragi-comedy of a contemporary people faced with ideological burdens of individualism, a dilemma never fully comprehended until it is too late. That scenario of living-in-anxiety can only be conveyed through a noir impulse, a collision of style, narrative, motif and aesthetics, all of which mimic a world as real and as allegorised as modernity, but which modernity never wishes to accept. In essence, that is the noir impulse: to present contemporary existential-political-social dilemmas in a manner that conveys their entrapment, while simultaneously alluding to the self-confinement with which modern culture's people so willingly delude themselves.

Noir aesthetics, theme and content certainly attract international filmmakers. Of course, there is an essential condition to black-and-white cinematography that lends itself to film noir visual techniques. Not all films, however, are noirs, even the slew of post New Hollywood, colour-saturated cinematography crime-action films from the 1990s onwards. What now appears to be the trend in noir is that *impulse* towards sustaining storyline, character, techniques and aesthetics not based solely upon the 1940s–50s American noir, but rather the mixed style of an International noir.

A case in point is Brian Helgeland's *Payback* (1999). This self-conscious noir recounts the relentlessly over-the-top story of a former driver, Porter (Mel Gibson), for 'the Outfit', who steals, fights, and kills his way up the corrupt crime ladder, with the help of a call-girl, Rosie (Maria Bello), in order to obtain the $70,000 that was stolen from him. The film opens with a voiceover narration from Porter, who punctuates the remainder of the film with his commentary on plot points, such as 'corrupt cops – are there any other kind?' That sum was part of the divided profits of $130,000 that Porter and ousted Outfit member, the sadomaschist Val Resnick (Gregg Henry), were to split after their daring head-on collision robbery of Chinese Tong money. At the split, Resnick complains that his cut is not enough to buy his way back into the Outfit. Porter's wife, Lynn (Deborah Kara Unger), abruptly shoots Porter, and Resnick and now supposed ex wife leave Porter for dead. The remainder of the film is Porter's systematic physical and psycho-social retaliation against the Outfit for taking his money, which escalates from one scene of malicious violence to the next. *Payback*'s significance remains its international noir style, adopting elements of the classic criminal revenge narrative from American film noir, but adapting the blue-tint, ultra-urban saturation look that pervades so much of Hong Kong noir. The violence by Chinese sex trade *maîtresse* (Lucy Liu) and her gang of anonymous, expensively suited triad henchmen signals the inclusion of Chinese narrative and aesthetic correspondence. This international noir aesthetic can be seen in neo-noir remakes of Hong Kong features, most specifically Martin Scorsese's *The Departed* (2006), based on Andrew Lau's and Alan Mak's *Infernal Affairs* (2002).

Payback, like *Un Prophet* (2009), *The Most Terrible Time In My Life* (1993), *Memories of Murder* (2003), *Män son hatar kvinnor* (*The Girl with the Dragon Tattoo*, 2009), recaptures, perhaps nostalgically, a world-weary sentiment that accounted for pervasive corruption, and creates, perhaps antisentimentally, a cynical re-evaluation of a contemporary world accountable for allowing corruption to be so pervasive. In all, they rely without question upon that global cinematic, technical and aesthetic *Weltanschauung* that can only be called noir. This volume will explore that noir *impulse* that underlies the narrative, thematic and visual mode that is so recognisable as international noir. This volume, along with its companion volume *Film Noir: Classical Traditions* in Edinburgh University Press's *Traditions in American Cinema* series, offers re-examinations, re-evaluations and re-appreciations of this fundamental and omnipresent cinematic aesthetic. In so many ways, noir defines the significant shifts, trends and movements that constitute the history of world cinema.

Notes

1. Paul Cooke, 'Introduction: World cinema's "dialogues" with Hollywood', in Paul Cooke (ed.), *World Cinema's 'Dialogues' with Hollywood* (New York: Palgrave Macmillan, 2007), pp. 4, 5.
2. Rosalind Galt and Karl Schoonover, 'Introduction: The impurity of art cinema', in Rosalind Galt and Karl Schoonover (eds), *Global Art Cinema: New Theories and Histories* (Oxford: Oxford University Press, 2010), pp. 11, 12.
3. Ned Sublette, *Cuba and its Music: From the First Drums to the Mambo* (Chicago, IL: Chicago Review Press, 2004), pp. 53–4.
4. Yingchi Chu, *Hong Kong Cinema: Coloniser, Motherland and Self* (London: Routledge, 2003), p. 34.
5. Richard Dyer, 'Resistance through charisma: Rita Hayworth and *Gilda*', in E. Ann Kaplan (ed.), *Women in Film Noir* (London: British Film Institute, 2000), pp. 120, 122.
6. Melvyn Stokes, *Gilda* (London: British Film Institute, 2010), p. 57.
7. Robert Miklitsch, *Siren City: Sound and Source Music in Classic American Noir* (New Brunswick, NJ: Rutgers University Press, 2011), pp. 237–41.
8. Kelley Conway, *The Chanteuse in the City: The Realist Singer in French Film* (Berkeley, CA: University of California Press, 2004), p. 135. This sequence relies upon close-ups of 'each woman's tired, longing face, as she stares at the singer mesmerized' in a 'dim and smoky' hall for pimps and whores, not the bright, modern lounge where Grace Chang performs her siren song (p. 136).
9. Dudley Andrew, *Mists of Regret: Culture and Sensibility in Classic French Film* (Princeton, NJ: Princeton University Press, 1995), pp. 208, 209.
10. Alastair Phillips, *City of Darkness, City of Light: Émigré Filmmakers in Paris, 1929–1939* (Amsterdam: Amsterdam University Press, 2004), p. 116.
11. Sheri Chinen Biesen, *Blackout: World War II and the Origins of Film Noir* (Baltimore, MD: The Johns Hopkins University Press, 2005), p. 150. As Biesen relates, the publicity campaign and reviewers used an 'A-bomb blast' to promote the explosive sexuality of *Gilda* (p. 151).
12. Merle Goldman, 'The Party and the intellectuals', in Roderick MacFarquhar and John K. Fairbank (eds), *The Cambridge History of China, Volume 14, The People's Republic, Part I: The Emergence of Revolutionary China, 1949–1965* (Cambridge: Cambridge University Press, 1987), p. 257. Goldman places the number of displaced intellectuals sent to rural labour reform camps from '400,000 to 700,000',

which meant that roughly a 'quota of 5 percent of the people in a unit were to be designated as rightists' (p. 257).
13. Chi-Kwan Mark, *Hong Kong and the Cold War: Anglo-American Relations, 1949–1957* (Oxford: Clarendon Press, 2004), p. 120.
14. Josephine Woll, *The Cranes are Flying* (London: I. B. Tauris/KINOfiles, 2003), p. 42.
15. Ibid., p. 33.
16. Boleslaw Sulik, 'Introduction', in Andrzej Wajda, *Kanal*, in *Three Films: Ashes and Diamonds, A Generation, Kanal* (New York: Lorrimer Publishing, 1984), p. 152.
17. *The Seventh Seal*, in *Four Screenplays of Ingmar Bergman*, trans. Lar Malmstrom and David Kushner (New York: Simon and Schuster, 1960), pp. 99–100.
18. Geoffrey Macnab, *Ingmar Bergman: The Life and Films of the Last Great European Director* (New York: I. B. Tauris, 2009), p. 97.
19. S. Alexander Weinstock, *Acculturation and Occupation: Study of the 1956 Hungarian Refugees in the United States* (The Hague: Martinus Nijhoff, 1969), pp. 38–9. Much of Weinstock's evidence comes from the Columbia University Research Project on Hungary.
20. Pierson Dixon's telegram (5 November 1956), as quoted in Edward Johnson, 'The Suez crisis at the United Nations: The effects for the Foreign Office and British foreign policy', in *Reassessing Suez 1956: New Perspectives on the Crisis and its Aftermath*, ed. Simon C. Smith (Aldershot: Ashgate Publishing, 2008), p. 172.
21. Ann T. Keene, *Peacemakers: Winners of the Nobel Peace Prize* (Oxford: Oxford University Press, 1998), p. 158.
22. Leslie Benson, *Yugoslavia: A Concise History* (New York: Palgrave, 2001), p. 84.

1. BRITISH NOIR

Jim Leach

>It was like living through a realistic nightmare.
>
>James Hadley Chase, *Flesh of the Orchid* (1948)

Anyone writing on British film noir has to confront not only the much-debated question of whether noir is a genre, a cycle or a sensibility but also that of whether, however it is defined, it is a uniquely American phenomenon (in which case, there may be no such thing as British film noir). There is no need to rehearse the arguments associated with the first question here, but it does have implications for identifying which (if any) British films should count as films noirs. Put simply, two basic elements figure in most definitions of film noir: 1) a corrupt and threatening urban setting in which crime is endemic, and 2) a visual style emphasising low-key lighting, deep shadows and unusual camera angles. The problem is that many films include one but not both of these elements, and most lists of films noirs accept many such films as bona fide examples. As Paul Schrader put it in 1972, in one of the first significant attempts to account for the phenomenon as it emerged in Hollywood during and after World War II, 'How many *noir* elements does it take to make *film noir noir?*'.[1]

In the case of British noir, an additional question would be: How far can a British film deviate from the Hollywood model, however that is defined, and still be considered noir? Most accounts of US film noir distinguish between the 'classical period', usually defined as running roughly from John Huston's *The Maltese Falcon* in 1941 to Orson Welles' *Touch of Evil* in 1958, presenting a dark vision of American society in marked contrast to the positive outlook usually found in mainstream Hollywood cinema. These films are usually seen as symptomatic of the social upheavals caused by World War II and its aftermath, while a revival, generally referred to as 'neo-noir', beginning in the 1970s, is associated with the questioning of established values by the social movements of the late 1960s. During these same time periods, similarly dark films emerged from British cinema, but, while some of these films are quite close thematically and iconographically to the Hollywood films, others develop a recognisably 'noir' outlook in quite different forms. Much then depends on what constitutes a film noir.

In Britain, as in the US, the term 'film noir' was unknown during the period when the films later designated as classic noir were produced. Although it originated in the 1940s in France, American filmmakers and critics did not take it up until the 1970s, and it was only during the 1980s that critics began to consider whether it might usefully be applied to British films, although it should be noted that Raymond Borde and Étienne Chaumeton did acknowledge the existence of 'an authentic British noir series' as early as 1955.[2] As in the US, the concept of film noir quickly caught on, and critics have retroactively identified hundreds of films as British films noirs, although there is still considerable disagreement about exactly which films should count as noir. In his useful and fairly comprehensive *British Film Noir* guide, Michael F. Keaney (2008) lists 369 titles, although in his accounts of the films, he admits that some are only 'marginal noirs', and many that he accepts without reservation push the definition of noir into areas quite remote from the classical Hollywood films.[3]

It must be acknowledged that critics have disagreed about the parameters of even the core films of Hollywood noir. Although some, such as Janey Place and Lowell Peterson, have regarded the visual style as the most important factor in defining American film noir, R. Barton Palmer has pointed out that 'the presence of noir visual motifs varies considerably from one film to another and ... hardly characterizes many films as a whole', and similarly only a handful of British films make extensive use of chiaroscuro lighting and canted camera angles, although there are a great many shadows and shots of rain-covered city streets at night.[4] A definition that seems more useful, especially in relation to British noir, is J. P. Telotte's succinct claim that film noir 'generally focuses on urban crimes and corruption, and on sudden upwellings of violence in a culture whose fabric seems to be unraveling'.[5] Unlike in the United States, British cities had suffered widespread damage during World War II, and the postwar years were characterised by economic hardship and a growing awareness that Britain was no longer a major world power. For many, the national culture did seem to be 'unravelling', and there was a widespread perception that violent crime was on the rise.[6]

As with so many later discussions of the phenomenon, Telotte's definition accords with that found in the first book on film noir, published in 1955, in which French critics Raymond Borde and Étienne Chaumeton argued that films noirs set out 'to disorient the spectators, who no longer encounter their customary frames of reference'.[7] Central to the noir sensibility, from this perspective, is the experience of a nightmare world that envelops the central characters and is vicariously experienced by the spectator. Accordingly, film noir has frequently been discussed in terms of the Freudian 'dream-work' or as a vision of 'a nightmare society, or condition of man'.[8] The noir visual style may contribute to this effect, but it can also be attributed to other factors, such as complex plots, in which flashbacks and coincidence are common features, and unreliable narration.

Alongside their emphasis on the dream logic of these films, Borde and Chaumeton insist, 'It's the presence of crime which gives film noir its most distinctive stamp'. What distinguishes these films from other crime films, however, is that crime is seen 'from within', from the point of view of the criminals, although, as they later allow, the protagonist does not need to be a criminal but can be someone, like a private detective, who is situated 'midway between order and crime'.[9] As Telotte suggests, the key setting in which these criminal entanglements are worked through is the city, although the influence of the corrupt urban world can sometimes spread into other settings. In the nightmare world of film noir, the modern city becomes a labyrinth in which the characters are trapped and rendered vulnerable in the crowded streets by day and the lonely streets by night.

As should be clear by now, critical discourses on British noir always start from a comparison with the American films. To some extent, this is inevitable, given the prestige and popularity of the Hollywood films noirs but also the close relations between the Hollywood studios and the British film industry. As in the US, most British films noirs were low-budget productions, many of them 'B films', intended as supporting features in the double-bills that were a prominent feature of exhibition practices at the time. The relatively few that were produced on more ample budgets required the involvement of Hollywood studios, and the two most high-profile British films noirs, *The Third Man* (Carol Reed, 1948) and *Night and the City* (Jules Dassin, 1950), had considerable American involvement and were released in different versions in the British and US markets. *The Third Man* was produced by Alexander Korda's London Films, but with the support of American producer David Selznick, and starred Orson Welles and Joseph Cotten. The differences between the two versions of this film involve the opening voiceover narration and the shortening of the extremely long take that ends the film, but more substantial changes were made in the US version of *Night and the City*, produced by the British subsidiary of Twentieth Century-Fox and starring Richard Widmark and Gene Tierney, including a completely different musical score.

These films offer perfect illustrations of James Naremore's observation that 'film noir occupies a liminal space somewhere between Europe and America'.[10] *The Third Man* is set in the divided city of Vienna, still suffering from the ravages of the war, and the presence of Welles and Cotten led many critics to compare its noir stylisation to *Citizen Kane* (1941), a film often regarded as a major influence on the noir sensibility. In *Night and the City*, the city is London, also showing many signs of wartime damage and deprivation, but, in this case, the director was from Hollywood and the star was already associated with Hollywood crime films, resulting in complaints that the film was British only in name. Yet one sequence does provide an iconic image of postwar London as a cosmopolitan city: when small-time crook Harry Fabian (Widmark) enters the American Bar in Leicester Square, there is a cut to a reverse shot showing the Café de l'Europe across the street.

Critics have debated the extent to which American noir was influenced by European filmmakers who had come to Hollywood in the 1930s to escape from fascist regimes, and a case can be made that British noir owed a similar debt to American filmmakers escaping from the blacklist that resulted from the investigations of the House Un-American Activities Committee into supposed communist infiltration in Hollywood. Dassin was expecting to be blacklisted while he was making *Night and the City*, and he was soon followed to Britain by Edward Dmytryk, Cy Endfield and Joseph Losey, directors who would all make significant contributions to British noir, often working under assumed names. In addition, American actors abound in British films noirs, cast to attract US audiences but often identified as Canadians in the films to make them more acceptable to British audiences. Critics often saw this involvement as a symptom of a more general Americanisation of the national culture, but, before the war, many of them had been equally concerned by the influence of émigré European filmmakers and actors who, along with a number of younger actors from the continent, continued to play a significant role in postwar British cinema.[11]

In the case of American film noir, the dark elements of the noir sensibility created tensions within the classical narrative style that dominated Hollywood production, whereas, in the context of British cinema, the postwar crime films challenged the critical canon of 'quality' cinema that emerged during the war and resulted in what became known as a 'golden age' of British cinema, based on the fusion of fiction and documentary techniques. British critics regarded the American crime films less as deviations from Hollywood norms than as especially distasteful examples of them. They became even more concerned when British filmmakers started to produce similar films.

As a result of this critical attitude, these crime films first came under attack and then, more damagingly, were largely ignored in accounts of the national cinema. The tide turned in the 1980s as a result of a more general re-evaluation of British cinema that called into question the canons of the past. In particular, in his 1986 essay on a 'lost continent' of British popular cinema, Julian Petley confidently asserted that, 'during the late 40s and early 50s Britain produced a fine crop of "films noirs" ... which match many of their Hollywood counterparts in terms of formal stylisation, sheer physical brutality, urban sleaze and underlying existential pessimism'.[12] While such formulations stress the similarities between the British films and American noir, later writers attempted to distinguish them by pointing to, usually vaguely defined, differences. Thus Lawrence Miller suggested that 'the British noirs ... have a distinctly British "personality" that distinguishes them from their American brethren', while Robert Murphy found them 'tantalisingly similar but fundamentally different from their American counterparts'.[13]

One notable difference derives from the importance of the past in British culture, reinforced by the visual presence of that past in the landscape. It is not surprising, then, that there has been a tendency to include historical films that exhibit a similar focus on crime and the criminal mentality in accounts of British film noir. Although Keaney rejects some of the titles that have been suggested, his list still includes a number of historical films, and Raymond Durgnat incorporates Gainsborough melodramas and other period films in his wide-ranging survey of British crime films.[14] However, while noir elements do spill over into some films set in the past, the core of British noir is to be found in the proliferation of crime films set in the present and produced during the postwar period. Even so, the past is inscribed in these films, in often ironic and ambivalent ways. *Night and the City*, for example, opens with shots of the city that evoke its past – even as they function in the present as icons of tourist London – and that contrast with the seedy underworld that Fabian inhabits and with the ruined buildings that bear witness to the recent past.

Glenn Erickson has suggested that, 'being a city that had taken real punishment from the war with its economic chaos and its rubble in the streets, bombed-out London has an advantage over Los Angeles'.[15] And while not all British films noirs are set in London (just as Hollywood noirs are not confined to Los Angeles), the visibility of the damage inflicted by the war is a major noir motif in the British films right up to the early 1960s. Similarly, the presence of Americans and icons of American popular culture in the postwar urban landscape acts as a reminder of the toll that the war had taken on the British economy and on traditional concepts of national identity. In order to identify the specific characteristics of British noir, then, we need to follow Charlotte Brunsdon's lead by looking at 'the way in which this British/American comparison is inscribed in the films themselves'.[16] If, as Palmer suggests, 'film noir ... offers the obverse of the American dream', Steve Chibnall points out that 'the American dream has never been confined to the USA', and the nightmare world depicted in British films noirs involves, as we shall see, a complex and ambiguous response to the impact of American popular culture on British society.[17]

Recourse is had to trauma, either wartime ... or Freudian[18]

In the opening sequence of *Obsession* (Edward Dmytryk, 1949) a group of middle-aged men sitting in a gentlemen's club discuss the neglect of the Empire and the costs of the war. One of them acknowledges that 'we' are now 'living on American dollars'. Among the group is Clive (Robert Newton), who goes home and surprises his wife with her American lover. It turns out that he is already aware of the affair and has devised a plan to gain his revenge. He kidnaps the man and chains him up in a derelict building, where he gradually fills a bathtub with acid so that he can dispose of the body once the hunt for the missing man has died down. During his regular visits, he and his victim engage in a series of barbed conversations that eventually bring about Clive's downfall because an alert policeman becomes suspicious when he says, 'Thanks, pal', which he realises is an 'Americanism'.

As this film makes abundantly clear, the vision of postwar Britain in films noirs is bound up with cultural discourses that stressed the political and moral decline of the nation. However, Palmer's observation about American noir, that 'most American films of the period were not dark – quite the contrary – so how can we say that the discontents of postwar culture in some way brought on film noir?' is equally relevant to the British situation.[19] Nevertheless there clearly is some relation between the darkness of films noirs and the social climate in which they were produced, and, for some audiences at least, British noir did offer a credible and meaningful response to postwar conditions, in which the open violence of wartime had been replaced by an uneasy and troubled peace in which many of 'their customary frames of reference' no longer seemed convincing.

The aftermath of the war is apparent in most of these films, visually in the bombed-out buildings but also in the characters whose lives have been disrupted. In *They Made Me a Fugitive* (Cavalcanti, 1947), Clem (Trevor Howard), suffering from boredom after being demobbed from the RAF, joins a gang of black marketeers. When he is accused of murders (which he did not commit), he finds it ironic because he had been trained to kill during the war. George (Jack Warner), in *My Brother's Keeper* (Alfred Roome, 1948), does commit murder, having deserted from the army after winning a medal. At the beginning of the film, he escapes from prison handcuffed to a slow-witted fellow prisoner, who gets blamed for the murder. At the end, however, the police close in on George, who refuses to give up, running across a minefield after shouting, 'I can tackle a minefield. I did it in the war, fighting for you', and is blown to bits. Peter (Derek Farr), another deserter, in *Man on the Run*

(Lawrence Huntington, 1949), becomes implicated in a robbery after he tries to sell the gun he has not used since he left the army. He claims that there are 20,000 deserters 'on the run', but the authorities make no allowances for 'human nature', and many are driven to crime.

There are also many characters, especially women, who struggle to cope with the loss of family members during the war, but the reminders of the war years also draw attention to the loss of a sense of the common purpose and community attributed to what had been known as 'the people's war'. The transition from the war against fascism to the less definite tensions of the Cold War is captured in *Seven Days to Noon* (John and Roy Boulting, 1950) when a scientist, who has worked on nuclear weapons but feels that 'the dream has become a nightmare', threatens to blow up London to draw attention to the insanity of war. He is first seen in a church outside which is a sign: 'Blitzed 10 years ago. Please help us rebuild'. The preparations for evacuation ordered by the government remind one of the workers of wartime evacuations from the city to the country, and an army officer in the operations room asks another, 'Does this take you back?'

A similar nostalgia appears in several films in which ex-servicemen are organised into impromptu armies to deal with criminal gangs: in *Dancing with Crime* (John Paddy Carstairs, 1949), Ted (Richard Attenborough) assembles his fellow cab drivers to avenge the death of his friend, and in *Noose* (Edmond T. Gréville, 1948), when Linda (Carole Landis), an American fashion reporter, becomes involved in exposing an Italian gangster, Jumbo (Derek Farr), her war hero fiancé, organises the members of a boxing club run by one of his wartime friends, to attack the gangsters. In a more sinister way, in *Cloudburst* (Francis Searle, 1951), John (Robert Preston), a Canadian who has stayed on in London after the war, enlists men who had served under him to assist in his revenge on a youth who ran down his wife. After he is arrested, the police are unable to make him betray them because he has learnt how to lie in the war.

'Film noir is a film of death, in all senses of the word', and the moral issue of the death penalty haunts British film noir.[20] It is linked to the idea that soldiers were trained to kill but are punished for doing so afterwards, encouraging a moral perspective from which capital punishment can be seen as state-sanctioned murder. *Daybreak* (Compton Bennett, 1946) opens with preparations for a hanging that are interrupted when the public hangman (Eric Portman) refuses to carry out his duties, and the main action then consists of a long flashback in which he reveals that he is guilty of the murder for which another man has been convicted. In the same year, Portman also starred in *Wanted for Murder* (Lawrence Huntington) in which he is first seen standing in front of a fairground booth where Punch is demonstrating a hangman's noose. It turns out that he is a serial killer, and, when he visits a waxworks that displays a likeness of his ancestor who was a hangman, he attacks it for haunting him and driving him to murder. A guard at the waxworks refers to the hangman as 'a strangler with a licence'. *Yield to the Night* (J. Lee Thompson, 1956) opens with a highly fragmented sequence, full of noirish camera angles, in which Mary (Diana Dors) shoots another woman at point blank range, but then the rest of the film is set in prison where she is deglamourised as she waits execution and narrates flashbacks to explain how she was driven to murder the woman who had driven her lover to suicide.

The flashbacks in *Yield to the Night* show Mary working at the beauty counter in an upscale department store – she meets Jim when he is looking for perfume for the other woman – and the motives for murder are thus associated with the emergence of the new consumer society that encourages the emulation of the glamour and lifestyle found in Hollywood movies (and the filmmakers were drawing on Dors's star persona as a 'blonde bombshell' and rival to Marilyn Monroe).[21] Although the film could be taken as preaching an 'undisguised anti-capital punishment message', the contrast between the affluent society outside the prison and the austerity inside creates an ambivalent view of a culture that is split between modern materialist and traditional puritanical values.[22] For many critics, the changes in British culture, especially evident among the younger generation, were linked to the widespread dissemination of 'mass culture' imported from the US, and the prevalence of British genre films was seen as contributing to this process.

According to Chapman, 'the critical hostility to the crime film ... arose from a combination of cultural opposition to Americanisation and a concern over the unflattering and disturbing picture that it presented of postwar British society'.[23] As early as 1927, the *Daily Express* had complained, 'the bulk of our picture-goers are Americanised ... They talk America, think America,

Figure 1.1   Diana Dors in *Yield to the Night*.

and dream America. We have several million people ... who, to all intent and purpose, are temporary American citizens'.[24] In the 1940s, critics expressed the hope that the emergence of a distinctly British 'quality' cinema would slow this process down, and they were dismayed that other British filmmakers turned to the popular genres associated with Hollywood. Their concerns were, ironically, mirrored in many of the crime films that depicted British characters behaving like Americans. One notable example is *The Woman in Question* (Anthony Asquith, 1950), made at the same time Akira Kurosawa was making *Rashomon* in Japan, in which five flashbacks represent very different versions of the events leading up to a murder from the point of view of suspects interviewed by the police. In the first of these, Bob (Dirk Bogarde) appears to be an American, described as 'the man in the cowboy hat' but actually dressed more like a Hollywood gangster, but in the second version he confesses that he was born in Liverpool (in other words, he is a temporary American citizen).

Critics complained that British crime films were themselves guilty of similar acts of impersonation. A few, such as *Joe Macbeth* (Ken Hughes, 1955) and *No Orchids for Miss Blandish* (St John Legh Clowes, 1948), were actually set in the US, with mainly British actors adopting more or less convincing American accents. While the critics simply deplored Hughes's rewriting of Shakespeare's tragedy as a gangster movie, the adaptation of James Hadley Chase's controversial 1939 novel created what amounted to 'a moral panic'.[25] In fact, the film toned down the lurid sex and violence of the novel considerably and played on the disparity between its British origins and American subject matter. The upper-class 'English' manners affected by the wealthy Blandish household in the opening sequence, almost suggesting the film may be set in Britain, contrast with the subsequent brutality of the underworld with its American accents and hard-boiled dialogue. Later, the distinction between traditional notions of 'class' and the vulgarity attributed to crime movies is called into question: when one of the gangsters who have kidnapped Miss Blandish comments, 'She's got class', another replies, 'They all got it now. It's the movies'. Far from being the drugged rape victim of the novel, she chooses to stay with her gangster lover, telling him, 'this is freedom compared to anything I have ever known'.

Joe Macbeth and *No Orchids for Miss Blandish* strive to eliminate local space altogether, along with the tension between British settings and generic plots that Brunsdon sees as a key feature of British crime films.[26] But they do not do so completely, since audiences could not miss the signs that 'America' in these films was created in British studios. More commonly, the films alternate between location shots of the city and studio interiors, both of which come to embody the nightmare space of film noir. Whether a film's style is predominantly realist or expressionist, there is a sense of entrapment that, to varying degrees of intensity, evokes a sense of collective trauma that grows out of the individual experiences of the characters. The source of the traumatic experience is often traced back to the war, but even when this is not overtly the case, as in *The October Man* (Roy Ward Baker, 1947) and *The Sleeping Tiger* (Joseph Losey, 1954), it is placed in the context of dislocations of family life that relate the effects of the war to the Freudian psychoanalytic paradigm. In these two films, psychological explanations come into conflict with the law, but both prove equally inadequate in resolving the mental problems of the victim of a bus crash (John Mills) in the first or a young hoodlum (Dirk Bogarde) in the second. As in British noir in general, these films depict individual traumas bringing out the tensions and passions hidden beneath the surface of 'normal' society.

> It is the task of the police to protect the normal citizen against the abnormal citizen, and not to pry too deeply into the various conditions of sexual repression that either might be suffering.
> Robert Fabian, *London After Dark*, 1954

After his retirement from Scotland Yard, Detective Superintendent Robert Fabian wrote two books about his experiences in the postwar London underworld that later formed the basis of a popular police procedural television series *Fabian of the Yard* (BBC, 1954–6). In his book of the same title, originally published in 1950, he insists there has been an increase in crime since the war and attributes it to the 'the influence of gangster films and novelettes, and the cheapening of life inherent in war itself'.[27] In *London After Dark* he focuses on 'sexual perversion' and argues that, 'whatever excuses are made for the individual, we must not blind ourselves to the fact that if vice is allowed to go unchecked it will destroy the moral stability of the whole nation'.[28] There are certainly overtones of 'moral panic' here, but Fabian is also aware of the need for legal reform. He points out that it was 'more than sixty years ago' that Freud began to publish the works on which 'nearly all of our modern theory of sex is built. Yet in this time the law has scarcely changed at all'.[29] The relations he suggests between sexuality, crime and national identity are also central to British film noir, and much has been written about a 'crisis in masculinity that emerged in crime films at this time', involving 'a feeling of a loss of war-time agency and an anxiety about the status of postwar women'.[30] The tensions around shifting gender roles can be effectively explored through two figures, the spiv (a frequent presence in postwar British crime films) and the femme fatale (a stock archetype of film noir).

The difficulties faced by ex-servicemen in postwar society were compounded by resentment against those who had stayed behind and prospered. According to Robert Murphy, 'during the war the spiv became a sort of generic term for someone who dressed flashily and had underworld connections', and his first screen embodiment was in Ted Purvis (Stewart Granger) in *Waterloo Road* (Sidney Gilliat, 1944).³¹ In this film, Jim (John Mills) deserts from the army because he has heard rumours that his wife has been tempted by the luxuries Ted can offer her. As Peter Wollen has noted, spivs were 'racketeers with roots in the working-class', and *Waterloo Road* depends on a contrast between the respectable and the 'rough' working class. In other films, the youthful working-class spiv is set against older figures representing more elite cultural values.³² *The Shop at Sly Corner* (George King, 1946) opens with a shot of a dark city street with a man lurking in the shadows wearing a raincoat and a trilby hat, while a classical violin concerto is heard on the soundtrack, eventually traced to a performance by the daughter of an antiques dealer. He comes from France but has become involved in the black market in London. His assistant (Kenneth Griffith), who blackmails his employer, is a spiv, and he complains that he was always made to feel out of place in the 'classy' shop. A similar, though less motivated, contrast is set up in the opening sequence of *Noose*, in which Bar Gorman (Nigel Patrick), a fast-talking spiv, hurries through the streets past a hall in which an orchestra is rehearsing a Brahms symphony, whose music continues over the rest of the sequence.

The old values are here associated with Europe, and this raises the question of the spiv's relation to popular depictions of the American underworld. Murphy argues that 'comparisons between the British spiv cycle and American *film noir* are inevitable but unhelpful' and that 'if one is to look for British *film noir*, then a more fruitful area to explore would be the series of "morbid" films which have in common an interest in psychology and neurosis'.³³ Yet the distinction is far from clearcut. In *Appointment With Crime* (John Harlow, 1946), for example, Leo (William Hartnell) identifies himself proudly as a 'spiv', but he clearly models himself on American stars like Bogart and Cagney, and reviewers saw the film as an attempt 'to create an English counterpart to the Hollywood gangster legend'.³⁴ As Murphy suggests, 'the spiv, as the representative of the black market, became something of a popular hero', and Wollen argues that it was 'official ideology' that depicted the spiv as 'an enemy of the war effort (and hence the people)'.³⁵ This is certainly true up to a point, but a spiv figure like Narcy (Griffith Jones) in *They Made Me a Fugitive*, who recruits Clem into his gang because he has 'class' and then frames him for murder, is cruel and vindictive, with more than a touch of the morbid and neurotic about him.

It is ironic that two of the most fully realised spiv characters are found in films adapted from pre-war novels, Graham Greene's *Brighton Rock* and Gerald Kersh's *Night and the City*, both first published in 1938. The film version of *Brighton Rock* (John Boulting, 1947) begins with a caption claiming that the Brighton it depicts no longer exists, which was inserted after pressure from the local authorities. Yet reviewers clearly saw Pinkie (Richard

Attenborough), the youthful and psychotic gang leader, as a contribution to the ongoing spiv cycle, and one of them praised the film as 'a serious analysis of spivery'.[36] In *Night and the City*, Fabian is apparently American, like the actor who played him, unlike Kersh's protagonist who is British but claims to be American, but, although he acts like a Chicago gangster, he is a small-time crook whose 'smart' clothes define him as a spiv in the British context, and he is so identified in the British version of the film.

As a product of the immediate postwar years, the spiv operated in a society of shortages and austerity, and by the 1950s, as James Chapman puts it, 'the time of the spiv had passed: the phasing out of rationing brought an end to the black market'. Yet his claim that 'the postwar cycle of underworld films had also run its course' is far from true.[37] These films continued, mainly in the form of B films, through the 1950s into the early 1960s, with frequent allusions to the effects of the war and with many characters who are recognisable descendants of the spiv. As late as 1963, in *The Small Sad World of Sammy Lee* (Ken Hughes), Sammy (Anthony Newley), a compere in a seedy strip joint, is constantly seen running through the streets of London, like Fabian in *Night and the City*, desperately trying to come up with ingenious schemes to pay off his debt to a local gangster. In the so-called affluent society that emerged in the 1950s, however, the spiv evolved into the 'juvenile delinquent', an equally ambivalent figure in the context of the consumer society that had been foreshadowed by the desire for luxury goods that the black market tried to satisfy and that was now associated with the influence of American popular culture.

A marked contrast between residual and emergent forms of masculinity is found in *The Blue Lamp* (Basil Dearden, 1950). This film is a police procedural whose ostensible focus is on a suburban London police station protecting citizens from what the opening voiceover narration calls 'the postwar increase in crime'. The avuncular PC Dixon, played by Jack Warner, is the main face of community policing whose jovial good humour is only tempered by the memory of his son killed in the war. In a shocking moment, midway through the film, he is shot down by Riley (Dirk Bogarde), a young thug who is seen as the product of a youth culture nourished on American popular culture. In an ironic reminder of wartime community, the police are able to capture him thanks to the efforts of professional criminals who band together to force him into the open. At the end, Dixon is replaced on the beat by Mitchell (Jimmy Hanley), a young constable of the same age as Riley but committed to the idea of public service. In view of this optimistic ending, and the focus on the activities of the police, *The Blue Lamp* is clearly not a film noir (although it is included in Keaney's *Guide*), but the noir elements associated with Riley threaten to unbalance the film. As Jeffrey Richards puts it, the audience may have been expected to prefer Mitchell, but he now 'looks rather bland, conventional . . . and sexless' compared to the edgy and unstable Riley.[38]

Figure 1.2   Dirk Bogarde as a young thug in *The Blue Lamp*.

A similarly ambiguous attempt to contain the noir questioning of gender norms and sexual roles is found in *Good-Time Girl* (David MacDonald, 1948), this time with reference to women. The main narrative is here presented as a moral example told by a magistrate in a juvenile court (Flora Robson) to dissuade Lyla (Diana Dors) from embarking on a life of crime. In the flashback that illustrates her story, Gwen (Jean Kent) is drawn into the underworld after escaping from her abusive home environment and eventually imprisoned for causing the death of two men, including the older man she has come to love. Several of the men who help send her on this downward course are spivs, and, as Murphy suggests, she becomes 'the female equivalent of the spiv, the good-time girl'.[39] However, it is clear that the female companions she meets in the 'Approved School', to which she is sent by the same magistrate who recounts her story, also encourage her later criminal behaviour. According to Murphy, 'there were accusations that the film celebrated the good-time life which ostensibly it condemned', and Viv Chadder argues that 'to identify with her desire for freedom in the world is to become complicit with her rejection of middle-class idealism and norms of femininity'.[40]

Lyla decides against becoming a good-time girl, but Diana Dors went on to become 'the country's first sex symbol' who 'presented her sexuality as a challenge to the fetid national culture of Britain'.[41] Despite her voluptuous physique, she rarely played the femme fatale, the major exception being *Yield to the Night*, but even there she does not cause her lover's death, and the emphasis is on what happens to her after the fatal shooting. In *The Last Page* (Terence Fisher, 1952), she plays a young assistant in a bookshop who tries to seduce and blackmail her American boss (George Brent), but she is seen as the dupe of her boyfriend who kills her when she tries to warn their victim.

According to Murphy, 'women in British films rarely exhibit the qualities associated with *femmes fatales*', but Keaney disagrees, insisting that he has 'found the opposite to be the case' in British films noirs.[42] As Melanie Bell suggests, this is partly a matter of definition since the 'benchmark for dangerous women remains predicated on a Hollywood model'.[43] In the British films, the distinctions between 'decent' and 'transgressive' women are often much less clear than in American noir. In *The Long Haul* (Ken Hughes, 1957), Dors plays a gangster's moll who becomes involved with Harry (Victor Mature), an American ex-serviceman working as a lorry driver because his wife refuses to move to the US. When his angry wife tells him that his son is not really his, she becomes the femme fatale who drives him into the criminal life he has so far resisted. Similarly, *Forbidden* (George King, 1948) features a wife who is the 'femme fatale' whose infidelity drives her husband to plan her murder, while Jeannie (Hazel Court) is both his mistress and the decent woman (despite herself). *Blind Corner* (Lance Comfort, 1963) is closer to the Hollywood model, but Anne (Barbara Shelley) is a very understated femme fatale who manoeuvres her lover into a plan to murder her blind husband, and only after he leaves to carry it out does the film reveal that she is really in love with another man whom she has pretended to hate. At the end, despite his blindness, the intended victim reveals he knows everything and refers to himself as 'the mate of a black widow spider'.

The relations between the sexes are as fraught in British noir as they are in the American films, but there is much more emphasis on the broken families that result from the breakdown of traditional gender roles. Many of the central characters are adolescents trying to play adult roles, like Pinkie in *Brighton Rock* and Riley in *The Blue Lamp*, or young people drawn into crime through their environment, like Gwen in *Good-Time Girl* and Roy in *Cosh Boy* (Lewis Gilbert, 1952), or simply 'child-like', as Fabian's girlfriend characterises him in *Night and the City*. This concern with the impact of the postwar world on the younger generation is found in a number of films that present the nightmare noir vision through the eyes of children.

A group of such films that appeared in the early 1950s may owe something to the American film *The Window* (Ted Tetzlaff, 1949), in which a young boy witnesses a murder and is hunted down by the killers, but the British films are less concerned with suspense and more with the strangeness of the adult world seen from the child's point of view. In the opening sequence of *Hunted* (Charles Crichton, 1952) a young boy runs through city streets and into a bombsite, where he stumbles on Chris (Dirk Bogarde), who has just murdered his wife's lover. Although the police believe the boy is in the clutches of a dangerous criminal, it becomes clear that he has left home because he is afraid of being beaten by his foster father.[44] The affection that Chris begins to feel for the boy contradicts the police version of the situation and negates the expected bloody ending, when Chris gives himself up because the boy is ill. A bombsite encounter also features in *The Yellow Balloon* (J. Lee Thompson, 1953) in which a boy is traumatised by the death of a friend who falls during an argument over a balloon just before Len (William Sylvester), an American deserter, appears out of the shadows. He exploits the boy in an effort to escape, and the events that lead to Len's death when he falls into the lift shaft of a disused Underground station are seen as if from within the consciousness of the boy. In *Bang! You're Dead* (Lance Comfort, 1954), an abandoned US base and the people living there in Nissen huts create an atmosphere of decay and instability in which the boy lives out violent fantasies that he has picked up from American westerns.

In *Tiger Bay* (J. Lee Thompson, 1959), a reworking of the situation in *Hunted*, the child is a young girl (Hayley Mills), who witnesses a Polish sailor (Horst Buchholtz) shoot his unfaithful girlfriend. They flee together, and he eventually sacrifices his chance of freedom by diving into the sea to save her when she falls overboard from the ship on which he is escaping. As in *Bang! You're Dead*, the 'real' violence is confused with that of children's games but is also associated with the socially sanctioned violence of a boxing match. The main difference between the girl in this film and the boys in the earlier ones is that she is much more in control of the situation. She weaves a web of improvised lies to hide her disobedience to her aunt and then to put the police off the trail. Her amoral resilience lessens the impact of the noir 'nightmare', foreshadowing the ways in which the youth culture of the 1960s will change the patterns of British cultural life.[45]

> *Neo-noir* is, quite simply, a contemporary rendering of the *film noir* sensibility[46]

According to Andrew Spicer, the first British neo-noir film was *The Strange Affair* (David Greene, 1968).[47] If we define the noir vision as involving a sense of nightmare linked with the city and crime, this film is certainly a film noir, in its depiction of a naive young police constable (Michael York) whose affair with a 'permissive' young woman makes him vulnerable to blackmail, first by the criminals and then by a police officer who makes him plant evidence so that he can get a conviction. Since Keaney, citing Murphy and Spicer, ends his *Guide* to classical British film noir in 1964, it is clear that the time lag between classical and neo-noir is much briefer than in the US.[48] As *The Strange Affair* amply demonstrates, the major differences are the replacement of black-and-white with colour and a more explicit treatment of sexuality and violence made possible by the relaxation of censorship. However, the term 'film noir' was not yet available to English-language filmmakers and critics in 1968, and the film was neither made nor received with 'the high degree of generic self-consciousness characteristic of neo-noir'.[49]

Todd Erickson argues that by the 1980s neo-noir had become 'a (new) genre that emerged from the overall movement, utilizing the subject matter that was at the very core of its existence: the presence, or portent, of crime'.[50] However, trying to pin down the parameters of this genre (if it is one) has proved as difficult as with the original films, and there is the additional complication that, as Ginette Vincendeau suggests, neo-noir 'can be understood both as simply coming after classic noir and as a reconfiguration or critique of it'.[51] Crime films have continued to be a significant factor in British film production, and received a major boost in the 1990s with a flood of gangster films apparently inspired by the darkly comic and graphically violent films of Quentin Tarantino. Some of these, notably *Sexy Beast* (Jonathan Glazer) and *Gangster No. 1* (Paul McGuigan), both released in 2000, are arguably films noirs, but most divest crime and violence of any vestiges of the dark vision of classical noir and are best categorised, in Chibnall's useful term, as 'gangster light'.[52] There is no room here to explore the full ramifications of British crime films of the past fifty years, but two strands of neo-noir can be briefly outlined, illustrating the distinction between those films that adapt noir plots and iconography to present-day settings and those that recreate the period of classical noir.[53]

The 'nightmare' experience of film noir could be used as an effective metaphor for the effects on British society of Thatcherism in the 1980s, setting Margaret Thatcher's law and order rhetoric and emphasis on entrepreneurship in a criminal milieu. In *The Long Good Friday* (John Mackenzie, 1979), Harold (Bob Hoskins) is a gangster who sees himself as a businessman with grandiose plans to restore the nation's former greatness but loses control of the London underworld when one of his men antagonises the IRA. *Stormy*

Figure 1.3 Information gathering in *The Long Good Friday*.

Monday (Mike Figgis, 1987) is set in Newcastle where Brendan (Sean Bean) becomes involved in a shady redevelopment scheme that brings together gangsters, politicians and businessmen. Both films also continue British film noir's ambivalent concern with American influence. Harold's plans in *The Long Good Friday* depend on investment by his 'American friends' from the Mafia, while *Stormy Monday* takes place during the celebrations for 'America Week' at the opening of which the Lady Mayoress delivers a Thatcher-like address welcoming the ruthless American entrepreneur in front of posters depicting Thatcher and Ronald Reagan.

The element of critique in the recourse to film noir in these and other films is less immediately apparent in those films set during the postwar period. Thatcherism, of course, appealed to past values in its 'heritage' mode, and nostalgia is a recurrent mood in postmodernist culture and recent British cinema. A continuity with earlier British film noir is found in the concern with the death penalty in *Dance with a Stranger* (Mike Newell, 1984) and *'Let Him Have It'* (Peter Medak, 1991). The former is based on the case of Ruth Ellis (Natasha Richardson), who was the last woman hanged in Britain in 1955, an event that coincided, perhaps fortuitously, with the production of *Yield to the Night*.[54] Unlike in the earlier film, the murder occurs at the end, and the issue of capital punishment is raised only as a final example of the deathly stifling culture of the 1950s that the film implicitly links to the condition of Britain under Thatcher. Medak's film deals with another notorious case in which Derek Bentley (Christopher Eccleston), a youth suffering from mental problems, was hanged in 1953 for his part in a robbery during which a police officer was shot by an accomplice who was too young to be sentenced to death. The opening sequence takes place during the Blitz when Derek is injured in a collapsed building, and a caption sets the action in 'London 1941', creating a distance in sharp contrast with the immediacy of the postwar films, as asserted in the opening caption to *The Sleeping Tiger*, which reads 'London this evening'.

The wartime experience is still a potent memory, however distanced, in British culture, and Medak's previous film, *The Krays* (1990), about the notorious twins who dominated the London underworld in the 1950s and 1960s, traces their villainy back to the impact of the war on the family and depicts a postwar culture immersed in nostalgic media representations of the war years. The title of a more recent crime film, *Spivs* (Colin Teague, 2003), also evokes the war but feels the need to provide a dictionary definition of a spiv as a 'man, especially a flashily dressed one, living from shady dealings'. There is no explicit reference to the war, and the modern-day spivs use electronic technology to carry out their con games. The earlier films' ambiguous relations to American culture is evoked when one of the gang buys a copy of Raymond Chandler's *Farewell My Lovely*, alluding to the American hard-boiled writing that was a major influence on film noir, but the allusion is double-edged, since it is also a reminder of a famous shot in a key British neo-noir, *Get Carter* (Mike Hodges, 1971), in which the title character reads the same novel. This shot of Carter (Michael Caine) reading Chandler next to a boy reading a comic has been described as evoking 'the postwar dismay at the Americanisation of British culture and moral panics about literacy, crime fiction and comics'.[55] In the later film, British spivery comes up against the might of the East European Mafia smuggling refugees into Britain to supply a prostitution ring, ironically suggesting that the coordinates of noir are changing now that Britain is a part of the European community as well as globalised networks of crime and violence.

Bibliography

Bell, Melanie (2010), 'Fatal femininity in postwar British film: Investigating the British *femme*', in Helen Hanson and Catherine O'Rowe (eds), *The Femme Fatale: Images, Histories, Contexts*, Houndmills: Palgrave Macmillan, pp. 98–112.

Borde, Raymond and Étienne Chaumeton (2002), *A Panorama of Film Noir 1941–1953*, trans. Paul Hammond, San Francisco, CA: City Lights Books [1955].

Bould, Mark, Kathrina Glitre and Greg Tuck (2009), 'Parallax views: An introduction', in Mark Bould, Kathrina Glitre and Greg Tuck (eds), *Neo-Noir*, London: Wallflower, pp. 1–10.

Brunsdon, Charlotte (1999), 'Space in the British crime film', in Steve Chibnall and Robert Murphy (eds), *British Crime Cinema*, London: Routledge, pp. 148–59.

Chadder, Viv (1999), 'The higher heel: Women and the postwar British crime film', in Steve Chibnall and Robert Murphy (eds), *British Crime Cinema*, London: Routledge, pp. 66–80.

Chapman, James (2008), '"Sordidness, corruption and violence almost unrelieved": Critics, censors and the postwar British crime film', *Contemporary British History* 22(2), 181–201.

Chase, James Hadley (2010), *Flesh of the Orchid*, Eugene, OR: Bruin Books [1948].

Chibnall, Steve (1996), 'Counterfeit Yanks: War, austerity and Britain's American dream', in Philip John Davies (ed.), *Representing and Imagining America*, Keele: Keele University Press, pp. 150–9.

——.(2000), *J. Lee Thompson*, Manchester: Manchester University Press.

——.(2009), 'Travels in Ladland: The British gangster film cycle, 1998–2001', in Robert Murphy (ed.), *The British Cinema Book* (3rd edition), London: British Film Institute, pp. 375–86.

Clay, Andrew (1999), 'Men, women and money: Masculinity in crisis in the British professional crime film 1946–1965', in Steve Chibnall and Robert Murphy (eds), *British Crime Cinema*, London: Routledge, pp. 51–65.

Cook, Pam (2001), 'The trouble with sex: Diana Dors and the blonde bombshell phenomenon', in Bruce Babington (ed.), *British Stars and Stardom: From Alma Taylor to Sean Connery*, Manchester: Manchester University Press, pp. 167–78.

Durgnat, Raymond (1970), *A Mirror for England: British Movies from Austerity to Affluence*, London: Faber and Faber.

——.(1996), 'Paint it black: The family tree of the *film noir*', in Alain Silver and James Ursini (eds), *Film Noir Reader*, New York: Limelight Editions, pp. 37–51 [1970].

Erickson, Glenn (1996), 'Expressionist doom in *Night and the City*', in Silver and Ursini (eds), *Film Noir Reader*, pp. 203–7.
Erickson, Todd (1996), 'Kiss me again: Movement becomes genre', in Silver and Ursini (eds), *Film Noir Reader*, pp. 307–29.
Fabian, Robert (1954), *London After Dark*, Toronto: Harlequin Books.
——.(1956), *Fabian of the Yard*, Kingswood: The World's Work [1950].
Greene, Graham (1980), *The Pleasure Dome: The Collected Film Criticism 1935–40*, ed. John Russell Taylor, Oxford: Oxford University Press.
Keaney, Michael F. (2008), *British Film Noir Guide*, Jefferson, NC: McFarland and Co.
Miller, Lawrence (1994), 'Evidence for a British film noir cycle', in Wheeler Winston Dixon (ed.), *Re-viewing British Cinema, 1900–1992*, Albany, NY: State University of New York Press, pp. 155–64.
Murphy, Robert (1986), 'Riff-raff: British cinema and the underworld', in Charles Barr (ed.), *All Our Yesterdays: 90 Years of British Cinema*, London: British Film Institute, pp. 286–305.
——.(1989), *Realism and Tinsel: Cinema and Society in Britain 1939–49*, London: Routledge.
——.(2007), 'British film noir', in Andrew Spicer (ed.), *European Film Noir*, Manchester: Manchester University Press, pp. 84–111.
Naremore, James (1998), *More Than Night: Film Noir and Its Contexts*, Berkeley, CA: University of California Press.
Oliver, Kelly and Benigno Trigo (2003), *Noir Anxiety*, Minneapolis, MN: University of Minnesota Press.
Palmer, R. Barton (1994), *Hollywood's Dark Cinema: The American Film Noir*, New York: Twayne.
Petley, Julian (1986), 'The lost continent', in Charles Barr (ed.), *All Our Yesterdays: 90 Years of British Cinema*, London: British Film Institute, pp. 98–119.
Richards, Jeffrey (1997), *Films and British National Identity: From Dickens to Dad's Army*, Manchester: Manchester University Press.
Robbins, Keith (1998), *Great Britain: Identities, Institutions and the Idea of Britishness*, London: Longman.
Schrader, Paul (1996), 'Notes on *film noir*', in Silver and Ursini (eds), *Film Noir Reader*, pp. 53–63.
Spicer, Andrew (2007), 'British neo-noir', in Spicer (ed.), *European Film Noir*, pp. 112–37.
Telotte, J. P. (1989), *Voices in the Dark: The Narrative Patterns of Film Noir*, Urbana, IL: University of Illinois Press.
Vincendeau, Ginette (2009), 'The new lower depths: Paris in French neo-noir cinema', in Bould, Glitre and Tuck (eds), *Neo-Noir*, London: Wallflower, pp. 103–17.
Weight, Richard (2002), *Patriots: National Identity in Britain 1940–2000*, London: Macmillan.
Wollen, Peter (2002), *Paris Hollywood: Writings on Film*, London: Verso.

Notes

1. Paul Schrader, 'Notes on *film noir*', in Alain Silver and James Ursini (eds), *Film Noir Reader* (New York: Limelight Editions, 1996), p. 54.
2. Raymond Borde and Étienne Chaumeton, *A Panorama of Film Noir 1941–1953*, trans. Paul Hammond (San Francisco, CA: City Lights Books, 2002), p. 126.
3. Michael F. Keaney, *British Film Noir Guide* (Jefferson, NC: McFarland and Co., 2008).

4. R. Barton Palmer, *Hollywood's Dark Cinema: The American Film Noir* (New York: Twayne, 1994), p. 39.
 5. J. P. Telotte, *Voices in the Dark: The Narrative Patterns of Film Noir* (Urbana, IL: University of Illinois Press, 1989), p. 2.
 6. According to Raymond Durgnat, in *A Mirror for England: British Movies from Austerity to Affluence* (London: Faber and Faber, 1970), 'the idea that the war explains an increase in violence, whereas the evidence, on balance, suggests that there was more violence before the war ... probably registers an increased sensitivity, and disapproval of, violence', p. 145.
 7. Borde and Chaumeton, *Panorama of Film Noir*, p. 12.
 8. Kelly Oliver and Benigno Trigo, *Noir Anxiety* (Minneapolis, MN: University of Minnesota Press, 2003), p. xvii; Raymond Durgnat, 'Paint it black: The family tree of the *film noir*', in Silver and Ursini (eds), *Film Noir Reader*, p. 38.
 9. Borde and Chaumeton, *Panorama of Film Noir*, pp. 5, 6–7.
10. James Naremore, *More Than Night: Film Noir and Its Contexts* (Berkeley, CA: University of California Press, 1998), p. 220.
11. In 1936, for example, Graham Greene wrote that the quota system, introduced to protect the British film industry from American domination, had only managed 'to surrender it to a far more alien control' (*The Pleasure Dome: The Collected Film Criticism 1935–40*, ed. John Russell Taylor (Oxford: Oxford University Press, 1980), p. 79).
12. Julian Petley, 'The lost continent', in Charles Barr (ed.), *All Our Yesterdays: 90 Years of British Cinema* (London: British Film Institute, 1986), p. 111.
13. Lawrence Miller, 'Evidence for a British film noir cycle', in Wheeler Winston Dixon (ed.), *Re-viewing British Cinema, 1900–1992*, (Albany, NY: State University of New York Press, 1994), p. 161. Robert Murphy, 'British film noir', in Andrew Spicer (ed.), *European Film Noir* (Manchester: Manchester University Press, 2007), p. 103.
14. There are certainly similar energies unleashed in the period melodramas produced by Gainsborough Studios, aimed mainly at female audiences, and the postwar crime films, aimed mainly at men. Both were equally reviled by critics at the time.
15. Glen Erickson, 'Expressionist doom in *Night and the City*', in Silver and Ursini (eds), *Film Noir Reader*, p. 203.
16. Charlotte Brunsdon, 'Space in the British crime film', in Steve Chibnall and Robert Murphy (eds), *British Crime Cinema* (London: Routledge, 1999), p. 148.
17. Palmer, *Hollywood's Dark Cinema*, p. 6. Steve Chibnall, 'Counterfeit Yanks: War, austerity and Britain's American dream', in Philip John Davies (ed.), *Representing and Imagining America* (Keele: Keele University Press, 1996), p. 150.
18. Durgnat, 'Paint it black', p. 49.
19. Palmer, *Hollywood's Dark Cinema*, p. 33.
20. Borde and Chaumeton, *Panorama of Film Noir*, p. 5.
21. Pam Cook, 'The trouble with sex: Diana Dors and the blonde bombshell phenomenon', in Bruce Babington (ed.), *British Stars and Stardom: From Alma Taylor to Sean Connery* (Manchester: Manchester University Press, 2001), pp. 167–8.
22. Keaney, *British Film Noir Guide*, p. 226.
23. James Chapman, '"Sordidness, corruption and violence almost unrelieved": Critics, censors and the postwar British crime film', *Contemporary British History* 22(2), 186.
24. As quoted in Keith Robbins, *Great Britain: Identities, Institutions and the Idea of Britishness* (London: Longman, 1998), p. 310.
25. Chapman, '"Sordidness, corruption and violence"', 194.
26. Brunsdon (1999), 'Space in the British crime film', p. 148.

27. Robert Fabian, *Fabian of the Yard* (Kingswood: The World's Work, 1956), p. 11.
28. Robert Fabian, *London After Dark* (Toronto: Harlequin Books, 1954), p. 6
29. Fabian, *Fabian of the Yard*, p. 46.
30. Andrew Clay, 'Men, women and money: Masculinity in crisis in the British professional crime film 1946–1965', in Chibnall and Murphy (eds), *British Crime Cinema*, p. 52.
31. Robert Murphy, *Realism and Tinsel: Cinema and Society in Britain 1939–49* (London: Routledge, 1989), pp. 149–50.
32. Peter Wollen, *Paris Hollywood: Writings on Film* (London: Verso, 2002), p. 189.
33. Robert Murphy, 'Riff-raff: British cinema and the underworld', in Charles Barr (ed.), *All Our Yesterdays: 90 Years of British Cinema* (London: British Film Institute, 1986), p. 304.
34. William Whitebait, as quoted in Chapman, '"Sordidness, corruption and violence"', 153.
35. Murphy, *Realism and Tinsel*, p. 150; Wollen, *Paris Hollywood*, pp. 185–6.
36. Joan Lester, as quoted in Chapman, '"Sordidness, corruption and violence"', 191.
37. Chapman, '"Sordidness, corruption and violence"', 197.
38. Jeffrey Richards, *Films and British National Identity: From Dickens to Dad's Army* (Manchester: Manchester University Press, 1997), pp. 144–5.
39. Murphy, 'Riff-raff', p. 299.
40. Ibid., p. 299. Viv Chadder, 'The higher heel: Women and the postwar British crime film', in Chibnall and Murphy (eds), *British Crime Cinema*, p. 70.
41. Richard Weight, *Patriots: National Identity in Britain 1940–2000* (London: Macmillan, 2002), p. 371.
42. Murphy, 'British film noir', in Spicer (ed.), *European Film Noir*, p. 85. Keaney, *British Film Noir Guide*, p. 2.
43. Melanie Bell, 'Fatal femininity in postwar British film: Investigating the British *femme*', in Helen Hanson and Catherine O'Rowe (eds), *The Femme Fatale: Images, Histories, Contexts* (Houndmills: Palgrave Macmillan, 2010), p. 100.
44. In this respect, the film reverses the message of *Cosh Boy*, which suggests that the delinquent's behaviour is the result of the lack of a firm hand in his upbringing (his father died in the war) and ends with his new Canadian stepfather beating him, to the evident approval of the policemen who are waiting to arrest him.
45. In *Whistle Down the Wind* (Bryan Forbes, 1961), also starring Mills, the noir vision recedes even further, as the plot centres on a group of children who mistake a murderer on the run from the police for Jesus come back to save the world.
46. Todd Erickson, 'Kiss me again: Movement becomes genre', in Silver and Ursini (eds), *Film Noir Reader*, p. 321.
47. Andrew Spicer, 'British neo-noir', in Spicer (ed.), *European Film Noir*, p. 114.
48. Keaney, *British Film Noir Guide*, p. 4.
49. Spicer, 'British neo-noir', p. 112.
50. Erickson, 'Kiss me again', p. 308.
51. Ginette Vincendeau, 'The new lower depths: Paris in French neo-noir cinema', in Mark Bould, Kathrina Glitre and Greg Tuck (eds), *Neo-Noir* (London: Wallflower, 2009), p. 105.
52. Steve Chibnall, 'Travels in Ladland: The British gangster film cycle, 1998–2001', in Robert Murphy (ed.), *The British Cinema Book* (3rd edition) (London: British Film Institute, 2009), p. 377.
53. This distinction is also apparent in American neo-noir, with films such as *Body Heat* (Lawrence Kasdan, 1981) telling a self-consciously noir story in a contemporary setting and others, like *Chinatown* (Roman Polanski, 1974), setting the action in the period of classical noir.

54. The filmmakers claimed that the screenplay had been completed before the Ruth Ellis case renewed the campaign against the death penalty (Steve Chibnall, *J. Lee Thompson*, Manchester: Manchester University Press, 2000, pp. 72–3).
55. Mark Bould, Kathrina Glitre and Greg Tuck, 'Parallax views: An introduction', in Bould, Glitre and Tuck (eds), *Neo-Noir*, pp. 6–7.

2. FRENCH NOIR 1947–79: FROM GRUNGE-NOIR TO NOIR-HILISM

Susan Hayward

Introduction

When I was first asked to contribute to this collection of essays on film noir, my original response was 'surely there is enough out there already?' Indeed, in the last decade, some hundred books on film noir have been published in the English language alone. The request, however, was to focus on French Film Noir (from 1930 to the new millennium). I felt there might be something new to say, even if (as with Borde and Chaumeton, 1955) I was not necessarily over-convinced that there is such a thing as French Film Noir; a noir aesthetic, yes – but a specific genre (or subgenre) within French cinema? But, having agreed to write a piece, I pressed forward.

My first move was to let the editors know that I did not consider I could write about French Noir from the 1930s until the present day. My view was that, if a noir period exists in its purest/purist sense, then it begins in 1947 and ends in 1979. First, with regard to the 'start date': whilst the term 'film noir' has had currency since the 1930s,[1] referring to certain 'dark/noir' movies of that period which we now more readily label poetic realist films, the concept of 'film noir' as a genre is nonetheless a postwar phenomenon. This generic label was coined in 1946 by French film critics to designate a particular type of American thriller-genre that suddenly made its appearance in French cinemas after the end of World War II.[2] As to the end date, there is an argument to be made (which I shall go on to do below) that the arc of French Noir coincides with what has been termed, in French economic history, *les trente glorieuses*, a thirty-year period of economic growth from 1947 to 1973, brought to an end by the two oil crises of 1973 and 1979, and that the demise of that economic growth (1973–9) and subsequent social decline can readily be identified with the dark nihilism of *Série noire* (Corneau, 1979).[3]

Ginette Vincendeau has published several lucid and comprehensive pieces in English on the subject of French Noir. In her study, '*Noir* is also a French word: The French antecedents of film noir', she argues for the impact of 1930s French cinema (particularly poetic realist films) on the American noirs of the 1940s and 1950s.[4] She makes the following valid points: first, that noir elements are an outcome of intertextual and transnational links between the American and French film industries; second, that noir aesthetics are prevalent in these 1930s French films; third, that the notion of the doomed protagonist is a recurring motif; and finally that at least seven American noirs are in fact remakes of these earlier 1930s French films.[5] Vincendeau's second study, 'French film noir', takes a broad look at what films could be determined as noir (although many are more readily gangster films). Beginning with the 1930s and ending in the early 1970s, Vincendeau offers 105 titles for consideration.[6] Her deliberate use of the lower case in 'film noir', however, points to a distinction between pure French Noir films and films inscribed with noir elements. Thus, some thirty films of the 1930s can come under the rubric of 'noir' with a small 'n' because of their noir aesthetic or pessimistic narrative. As for a number of films of the 1940s and 1950s, some of which are *polars* (police thrillers, about ten films), but most of which (about thirty-three films) have historically come under the label of *réalisme noir* (noir realism), again the argument for their inclusion in a film noir listing can be convincingly made (because they are dark and pessimistic). Finally, of the films of the 1960s and 1970s (some thirty-two on Vincendeau's list), in their deliberate play with or homage to the American Noir tradition, they surely merit a noir label – even though those that can truly be considered French Noir remain a handful (in my view, ten, see below).

Vincendeau's third study is her magisterial book-length analysis of the French master of noir: Jean-Pierre Melville (*Jean-Pierre Melville: An American in Paris*, 2003). Here, Vincendeau reveals the patterns of cross-fertilisation between American and French Noir traditions as embodied by Melville's oeuvre. She also discusses Melville's originality and cinematic contribution to the film noir genre, including close analyses of style, narrative and characterisation (particularly of the male protagonist).

As you will begin to perceive, my concern was what more I could possibly add. I thought that I might pick up on some of my own discussion of the lack of a femme fatale in French Noirs – I had done this in relation to Simone Signoret (especially her roles in *Les Diaboliques*, but also some earlier *réalisme noir* films, *Dédée d'Anvers* and *Manèges*).[7] But, then, when I turned my attention to a recent book entitled *French and American Noir: Dark Crossings*, by

Alistair Rolls and Deborah Walker (2009), I discovered that an entire chapter had been devoted to this subject (kindly crediting my work, it must be said) – so I encountered yet another impasse! Indeed, Rolls' and Walker's book provides a useful overview of the cross-fertilisation process between American and French noir traditions (taking on board such issues as the literary tradition of noir films and the importance of jazz and its significance as a marker of counter-cultural defiance).

Finally, I turned to Phil Powrie's study of the post-1970 French Noirs, 'French neo-noir to hyper-noir'.[8] My own feeling in relation to this particular noir labelling is that it casts the net too wide and empties the 'noir' of any helpful meaning. Powrie readily admits that few of the films included in his corpus have what could be considered a 'typical noir sensibility'.[9] Indeed, most of the films included in his list are *polars* (albeit with noir elements); and it is doubtless for that reason that Powrie categorises his selection of films under two headings: the Political Thriller (mostly of the 1970s) and the Postmodern Thriller (1980s onwards, Beineix and Besson being the more renowned directors in this domain with their techno-neo-noirs).

For all the above reasons, I decided to focus on what can be considered French Film Noir in its purist form, limiting the number of films in terms of timescale and their adherence to the definitions that, to my mind, embody the spirit of this generic typology. Film noir is associated with a particular moment in twentieth-century history: World War II and the postwar Cold War period up until the late 1950s. Film noir emerged, then, from a period of political instability. The dominant mood in noir narratives, unsurprisingly, is one of anxiety and paranoia, pessimism and social malaise. Noir creates an environment in which the male protagonist seeks to assert his identity, often through violent means – thus pointing to an overriding sense of masculinity in crisis which can, in turn, be associated with the political culture of the moment in which national identity comes seriously under question. Let us not forget that men, having fought in a major world war, upon returning home found that the old societal patterns had changed (women occupied workplaces that had previously been the province of the menfolk; economic security, in the form of decent jobs, was far from assured). Nor were nations secure. Almost immediately, the capitalist West and the Eastern communist bloc were at loggerheads. This time, however, in a post-nuclear world, the stakes were even higher (where the arms race and espionage were the key elements of the Cold War). But we need to recall that for France this war experience was singularly different: France was an occupied nation – men were not fighting; they were either taken into forced labour to Germany or were at home having to cope with the occupying enemy (at worst collaborating, at best joining the Resistance, or keeping a very low profile). Thus, masculine identity was crucially aligned with the nation and, in this instance, it was not an easy one to confront – a weakened, submissive, emasculated identity with which, arguably, the nation has still yet to come to terms.

Setting the Parameters of French Film Noir

Whilst few will dispute what are the visual characteristics of noir, not all agree on what, in narrative terms, can be defined as noir. Thus, film noir's distinctive cinematography emphasises the impression of night-time photography with high-contrast lighting (chiaroscuro), occasional low-key lighting, deep shadows and oblique angles – all of which serve to create an atmosphere of dread and anxiety in which the male protagonist (it is always a male) finds himself claustrophobically enveloped. This atmosphere acts as a foil for his state of mind. The French noir protagonist is an embodiment of solitude; he has an interiority that manifests itself in a number of different ways: paranoia, suspicion, timidity (to name but some). It is this individuality and interiority – a psychology if you will – that helps us to demarcate the noir film from gangster films. The film noir protagonist is above all else a loner. Even if he brings a gang together around him to commit a crime, his solitude and individualistic drive mark him out as a lone figure. If the noir protagonist is involved in criminal activity (theft and murder), then the narrative outcome is ineluctably death. Often, it appears that the protagonist's trajectory is one long suicidal death wish – as if he finds himself enmeshed in an existential angst from which there is no exit. This fated protagonist follows an ineluctable route, one chosen by *himself* (a last job, a score to settle, a point to prove), not a femme fatale figure, who to all intents and purposes does not really exist in French noir. Thus, we can speak more readily of the central protagonist as the *homme fatal* (or, occasionally, a secondary male character linked to the protagonist). Finally, on this issue of male noir characterisation, the other type of protagonist in noir, also a loner, is of course the detective – in French noir, most often a policeman. Less frequent in French film noir, this detective-loner has a fairly pessimistic view of humanity (including the police), perceives mankind as flawed, understands the ambiguities of human nature well enough to exploit them to his advantage and finally nail his criminal or gangster.

It is this rather purist take on noir that informs my own corpus. My first point of reference (after visual stylisation) is characterisation; my second, narrative. Thus, my corpus of films for this thirty-year period comes to some seventeen titles (see Table 2.1). A far cry from Vincendeau's 105, I admit. Based on the above definitions, I am leaving *réalisme noir* films and most gangster films to one side (whilst acknowledging that a looser definition of noir might encompass them). I begin, therefore, in 1947 with Clouzot's *Quai des Orfèvres* and end, in 1979, with *Série noire*. In imposing my criteria, however, I came up against one stumbling block in relation to two 1950s films that have

Table 2.1 Chart of French Film Noir Corpus (1947–79)

Date	Title	Director	Novel/original scenario	Director of Photography
1947	*Quai des Orfèvres*	Henri-Georges Clouzot	S. A. Steeman (Belgian/novel)	Armand Thirard
1948	*Impasse des deux-anges*	Maurice Tourneur	Jean-Paul Le Chanois (French/original scenario)	Claude Renoir
1954	*Les Diaboliques*	Henri-Georges Clouzot	Boileau & Narcejac (French/novel)	
1954	*Touchez pas au grisbi*	Jacques Becker	Albert Simonin (French/novel)	Pierre Montazel
1955	*Du rififi chez les hommes*	Jules Dassin	Auguste Le Breton (French/novel)	Philippe D'Agostini
1955	*Razzia sur la chnouff*	Henri Decoin	Auguste Le Breton (French/novel)	Pierre Montazel
1958	*L'Ascenseur pour l'échafaud*	Louis Malle	Noël Calef (French/novel)	Henri Decaë
1960	*À bout de souffle*	Jean-Luc Godard	François Truffaut (French/original scenario)	Raoul Coutard
1960	*Tirez sur le pianiste*	François Truffaut	David Goodis (US/novel)	Raoul Coutard
1963	*Le Doulos*	Jean-Pierre Melville	Pierre Lesou (French/novel)	Nicolas Hayer
1963	*Le Deuxième souffle*	Jean-Pierre Melville	José Giovanni (French/novel)	Marcel Combes
1967	*Le Samouraï*	Jean-Pierre Melville	Joan McLeod (US/novel)	Henri Decaë
1970	*Le Cercle rouge*	Jean-Pierre Melville	Melville's own scenario	Henri Decaë
1971	*Comptes à rebours*	Roger Pigaut	André-Georges Brunelin (French/original scenario)	Jean Tournier
1972	*Un Flic*	Jean-Pierre Melville	Melville's own scenario/script	Walter Wottitz
1976	*Police Python 357*	Alain Corneau	Corneau's own scenario	Étienne Becker
1979	*Série noire*	Alain Corneau	Jim Thompson (US/novel)	Pierre William Glenn

consistently been heralded as part of the noir canon, but which arguably do not belong. Should I keep them in? The first is Becker's *Touchez pas au grisbi* (1954). Strictly speaking this is not a noir, since the central protagonist, Max (played by Jean Gabin), an ageing gangster, does not perish at the end of the story. In fact, he is obliged to 'carry on as normal'. Condemned to live on in a future without his best friend Riton (René Dary), an existential emptiness looms large. Furthermore, as the narrative unravels it is clear that noir dynamics propel the story forward, most especially in the form of Riton who 'betrays' (albeit inadvertently) his friend and thus constitutes an *homme fatal*. This film stays in my corpus. In the second instance, Melville's *Bob le flambeur* (1956), the case for exclusion is clearer. It is the director himself who states that his film is not a noir film but a 'comedy of manners'.[10] Indeed, the central protagonist, Bob, fails to accomplish his heist because he has been too busy gambling. As the film closes, his arresting officer jokingly remarks that he will only get a five-year sentence, after which he can enjoy the fruits of his winnings! Thus, this second film is not included in my corpus.

The above seventeen films trace an interesting arc when examined against the evolving economic climate of this thirty-year period. Thus, the first three films, *Quai des Orfèvres*, *Impasse des deux-anges* and *Les Diaboliques*, with their grunge-noir look, coincide with the period of economic hardship and moral rehabilitation post war; the second swathe of noirs, *Touchez pas au grisbi*, *Du rififi chez les hommes* and *Razzia sur la chnouff*, all refer in a very distinct fashion to the reconstruction and modernisation of France. These two cycles of noir also demonstrate, in a number of ways, the transition from a parochial, localised, grubby and penny-pinching *petit-noir* environment to one with a more sophisticated, international feel. Luxury objects, so predominantly absent from the first cycle, make their appearance in numerous forms in this second cycle: flash cars, expensive nightclubs, nice apartments, well-cut suits. So, too, do elements from an unsavoury criminal underworld such as drugs and all types of ballistic technology (from revolvers to machine guns).

The third cycle (1958–60) is made up of three films from directors associated with the *Nouvelle Vague* (New Wave) (Malle, *L'Ascenseur pour l'échafaud*; Godard, *À bout de souffle* and Truffaut, *Tirez sur le pianiste*). This period of the late 1950s to early 1960s was marked by the return of General de Gaulle to power, and with him a new Fifth Republic. De Gaulle's return as the elder statesman, patriarch-saviour of a France on the brink of civil war (due primarily to the Algerian conflict) was at odds, however, with the demographic reality of a rejuvenated nation. In the postwar period and throughout the 1950s, France's birth rate reached its highest in 150 years (at 20 per cent). The youth class therefore became a significant presence and, although it could not yet vote, it showed considerable irreverence to the status quo – through its look, its music and, where our New Wave directors are concerned, through a playful engagement with American noir codes and conventions.

The final cycle (1963–79) represents the very darkest collection of noirs. Here revenge narratives dominate. Over these sixteen years, starting under de Gaulle, presidential power became increasingly autocratic (censorship, centralised power, tough policing), all but disenfranchising the citizen. Moreover, in this post-industrial age, technology replaced masculine labour and economic crises compounded unemployment, which brought in its wake renewed hardships. A sense of redundancy pervades these noirs, therefore, in which asserting a masculine identity seems a virtual impossibility as, one by one, the protagonists fail in their pursuit of some imaginary holy grail. Thus, there are 'last heist' films that end in death (*Le Doulos, Le Deuxième souffle, Le Cercle rouge* and *Un Flic*); tragic hymns to the ascetic solitude of the lone wolf: one a hired assassin (*Le Samuraï*), the other a tunnel-visioned cop (*Police Python 357*). *Série noire*, the last film in the corpus, is an amalgam of all three narrative lines: revenge, stealing and ascetic solitude and is the most pitifully dark of all.

Cycle One: Grunge-noir 1947–54

The immediate postwar period through to the early 1950s was known as *les années noires* (the dark years) and so they were, for a number of political as well as economic reasons. Poverty was rife, resources scarce and the winters fierce – people were living a dystopian reality. This was a period of huge civil unrest with acts of sabotage and thousands of strikes, often brutally repressed by the police. This unrest was matched by political instability, with eight governments succeeding each other in the four-year postwar period (1947–51). To compound this unease, the political right wing, which had been most readily associated with collaboration during the war, engaged in a form of resistance to the national government. The Right chose to ignore the call for national unity and engaged in a *guerre franco-française* in which they accused the government of aggressive retribution (through the *Épuration* (Purge) of wartime collaborators) and of holding up a false image of the Resistance (dismissively labelling it *résistentialisme*). The humanism of the Liberation discourse was ridiculed. Further, as part of the right-wing counterattack, existentialism was ironically labelled the 'official philosophy of the régime'.[11]

This period was also known as a *politique de redressement* (politics of recovery) that was both physical and moral – a physical reconstruction of France, but also a moral one (*redressement* also means the righting of wrongs). Yet, to all evidence, if the physical recovery did happen and economic growth began to kick in, the moral one was far from assured. A prime example was the 1951–2 amnesty – sanctioned in the name of national unity – of those who had been condemned under the *Épuration*. Thus, by 1951, former collaborators were back in political office. This cynical opportunistic behaviour in the political-cultural realm compounded the ambiguities already felt by the national psyche and found expression in the films of the period, particularly the *réalisme noir* films and of course the films noirs. Elsewhere on the cultural scene, the existentialist theatre of engagement exposed this cynical expediency as bad faith – and asserted that moral accountability had to be assumed for one's actions (Camus' and Sartre's plays in particular). The theatre of the absurd pointed to the unreliability of the spoken word and the ultimate meaninglessness of existence (Ionesco and Beckett).

Moral preoccupations ran deep in the nation's psyche; this was, after all, a country that had capitulated to the enemy (in the Occupation, 1940-4) and denounced itself to itself – during the Occupation some 3–5 million anonymous letters of denunciation were sent to the Vichy government alone.[12] Suspicion and paranoia were rife, as too was jealousy (often the root cause of letters of denunciation); the very essence of noir was a lived reality during this painful period of France's history. Thus, it is hardly surprising that betrayal is a major trope of the French film noir – a betrayal that can be read (allegorically at least) as pertaining to the nation.

Although none of the three films in this cycle makes a single mention of the war, the Occupation period or the Resistance, that recent past is nonetheless there as a structuring absence. *Quai des Orfèvres* is a film that speaks directly to the postwar mood of jealousy and despair, *Impasse des deux-anges* to the need to rebuild a broken France and *Les Diaboliques* to the cold cynicism of material advancement regardless of the cost to others. In *Quai des Orfèvres* the murder of a salacious promoter-entrepreneur, Brignon (Charles Dullin), becomes the focus of investigation for world-weary, ageing Detective Antoine (Louis Jouvet). Brignon, an elderly, hunchbacked individual, enjoys collecting photographs of nude women whom he has procured for that purpose (with possible spin-offs for financial gain too). Three major suspects come under Antoine's purview: the aspiring music-hall artiste Jenny (Suzy Delair), who hopes to impress Brignon with her singing talents and get into film, although he is more interested in her physical attributes; her husband-accompanist Maurice (Bernard Blier) whose jealousy drives him to hunt down Brignon and kill him, only to arrive too late (he is already dead); finally, Dora (Simone Renant), a professional photographer who, because of economic necessity, supplies Brignon with his photographs (she tries to protect both Jenny and Maurice from suspicion, the former because she is secretly in love with her, the latter because he is an old friend).

The film plays skilfully with its audience, asking the question: who is the noirest of them all? For during the first half of the film, the central noir character is undoubtedly Maurice. Once he gets wind of Jenny's deception (she claims she is going to see her sick grandmother when in fact she is going to Brignon's private mansion), the whole tone of the film turns to noir. Lighting in Maurice's apartment becomes chiaroscuro, casting shadows as he looks at his despairing reflection in the mirror, takes his gun, plans the murder, constructs an alibi and chases off in the night to Brignon's house. But then, once Detective Antoine comes into the story, it is he who becomes more obviously the central noir protagonist. We first encounter him in his miserable lodgings, which he shares with his son (a mixed-race boy). The cheerless, freezing rooms are matched by his down-at-heel sartorial shabbiness and cynical world-view. But most significantly, the chiaroscuro lighting that first came into play as Maurice developed his murderous plot now goes into overdrive. Shadows cast against the walls and ceiling in Antoine's room are gigantic and seemingly completely out of synch with the context (Antoine nurturing his son, then getting dressed for work). Yet, metaphorically, Antoine looms large in this investigation, casting a long shadow of fear over the suspects, as he slowly exposes their weaknesses and uncovers the truth.

In the end, none of the three suspects is the murderer (a local hood was the perpetrator). But what stands out is their desire to cover up the truth for each other and even take the blame – including Jenny, whose grubby pursuit of fame led to the misadventure in the first place. Most honourable of all (as Antoine acknowledges) is the social 'misfit', the lesbian Dora. To save both Maurice and Jenny from the guillotine, she claims she murdered Brignon. Decency is a thread that runs through this film, an interesting twist in noirness. At several junctures, people stand up against the idea of denunciation – '*je ne suis pas mouchard*' ('I am not a grass'), a theme close to Clouzot's heart, one suspects (he had been unfairly suspended under the *Épuration* laws). It is as if Clouzot, for whom this film marked the return to work, was making a statement to his audience: 'look what you have been missing, the master of suspense is back'.[13] Indeed, a hallmark of Clouzot's thrillers is to lead his audience down one path, only to reveal in the end that it was the wrong one – things are not what they seem.

A similar, albeit far more sinister subterfuge is at work in Clouzot's *Les Diaboliques* where we are led to believe it is the two women who are plotting to kill the male character. In fact, in this triangular relationship (wife, mistress, husband) it is the husband and his mistress who try (and succeed) in doing away with the wife with the intention of getting their hands on her fortune. In this film, set in a decrepit boarding school, the children are poorly fed and the wife Christina (Vera Clouzot) and mistress Nicole (Simone Signoret) serially abused by the husband Michel (Paul Meurisse). Cruelty and guilt are at the core of this narrative of triangular sado-masochistic relationships. The suspense and terror is ratcheted up once Michel has apparently been murdered; the women first drown him in a bath then sling his body into the school's murky swimming pool. Christina can barely live with her guilt and fear of discovery (much like Maurice in *Quai des Orfèvres*, who at one point attempts suicide). After this turning point, mysterious goings-on occur at night; shadows move across windows, sounds magnify in the dark, evidence of Michel's ghostly return abound, finally terrorising Christina to death as he rises fully clothed (and alive) out of the bathtub. Needless to say, the truth is slowly unravelled by Fichet (Charles Vanel), a scruffy, shabbily dressed policeman (much as Antoine in *Quai des Orfèvres*) turned private detective.[14] The venal pair are apprehended and sent away for a long time.

Figure 2.1 Paul Meurisse in *Les Diaboliques*.

With both these films (made some seven years apart) guilt is what drives the narrative, even if the tonalities are distinct. The shadows of the past, the legacy of the Occupation, are cast long; no one, it seems, is immune – even Antoine admits his job is a dirty one. In *Quai des Orfèvres*, the guilt experienced is mostly an outcome of irresponsible actions, often due to the compromises that have to be made in this time of postwar penury (Dora and Jenny in particular, but also Maurice in his jealousy and cowardice). So bad faith plays its part until, in the end, all three take responsibility for their actions. In *Les Diaboliques*, the drab décor matches the sordid motives of the central couple whose penny-pinching avarice will be their final undoing. As for guilt, with the exception of Christina, whilst it is pervasive, it remains ungraspable, much like Michel's ghostly body.

Confrontation with the past is ultimately the only way forward, as Tourneur's *Impasse des deux-anges* makes clear. Indeed, the penultimate lines of the film, spoken by Marianne (the name is symbolically Republican to the core) are: 'I had a past. I no longer have one. Now I am free.' Yet what is intriguing here is that the confrontation is mediated through the female body – Marianne (Signoret) confronts her past, something her male counterparts are seemingly incapable of doing. In this film, a former lover, Jean (Meurisse) resurfaces into Marianne's life after a seven-year absence. Briefly, she is tempted to forego her marriage to a rich marquis, Antoine (Marcel Herrand) and leave with Jean. She joins him on a nocturnal walk that takes them to their old working-class haunts in the Impasse des Deux-Anges (in the sixth arrondissement of Paris, just a few streets behind her posh apartment in Saint-Germain). They catch up on their past, through a series of flashbacks. She learns that when he disappeared from her life seven years ago, unbeknownst to her he was under arrest for theft and sent to jail. He is now a top safe-cracker and jewel thief and back in Paris (his nom-de-plume is 'Le Spécialiste'), brought in by some mobsters to steal her necklace (although he had no way of knowing it was hers since she had changed her name). She, meantime, has built herself a successful career on the stage, which she is about to relinquish in order to marry the marquis. Jean accuses her of betraying her class; she retorts she has nothing to reproach herself for, yet her renaming (from Anne-Marie to Marianne) belies this – she clearly did want to leave her past behind. The two angels in the film title are hyphenated, suggesting an inextricable link between Jean and Anne-Marie/Marianne. Yet which is the good angel and which the bad: the man with a criminal past or the woman in denial of hers? The flashback trajectory clarifies this impasse. Jean is incapable of change; Marianne sees through his bad faith when he blames her for his inability to go straight and it is that, plus his violence and cruelty towards those who get in his way, which clarifies her own past (she acknowledges how her passion for Jean blinded her to the truth) and leads her to leave him. Bereft, he elects to die: he returns the stolen necklace, thereby defying the mobsters' orders, knowing full well they will come and gun him down – an honourable Samurai-type of suicide which Melville's hero, Jef Costello, reprises twenty years later (*Le Samuraï*). At last he takes responsibility for his actions – it is therefore an existential death. But it is also an absurd one, for, as he lies dying in the street, he manages to utter the very last words of the film, '*c'est pas la peine*' ('it isn't worth it'). (Michel's dying words in *À bout de souffle*, '*c'est vraiment dégueulasse*' ('it's really disgusting') echo this absurdist view.)

I want to close this section with a few words about noir iconography and sexuality. The first point concerns set design. Typically it should act as a foil to the narrative and, in *Quai des Orfèvres* and *Les Diaboliques*, Max Douy and Léon Barsacq's restrained style does just that. Douy's sets match the temperament and economic reality of the *Quai des Orfèvres* characters: the cramped effervescence of the music-hall and backstage environs; the art-nouveau cafés of Jenny's world (all rather artificial); the straight lines and functional art déco of Dora's apartment, which tell us a great deal about her professional precision and empty love life; Maurice and Jenny's apartment, aspiring to be bourgeois yet dingy and unkempt (especially in the kitchen); Antoine moving from one drab, spartan environment (his freezing cold rooms) to another (the equally freezing police headquarters). Similarly, Barsacq's décor for *Les Diaboliques* is entirely consonant with the different characters' personas (Michel's stark wood-panelled office, Christine's overly Catholic bedroom, Nicole's stingy flat in Niort where the rattling of old pipes in the bathroom ultimately gives the murderous plan away). Only Jean D'Eaubonne stands out with his excessive décors for *Impasse des deux-anges*, with the rich, overstuffed interiors of

Marianne's Saint-Germain apartment and its many mirrors, suggesting there is some decluttering and taking stock or self-examination to be done. But these are intended for contrast with the excessively desolate set of the Impasse that is more hyper-real than real. It is an imaginary Impasse, with a view beyond its dead-end to Paris's Montmartre (in fact no such view is possible). For twenty-two minutes, caught between night and daybreak, Marianne and Jean negotiate their own histories in this murky, dimly lit area (fantastically shot by Claude Renoir with side-lighting, low-key lighting and chiaroscuro effects). The derelict buildings, ripe for demolition but still inhabited by a couple of homeless people, make a fine backdrop to the final exposure of Jean as a cruel and ruthless individual whom Marianne cannot possibly follow. As indeed she tells him, he is responsible for his past, she for hers. The set acts, then, in its excess of dereliction, as a moral metaphor for the inescapability of Jean's criminal past and it is possible, furthermore, to read this dynamic as an allegory for the nation's relationship to its own recent murky history.

In all three films, female sexuality is far from fixed. Dora and Nicole for example – central characters in the two Clouzot vehicles – hold down more readily masculine-identified jobs (a portrait photographer and a science teacher, respectively). Both have a queered sexuality, Dora is a lesbian (and out to all but Jenny and Maurice), Nicole's masculine attributes (short hair, unfeminine attire) and gestures (she stomps about) mark her out as the butch partner-in-crime to Christina's overinvested feminine femme.[15] Even Marianne in *Impasse* is not exempt from queer associations. When we first meet her, at the theatre, she is cross-dressed as an eighteenth-century marquis (as if a parody of her own fiancé). A cigarette hangs from her mouth as she poses for a group photograph in which she gazes 'adoringly' into the eyes of her understudy. Who wears the trousers, one wonders? Especially when we see her repeatedly rejecting the marquis' attempts to dominate her and refusing to let Jean blame her for his criminal life.

This queerness is intriguing when we consider that, in all three films, the central female characters were dressed by top couturiers (Fath, Carven and Heim) all of whom were committed to redress the over-masculinised fashion of the war years by introducing a style of opulence that would refeminise women (starting with Dior and his New Look of 1947). The feminine masquerade, at least where our characters are concerned (Dora, Jenny, Nicole and Marianne), fails to neuter their inherent strength and steel. As to the men, none quite passes muster. Maurice and Antoine (*Orfèvres*) wear ill-fitting suits and bear no insignia of their profession. Small wonder Jenny failed to recognise Antoine as a detective because he did not have a trenchcoat (it was stolen, he tells her, perhaps by the murderer, the only one to wear such a coat in the film). Jean (*Impasse*) and Michel (*Diaboliques*) are snazzy dressers (they wear double-breasted suits of expensive cloth) – displaying a status to which they clearly feel entitled. However, if fetishistic iconography is anything to go by, they should beware. Jean is without his trenchcoat once he embarks on the theft, and Michel's Prince of Wales suit is ruined from several soakings (bathtubs and swimming pool). In these last two embodiments of the noir protagonist (Jean and Michel) we see the emergence of a new phenomenon: the criminal male as enigma, as the identity to be probed, the *homme fatal* around whom the narrative revolves. This *homme fatal* proffers a disturbing image of masculinity in crisis that is quite distinct from that of American noir: a cynical, ruthless, yet cowardly masculinity which cannot survive – an embodiment of a past lack of moral fibre that the nation must expunge, as Republican Marianne does in *Impasse*.

Cycles Two and Three:
Bourgeois Noir and its Deconstruction 1954–60

If messages of moral rehabilitation abound in the first cycle of noirs, no such message is present in the second. These noirs are about a modernising France, the building of a new, shiny, technologically advanced nation. The majority of the gangsters have already attained bourgeois comforts (if not status) and live in plush apartments or bachelor pads. They can afford the luxuries of life: nice clothes, smart cars, elegant women. Truffaut was right when he said that these mid-1950s thrillers merely gave an inverted image of bourgeois values.[16] And it is for this reason that the second and third cycles of noirs seem naturally to come together as generic opposites to be considered: the former working to consolidate bourgeois values, the latter to deconstruct them.

The mid-1950s marked the beginning of the boom years. France experienced tremendous economic growth (by 1958, to 5 per cent annually, a figure sustained until 1973 when the first oil crisis hit hard). By the end of the 1950s, 22 per cent of all households had a fridge and other electronic goods in the house (compared with 5 per cent in 1951); by 1954, most households in the major cities had running hot water and bathrooms (compared with only 3 per cent in 1949), and the automobile industry had grown by a third (the Citroën DS dates from 1955). From 1954 to 1964, slums were cleared and there was a huge increase (30 per cent) in social housing. If, in economic terms, France was expanding rapidly, such was not the case where its foreign affairs were concerned. First came the humiliating defeat in 1954 in Indochina; second, in 1955, the armed conflicts with France's northern African territories: Algeria, Morocco and Tunisia – the latter two countries were granted independence in 1956. Algeria was a territory France was unwilling to lose. A tenth of its inhabitants were French colonials, but oil and gas were also major considerations for holding on. By June 1956, beginning with the Battle of Algiers, France was fully engaged in a colonial war, known as a *sale guerre* (dirty war) because of terrorist and torture tactics on both sides. Conflict lasted until 1962 when, finally, France gave up the fight, and independence for Algeria was granted by referendum of the French electorate (by 99.72 per cent).

The image of France to prevail, therefore, is of modernisation, economic growth and cleanliness at home, but difficult and dirty decolonisation abroad. Of the six noir films we are considering here, only one, from the third cycle, Malle's *L'Ascenseur pour l'échafaud* (1958), speaks to this image of a nation in conflict (a brave step given censorship laws of the time, especially in this peak year of the troubles). The central male character is a former paratrooper who fought in both Indochina and Algeria; his boss (whom he murders) is a magnate in the oil business (laying pipelines) and has made his fortune exploiting Algeria; the secondary character, a troubled youth, has a barbed exchange with a German tourist (whom he murders) over the effects on French morale of both the Occupation and the colonial wars.

The focus in the second cycle is on a modernising France, where the concept of honour amongst thieves (*Grisbi*), the importance of family (*Rififi*) and keeping France clean (*Razzia*) prevail. However, there is an undercurrent of nostalgia for a pre-war consciousness when France was an honourable nation, in that these three films are all constructed around a similar premise: the old order versus the new, wherein the new order is not necessarily always seen as the best. In *Rififi* and *Grisbi* the new order is the rival gang that doesn't want to work for its money. The leader of the rival gang is a foreigner and is involved in selling drugs (in nightclubs) and thinks nothing of stealing the loot from the likes of Tony-Le-Stéphanois (Jean Servais) in *Rififi*, and Max in *Grisbi*, two old-style gangsters who have worked very hard to pull off what they hoped was their last heist. Indeed, in *Rififi* we are witness to the labour involved (in a twenty-five-minute central section of the film). In *Razzia*, the new order is epitomised by a get-rich-quick culture of drug manufacturing (*la chnouff*) and sleazy jazz clubs where marijuana is freely smoked. This 'stoned' generation (literally, several personages are complete zombies) and those who supply their habits must be eradicated – and they are, thanks to the hard endeavours and clever work of undercover cop Henri Ferré, aka 'Le Nantais' (Jean Gabin), a man of strength and long service to law and order.

The new order in these three films is also the greater materialism of the age, evidence of which is to be found in the domestic interiors, clothes and the very fancy cars. But, again, this is revealed in a contrastive manner, casting a shadow on its intrinsic worth. To this effect, domestic interiority has a significant role to play. In *Rififi* the contrast between the modern luxury of Jo's apartment and Tony's dingy bedsit immediately signals the price Tony has paid (including his poor health) in taking the rap and going to jail for Jo. The cleanliness and elegant modern design of the furniture in Jo's apartment, and the value placed upon it, is mirrored by the attention his wife, Louise, pays to it (we first see her in an apron running a vacuum cleaner around the apartment). As Jo explains to Tony, he remains in crime so he can satisfy his wife's materialism. Mario, another member of the gang, also lives in comfort with his girlfriend Ida. His apartment is a more traditionally furnished space and rather cluttered, but he has television (very unusual in those days), a draughtsman's table (pointing to his technical skills) and a nice bathroom wherein at one point we see the maternal Ida giving him a bath. Yet it is in this very space of domestic well-being that the couple will be brutally murdered by the rival gang.

Grisbi offers an interesting mix of domestic interiors, all linked via the character of Max. He owns two apartments: the more conventionally furnished one from which he has to escape, over the Paris rooftops, when the rival gang comes after him; and the sparse but manly and elegant art-deco bachelor pad (including a sleek black-tiled bathroom) where he holes up with his friend Riton. Max's wealthy environs contrast with Riton's crummy single room which has a sink and bidet tucked away behind a nasty plastic shower curtain. These contrasting spaces, therefore, tell us a great deal about their friendship. It is evident that, without Max, Riton would sink into the abyss. And, it is Max's commitment to Riton that will cost him his loot (*grisbi*).

Finally, *Razzia*, where again domestic and work environs overlap. Le Nantais runs a chic restaurant as a cover for his drug activities. But he lives upstairs in considerable comfort – as we can determine from his modern-looking bedroom with its en-suite bathroom. In these spaces, his lover, Lisette, tends to his every need: preparing nice food (served in the restaurant downstairs after hours), running baths, ministering to his wounds and so on. The other domestic space, the suburban house where the drugs are cut and packaged by a husband-and-wife team, is the complete opposite. Although inhabited, it feels desolate; there is not one sign of domestic practice – everything is geared to the drugs business. The wife wears a slovenly dressing gown and her husband's attire is equally shabby. Thus, in *Razzia*, domestic environs are double-edged in that they serve either to conceal or reveal the existence of criminality.

The third link between the second-cycle noirs is the very visible presence of the maternal, be that in the form of a real mother (Louise in *Rififi*) or proto-mother (Ida in *Rififi*, Mme Bouche in *Grisbi* and Lisette in *Razzia*) and a sense of the family, be it in its real form (Louise, Jo and their son Tony in *Rififi*), or the central male protagonist and his proto-son (Tony Le Stéphanois and Jo in *Rififi*; Max and Marco in *Grisbi*). But be warned. The family is far from secure. In real or surrogate form it is constantly under threat from its own criminal fathers. Furthermore, the proto-fathers fail their sons: Max to save Marco who dies in a shoot-out trying to retrieve Max's loot; and in a curious reversal of the concept of protection, it is Jo who looks out for Tony Le Stéphanois. Indeed, every time he gets into trouble, Tony telephones Jo (rather than the other way around). The mother-nation is, it seems, a forlornly longed-for but lost entity.

These bourgeois noir characters, with their bourgeois values, their sleek bathrooms and electronic household goods standing as a symbol of having arrived, seek to settle down to a quiet life. However, it is not external forces that will give their secrets away (as in *Diaboliques*). What will is a masculinity that is unable to be strong. Tony Le Stéphanois' (*Rififi*) wracked body is an excellent metaphor for this concept of a weak and ailing masculinity. He could have saved Jo from death if he had managed to make that one last phone call instead of being bent on revenge and going after his rival. His specialist safe-breaker, Césare (Jules Dassin),[17] also shows weakness by breaking the code of trust when he steals an extra ring for his girlfriend (it is this gift that gives the secret away); similarly Riton in *Grisbi*. Only the undercover cop, Le Nantais in *Razzia*, has any mettle and is unafraid to confront the drug underworld, and, of the gangsters, only Max in *Grisbi* lives on (difficult, perhaps, to kill off Gabin, the *monstre sacré* of French cinema).

Bourgeois values are a far cry from two of the three iconoclastic New Wave noirs, *À bout de souffle* and *Tirez sur le pianiste* – less so in *L'Ascenseur pour l'échafaud*, for Florence (Jeanne Moreau) may well want to leave the stifling nature of bourgeois life, in the form of her rich husband, but not necessarily its trappings. Fortunately, her lover, former paratrooper Julien (Maurice Ronin), is well-equipped, physically, to carry out the perfect crime (by abseiling up and down the building to murder her husband) and, if his expensive sports car is anything to go by, wealthy enough to maintain her lifestyle. Crucially, however, he leaves the rope behind and has to trace back his steps, this time in the lift. It gets shut down overnight – and he is stuck. Meantime, the youth, Louis (Georges Poujoly), has stolen Julien's car to impress his girlfriend, Véronique (Yori Bertin). In an absurdist gesture of fury he shoots dead two German tourists with Julien's gun (left in the car's glove compartment). The twist of fate could not be more cruel – a catch 22 in which either way, Julien will be found guilty of murder – and, of all ironies, it is new technology that is the undoing of both murderers (Julien's miniature spy camera reveals the truth).

This cold, slowly seething noir is spectacularly shot in the night hours of Paris (Decaë at his documentary best) as Florence trails around the city looking for her lover, her trajectory coolly underscored by the improvised jazz of Miles Davis's trumpet, discreetly backed by the rest of the quartet. It is a 'no exit' noir, sad and tragic; wasteful where Julien's and Louis' lives are concerned (Julien to a long prison sentence; Louis to the guillotine); a desperate dashing of Florence's and Véronique's hopes for fulfilment in love. What *L'Ascenseur* introduces to the French noir is the sense of futility not just of the gestures of crime (compared with the great craftsmanship of the heist in *Rififi*), but of aspirations, of hopes for a better life. Instructively, it is the youth (the new demographic class), Louis, who most readily embodies this despair and who encapsulates this morose mood of the nation when he speaks of France 'having a lot on its mind' (he is referring to the Occupation and the Indochina and Algerian crises).

Truffaut said of *Le Pianiste* that he wanted to make a film *sans sujet* (without a subject).[18] And that 'lack' is precisely what tips the scales – the central protagonist's timidity makes him ineffectual, a rather cowardly creature (*un salaud* in existential terms). Similarly, in *À bout de souffle*, although Michel (Jean-Paul Belmondo) accuses all around him of cowardice, especially Patricia (Jean Seberg), his American girlfriend, it is his own arrogant bravura that makes him the coward he is (stealing from the weak and unsuspecting; taking what is not his without a thought; full of empty gestures and maxims). His ineffectual pose as a gangster is marked sartorially. First, he loses his tweed jacket and trilby hat. Second, he mixes sartorial metaphors, wearing silk socks with a tweed jacket; later, he is seen sporting a tweed cap. Third, he completely undermines his hard-man act when, in the long, central sequence in which he and Patricia talk about life, we repeatedly see them wearing each other's clothes (for example, he, her dressing gown; she, his shirt). Noir sartorial iconography is at its most unstable here. Finally, in the closing sequence, his signature sunglasses have lost a lens, as if indicating that he is no more than the sum of his contradictions. No wonder he says '*je choisis le néant*' ('I choose nothingness') – in Sartrean terms the *salaud*'s bad faith escape – and elects to run down the street knowing he will be shot in the back by the police.

Truffaut called *Le Pianiste* '*un pastiche respectueux*' ('a respectful pastiche') of American cinema. Coming on the back of his very successful *Les 400 coups*, he wanted to avoid being pigeonholed and so made this film with the intention of disconcerting the audience. It is a mélange of generic tones, mixing the burlesque with the surreal, the lyrical with the noir.[19] But, despite the noir iconography being in place, nothing makes a great deal of sense (the lack of subject again). Even though Charlie (Charles Aznavour), the timid pianist, unwillingly gets enmeshed in his gangster brother's problems (the criminal element of the film); the only part of the narrative that is 'follow-able' is his own personal story. We learn how he gave up classical playing when his wife committed suicide. Then, as now, he is obsessed with failure and his trajectory is a solitary one – 'even when he is with someone he is alone', his girlfriend Lena (Marie Dubois) remarks. It is his failure to connect fully to another that makes him the *homme fatal* and causes the death of the two women who love him (his wife and Lena). With *À bout de souffle* and *Le Pianiste*, the protagonists are counter-noir in their lack of heroism. Indeed, both characters are straining to get either into or out of noir narratives. Michel starts off in *Detour*, ends up in *Dillinger*. He yearns to be a French Bogey, but remains a sorry pastiche. In the end, both Godard (in a cameo role) and Patricia denounce him. In this parodic doubling-up of the femme fatale, first the director turns *homme fatal* – he's

Figure 2.2 Charles Aznavour in a Bogartesque trenchcoat in *Le Pianiste*.

seen enough – then Patricia, for she too is tired of Michel's gangster narratives (Godard is clearly ironising the ubiquitous femme fatale of the American noir here). As for Charlie, he simply wants to disappear: one shot of him in the bar at his piano has him squeezed up in the right-hand corner of the frame, almost pushed out of sight, therefore exactly where he'd like to be, the embodiment of the lack of subject.

A striking feature of all three New Wave noirs is their slowness, a seeming oxymoron where noir aesthetics are concerned. Time is given to follow Florence as she trails through the streets of Paris; to observe Julien trying to escape from the lift; for Louis' fury to mount. In *À bout de souffle*, the only quick moment is the killing of the cop at the beginning (all done in a series of jump cuts); the rest is a series of meanderings through Paris on foot or in stolen cars, and much discussion, especially in cramped hotel bedrooms. In *Tirez sur le pianiste*, apart from the opening sequence (of a man running through the streets), the camera is never in a rush to move on – we *will* hear the interminable song about breasts ('Framboise'), and the pianist repeatedly tinkling out his tune. This cinema of slowness owes a great deal in terms of its look to cinematographers Decaë and Coutard, both of whom trained as photojournalists and served in France's wars (World War II and Indochina, respectively). Their documentarist's style is much in evidence in these three films, with a raw grainy realism being created by hand-held cameras and shooting on location and in natural lighting. It is a style that offers an anatomy of noir, in the sense that it allows for the exposure of the randomness of a gesture or a set of conditions, the split second, the seemingly insignificant detail or nothingness (*néant*) that can bring about terrible consequences. That nothingness exposed here will be the starting point of the last cycle of noirs, in which cowardice and weakness, so much a marker of the first three cycles of noir, are replaced by a sublime impotence – sublime because the gestures of crime are in excess; sublime because death is the noir protagonist's desired goal.

Cycle Four: Noir-hilism – Identity Erasure 1963–79

In the aftermath of the Algerian crisis and the loss of other colonies, de Gaulle was determined to reassert France's importance in the world. He conducted a 'politics of grandeur' which entailed, amongst other things, imposing the supremacy of executive/presidential power. This progressive curbing of parliamentary powers, which the national uprising of May 1968 did little to effect and which was perpetuated by both Pompidou and Giscard d'Estaing (de Gaulle's successors), led to a gradual divestment of power among the citizenry. This disempowerment was not helped in the late 1960s by the development of big capital instigated by Pompidou who was fully committed to a concerted programme of building on a huge scale and to economic expansion in the form of exposure to foreign competition (bringing in multinational companies). The effect was socially and economically disastrous. Accelerated urbanisation (much of it driven by high-finance cronyism and fraud) led to brutalist architecture with unsocialised, drab concrete high-rise masses; the car became king and *autoroutes* were ruthlessly pushed through city centres. In economic terms, along with other Western countries, France entered a period of stagflation, productivity slowed down, unemployment rose, inflation accelerated; automated technology meant that workers' conditions worsened. Economic decline worsened further with the impact of the two oil crises bringing severe recessions in their wake, increasing inflation and intensifying unemployment.

Paradoxically, in this harsh socio-economic environment, women's rights made numerous advances. Laws governing the woman's marital status changed. Before 1965, she was under her husband's control; now, she could choose her own employment; manage her own assets; open her own bank account. By the late 1960s, the contraceptive pill was legalised; in 1971, the law for equal pay was passed; by the mid-1970s, abortion on demand was available; and a wife could sue for divorce. Financially and corporeally the woman was a fully fledged citizen. Masculinity, therefore, was under threat not just in economic terms, but also in the politico-social *and* domestic arenas.[20] And yet, as we shall see, of the eight films in this cycle, women are all but banished and there is very little evidence of heterosexuality. Instead, revenge narratives dominate.

With these eight films, all elements of earlier stages of noir coalesce. However, a different, bitter-tasting noir emerges, matching the progressive decline of masculine power in both the work and domestic spheres (as explained above). Lyotard defined this period as the 'postmodern condition' in which man finds himself positioned as an ahistorical subject.[21] Unable to face the weight of history, he is without one. Virilio, for his part, speaks of the speeding up of life (thanks to technology) and how it brings us more rapidly towards death.[22] The focus of the last cycle of noirs is the impenetrable solitude of the central protagonist which nothing can redeem except a wished-for suicide. As we move towards the end of the 1970s, the protagonist becomes increasingly a hysterical figure, a shadow glancing in a fractured mirror – masculinity at its most fragmented, rushing death *towards* them. Stymied in all areas (economic, political, social and domestic), masculinity has reached its own impasse.

Tonally these noirs are much darker; icy cold – a temperature matched by the extreme wintry seasons in which they take place (with rain, snow, wind). The palette of the colour films (all Eastman Kodak except for *Série noire* which was shot in Fujicolor) is metallic blue, steely grey (plus dark browns and greens in Corneau's Fujicolor film) – unusually bleak tones for these types of film emulsions. We have moved on a gear from the previous cycles and especially the nihilism of *L'Ascenseur*. Now melancholy mixes with bleak ennui, futility with a pursuit for ritualistic order and a fetishitic fascination with guns (including making one's own bullets: Yves Montand's characters in *Le Cercle rouge* and *Police Python 357*). Silence and gesture replace speech.

On a visual level, the former slow-paced New Wave noir has progressed to what McArthur calls a cinema of process,[23] whereby the camera is fascinated by the extent of the labour involved in whatever procedure is being conducted, be it pulling off a successful heist, interrogating witnesses, or staging a jazz or dance routine (thus making the spectator a witness to the skills involved). The protagonists have no past, merely a mention of a prison sentence. They have no place, living in other people's apartments, hotel rooms or their own minimalist, anonymous and shabby environs. Bathrooms are either invisible or scruffy. Mirrors are plentiful, sometimes cracked, sending back confusing or shattered reflections. These characters are less individuals than archetypes upon whom the tragedy of friendship, betrayal, solitude and death is played out. Their world is almost entirely masculine. As such it is hard and brutal; and, despite a code of honour, whereby the most heinous crime is to grass, there is very little morality: men (even their own) die or are eliminated, all in the pursuit of the heist. Indeed, in this milieu, so fine is the line between the code of honour and lack of morality that betrayal is rife in all of the films. In *Doulos*, Faugel (Serge Reggiani), believing Silien (Belmondo) is a snitch, orders his assassination – but he has misread the 'evidence'; all the time Silien was protecting him. In *Deuxième souffle*, Gu (Lino Ventura) also misreads the situation when the police, disguised as gangsters, hijack him and trick him into giving up fellow gangster Paul (Raymond Pellegrin). Under police interrogation/torture, Louis (Michael Conrad) grasses on his fellow gangsters (*Un Flic*). In *Cercle rouge*, rival gangster Rico (André Ekyan), intent on revenge, grasses up Corey (Alain

Delon); and Poupart (Patrick Dewaere) is subject to blackmail by his unscrupulous boss (*Série noire*). Women of the milieu are, for the most part, rarely a threat. They remain peripheral, in the form of nightclub cabaret dancers, a wife or a mistress from whom these men refuse to accept help of any sort. If they do snitch, it is under duress – Valérie (Caty Rosier) in *Le Samuraï*; Léa (Signoret) in *Comptes à rebours*. In a shocking twist on this pattern of repeated denunciation – because it concerns a men from the other side, namely the law enforcers – a fellow policeman tries to implicate his colleague in a murder he has committed (*Police Python*).

Cops are as much transfixed by their own sense of order and routine; but, as opposed to their criminal counterparts, whom they resemble in almost every way (sartorially and morally), they are the talkers who weave intricate webs to catch their man, knowing all the while that it is the smallest of things that will lead to an arrest. For this reason, in several of the noirs there is a pairing between gangster and cop where, in their characterisation, two forces are pitched against each other in a curious reverse mirroring. Inspector Blot (Meurisse) is the cerebral player who slowly undermines Gu's physical game (*Deuxième souffle*); Inspector Coleman (Delon) the cool voyeur who slowly unravels his opponent, action man Simon (*Un Flic*). The inscrutable Inspector Mattei (Bourvil) eventually corners the overly transparent Corey (*Cercle rouge*). In a last pairing (*Police Python*), police commissioner Ganay (François Périer) and Inspector Ferrot (Montand) play out two sides of a same coin: police corruption, whereby the former attempts to frame the latter and the latter destroys all evidence that might implicate him.

Central protagonists from this last cycle are unfathomable, often referred to as shadows. In part this unknowability is marked iconographically by the notable transferability of the trenchcoat (both sides wear it), rendering its original meaning unstable. For the trenchcoat is interpreted as a badge of professionalism (because of its provenance from World War I and its association with officered soldiers). So if both sides are seen wearing it, whose professionalism are we regarding? Obviously, its original meaning is queered (in the sense of undermining its original value, as a metaphor for a respectable professional). Intriguingly, up until this last cycle, where it is quite ubiquitous, the trenchcoat has only made an appearance in three films of our corpus (*Impasse*, *Razzia* and *Le Pianiste*). We saw how Jean, in *Impasse*, never again reappears with his coat after the first time he arrives on screen as Le Spécialiste – it is as if he loses his badge of professionalism; Detective Antoine in *Quai des Orfèvres* complains that his was stolen – this rendered him unidentifiable. As for *Razzia*, the undercover cop, Le Nantais, wears his trenchcoat on three occasions only (the rest of the time he sports a very smart double-breasted camel-haired coat). Each time he is trenchcoated, members of the drugs cartel are killed. He is on duty, a professional, but in which capacity – cop or gangster? An ambiguity resonates, but, whichever way, the trenchcoat becomes a mantle of death. In *Le Pianiste*, both Charlie and Lena wear a trenchcoat, thus pointing to its gender-free nature (worn by women as early as the 1920s, incidentally). This transferability across the sexes renders it bisexual/hermaphrodite (the buttoning-over switches its sex). In this instance, it becomes again something of a queered entity. It is also a mantle of death since Lena is shot dead in hers.

In the last cycle of noirs, the queerness and mortal value ascribed to the trenchcoat comes into full display. In *Le Doulos*, the two main characters, Faugel and Silien, wear one, but Faugel's is grubby and Silien's clean (almost Teflon clean, since nothing seems to stick to him). Throughout the film, Silien is the *meneur-du-jeu*, but none of us, especially Faugel, knows which game he is in: a grass or a true friend. Faugel is a shadow of his former self (at various points in the film, he is described as weak); he fails in his heist and ends up killing a cop. His shabby trenchcoat is a marker of his own dereliction, a has-been gangster of the old guard. Silien, in his crisp new trenchcoat, has all the efficiency of the ruthless modern gangster (he disposes of anyone who threatens). And yet both end up dead in a case of mistaken identity. Faugel, believing Silien to be a grass, engineers his murder through a third party, Kern (Carl Studer). Only when it is too late does he discover Silien is a true friend. He rushes to Silien's country house (where Silien plans to retire now he has given up gangsterdom). But when he enters through the french windows, he is back-lit and Kern mistakes his trenchcoated silhouette for Silien and shoots. Silien turns up a few minutes later and shoots Kern, but not before Kern has mortally wounded him. Two men, same coat, both dead.

In *Le Samuraï*, once Jef Costello (Delon) is wounded in the arm when wearing his trenchcoat, he has to abandon it. This, after all, is the meticulously clean, ritualistic hired assassin for whom everything must be right, down to the last detail. It is instructive that from this moment forward, Costello's world starts to implode. His formerly safe haven of a minimalist *in extremis* apartment is intruded upon by gangsters and cops alike (the former to kill, the latter to plant surveillance bugs); even his pet female bullfinch who warns him of these intrusions cannot save him from the inevitable. Costello's saving grace, however, is his deep commitment to ritual. As he puts it, 'I never lose, not really'. Seeing that his time is up, he chooses his own death – a true Samurai.

In *Le Cercle rouge*, both Inspector Mattei and Corey wear trenchcoats (as do various other characters on both sides). Mattei wears a traditional light-coloured one with epaulettes and a capelet at the back. Corey's is more modern, grey and lacking in the two aforementioned features. Both men are represented as entirely decent. Corey is fair in all his transactions with Vogel (Gian-Maria Volonté), his co-conspirator on the heist, and Janner the marksman (Montand); he plays by clean rules (more so even than Mattei) and lives by a strong code of ethics (he may carry a gun but he doesn't kill; he will help out fellow criminals by sheltering them). Despite his moustache, however, Corey gives out an aura of ambiguous sexuality, which his demilitarised trenchcoat only serves to reinforce. Vincendeau, in her study of this film, suggests that heterosexual sexuality is renounced (women are banished) and describes the relationship between Corey and Vogel as homophilic (where an attraction between the two men is explicitly present).[24] Indeed, they share Corey's apartment, Corey is tender in his gestures when he helps Vogel down the rope ladder during the heist and so on. As the film draws to its conclusion, Vogel attempts to step in and rescue Corey from the trap Mattei has set him (he disguises himself as a fence for the stolen jewels), but ends up dying for him. Corey runs up to his body and gently caresses him before dashing off and being shot himself.

A similar homophilia colours Melville's last film, *Un Flic*. There are numerous matching eyeline shots of the two men, Inspector Coleman (Delon) and Simon (Richard Crenna), glancing at each other in close-up. But perhaps the most intense exchange occurs when the two of them are seated at the bar (in Simon's nightclub) with, in the middle, Cathy (Catherine Deneuve) – the woman who is sexually shared by both men. The exchange of looks between the two men makes it clear that they both know they are phallically linked through her. We are not even sure they haven't been in the know about each other (criminal and pursuant) all along. This queerness is compounded by the presence of a transvestite who is one of Coleman's chief grasses – whose over-invested femininity pastiches Cathy's ethereal beauty – and who puts Coleman onto Simon's extravagantly planned heist (stealing contraband heroin off an overnight express train). The exchange of looks between Coleman and the transvestite unambiguously expresses desire (unfulfilled or otherwise); and when Coleman beats her up and orders her to become a man, one suspects again that homophilia may be at work here. The icing on this queering comes in the final showdown between Coleman and Simon. Coleman plays along with Simon's last mise-en-scène of himself: dressed in his ever-present trenchcoat (his badge of professionalism), he pretends to reach for a gun but is shot down by Coleman. Aided and abetted by Coleman, Simon's death becomes a heroic suicide (rather than a sordid one in prison, as Coleman explains to his Detective Sergeant).

These noirs are beyond the realm of the real, with Melville leading the way. These suicidal gangsters, hiding in the light in a hysterical reaction to the erasure of identity, are driven by an ineluctable desire to be seen and thereby killed – a form of visible anonymity. The repeated use of urban wastelands – where city renewal has been halted; of bleak rural non-spaces; of modern architecture that is brutish in its angular meaninglessness (all of which is underscored by enhanced natural sounds: fierce winds, incessant car tyres on wet tarmac and so on) – contributes to the construction of a national dystopia that reaches its climax in *Série noire* where everything is in freefall and in which Frank Poupart, a travelling salesman, dances and dices his way to a total annihilation of his being. The *homme hystérique* erases the *homme fatal*.[25] Poupart's manic behaviour readily embodies the 'energy of despair' that typifies the post-industrial world he inhabits.[26] For all that his trenchcoat remains pristinely clean throughout; for all that his dingy apartment (once his wife leaves) is returned to order and cleanliness; for all that, from his distorted vision of things, he rescues a young woman from her abusive aunt (and in so doing kills the aunt and steals her money) – thus fulfilling his imaginary gangster narrative which we see him enacting at the very beginning of the film (on a wasteland, to which he returns whenever stressed) – nonetheless, the noir protagonist is at an end.

Bibliography

Birchall, Bridget (2007), 'Patrick Dewaere and gender identity in Giscardian France (1974–1981)', unpublished dissertation, University of Exeter.
Borde, Raymond and Étienne Chaumeton, (1955), *Panorama du Film Noir Américain*, Paris: Éditions de Minuit.
Hayward, Susan (2004), *Simone Signoret: The Star as Cultural Sign*, New York and London: Continuum.
——.(2005), *French National Cinema* (2nd edition), London and New York: Routledge.
——.(2005), *Les Diaboliques*, London: I. B. Tauris.
Insdorf, Annette (1995), *François Truffaut*, New York and Cambridge: Cambridge University Press.
Lyotard, Jean-François (1979), *La Condition postmoderne*, Paris: Éditions de Minuit.
McArthur, Colin (2000), 'Mise-en-scène Degree Zero: Jean-Pierre Melville's *Le Samuraï* (1967)', in Susan Hayward and Ginette Vincendeau (eds), *French Film: Texts and Contexts* (2nd edition), London and New York: Routledge, pp. 189–201.
McMillan, James F. (1985), *Dreyfus to De Gaulle: Politics and Society in France 1898–1969*, London: Edward Arnold.
Phillips, Alastair (2009), *Rififi*, London: I. B. Tauris.
Powrie, Phil (2007), 'French neo-noir to hyper-noir', in Andrew Spicer (ed.), *European Noir*, Manchester: Manchester University Press, pp. 55–83.
Rolls, Alistair and Deborah Walker (2009), *French and American Noir: Dark Crossings*, London: Palgrave Macmillan.
Vincendeau, Ginette (1992), '*Noir* is also a French word: The French antecedents of film noir', in Ian Cameron (ed.), *The Movie Book of Film Noir*, London: Studio Vista, pp. 49–58.
——.(2003), *Jean-Pierre Melville: An American in Paris*, London: British Film Institute Publishing.
——.(2007), 'French film noir', in Spicer (ed.), *European Noir*, pp. 23–54.
Virilio, Paul (1997), *Pure War*, New York: Semiotext(e).
——.(2004), 'The information bomb', in Steve Redhead (ed.), *The Paul Virilio Reader*, Edinburgh: Edinburgh University Press, pp. 198–208.

Notes

1. See Ginette Vincendeau, '*Noir* is also a French word: The French antecedents of film noir', in Ian Cameron (ed.), *The Movie Book of Film Noir* (London: Studio Vista, 1992), p. 31.

2. Upon the Liberation of France (in 1944) the ban on the importation of American films (imposed by the German Occupier) was lifted.
3. It is worth making the point here that this film title refers to the marketing label *série noire* used by Marcel Duhamel to launch, in 1945, the successful publication of hard-boiled American detective fiction (in translation) and, a little later, of French detective novels.
4. Vincendeau, '*Noir* is also a French word', pp. 49–58.
5. Ibid., p. 51.
6. Ginette Vincendeau, 'French film noir', in Andrew Spicer (ed.), *European Noir* (Manchester and New York: Manchester University Press, 2007), pp. 23–54.
7. Susan Hayward, *Simone Signoret: The Star as Cultural Sign* (New York and London, Continuum, 2004).
8. Phil Powrie, 'French neo-noir to hyper-noir', in Spicer (ed.), *European Noir*, pp. 55–83.
9. Ibid., p. 55.
10. See reprinted (1966) Melville interview in *L'Avant-Scène Cinéma* 525 (October 2003), 3–9, at 4. 'For me *Bob* is not a noir, but a comedy of manners ... *Le Deuxième souffle* is a noir'.
11. For much more detail see the special issue on this period, 'Culture and the Liberation', *French Cultural Studies* 5(15).
12. James F. McMillan, *Dreyfus to De Gaulle: Politics and Society in France 1898–1969* (London: Edward Arnold, 1985), p. 133.
13. For details of Clouzot's suspension, see Susan Hayward, *Les Diaboliques* (London: I. B. Tauris, 2005), pp. 4–5.
14. For a detailed analysis of *Les Diaboliques* see Hayward, *Les Diaboliques*.
15. For a detailed analysis of their relationship, see Hayward, *Les Diaboliques*, pp. 47–55.
16. See Truffaut interview supplement, *Tirez sur le pianiste* DVD (MK2, 2006).
17. There is no space here to expand on Dassin's blacklisting by HUAC in the USA. But see Alastair Phillips, *Rififi* (London: I. B. Tauris, 2009), an excellent study of *Rififi* which includes a full discussion of Dassin's circumstances.
18. Annette Insdorf, *François Truffaut* (New York and Cambridge: Cambridge University Press, 1995), p. 27.
19. All on Truffaut interview supplement, *Tirez sur le pianiste* DVD, see note 16.
20. See Susan Hayward, *French National Cinema* (2nd edition) (London and New York: Routledge), pp. 210–11, 239.
21. Jean-François Lyotard, *La Condition postmoderne* (Paris: Éditions de Minuit, 1979).
22. Paul Virilio, *Pure War* (New York: Semiotext(e), 1997), pp. 50–6.
23. Colin McArthur, 'Mise-en-scène Degree Zero: Jean-Pierre Melville's *Le Samouraï* (1967)', in Susan Hayward and Ginette Vincendeau (eds), *French Film: Texts and Contexts* (2nd edition) (London and New York: Routledge, 2000), p. 191.
24. Ginette Vincendeau, *Jean-Pierre Melville: An American in Paris* (London: British Film Institute Publishing, 2003), pp. 197–8.
25. For an illuminating study of this film see Bridget Birchall, 'Patrick Dewaere and gender identity in Giscardian France (1974–1981)', unpublished dissertation, University of Exeter, 2007, pp. 280–313.
26. Paul Virilio, 'The information bomb', in Steve Redhead (ed.), *The Paul Virilio Reader* (Edinburgh: Edinburgh University Press, 2004), p. 202.

3. FRENCH NEO-NOIR: AN AESTHETIC FOR THE *POLICIER*

Maureen Turim

Is there such a genre as French neo-noir? Do elements inherent in a group of films determine genre, or rather is it critical recognition that demonstrates how films might correspond to each other to form a set? Is genre a naming of filmic commonality, or a partial reading? In truth, a bit of both. This doubleness of the historical emergence of genres will be crucial to our investigation of French neo-noir, for it is hard to demarcate neo-noir as a historical successor to French classical film noir, as those lines blur. Yet, beginning with Jean-Pierre Melville's films, the French *policier* and gangster genres turn to a self-conscious reworking of US film noir; this self-conscious reworking serves as our very definition of neo-noir. As such, Melville's films might be read as neo-noir productively, even though they were made quite early, before the term 'neo-noir' had currency.

Yet, complicating this, all of the films we might think of as French film noir, let alone French neo-noir, might easily be seen as permutations of other genres: most notably what the French term the *film policier* or the *polar*, terms that correspond to an American notion of the police procedural, on one hand, and of the gangster film on the other. As the police procedural was one of the threads of film noir in the US, it is easy to see how film noir might be a category applied to these films; yet, those police films without noir stylisation would not merit the noir etiquette, and many French, as well as US, cop or gangster films have little or none. Also the two genres, gangster and police procedural, may overlap, while a subset of the gangster film, the heist film, is sometimes distinctly named as a genre. In addition, the thriller (including its psychological subset), the spy film, the black comedy and the mystery story are other genres with clear overlaps with what many call French film noir, classical or neo. I prefer a more restrictive definition: if there is no noir stylisation, the film will not be considered here as neo-noir.

Neo-noir defined temporally as later noir often synthesises diverse genres, while foregrounding the scaffolding of film noir. In this chapter, I will embrace the term 'neo-noir' as appropriate to group together a set of French films from the 1960s to the present, when the 'bones' of film noir still hold together the body of the film. However, I will not consider certain films that by their violence or cynicism others, such as Phil Powrie, have called French neo-noir or hyper-noir, if they have few or no other qualities that merit inclusion in the genre. The 'new French extremity', as some have termed the genre of these violent films, features characters who may commit violent crimes, but without the motivations and narrative patterns associated with film noir, and certainly without noir style, despite some use of urban, night-time settings.

I trace the story of French neo-noir to the films of French director Jean-Pierre Melville; one could argue that all of neo-noir as it branches diversely into a global genre can make more sense by considering Melville's films as intertexts and, in some cases, exemplars. Neo-noir might be as linked to Melville as it is to US films; as I shall discuss, the interconnections between developments in the US and France are strong, with Martin Scorsese in the past forty years setting a benchmark for the French in a manner similar to Melville for his US admirers. The permutations enacted on film noir by Melville in five gangster films made in the 1960s and 1970s demonstrated the potential of neo-noir: *Le Doulos* (1962), *Le Deuxième souffle* (1966), *Le Samouraï* (1967), *Le Cercle rouge* (1970) and *Un Flic* (*Dirty Money*, 1972). In fact, the precedent for neo-noir may be established by Melville as early as 1956 in *Bob le flambeur*, and I would place that quirky and wonderful film as so anomalous within French film noir as to serve as transitional to neo-noir despite its very early date, at a time when US film noir is still entirely active as a genre.

The historical forces behind Melville's permutation include his grasp of the philosophical and formal stakes of film noir in the way that other, even quite excellent *policiers* from the time do not. For Melville makes a strong case for defining neo-noir not merely by subject matter, nor by iconographical motifs, but by a more comprehensive evaluation of form as well: a specific consistency in narrative structure, style of lighting, style of dialogue and tone.

It has often been remarked that the naming of film noir by French critics in 1946 in reference to American postwar detective film itself involved a borrowing from the French name for the book series published by Gallimard, *Série noire*, which published hard-boiled American detective fiction alongside French crime, detective and gangster novels. In the mid- 1950s, the notion of film noir was yet to be applied to French crime films. To mark the significant self-conscious deviation that Melville pursued seems to be a transition to neo-noir, emerging first with his famous *Bob le flambeur*, then really taking hold with his subsequent gangster films.

Looking back at *Bob le flambeur*, one aspect of its innovation is to highlight the Montmartre and Pigalle conjoined areas of Paris as the visual grounds for the film, shot on location. This is a formal shift from what we retrospectively might call 'classical French film noir', but which was known at the time as murder mysteries or thrillers: Jacques Becker, René Clement, Henri-Georges Clouzot and Jacques Tourneur (in his French films). The small bars and nightclubs Melville explores each has its own character.

The move away from the studio towards location shooting was already operative in some US films noirs, though not as consistently as we see in *Bob le flambeur*. As Ginette Vincendeau notes, *Bob le flambeur* is thus tonally quite different from the three gangster films starring Jean Gabin made the year before, in studio.[1] Yet Vincendeau contrasts Melville's location shooting in Paris with what she calls the 'anonymous city of Hollywood film noir', a claim that is mystifying, as many US films noirs have very specific settings in New York City and Los Angeles, especially: for example, Billy Wilder's *Double Indemnity* (1944), for Los Angeles, and Samuel Fuller's *Pickup on South Street* (1953) for New York, to name just two steeped in their specific city locales. Noir is often city specific, as much recent critical writing attests. Melville's insistence on the atmosphere of Montmartre and Pigalle should be recognised as supplying a French equivalent to such use of urban locations, one that signifies 'Frenchness', in a reflexive manner, especially since it is also mixed with appropriations of US film noir style. It is this reflexivity about place, inscribing

Figure 3.1   Montmartre, with Sacré Cœur silhouetted in the background, above Pigalle from *Bob le flambeur*.

both specific reference and genre abstraction, that may be considered how neo-noir updates a film noir characteristic by taking into account how cities have changed since the age of classic noir.

We should also note that Montmartre and Pigalle were actual organised crime encampments historically, and that this corresponds to Melville's interest in reworking actual organised crime history in France, something the symbolic and philosophical bent of his films tends to obscure. *Le Doulos*, *Le Deuxième souffle* and *Le Cercle rouge* were sourced from novels drawn from actual gangster crimes.

The Montmartre-Pigalle representation finds its most startling inscription is the depiction of Bob's apartment as an artist's studio with a large ceiling-to-floor picture window framing Sacré Cœur cathedral. This bizarre detail serves not realism, but rather Melville's multilayered system of references, in that it links Bob to the residences of French avant-garde artists in Montmartre in the 1910s–1920s that would give birth to cubism and other artistic innovations, though none of the artists had such stunning apartments. This high cultural reference may be read as an assertion of French cultural identity by the film, a reflexive gesture claiming France's rich visual arts traditions; Melville will place small abstract paintings in the protagonist's reclaimed apartment in *Le Cercle rouge* to the same effect. In both cases, these references to art point to the film's mise-en-scène reflexively, requesting aesthetic appreciation of abstract composition.

Anne, who will eventually become the film's femme fatale, is introduced in the opening scenes as a random passerby to whom Bob's attention is drawn. As a future femme fatale, she is literally picked out of the crowd. She will be someone to be saved by Bob from the dangers of Montmartre, someone he assumes to be too innocent to let the city, especially one of its harshest localities for women, spoil. Femme fatales in film noir are often women whom men think they can save: *Out of the Past* (Jacques Tourneur, 1947), for example, introduces Cathy as someone to be saved from the gangster boss who controls her. Yet the difference here is the paternal attitude of Bob towards both Anne and his protégé, Paulo. Instead of taking Anne's offer of sexual favours, he tries to give her to Paulo, who becomes fatally attracted to her. This paternal displacement of the sexuality of the femme fatale is one of the most intriguing aspects of the film, as is Anne's characterisation as a woman determined to remain independent; she continues to sleep with others, flouting both Bob's and Paulo's attempts to restrain her.

Upon first seeing Bob's apartment's interior and view, Anne remarks that he must have inherited wealth. The irony of this remark is later underscored by the car trip on which Bob takes Anne to see his origins, a run-down house, presumably in the working-class north-eastern suburbs, as we see Montmartre in the far distance behind their car. A suburb whose distance from Montmartre is visually encapsulated in an image will significantly occur again in Melville's next film, *Le Doulos*, at the end of the famous tracking shot that accompanies the credit sequence, indicating just how self-conscious Melville can be about his framing of symbolic cityscapes from film to film.

In fact, the contrast of the natal house with the modernist artist's studio flat is typical of the way French neo-noir will depict run-down postwar settings versus modern or contemporary architecture, contrasting grit with gleam as two aspects of the same cityscape and gangster milieu. Another aspect of the mise-en-scène worthy of note is the slot machine Bob keeps in his closet, a visual emblem of his being an obsessive gambler, but also a surreal element in its own right; Melville will set his scenes with just such elements, which neo-noir stagings to come will take to new heights in what has been called the 'cinema du look', in Jean-Jacques Beineix's *Diva* (1981), whose vaguely surreal interiors we shall examine shortly.

Similarly, as Bob trains his assembled gang in a field, reminiscent of a military drill, the abandoned cars in the background are significant as a precursor of the sets in *Diva*. The military allusion made by this scene is also iterated as Bob plans his casino heist with maps and diagrams. If, as Vincendeau has suggested, the macho of French film noir may be read in terms of a postwar compensation for France's defeat by the Germans, then the failure of the casino heist here replays the French army collapse. This military mode of preparation serves to set up *Bob le flambeur*'s ironic ending, as Bob loses track of his heist, because his winning at the casino distracts him. He loses because he wins. This comic ending also foretells Truffaut's admixture of noir and comedy that I will consider as a branch of neo-noir later in this chapter.

Le Doulos takes neo-noir stylisation further. I have already highlighted the end of the tracking shot that opens the film, but let me say more about this shot's abstraction, to indicate how such temporal composition becomes paradigmatic in a strain of neo-noir. This tracking shot follows the protagonist, Maurice Faugel (Serge Reggiani), newly released from prison, from the side as he walks along a lower sidewalk underneath a series of train trestles, whose shadow and soot are followed by moments of sunlight to create alternating segments of dark and light in the image, with the darkness periodically obscuring the walking figure until he is revealed again. As a poetic encapsulation in abstract terms it maps the film's oscillation between gains and losses. Faugel's successful revenge attempt, which includes his appropriation of the goods of a heist, contrasts with the fateful doom that shadows him, as others try to recover his loot. The tracking shot translates film noir's concern with shadows and chiaroscuro lighting into a principle of temporal composition of a filmic sequence.

The successful 1957 Pierre Lesou *Série noire* novel had made famous the slang term for informer, *le doulos*, as its title, supposedly derived from the slang for hat (I can find no corroboration of this preceding Lesou's novel, nor any subsequent mention of this particular slang term outside of commentary on the novel and this film). For Melville, that *doulos* also means 'slave' in Greek might have had resonance, as an Hegelian master-slave dialectics inform gangster hierarchies and rivalries. As Vincendeau suggests, *doulos* echoes the French *douleur* (pain and sadness), evoking the tone of Melville's films that inflects much neo-noir; if US film noir celebrates its doomed heroes, French film noir more consistently examines their sadness. Already in Jacques Becker's *Touchez pas au grisbi* (1954), and continued in Claude Sautet's *Classe tous risques* (1960), we have narratives in which a gangster escapes from prison to head back to collect cash owed him from his former gang in order to then move on to a better life. When such redemption is delayed or negated, these French film gangsters pursue one last heist in order to retire, having otherwise lost their former enthusiasm for crime. Melville frames his neo-noir protagonists in a deliberately slower-paced poetics than either Becker or Sautet, one that extensively explores this mood of resignation and weariness, though it is also coupled with a cool determination for the tasks at hand.

The pervasive misogyny of Lesou's writing is mostly mitigated in Melville's rendering, but Silien's nasty treatment of Faugel's girlfriend, while anomalous in Melville, becomes a precursor to the extreme violence that will later fill some neo-noirs. Silien binds her hands and feet, slaps her and then pours whisky over her head, creating an image reminiscent of the most lurid US hard-boiled fiction dime novel covers. While today's spectator, used to extremes of violence, might well fear that next he will set her alight, horror is for the moment restricted to her dishevelled appearance, a dishevellment not rendered as sexy, but as so profound as to be an unfeeling trashing of her being. Silien subsequently kills her, though her murder will be told only in his later flashback recounting to Faugel and is visually discrete, occurring when the car in which she is bound is pushed off an embankment. This scene is misogynous, and as Ginette Vincendeau remarks, many critics complained that the binding and brutality scene went too far; my point is that neo-noir representations restore the misogyny and violence that the Hollywood versions of hard-boiled detective novels mostly excised, and here, too, Melville introduces a tendency to not temper the source novel, introducing a graphic filmic violence that we might characterise as neo-noir.

Silien becomes a figure of paradox; a rumoured informant, he nonetheless continues to be considered as possibly only an independent operator, useful to the various gangs. If his name Silien might be a shortened form of *Sicilien* (Sicilian) it also asks in French 'to whom is he tied?' (*si lien?*) Later, Silien pressures and cajoles a woman into his version of events, convincing her that she witnessed something she did not. Malleability, as well as ambiguity, persists for the duration of the film; Flaugel's dependence on Silien seems to be fraught with danger, with him, as well as the audience, wondering if he has been taken.

The trenchcoats and hats, which continue to be self-conscious gangster emblems in Melville's films beyond their fashion currency, set up the final confusion of one character with another, the fatal mistaking of Flaugel for Silien by Silien's adversary in a final shoot-out. Yet even before this, trenchcoats provide the police in this film with material evidence, a materiality that is somewhat rare in French crime films. They deduce from the wrinkles in a dead gangster's trenchcoat that the wearer had been physically supported by Flaugel, after being shot as they attempted to escape the police. Later, a torn piece of another trenchcoat will provide evidence of the identity of Silien's accomplice, who helped dispose of the girlfriend's body. In *Le Samouraï*, Melville again self-consciously inscribes the iconographic trenchcoat and hat as not simply an element of mise-en-scène, but as a major narrative device, when the fact that the hitman wears them when he both enters and exits the nightclub becomes a central clue to the hired killer's identity. Yet, ironically, a witness recombines the now dispersed elements of the ensemble (that hat, with that coat, but with this face) to corroborate an alibi, temporarily exonerating the guilty perpetrator, indicating how much the iconography has become a device within a formal structure, beyond any plausibility that will be the hallmark of other, more realistic, *policiers*.

In *Le Doulos,* as in other Melville films, gangsters do one another in to the tune of cool jazz, with a packet of Kool cigarettes placed strategically at one point in the image to underscore this cool mode of depiction. The slow-paced jazz establishes a Parisian lounge-time solitude, to use the term with which Vivian Sobchack delineated bar scenes in such films as *The Blue Dahlia*. However, I resist those who would too quickly label Melville's mise-en-scène as primarily being an American homage; what fascinates me is his insistence on a particular Frenchness in his films; he depicts Paris and Marseilles as modern cities that remain distinctly French. These cities in his films adapt American or other national tropes to a different end, and with a different mode and style. The cabarets with stripper shows and musicians that one sees in Melville's films were typical, historically, of the organised crime milieu of these two French cities, though their formal elements are exaggerated here. In addition, as I will show, his forays outside the city make distinctive use of such landscapes as the Normandy seaside or the Marseillaise cliffs, and his use of the Parisian *banlieues*, the ex-urban ring of suburbs that has mixed historical town and village centres with dense new development, borrows from Marcel Carné's *Le Jour se lève* (1939), even as it prefigures such *banlieue* films as Mathieu Kassovitz's *La Haine* (1995). In this way his films chronicle the beginnings of the postmodern era that one associates with neo-noir, when globalisation has permeated the distinctly national, to move the city and the surrounding landscape away from their historical primacy as signifying the nation.

Many have remarked on the mirrors in Melville, and this film has two notable inscriptions: the sunburst mirror in which Silien sees himself reflected towards the end of the film may suggest a promise of Apollonian ascendance but also recalls the broken mirror in which Flaugel regards himself earlier. The contrast in mirrors inscribes the master-slave dialectic that the pair cannot escape, for the invincibility of ascendance to mastery occurs only as a brief illusion, to be destroyed by the film's end.

Already in *Le Doulos*, and repeatedly in Melville's films, his police and gangster interactions, and his inter-gang guerrilla warfare parallel both his experience of the French Resistance and his three films depicting the Resistance: his characters are hunted, not knowing whom to trust. In fact, the personal liaison between Melville and Jacques Becker underscores how both directors may have channelled their Resistance activities into their depiction of gangsters, displacing onto this other world the life-and-death pressures of Occupation France. Melville's series of films about the Resistance alternated with his gangster films, yet the latter play out the tensions of the Resistance, displaced.

In his 1972 book of interviews with Rui Nogueira, Melville is aware of the irony that the gangsters participated in the Gestapo. Melville calls the book upon which *Le Deuxième souffle* (1966) is based, *Un Règlement de comptes* by José Giovanni, 'an absolutely authentic document on the Marseillais *milieu* [underworld] which gave birth to the rue Villejust Gestapo' (which, he explains, 'was the Parisian section of the Corsica/Marseilles Gestapo').[2] Author Giovanni, whose real name was Joseph Damiani, had been a convicted gangster before turning to writing upon his prison release; his novel was later republished under the title Melville gave the film. The novel is based on the story of real-life gangster Gustave Méla, whose career began in the late 1930s and lasted until his demise in the 60s. Melville's film concentrates on the events in the mid-1960s leading up to Méla's death. False papers and clandestine movements characterise both novel and film.

Melville says, in addition, 'The seven Paris Gestapos were all formed in the same way'.[3] This remark is telling, for the connection of French organised crime to the French collaborationist Gestapo was not something often directly discussed in France. Giovanni as *Série noire* author had been rehabilitated and his postwar conviction for murder commuted, when he was later found not himself to have been the assassin. Only in 1993 would Giovanni's ties to the Gestapo during the war become known, though Melville seems to suspect it even as he adapts the novel.

While drawn to Giovanni's novel, Melville tries to inscribe what he knows of Giovanni's past in the film. He adds a mark, a *mogen David* (star of David), to the interior of the boxcar in which Gu escapes in the opening sequences of the film. This is both a pointed reminder of the fact that French national railway company (SNCF) collaborated during World War II in the deportation of Jews and other prisoners from France to concentration camps, and to the gangsters' own collaborations with the Nazi regime in the Paris Gestapos.

The prison escape which opens the film is entirely abstracted in parallel to the opening sequence of *Le Doulos*, and in contrast to the prison escape in Jacques Becker's *Le Trou*, also adapted from a Giovanni novel. French critics tend to call such sequences 'pure cinema', by which they mean to extol cinema which, without compromise, celebrates formal qualities unique to the moving image. Here this takes the form of an image that is filled with abstract geometric shapes, mysterious until the escapees' heads emerge to define these shapes as elements of prison architecture.

Despite this initial abstraction, as a narrative drawn from the biography of a real gangster, there is much that connects this to Jean-François Richet's two-part *Mesrine* films, both from 2008, in which Vincent Cassel plays Jacques Mesrine, a notorious gangster whose heists and prison escapes garnered much press and popular attention from the 1960s to the 1980s; my consideration of the neo-noir aspects of *Mesrine* will rest on what they have in common with this film by Melville. In that light, it is intriguing to note that Giovanni's story of Méla was remade as *Le Deuxième souffle* in 2007, by Alain Corneau, with considerable shifts in emphasis and stylistic differences from Melville's film. The gangster biography would seem to be the subset of the gangster genre that has the least in common with the film noir genre, as its reference to a real, known life (even if highly fictionalised) prides itself on a verisimilitude at odds with noir stylisation. Melville's film may be considered *more* neo-noir than the more recent ones by Richet and Corneau, more interested in blending noir with gangster biography.

The poor interiors with fading wallpaper of the hideouts in *Le Deuxième souffle* contrast with the luxury to which the gangsters aspire. '*Gitan*' is the word used to racially characterise a young gangster, which also serves to suggest the ethnic *Manush* and ethnic *Yeniche* factions of the Parisian underworld. As we shall see, while French gangster films often included Italians as part of the underworld, one of the characteristics of neo-noir is to include a wide range of ethnicities and national origins beyond the French and Italian contexts, responding perhaps to the evolution of organised crime in France into clans of distinct ethnicities, as well as interactions between these diverse groups within certain gangs.

The mistral winds of the *corniches* (cliffs) east of Marseilles provide the setting for the final platinum heist of the film. Wipes left to right across the image punctuate this segment, as they will in Melville's next film, punctuation devices that might suggest nostalgia for an earlier period of filmmaking, but which also serve to emphasise the attention to spatial composition.

Le Samouraï (1967) marks a new stage in the growth of French neo-noir as a reflexive rethinking of the US film *This Gun for Hire* (Frank Tuttle, 1942).

A line from Melville's film, 'Why don't you tell me what this is all about?' receives a curt answer, 'Talk takes time', that becomes emblematic of the stripping of dialogue from a film that would rather show, would rather give time to actions meticulously executed. This film constructs a blue-grey tonality in many scenes, while others emphasise a deep black and sharp white light contrasted to grey, as in the sculptures and modern lights that are so evocatively displayed in the vertical stripes of the upscale club, Martey's, where the first killing takes place. Martey's as a name might indicate a nod to the American style, but the owner's brief exchange with his assassin borrows its laconic French from the understatement of Robert Bresson. The office, in shades of blue with modern paintings on the wall, and the police headquarters characterised by its black and grey web of interlocking offices and long corridors, create the sense of an extremely designed film in which colour and long corridors will be motifs. *This Gun for Hire*'s rented bedroom in a San Francisco rooming house and the kitten the hitman feeds, whose abuse by a maid incites his first violence, a lashing out at that woman, are transformed in Melville's film into a single-room apartment, in tonalities of mottled grey, with a birdcage as its centrepiece, prefiguring as a studied interior the loft spaces we will see in *Diva*. Unusual for the gangster film is the perspective on a minor player, the hitman, with this focus adding to the philosophically noir aspects of both the US film and its French homage, as the hitman by definition is a pawn, hunted by police and gangsters alike, once he has been used by his gangster employers, only to be discarded, according to their convenience.

Alan Ladd and Alain Delon both have youthful, good-looking faces that can hide emotions. Delon offers silent, stilled reactions, similar to the noir characters played by Robert Mitchum. Melville takes this to new extremes in directing Delon, self-consciously commenting on the genre, and also as invocation of an aesthetic he shares with Bresson. Lines are terse, spare. The payoff betrayal scene on an elevated walkway over train tracks is a study in extreme deep perspective, a no-exit corridor bordered by iron fencing.

Edward Dimendberg, in his *Film Noir and the Spaces of Modernity*, analyses how US film noir portrays two different sorts of urban environments: the centripetal city of verticality, high density and public transport versus the centrifugal city spread into suburban and ex-urban accretions. New York City would be the model of the centripetal, Los Angeles, the centrifugal. He also reflects on how the two different cityscapes can coalesce. The Paris of *Le Samouraï* is first explored as centrifugal as Jef Costello steals cars, then drives to an isolated mechanic to change their licence plates before performing a hit, a vehicular mobility often taken as a token of Melville's obsession with American tropes, especially since the cars are often large US models. If this seems contrary to a central Paris known for its intricate web of public transport, its metro and buses, we should remember that Paris is not all that dense or vertical in its central *arrondissements*, and has spread continuously over the twentieth century into ever enlarging bands, with specific suburbs noted for high-rise housing developments and thus more density than the centre itself. Though the film begins with murders performed by car, it moves towards a subway subterfuge that will allow the tailed Jef Costello to lose the police tracking him, and to wend his way under the city to the payoff site. Later, a subway escape centres on the police detectives following the trajectory through lights on an electronic map of the subway system (ironically, much like the electric light subway maps used historically to help tourists and newcomers in some subway stations). Here the game playing concentrates on the singular loop of the subway serving Belleville, the only part of the *métro* in which the train circles back on itself. Melville thus ends the earlier excursions through the centrifugal Paris with a chase through its centripetal structures, culminating in an endgame, a return to the car, a return to the isolated, suburban garage of the dealer in licence plates for stolen cars and guns, one last time. Neo-noir Parisian films to follow will return to centripetal Paris, to the motor scooter, and to the subway in striking ways, as we shall see.

Elements of more classical French films noirs, *Rififi* (Jules Dassin, 1955) and *Touchez pas au grisbi* (Jacques Becker, 1954), are reworked as neo-noir in *Le Cercle rouge*. Melville takes the heist gangster film in a different direction, exploring contemporaneous surveillance technology and high-powered weaponry against a police background as concerned with terrorism as it is with organised crime or jewellery robbery. A newly released con, played by Alain Delon, enlists the aid of a prison escapee whom he wordlessly helps to elude a dragnet. They then seek the services of a former cop and top marksman (Yves Montand), who jettisons his alcoholism to aid in the heist.

Three scenes at a nightclub, Santi's, are not only pivotal to the narrative, they introduce elements of neo-noir staging, in their self-conscious variations, one to another. In the first of these scenes, the inspector visits the club, whose

Figure 3.2   Dancing girls at Santi's in *Le Cercle rouge*.

glass doors marking the entrance are a level lower than the street. The chorus girls are bedecked in blonde curly wigs, first reflected in the glass. Their costumes are reminiscent of his former lover, whose photos from before his incarceration, and whose disloyalty, have already figured in the film.

A latter meeting with the marksman depicts his identical entrance to Santi's. This time, flapper costumes on the dancing girls fill the frame behind the meeting. Both men no longer have female lovers, and the chorus girls situate self-consciously their distance from 20s and 30s gangsters of New York and Chicago. The third time at Santi's, conga drums and African beaded costumes fill the frame between the hands of the Playboy-costumed flower seller, followed by a cigarette lit by the 'fence', whose hand comes into the foreground. The audience knows the fence to be the inspector in disguise; his remark that 'Santi will vouch for me' conceals the pinch he put on Santi to introduce him into the post-robbery plans of this otherwise carefully planned heist.

The architecture as the gang drives through the city planning the heist is all high-rise, probably meant to represent the new construction around La Défense, the area of western Paris devoted to corporations and finance. In sharp contrast to this is the Louveciennes mansion, in which the final revelation occurs that the inspector was impersonating a fence as a police trap, leading to a final shoot-out on the lush grounds of this wealthy estate. This is the wealthy Parisian ex-urban enclave of a Claude Chabrol mystery thriller, with the same attention to class and to surreal overtones, where the final shoot-out will take place.

Finally, *Un Flic* opens on the rain and wind of the Normandy coast as a prelude to a bank robbery in a branch bank on the ground floor of a contemporary high-rise office building, before the introduction of the double-gated security entrances that would soon adorn all banks in France. The gang conducting the robbery includes Simon (Richard Crenna), who is the unlikely friend of a detective (Delon). As a filmic permutation on Delon's two earlier Melville films, this closeness between the cop and the suspect is accompanied with the twist that the prostitute qua femme fatale, played by Catherine Deneuve, is having an ongoing romance with the cop. The scene that introduces this liaison deceives the audience into thinking they are witnessing a brutal, sexualised interrogation; this strange scene turns out to be simulation, amorous role-playing on the part of the longstanding lovers. It is such twists that again move Melville's films into the territory of neo-noir, in which self-conscious staging and narrative structuring become embedded as filmic jokes.

This is perhaps the moment to consider remarks Jean-François Lyotard made about the periodisation as regards the postmodernism: he held that it was less a question of what followed modernism historically as a sequence than a differentiation that theorists could make on the basis of how cultural forms functioned, regardless of their moment of historical emergence. Still, if one considers the neo-noir in France contemporaneous to or after Melville, there are two major possibilities: films that are associated with the Nouvelle Vague and its aftermath, and films that are either crime films or include aspects of the crime film in their multi-genre weave, while sharing with Melville an attention to staging and style.

While it is worth noting how the more recent documentary-style police procedurals that mark French production, such as *Police* (Maurice Pialat, 1985) and *L.627* (Bertrand Tavernier, 1992), renew a tradition that includes Dassin's *Rififi*, Henri-Georges Clouzot's *Quai des Orfèvres* (1947) and Claude Sautet's *Classe tous risques* (1960), and the US films noirs *The Naked City* (1948), *The Street with no Name* (1948), *T-Men* (1947), *Border Incident* (1949) and *He Walked by Night* (1948), while they are recalibrated in a register that is quite the opposite of film noir. So I will consider here as neo-noir only police procedurals that retain noir aspects. The inheritors of Melville and the New Wave, who add to this mix a cross-fertilisation with international neo-noir, especially US neo-noir, include the following group of films, chosen for their place in shaping our sense of the specificity of French neo-noir: *Série noire*, *La Balance*, *Diva*, *Le Cousin*, *De battre mon cœur s'est arrêté*, *Place Vendôme*, *Le Prophet* and the two-part *Mesrine*.

First, let us look at how the works of Godard, on the one hand, and Truffaut, on the other, that reference noir set a tone for the French neo-noirs to follow, introducing elements of the renewed genre's sensibility and style.

The Godard films in question with the most obvious debt to film noir mostly date from the late 1950s and 1960s, including *À bout de souffle* (1959), *Bande à part* (1964), *Alphaville* (1965), *Pierrot le fou* (1965), but also the much later *Détective* (1985). In each case the hermeneutics of noir and its suspense structure becomes subject to digressions, some simply more lengthy suspensions than one would find in film noir, but others that are nearly extra-diegetic. Other concerns such as the variation on what might constitute a film scene and its sound and image articulation are foregrounded, as are the philosophical overtones of an investigation into language and gesture. Not embellishment, nor even mere interlacing, these concerns constitute a displacement of genre, for which a new mode of expression substitutes.

Despite this, it is worth remembering how classical the bones of the narrative structure of *À bout de souffle* remain when seen in the context of French film noir: a gangster travels from Marseilles to Paris to receive payment owed to him and also to reunite with his girlfriend, hoping then to leave the *milieu* by travelling away from France. Of course, the unlikely girlfriend, an American student abroad who has her sights set on a career in journalism, signifies a shift out of genre, into the film's exploration of language and contemporary culture analysed so well by Marie-Claire Ropars. Yet the interim stop by a policeman that adds murder to the potential car-theft charges against our protagonist functions similarly to the prison escape, car theft and murder of a policeman that will later appear in Melville's *Le Doulos*, while other elements of intragang debt collection correspond not only to that film, but also to Jacques Becker's earlier *Touchez pas au grisbi* and Claude Sautet's nearly simultaneous *Classe tous risques*. *À bout de souffle*'s motif of serial car theft will appear in Melville in *Le Samouraï*.

Consider another film noir element that undergoes renewal in *À bout de souffle*: the rendezvous between gangsters that takes place at night outside the café-bar-restaurants on the boulevard du Montparnasse. The lounge scene of film noir that Melville had already begun transforming in *Bob le flambeur* to the Montmartre cafés here takes place from a passing convertible on Boulevard Montmartre, as Michel speaks to those lining the pavements in front of the bars. It extends Melville's establishment of neo-noir Paris as a city in vehicular motion to create one of drive-by negotiation, a variation that prefigures Melville's own permutations on automobiles and bars in his films of the 1960s and 70s. Finally, *À bout de souffle*'s shoot-out ending on the rue Campagne-Première (a street known for its artists' lofts) is a flamboyant addition to the paradigm of film noir endings.

Bande à part extends the automobile mapping of the city to Joinville, a northern banlieue, trading the mostly modernist settings of *À bout de souffle* for the dreary suburbs that Melville visited two years earlier in *Le Deuxième souffle*. Aspects of *Bande à part* also rework elements of Francois Truffaut's *Tirez sur le pianiste* (1960), which, along with Truffaut's *The Bride wore Black* (1968), *Mississippi Mermaid* (1969) and the much later *Confidentially Yours* (1983), mark that director's foray into his characteristic blending of two 'black' genres, the black comedy and film noir. Similarly to Truffaut's neo-noirs, it is a loose adaptation of an American crime novel, Dolores Hitchens' *Fools' Gold* from 1958, and similarly it pushes the novel towards tragicomedy, echoing the musical interludes in *Tirez sur le pianiste* with its own insertion of a musical number, performed to reflexively remark upon genre conventions and filmic style.

Cinematic elements boldly stage its humour, while a sympathetic portrayal of characters is oddly infused into its dark comedic genre. My point is that the Truffaut and Godard films are riffs on film noir that present for French neo-noir to follow the extreme liberties with genre that may be taken and the meta-cinematic consciousness that may be playfully explored in rethinking film noir.

This heritage of Godard, in particular, is part of what differentiates *La Balance* (1982), by Bob Swaim, an American-born expatriate director, from the more documentary police procedurals that surround it. *La Balance* is especially worthy of being considered a neo-noir not only for its inheritance of some aspects of New Wave mise-en-scène, but what it has in common in tone and style with US neo-noir such as Scorsese's *Mean Streets* (1973) and *Taxi Driver*

(1976). This *policier* with noir overtones moves to Belleville from Melville's Montmartre, another hill sector of Paris that at the time of the film's shooting had seen its transition from working-class slum (featured in Jacques Becker's 1951 *Casque d'or*, set at the turn of the century) to an ethnically diverse neighbourhood, home to many of Arab and of Jewish *pied-noir* backgrounds; it is just beginning to move towards gentrification, with many construction sites in evidence. This 80s Belleville environment features restaurants specialising in Moroccan, Tunisian or Algerian cuisines used prominently in the film, including one with a particularly garish interior featuring a statue of a black servant, which may be seen as paradigmatic for the self-conscious but often troubling representation of race throughout the film. The first scene chronicles a hit on an informer by the gang led by Roger Massina (Maurice Ronet) to serve as an introduction to the neighbourhood, as the informer exchanges salutations with everyone he passes on the way to an all-night grocery to pick up what is remarked upon by the storekeeper as 'his usual' bottle of vodka. This bottle is soon to be shattered in the gutter when his body is peppered with bullets in a drive-by assassination. That this informer, by appearance and dialogue marked as of Arab ethnicity, buys alcohol succinctly marks the assimilated mores of these streets in a manner characteristic of the neo-noir policier. The genre will engage contemporary Paris, making ethnicity and racism both elements of its discourse.

Mathias Palouzi (Richard Berry) and his partner from the *brigades territoriales*, a special undercover police unit devoted to stopping organised crime, appear at a crime scene already being studied by other policemen, as the victim was one of their key informants. This introduces the need for the brigade to replace this informant, drawing Palouzi and his compatriots to target a low-level pimp, Dédé, and his prostitute girlfriend, Nicole, who were once in Massina's inner circle. Both a prison sentence that Dédé served in Massina's stead, and Massina's seduction of Nicole have led the pair, now reconciled, to sever all ties to the gang, surviving on their own through Nicole's activities as prostitute in the upscale district near the Madeleine church, far from Belleville. Much of the film centres on the unusual romance and deep loyalty enjoyed by this couple, playfully enacted in scenes such as one in Fauchon, the expensive purveyor of prepared food by the Madeleine, in which a long take depicts their flirtatious double-entendres.

The film stages a series of scenes in several of the prostitution districts of Paris: venues as distinct as the rue St Dénis and the Bois de Boulogne become sites that Palouzi's brigade use to pressure prostitutes, and particularly Nicole's friend, Sabrina, into informing; the film makes use of the local colour of these districts in a manner similar to Scorsese's exploration of neighbourhoods in New York. Much of the narrative rests on two particular aspects of French prostitution in the second half of the twentieth century: that prostitution itself

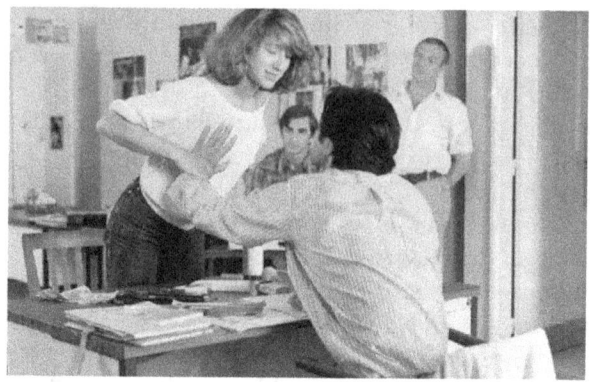

Figure 3.3   Nathalie Baye as Nicole handling the cops in *La Balance*.

is legal, but pimping is against the law; and that, nonetheless, organised crime exerts considerable control on prostitution. Another contemporaneous film, *Le Grand Pardon* directed by Alexandre Arcady earlier in 1982, was a fictionalised treatment of the Zemour brothers' crime family of Jewish *pied-noirs* who in the 1970s controlled prostitution in the French capital before they were assassinated in the early 1980s. *La Balance* revisits the connections between organised crime and prostitution, but it does so to focus on how the undercover police units operate through coercive tactics seemingly learned from the crime families themselves, while tracing the investigators' interactions with the prostitutes.

Yet this study of brutality owes other of its concerns to the New Wave's intervention in neo-noir, rarely remarked upon in the critical assessments of this film that reached a broad popular audience, and was seen by many critics as primarily an Americanisation of French film. One aspect is the self-conscious treatment of cinema as experienced in Paris. A series of film posters dot the film, primarily in the undercover police squad's offices, but also in a scene at the entrance to a cinema; they include posters of Steve McQueen in *La Chasseur* (*The Hunter*, 1980), of *Taxi Driver* (1976) and of *Star Wars* (1977). Granted, these US films are somewhat coterminous with *La Balance*'s production, and films which cops and the gangsters they trail might be likely to see, but this is also a nod to cinephilia.

More particular is the film's scenography that owes much to both *La Chinoise* and to the Bouvard and Pecuchet sequence in *2 ou 3 choses que je sais d'elle* (Godard, 1966), as conversations between the brigade members show them seated behind tables, their brightly coloured clothing set off against the white tables and walls hung with images. The traffic jam the squadron orchestrates to catch Massina in a heist, which through their informant they have been observing from its inception, recalls *Weekend*'s elaborate traffic jam, though there is some cutting between the tracking shots that capture cops and gangsters moving, guns drawn between the automobiles immobilised in which little vignettes of peoples' reactions of curiosity or fear pose diorama-like in front of or between the action. This mise-en-scène is crucial to the sense of ironic extended failure of the plan hatched by the brigade. As they walk through the wreckage, the wounded and dead civilians, the dialogue acknowledges the failure as their fault.

Yet if the film presents a critique of the brigades, it inscribes as well the racism and sexism rampant in French popular film of the period, even as this racism and sexism is self-consciously noted by dialogue and mise-en-scène. Consider an earlier chase scene, as gang members think they have eluded an all-points police chase only to have squad cars break through a fence surrounding the construction site in Belleville to which they have escaped; it draws its style from French comedies and their tendency to mock ethnic characters. The bold and self-aware prostitute, Nicole, whom Palouzi admires for her brassy responses to police interrogation, is chastised by him when she refuses a customer of Arab descent: 'Even prostitutes are racist!' There is a running critique of a right-wing member of the brigades whose nickname 'Captain' stems from his French army service in Algeria. Yet this Captain is given a line whose irony can be received by the film's audience in opposite ways: 'We lost Algeria, but we won't lose Belleville'. As is the case with Scorsese's films of the 1970s, the trenchant and dark view of crime and insanity in the city characteristically is treated with an irony that comes to pervade neo-noir. That irony can entertain social critique, but it just as often partakes of the biases it exposes; the dense and contradictory street scenes these films offer, such as this film's repeated scenes of brutality against the old-fashioned outdoor toilets still operative in the poor courtyards of Belleville's oldest housing, speak to a disgust with poverty itself and the desperation of the inhabitants of such places.

If Nicole, the prostitute, has climbed her way into the white raw-silk high-fashion outfit with which she taunts the policeman – 'You could never buy this for your wife' – by the film's close she has turned informer, sending her lover, Dédé, into police custody as the lesser of two evils, as she knows he will be killed by the gang in retaliation for his murder of Massina. Here we have a variation on the femme fatale who informs to offer her lover at least the chance of survival, and a variation as well on the ends of so many films noirs, a bleak fatality in which many have been killed, while the survivors become compromised, as the lovers are separated from the glimmers of pleasure they once enjoyed.

Diva, on the other hand, is a neo-noir as obsessed with interior decoration as it is with stylish location shooting. In fact, the set design reaches towards installation art as emblem of the eccentricities and taste of the two male protagonists, a young postman, Jules (Frédéric Andrei), and Gorodish (Richard Bohringer), the burned-out classical pianist who has turned philosopher after acquiring a fortune through shady but unspecified activities. The loft Jules rents, which he found already decorated by a previous artist-tenant, is filled with junked-car motifs, taking the vehicular circulation of this and many other film noirs and neo-noirs into its interior spaces. Filmed as a fragmentary backdrop, the car installation recalls the use of the mural in Rainer Werner Fassbinder's *Die bitteren Tränen der Petra von Kant* (*The Bitter Tears of Petra Von Kant*, 1972), and the cinematography by Michael Ballhaus of that and other Fassbinder films. In fact, much camerawork reminiscent of Fassbinder/Ballhaus on the movement of characters in planes of the space defines the style of this film.

The film adapts the novel *Diva* (Seghers, 1979) by Delacorta, written as the first of a series of novels that centres on Alba and Gorodish, an unlikely postmodern crime-solving duo, inheriting the focus on the interaction of the couple from Nick and Nora, characters from *The Thin Man*. In the film, Alba (Thuy An Luu) is a young orphan of Vietnamese descent, whom Gorodish shelters and with whom he collaborates; the novel, on the other hand, presents this character as a thirteen-year-old blonde girl. In both cases, she serves as emblem of Gorodish's eccentricity, a work of art that he has collected but does not touch, though she rollerskates around his loft and lounges there seductively; the addition of Vietnamese ethnicity adds to this film's setting in an ethnically diverse Paris, a characteristic I have already noted as prevalent in French neo-noir.

Jules and Alba 'meet cute' (the Hollywood term for chance meetings of couples) as they are each shoplifting records early in the film. From this emphasis on recorded music grows both their friendship and the intrigue that comprises the film's neo-noir underpinnings. Two tape recordings are at the centre of crossing storylines: one a surreptitious recording of a performance of the diva Cynthia Hawkins (opera singer Wilhelmina Wiggins-Fernandez) that Jules relishes in fetishistic solitude, the other a recording made by the black prostitute Nadia that implicates police detective Saporta (Jacques Fabbri) as mastermind of the largest prostitution and drug activity in Paris. When Nadia deposits her tape in the mailbag of Jules' scooter, he will be hunted for both tapes by two different groups of assailants: a pair of Taiwanese men hoping to seize the opera recording for their own blackmail or exploitation, and Saporta's gang. Thus two black women, one an opera star and the other a prostitute, are connected to Jules' two tapes, so that he meets with each of them as he tries to elude his would-be captors with the help of Gorodish and Alba.

Gorodish's loft, which features a large wave sculpture, an open claw-footed bathtub and a glowing blue puzzle that he is seen working on in luminous overhead shots, is a blue- and-black-toned space of performance and posing.

If one the challenges of neo-noir has been to substitute a colour palette for the remarkable shadows of high-contrast black and white of classical film noir, deep blue tones has been one solution, and it is the one adopted with great flourish in the rendering of Gorodish's loft, supplemented by an abstract neon circle that substitutes for the street-neon of film noir. The preoccupation with interiors may be compared to Melville's, though in *Diva* excess and redundancy is substituted for Melville's minimalism.

Fredric Jameson, in his 'Diva and French Socialism' chapter of *Signatures of the Visible*, proposes an allegorical reading of the film as supplanting both Godard's and the French nation's evolution into revolutionary politics with a stylised reconciliation of the French working-class everyman with the demands of global capital and diversification of the French populace, consonant with the election of Mitterrand and the Socialists in 1981. Clearly, French neo-noir as a genre lends itself to such allegorical readings, forging as it does a series of parallels between law enforcement and gangsters, while films as different from one another as *La Balance* and *Diva* depict the working class as caught between these forces, somewhat helplessly. Yet *Diva* seems also to want to be an allegory for art and philosophy infusing everyday life, an ode to recognising and preserving freedom of spirit and creativity, once everything is not only for sale, but reduced to traces that serve as fetish, with the experience of performance either lost or stolen. Yet the film operates within the contradiction of collecting and reproducing its artistic set designs as a staging to be sold within a genre; it pivots, as the rollerskater Alba does, between the horror of recording and the value of recording, exploring the contingencies of appropriation.

Thus the chase scene in the metro here takes place on a motorbike that has been customised to permit speeds the standard-issue postman's bike would not. If French films noirs often have protagonists abandoning their fancy cars to escape into the anonymity of the metro, here the prowess of the driver glorifies an unlikely chase scene by moving the vehicle itself into the subway. *Diva* represents a neo-noir appropriation and reference to style that will permit a creative embellishment, rather than a more thorough *détournement* (political undercutting) of the genre.

In *Le Cousin* (Alain Corneau, 1998), a combination of the thriller and *policier*, two actors known for comedy, Alain Chabat and Patrick Timsit, are cast in the dramatic roles of a police detective and his informer. Corneau's earlier foray into neo-noir is his *Série noire* (1979), adapted from Jim Thompson's *A Hell of a Woman* by Georges Perec, a writer known for his experimental approach to language and structure. In fact Perec's dialogue, while pointedly of the genre, is terse, yet manic, self-consciously repetitive and delivered with great irony by Patrick Dewaere as Franck, a hapless door-to-door salesman who is baited into a murder-for-profit by Mona, the strange granddaughter of his victim, played disarmingly by a young Marie Trintingant. Often called a comedy, *Série noire* has little in common with the black comedy of Truffaut heritage, and more in common with theatre of the absurd, as the pathos it explores exceeds that of Truffaut's films. It offers a desperate view of marginal survival by intensely misanthropic characters.

Both novel and film seem like an even bleaker variation on James M. Cain's *The Postman Always Rings Twice*, a novel that was bleaker and more raw than any of the film adaptations of it. In an opening scene whose setting reappears later in the film, Franck pulls his station wagon into a desolate space in the Parisian suburbs, a barren lot whose future is predicted by the high-rise apartments that line the horizon in the distance, where he delivers a monologue that schizophrenically traces his woes and ambitions. As prolix as Franck is, his pauses provide telling gaps, while Mona will be nearly mute, communicating only through her stare and impulsive actions. Franck will kill the aunt whose stashed nest-egg and whose abuse of Mona as sexual commodity in her system of barter motivates Franck's attack, but the actual murder is almost an accident, as the elderly woman's head is bashed as she falls against a stone staircase in the once elegant, but now dilapidated house in which she and Mona live. Franck shoots his male companion in the would-be heist, then places the gun in the old woman's hands, somehow fooling the police as to the nature of these murders.

However, Franck's role in the crime begins to be clear to both his wife, who has returned, and to his boss in the door-to-door pay-by-credit operation. She is choked to death by Franck, but the boss claims to have deposited a letter that will point to Franck's guilt should he not return from Franck's apartment, thus allowing him to escape with all the money stolen from the aunt. In the end Franck embraces Mona, who has been waiting outside, as the film ends on their twirling delusions, the demise of which Mona is not yet fully aware, as Franck promises her that there is 'nothing left to fear any more' (*plus rien à craindre*). *Série noire* showcases the brilliance of its lead actors, in their contrasting verbosity and mutism. It also underlines the US–French connection of film noir permutations, with its borrowing from Thompson, reinscribed with French literary and cultural layering.

Le Cousin, on the other hand, continues the French neo-noir fascination with the consequences of the demise of an informer that marked *La Balance*, while much of the film takes place at night in Rungis, a northern suburb of Paris transformed into a bizarre environment of shopping malls and fast-food restaurants. In the opening scenes, Inspector Philippe Maurin stops to purchase videos for his children in an *hypermarché*, an exaggeratedly huge grocery and department store located on the outskirts of French cities. Returning home, he tries to tell his wife of the legal trouble he finds himself in, but her indifference towards his fate and her resentment over a cancelled holiday leads him to a despairing, violent suicide. Chabat plays Gérard Delvaux, the policeman who must pick up the pieces and cover his dead buddy's misdeeds with Nounours, the nickname of an informer whose special arrangement with the police facilitated his own drug dealings, with police complicity. Marie Trintigant plays Judge Lambert, who had charged Maurin and continues to investigate Gérard and the narcotics squad to which he belongs, while Nounours offers Gérard an enormous heroin trafficking bust run by Africans whose impeccably tailored suits and expensive cars signal not only their drug operations, but their diplomatic passports and licence plates.

As is the case with many of the neo-noirs we have looked at, the Parisian suburbs are the focus, combining here the night patrols through commercial spaces with the apartment environments that display the kinds of interiors one would purchase at these big box merchants. This interior design meant to establish the bereft lives of the police inspectors contrasts with the stylisation of *Diva*'s artistic lofts, offering a bleak view of a Paris without good taste. Nounours' apartment, in contrast, shows elements of a North African ethnicity, an ethnicity not apparently that of his wife and daughters, and his family remains loyal and loving, in contrast to those of the inspectors. The pointed drawing of this ethnic background through décor, as well as that of the African heroin traffickers, raises once again the same problems seen in *La Balance* of a white law establishment coping with criminals of colour or distinguished by ethnicity, though here the issue is not as directly addressed as in the earlier film; clearly, making Nounours' family sympathetic serves to counteract xenophobic elements of the Africans. Once again police are tainted by the traffickers they investigate, yet the female judge who aims to purge their operations of corruption must uphold the corrupt international legal loophole that allows the worst of the traffickers to break the law that would apply to French citizens and non-diplomats.

If feminism seems in short supply in French neo-noir, Nicole Garcia's *Place Vendôme* (1997) can be seen as an attempt to restage a noir centred on a female protagonist, Marianne Malivert (Catherine Denueve). With the suicide of her husband, the alcoholic widow reforms, and reanimates her moribund life, her motivation the resale of illegal diamonds that were her husband's legacy, with her rediscovery of her sexuality a by-product of her endeavour. Set in the elegant streets and interiors of Paris's most exclusive retail and residential areas, the film contrasts deeply with films such as *Le Cousin* in its display of the upper-class elegance enjoyed by its thieves and double-crossers. In fact, the close-ups on shining jewels define the style of the film, recalling not so much film noir as Alfred Hitchcock's *To Catch a Thief* (1955) or the surreal play on this genre in Luis Buñuel's *Belle de Jour* (1962), a comparison made evident by the casting of the same actor who played Deneuve's husband in that film as her husband here (Bernard Fresson). An uncanny resemblance between a young jewel expert working for the Malaverts, and Marianne, including the similarity of their blonde chignons, serves to underscore these two women's links sexually with many of the male protagonists in the fight for the jewels. Clearly, the younger woman is Marianne's doppelganger, reminding two of the men, Battistelli (Jacques Dutronc) and Vincent Malavert, of the object of their mutual desire eighteen years earlier, at the moment Battistelli betrayed Marianne and Vincent Malavert rescued her from arrest to trap her in a suffocating marriage. Garcia's film is a slow-motion, understated version of a thriller, using elliptical exposition and development until its final moments of Marianne's attempted escape from the others once reunited with Battistelli. As such, it has something in common with Melville's films, in that it re-establishes a French mode of noir as a differentiated filmic style.

Yet if the thriller is also a dark genre of betrayal, I hold to its difference from film noir, and have not included the films of Claude Chabrol as neo-noir in this essay for that reason. The night-time traversals of the most aristocratic streets in Paris, and the mixture of sexual pasts and presents with the illegal jewel trade do invite inclusion in the genre. As such, Deneuve's magisterial performance, as well as Garcia's and co-scriptwriter Fleschi's emphasis on the recovery of female selfhood, make this an important film to consider as an alternative to the sort of fixation on male central characters in other neo-noirs.

One such is *De battre mon cœur s'est arrêté* (2005), whose inclusion as neo-noir is predicated on its being a remake of James Toback's *Fingers* (1978), and considered neo-noir in its casting of Harvey Keitel as the debt collector son of an Italian gangster with fantasies of becoming a concert pianist like his Jewish mother, therefore escaping the life of petty crime within which he is enmeshed. Coincidentally, *De battre mon cœur s'est arrêté* continues the motif of the failed musician in French neo-noir seen in *Shoot the Piano Player* and alluded to in *Diva*. The illegal enterprise the protagonist Thomas Seyr (Romain Duris) undertakes for his low-level gangster father includes violently evicting squatters, allowing the film to explore shady real-estate practices whose immediate targets are the homeless immigrant population. The dynamics between son and father (Niels Arestup) are a down-and-out version of the reluctance of Michael Corleone to assume his designated place in the mafia in *The Godfather*, leading to compelling scenes of confrontation between the two, still not reconciled upon Thomas's discovery of his father, dead, among his ransacked belongings. Escape, not revenge, becomes Thomas's goal, as the classical piano training Thomas returns to, having abandoned it after his parents' divorce, veers the film into another direction. Unlike *Fingers*, *De battre mon cœur s'est arrêté*, centres its later segments in this world of concert preparation with only a late return of his gangster past threatening the new job to which Thomas has reconciled himself: manager of the concert career of his former piano teacher.

Recently, it has become harder to find consistently neo-noir films in the French film repertoire, though the gangster biography has had some huge successes with *Mesrine : L'Instinct de mort* and *Mesrine : L'Ennemi public No1*, both directed by Jean-François Richet, as well as *Carlos*, the biography of the figure whose militant political leanings led to terrorist activity close to gangsterism. *A Prophet* (2009), a prison drama directed by Jacques Audiard and based on a story by screenwriter Abdel Raouf Dafri, who also wrote the two Mesrine films, takes up the struggle between Arab and Italian gangs, once arrested, thus overlapping with the neo-noir concerns with rival criminal gangs.

Finally, we see how important reference to film noir has been to the history of French film over the last sixty-five years, though the genre is, as we have seen, often decentred or reconstrued by other concerns of the film. After Godard's deconstructed noir narrative, *Détective* (1985), in which the hermeneutics of noir circulate as if simply so much detritus visible in a film armed in the contestation of genre recycling, we have noted a resuscitation of the genre with considerable success augmented by intriguing performances and variations in location, social commentary and filmic style.

Bibliography

Austin, Guy (1996), *Contemporary French Cinema: An Introduction*, Manchester & New York: Manchester University Press.

Barat, François and Jean-Pierre Melville (1999), *L'Entretien avec Jean-Pierre Melville*, Biarritz: Atlantica.

Beugnet, Martine (2007), *Cinema and Sensation: French Film and the Art of Transgression*, Carbondale, IL: Southern Illinois University Press,

Buss, Robin (1994), *French Film Noir*, New York: Marion Boyars.

Conard, Mark T. (2007), *The Philosophy of Neo-Noir. The Philosophy of Popular Culture*, Lexington, KY: University Press of Kentucky.

Dickos, Andrew (2002), *Street with no Name: A History of the Classic American Film Noir*, Lexington, KY: University Press of Kentucky.

Dimendberg, Edward (2004), *Film Noir and the Spaces of Modernity*, Cambridge, MA: Harvard University Press.

Forbes, Jill (1992), *The Cinema in France after the New Wave*, London: British Film Institute.

Gorrara, Claire (2003), *The Roman Noir in Postwar French Culture: Dark Fictions*, Oxford & New York: Oxford University Press.

Goulet, Andrea and Susanna Lee (2005), *Crime Fictions*, New Haven, CT: Yale University Press.

Greene, Naomi (1999), *Landscapes of Loss: The National Past in Postwar French Cinema*, Princeton, NJ: Princeton University Press.

Hughes, Alex and James S. Williams (eds) (2001), *Gender and French Cinema*, Oxford & New York: Berg.

Jameson, Fredric (1990), 'Diva and French Socialism', in Fredric Jameson, *Signatures of the Visible*, New York: Routledge.

Kline, T. J. (2010), *Unraveling French Cinema: From L'Atalante to Caché*, Chichester & Malden, MA: Wiley-Blackwell.

Konstantarakos, Myrto (2000), *Spaces in European Cinema*, Exeter & Portland, OR: Intellect.

Mazdon, Lucy (2001), *France on Film: Reflections on Popular French Cinema*, London: Wallflower.
Melville, Jean-Pierre and Rui Nogueira (1972), *Melville on Melville*, New York: Viking Press.
Menegaldo, Gilles (2006), *Jacques Tourneur, une esthétique du trouble*, Condé-sur-Noireau: Corlet Éditions Diffusion.
Nogueira, Rui, Philippe Labro and Jean-Pierre Melville (1996), *Le Cinéma selon Melville: Entretiens avec Jean-Pierre Melville*, Paris: Cahiers du cinéma/Gallimard.
Oscherwitz, Dayna (2010), *Past Forward: French Cinema and the Post-Colonial Heritage*, Carbondale, IL: Southern Illinois University Press.
Palmer, Tim (2011), *Brutal Intimacy: Analyzing Contemporary French Cinema*, Middletown, CN: Wesleyan University Press.
Powrie, Phil (1999), *French Cinema in the 1990s: Continuity and Difference*, Oxford: Oxford University Press.
——.(2001), *Jean-Jacques Beineix*, Manchester & New York: Manchester University Press.
——.(2007), 'French neo-noir to hyper-noir', in Andrew Spicer (ed.), *European Film Noir*, Manchester: Manchester University Press, pp. 56–83.
Sellier, Geneviève (2008), *Masculine Singular: French New Wave Cinema*, Durham, NC: Duke University Press.
Sobchack, Vivian (1998), 'Lounge time: Post-war crises and the chronotope of film noir', in Nick Browne (ed.), *Refiguring American Film Genres*, Berkeley, CA: University of California Press, pp. 129–170.
Spicer, Andrew (ed.) (2007), *European Film Noir*, Manchester: Manchester University Press.
Tassone, Aldo (2000), *France Cinéma 2000: Retrospettiva Jacques Becker*, Milan: Il Castoro.
Vincendeau, Ginette (2003), *Jean-Pierre Melville: An American in Paris*, London: British Film Institute.

Notes

1. Ginette Vincendeau, *Jean-Pierre Melville: An American in Paris* (London: British Film Institute, 2003), pp. 104–5.
2. Jean-Pierre Melviile and Rui Nogueira, *Melville on Melville* (New York: Viking Press, 1972), p. 113.
3. Ibid., p. 113.

4. EARLY JAPANESE NOIR

Homer B. Pettey

In the Japanese language, 黒 (*kuro* or *koku*) shares similar meanings with the French word *noir*, such as the visual absence of colour, black, dark and shadowed, as well as the metaphorical associations with emptiness, mystery and evil. The complex aesthetic history of Japanese filmmaking, however, reveals not only its adaptation of proto-noir and noir techniques, but also the development of its own noir sensibility. Shifting values of modernism, existential angst and paranoia, crises of socio-economic identity, a sense of doom, pervading neurasthenia and resignation to failure, sceptical views of progress as well as ambivalent views of the past, the penchant for violent and sexual narratives, and the creation of a chiaroscuro aesthetic that mirrored psychological and ethical problems – these certain tendencies of film noir were already ingrained within the Japanese literary and artistic consciousness. While early Japanese filmmakers, very much like their American counterparts, relied upon modernist technological, narrative and aesthetic experiments from Europe, they did so by adapting and transforming them into a twentieth-century Japanese art form. Both proto-noir and early Japanese noir reveal a cultural fascination for modernity and its re-evaluation of social and gender roles for those struggling at the margins of contemporary urban life.

The concept of blackness frames American aesthetic, cultural and political influences on modern Japan. Two significant intrusions upon Japan have been characterised in the Japanese language as blackness. In July 1853, the opening of Japan occurred with the arrival in Kanagawa (now Yokohama) harbour of Commodore Matthew Perry's black ships (*kuroi fune*), four warships with sixty-one guns and nearly 1,000 men.¹ In August 1945, the radioactive fallout from the Hiroshima and Nagasaki atomic bombs produced black rain (*kuroi ame*), the result of irradiated material combining with thermal currents to create precipitation of dark, viscous and poisonous liquid. Perry's opening of Japan led to the introduction of Western culture and technology that eventuated in the supremacy of the new modernised Japanese navy dominating the northern Pacific after its victory in the Russo-Japanese War. The Treaty of Portsmouth of 1905, negotiated by President Theodore Roosevelt, ended that conflict by ultimately dividing the Pacific, with Japan gaining control of Korea and the United States maintaining dominance in the Philippines. From that moment, Japan's nationalist militarist politics would lead to its successive invasions throughout Manchuria, China, Southeast Asia and the southern Pacific islands, resulting in World War II. Japan would adapt to its own nationalistic needs models of United States technological might and economic and military policies of imperialism. At the same time, Japanese political and technological innovations would result in their own form of blackness and destruction.

Japanese metaphorical use of black indicates a cultural ambiguity, even polarisation, of its usage for both death and beauty. For the Japanese, death is represented by blackness, which serves as the hue for traditional mourning clothes (*kurofuku*). As the black shade (*kuroi kageri*), it represents that region divided from life, and since medieval times, this separation has been maintained in order to protect the 'living and the gods from death pollution' or black pollution (*kuro fujo*).² *Kuro* or *koku* also characterises Japanese cultural aesthetics of physical beauty, such as the raven-black hair (*kurokami*) of women and their dark pupils (*kuroi hitome*), as well as artistic beauty with traditional black lacquer (*kokushitsu*), calligraphy and black ink drawings (*sumi-e*), *kokuei* (literally 'black painting') for silhouette and the black outlines of *ukiyo-e* (floating world prints) of Hiroshige, Utamaro and Hokusai.

Metaphorically, *kuro* or *koku* points to both winning and losing, as in *kuroboshi* for both a success (the bull's eye) and a failure (a black mark). Absence, failure or being wrong is typified by blackness, as it also indicates the Japanese cultural abhorrence for imperfections and defilement, as in dirt, filth, smut and being charred. Socially, homogeneous Japanese society performed a type of cultural cleansing through the auto-segregation of its own people, the *burakumin* or 'villagers'. In the Edo period, these marginalised people were associated with unclean occupations, such as butchering animals or working with leather goods, in accordance with Shinto and Buddhist abhorrence for blood and death. Japanese castigated them as other and deprived them economically and politically. Moreover, *burakumin* were culturally alienated as diseased, leprous, contagious outcasts with 'black blood' (*kuroi chi*).³ Due to their outsider status, *burakumin* would comprise a substantial portion of the Japanese underworld, the *yakuza*, especially in the Kansai region and its major cities, such as Osaka.

With the postwar democratisation of Japan came restrictive economic controls of market goods and products. Economic disparity, especially in the large cities, accounted for increased black marketeering in illicit drugs, prostitution and extortion. In July 1946, Tokyo's Shinbashi market became the site of the first open and successful battle for what would become the *yakuza*, when over 1,000 of the Matsuda-*gumi* defeated Taiwanese merchants for black market control.[4] Criminal behaviour, organised crime syndicates and scandals share the power of darkness. The black mist (*kuroi kiri*) refers to the notorious history of *yakuza* 'dirty tricks and corruption'.[5]

Western technological innovations were not limited to warfare in Japan. From magic lanterns to early film, Japan was fascinated by new experiments in visual culture. While magic lantern slides of Japan were popular in Europe, *ukiyo-e* occasionally depict a Japanese woman in Victorian dress before a projected magic lantern screen. As early as 1896, Edison Kinetoscopes were available in Japan, as were public screenings of Lumière Cinematographs. After the Russo-Japanese War of 1904–5, the national film industry boomed, especially with patriotic films depicting the recent victory. Within a decade, Japanese films had expanded to include detective series, melodramas, romances, adventures and modern themes. On the sixth page of the *Tokyo Asahi Shimbun* of 13 October 1912, police guidelines for film exhibition listed warnings against adultery, cruelty, obscenity and conduct contrary to morality. Of course, these are mainstays of film noir.[6]

Makino Shozo, who began showing occasional short films in his small theatre in 1907, had created a sensation of 168 one-reelers between 1909 and 1912.[7] The majority of these early films, and even cinema throughout the 1920s, relied upon static proscenium camerawork. The Pure Film Movement (*jun'eigageki undo*) instead followed avant-garde European and American models by emphasising preproduction planning and film's necessary separation from traditional theatre. The Pure Film Movement gave prominence to scriptwriting, to intertitles instead of the *benshi* (contemporaneous narrator or lecturer of the film) and to the inclusion of female roles actually performed by women as opposed to female impersonators (*oyama* or *onnagata*). To move away from *benshi*-oriented films, *eiga*, which could mean 'descriptive pictures', 'reproduced pictures', 'projected pictures' or 'attractive pictures', replaced *katsudo shashin* or 'moving pictures'.[8] In her admirable study, Joanne Bernardi provides excerpts from several Pure Film Movement screenplays, among them Tanazaki Jun'inchiro's adaptation of *Ugetsu monogatari* (*The Lust of the White Serpent*) (1921), which has a scene described as though it were to be shot with noir lighting:

> Scene #18. Interior. Inside the hut
> The interior is a dim space enclosed by wooden boards and a low ceiling. Sunlight shines faintly through the thatched eaves in front of the hut. No planks cover the dirt floor, which had been spread with straw mats.[9]

Of course, this lighting effect resembles the ubiquitous shadows of venetian blinds and stairway rails and spindles, with the dim interior providing the chiaroscuro effects of film noir. Such movements give insight into the proto-noir aspects of early Japanese filmmaking. By the late 1930s, Japanese cinematographers, directors and film critics were fascinated by the photographic treatments and experiments with light and shadow, especially the *'attraction of black and beauty of darkness'*.[10]

Japanese film industry and its distribution, utilising sanctions by imperial powers and police authorities, welcomed a boycott of Hollywood films in 1924, which was in direct response to the US Immigration Act of the same year. In the September of the previous year, a earthquake registering 7.9 had devastated Tokyo and its cosmopolitan area, killing nearly 150,000 people and destroying much of the urban industry, including a majority of its film production. Such economic stress added to the studios' demands for a boycott. Overall, the boycott was not much of one, since moviegoers continued to go to see foreign, especially Hollywood-made, films. The boycott's failure pointed to Japanese continued interest in Western filmmaking, because Japanese production crews still needed 'to use Eastman film, movie cameras made by Simplex and Powers, all manufactured in the US', as affirmed by the *Kinema Junpo* of 21 June 1924.[11] Moreover, Japanese audiences found American films, their subject matter and their cinematic experimentation very appealing. Thus began Japanese modernity, a cultural transformation that resisted, at least during the mid-1920s, oppressive nationalistic intrusion into popular taste, morality and conduct.

Two modernist films whose proto-noir techniques would influence later films are Kinugasa Teinosuke's *A Page of Madness* or *A Crazy Page* (*Kurutta ippeiji*, 1926) and *Crossroads* (*Jujiro*, 1928). Today, they stand as reminders of the broad interest in modernism in Japan during the 1920s and its avant-garde movements in cinema, especially the Pure Film Movement. Like American proto-noir, early Japanese noir was influenced by Futurism and Dada, which had found an enthusiastic reading public for their manifestos and concepts:

> Marinetti's *Futurist Manifesto* (1909) was translated five times by 1924, initially by Mori Ogai in 1909. Dadaism was introduced somewhat later through a series of articles in the newspaper *Yorozu choho* (Universal Morning Report) in 1920 and proved to have strong appeal for several Japanese writers.[12]

The obsession with mechanisms and their rhythms, the fetish for automobiles and the fascination with speed – all reveal themselves in the swift, sometimes chaotic editing of *A Page of Madness*. The anti-art elements of Dada, as well as its political critique of post-World War I power structures of the military and imperial power, find their way into the thematic content. The hallucinatory qualities of Dada, later Surrealism, are also evident, as they are in later noirs of the late 1940s and 1950s. Of course, German Expressionist films were screened in Japan almost as soon as they were produced; their influence, especially the camera movements of F. W. Murnau, can be observed in these early proto-noirs.

The original story and script for *A Page of Madness* combined the talents of the modernist author Kawabata Yasunari and the director Kinugasa Teinosuke. A surrealistic film narrative concerns an old janitor (Inoue Masao) in an insane asylum where his wife (Nakagawa Yoshie) is a patient and the arrival of their daughter (Ijima Ayako) who informs them that she is to be married. Yet the film has no clear narrative structure. Japanese critics hailed this lack of overt narrative structure as original, innovative and thoroughly modern:

> Influenced by both German Expressionism and French Impressionism, Kinugasa's film went without intertitles and was thus hailed by some critics like Iwasaki Akira as 'the first film-like film born in Japan'. Its non-narrativity itself was the object of celebration. The emphasis on the film's purity led many to denigrate the contribution of Kawabata Yasunari and the Shinkankaku modernist literary group made to the film. This finally was cinema, not literature.[13]

Since there are no intertitles, Kinugasa relies upon visual repetitions and signature use of lighting to provide a semblance of coherence to a tale of madness. The film indulges in experiments with montage, shifting camera angles and particularly variant lighting. *A Page of Madness* uses a number of innovative techniques that anticipate film noir, especially 'two barred windows in *chiaroscuro* interior'.[14] The Expressionist use of shadows, particularly the long shots of alternative spaces of darkness and light for the asylum's interior, articulates shifts in time, but these shadows also represent the existential crisis of confinement, entrapment and alienation so prevalent in noir. The opening shot is a nightmarish movement from sensuality to confinement. Harsh lightning shifts to stage-lighting to reveal the transition from hallucination to reality: a dancing female figure sways before a rotating ball of black-and-white stripes, then, as the camera pulls back, the view is from vertical cell-like bars; a black fade transitional frame then reveals the dancer in silhouette, seen through vertical lattices of the cell; finally, a cross-dissolve reveals a female mental patient dancing before the vertical shadows of cell bars on the wall. Vertical lines superimpose over cell numbers as individual mental patients are viewed in oblique angles as a cut occurs of a nurse walking down a long, dark corridor, partially illuminated by the vertical shadows of cell bars. These vertical lines are the central visual motif of the film and they punctuate the Expressionist transitions in the narrative.

Visually, *A Page of Madness* owes much to German Expressionist subjectivity, but its experiments with lighting, oblique angles and inventive camerawork point the way to Japanese noir. The film narrative portrays a family's disturbing psychological relationships: the father figure is the old janitor trapped in this bizarre mental institution; his psychologically disturbed wife resides as a patient, having gone insane due to her drowning their baby; and their daughter harbours an Electra-like resentment for her father. When the daughter arrives to announce her proposed marriage, tormenting guilty revisits upon the janitor disturbing memories and dark visions that also portend a chaotic future. *A Page of Madness* employs flashback sequences and hallucinatory moments that reveal the maniacal atmosphere of the asylum and the progressive anxiety of the old janitor. The climax of the film occurs when the janitor envisages his daughter driving away with one of the perverted inmates, a moment that calls into question the janitor's own sanity, visually portrayed with patients donning Noh masks. The conclusion of the film returns the viewer back to the mundane reality of the institution, with the dancing female patient and a parade of other inmates, while the janitor mops the floor. This page of madness has turned, but only to recur endlessly.

While continuing, although to a less radical extent, Expressionist and proto-noir experimentation, Kinugasa Teinosuke's *Crossroads* relies upon the Japanese penchant for emotional subjectivity to convey psychological realism. Set in Edo's Yoshiwara, the pleasure quarters for courtesans and geisha, the film employs feudal-era costumes and rituals as backdrops for a modernist tale of fetishistic fixation and its disastrous outcome. This narrative of lust and obsession concerns Rikiya (Junosuke Bando) and his sister Okiku (Chihaya Akiko). Rikiya pines for O-Ume (Ogawa Yukiko), a haughty, highly desirable geisha who takes delight in humiliating her victims. During a public festival, Rikiya is blinded with white ash (white dots upon the screen) by a rival for O-Ume's affections, whom Rikiya then attacks with a sword in a literal blind rage. Daisuke Miyao views this blindness as representative of the material conditions of cinema: 'The sudden appearance of white dots not only reveals the existence of the camera, but also draws the viewers' attention to the very fact that cinema is a visual medium and a spectacle of light'.[15] Rikiya's blindness also points to a common noir visual expression of the division between sensual appearances and ethical insight, of the inability to distinguish between virtue and depravity, between illusion and reality. Okiku tries to care for her afflicted brother, who now believes that he has killed his rival. Using that misperception to his lying advantage, a perverted constable forces Okiku to decide between loss of virtue or loss of her brother's life. Of course, the imperilled sister's virtue corresponds to O-Ume's amorality.

Crossroads relies upon Expressionistic experiments, gloomy interiors and evocative lighting to convey the hallucinatory moments of madness that Rikiya displays. As evidenced from the screenplay, *Crossroads* uses conventions of Weimar street films with severe contrasts between visible and adumbrate space:

> 01. A pitch-dark street. There is a row of houses with slanting roofs along the street. Besides, there is a long stretch of winding road. The road is completely deserted. A man with a large shadow behind him suddenly emerges from the street corner ... The scene fades away with the dark street which at first was seen as though in a painting.[16]

Kinugasa shot *Crossroads* at night in order to achieve the maximum effects for the attraction of blackness. Moreover, the extensive use of shadows and darkness reflects a commentary on modernity as well as the illusory effects of luminosity, which represents the allures of the city. Yoshiwara of the Edo period is a not-too-veiled depiction of the immorality and corruption of Asakusa, the modern pleasure district of Tokyo. Rikiya invariably returns to Yoshiwara, centre of commerce, exploitation and the luminous world of false appearances. *Crossroads*, like so many later noirs, calls attention to the dichotomy of vision and blindness as man's predicament in the modern world, as well as the nature of cinema both to accentuate and to exacerbate those conditions.

Ozu Yasujiro's *Dragnet Girl* (*Hijosen no onna*, 1933) serves as a transitional Japanese film between these early Expressionist experiments and a more fully realised noir aesthetic. In the early 1930s, *ankokugai eiga* (underworld films) developed as a new genre, expressing a new view of marginal figures in Japanese society and liminal aspects of those outside traditional roles, especially women. These films appealed to Japanese audiences, since their Western-style manners and presentations of self were part of the urban scene, especially in Tokyo and Osaka: 'Interwar popular culture was fully engaged with alternative identities – the underworld street gang, longshoremen, dance hall girls, barmaids, prostitutes, and urban strollers, flâneurs and flâneuses in the urban space'.[17]

A significant contribution to both literary and film modernism was Kawabata Yasunari's *Scarlet Gang of Asakusa*, an experimental novel that aptly depicted sights and sensations from the new urban scene of Tokyo's familiar pleasure district:

> *Asakusa is Tokyo's heart...*
> *Asakusa is a human market...*
> The words of that popular writer Soeda Azenbo; Asakusa is Asakusa for everyone. In Asakusa, everything is flung out in the raw. Desires dance naked. All races, all classes, all jumbled together forming a bottomless, endless current, flowing day and night, no beginning, no end. Asakusa is alive... The masses converge on it, constantly. Their Asakusa is a foundry in which all the old models are regularly melted down to be cast into new ones.[18]

The novel presents a number of identifiable modern elements of popular culture from new styles of dress to manners of speech. To depict this contemporary world, Kawabata deploys mixed media references, including theatre, radio and particularly film. While *Scarlet Gang of Asakusa* was being serialised, its film version was under completion, which affected the composition of the novel: 'In the second half of *Scarlet Gang of Asakusa*, the narrative refers to the film version of the novel'.[19] Like the hard-boiled tradition, Kawabata's novel breaks down the divisions between high and low culture, especially between Japanese pure literature (*junbungaku*) and mass-market fiction. Moreover, Kawabata reflects the same mixing of genres that characterised European avant-garde artistic movements. The significance of *Scarlet Gang of Asakusa* remains its noir-like portrayal of liminal, delinquent figures on the margins of Japanese modernity, and its kaleidoscope of journalism, poetry and pulp narrative. It has a narrative style Kawabata once described as 'the succession of images in a newsreel film'.[20]

Dragnet Girl represents a move beyond parody of American gangster films. The opening shot sequence reveals several noir stylistic elements. An overhead shot of an urban street square places two anonymous figures moving diagonally in opposition to another across the space. Here, Ozu relies upon the modernist aesthetics of the New Photography (*shinko shashin*) of the 1920s and early 1930s, such as Seiyo Sakakibara's *Street with Train* (1922) and Nakaji Yasui's *Secessionist Building and its Surroundings* (1922), with the emphasis upon new angles to view the urban environment, especially the relationship of human subjects to buildings and machinery.[21] Ozu cuts to an empty window frame with a set of bamboo slated blinds, whose lined shadows then appear across two clock faces of time-punch machines. Cut again to a rack of pegs for fedoras, with parallel blinds still casting horizontal shadows, to a single clock face with horizontal line shadows, and then back to a hat falling from the peg to the floor. The camera then dollies down a line of typists, returns to the hats and dollies along the same left-to-right direction back to the typists, before settling upon a empty space before a typewriter. Enter the heroine Tokiko (Tanaka Kinuyo) before her typewriter. In this simple sequence, Ozu offers noir commentary on modernity, the alienation and isolation of urban space, the spatial-temporal mechanised existence of capitalism and the sense of entrapment that these conditions impose, particularly upon the new woman (*atarashii onna*). Ozu repeats this sequence in reverse as the typists leave for the day, emphasising the connection between the human and the mechanical in urban capitalism.

Stylistically, Ozu relies upon proto-noir foreground objects as 'synecdoches to establish every locale', but he also employs chiaroscuro lighting effects to reflect psychological states, as evidenced by the partial concealment of facial features to suggest hidden desires, oppositional passions and emotional transformations.[22] The narrative of *Dragnet Girl* follows a familiar pattern of love, loss and redemption that characterises much of the American gangster genre, but the focus upon the women's roles in both corporate and underworld communities signifies a shift. Tokiko lives with a small-time hoodlum, Jyoji (Oka Joji), who is infatuated with Kazuko (Mizukubo Sumiko), the sister of a new member of the gang, Hiroshi (Mitsui Hideo). The office world shifts among the Toa Boxing Club, pool hall and the Florida Cabaret, worlds dominated by men and violence. Complications ensue, with tensions between Tokiko and Jyoji. Tokiko feels the need to reform him, but she is also torn because of her need to protect Hiroshi and Kazuko. In order to repay money stolen by Hiroshi, Jyoji will pull off one more robbery, this time with Tokiko helping to rip off her employer.

Ozu extends the final scene of Tokiko and Jyoji fleeing the police to over ten minutes. He creates a noir night street sequence that corresponds to the daytime opening of the film. The visual prophecy of alienation and entrapment is fulfilled by the adumbrated street lined with vertical iron fence bars, with the angle of movement from right to left, in opposition to the initial pattern

Figure 4.1   *Dragnet Girl.*

of the first shot sequence. The vertical bars foreshadow jail cells. Tokiko tries to dissuade Jyoji from continuing a life of crime and his gangster ways. He responds by slapping her and taking off. Held in centre frame, Tokiko's face, which had just been fully lit, now becomes half in shadow as she points a revolver and shoots Jyoji in the leg.

He falls, then gets up and hobbles off. Tokiko runs to him, as Ozu frames her directly opposite from the shooting moment, her face now becoming more illuminated. She convinces Jyoji to surrender. She bandages his leg with her scarf and, as police officers arrive, the couple embrace, are handcuffed together and are led away into the urban darkness, illuminated only by a single lamp post. Ozu, however, does not conclude with that scene. Instead, a young policeman finds Tokiko's knitted bootees, suggesting her pregnancy. The film's final shot is of the window of their apartment that frames a potted plant. Backlighting increases upon the enframed plant, suggesting a natural movement of time as opposed to the artificial, mechanised time that began *Dragnet Girl*. Ozu's sentimental conclusion does offer a visual ray of hope, but it is also a commentary on what has been lost in modernising Japan, that sense of connection with the natural, not urban, world and its order.

Dragnet Girl serves as a transitional film between the avant-garde aesthetics of modernist film experiments and the proto-noir imitations of American gangster films. Ozu's film stands out for its focus upon the woman's predicament and perspective. Certainly, *Dragnet Girl* sets the stage for women's films of the 1930s. Mizoguchi Kenji's mid-1930s films on women's life during imperial Japan – *Osaka Elegy, Sisters of Gion* – represent the first stage of feminine film noir, while his postwar films, *Women of the Night* and *Street of Shame*, are the feminine counterpart to the underworld depictions of masculine displacement in postwar Japan. The suppression of leftist films by police, censors and governmental policies, and the lack of adequate funding did not afford any opportunity for *ProKino* (proletarian cinema) to produce narrative and dramatic films. That censorship, however, did not impede films with social commentary and political critiques. In the same way that filmmakers went around the Breen Office and the Production Code, Japanese directors, especially Mizoguchi in his films of the 1930s, slyly incorporated social analysis into the narrative and thematic structure. Both *Osaka Elegy* and *Sister of Gion* are social commentaries on the plight of modern women stuck between restricted traditional roles and contemporary freedom.

In *Osaka Elegy* (*Naniwa Erejii*, 1936), Ayako (Yamada Isuzu), a switchboard attendant for Osaka's Asai pharmaceutical company, is torn between the affections of her beloved Nishimura (Hara Kensaku) and the lecherous propositions of her boss, Asai (Shiganoya Benkei). Even though Ayako wants to marry Nishimura, she is faced with the dilemma of her father's embezzlement and an obligation for her brother's college expenses, as well as the daily subsistence for her younger sister, that radically alter her plans and her life. Their impecunious future forces Ayako, a modern girl, to resign herself to being mistress to her libidinous boss. Once Asai's wife nearly discovers the illicit affair, due to Ayako adopting the hairstyle of a married woman, a new sexual economic dilemma imposes itself. Ayako must, due to her family's financial constraints, comply with the propositions of her boss's friend, Fujino (Shindo Eitaro), to now become his mistress. Ayako, however, realises that she is falling deeper into infamy.

Ayako plans to use Nishimura to pose as a vicious underworld tough in order to intimidate the persistent Fujino. Initially, the apartment scene is shot through sheers in order to reinforce visually her predicament. On the ceiling, the lighting forms a combination of modernist and traditional floral patterns, suggesting again her dual feminine identity. Using Nishimura to intimidate Fujino backfires and lands them in a prefectural police station under charges of solicitation. There, Nishimura claims to have been taken in by Ayako and repudiates her. Returning home, Ayako discovers that even though she has successfully alleviated her family's financial burdens, they disown her. Ayako's plight is emblematic of women in a hypocritical modern world. Mizoguchi employs harsh contrasting lighting to convey not only Ayako's predicament, but also the strict binary oppositions of Japanese cultural views of women. The police resolutely refuse to grant any leeway to Ayako. Mizoguchi chooses to shoot her interrogation with the detective's back to the camera and his face obscured in shadow, thereby accentuating Ayako's humiliation. Released to her father with a police warning for him to keep an eye on her, Ayako then suffers indignities from her ungrateful, hypocritical father, brother and sister. With family members dominating the foreground in shadows and Ayako's face illuminated, the scene nearly repeats her humiliation at the police precinct, as Kirihara points out about this chiaroscuro effect in the scene: 'figures that may have deeply shadowed features in one shot lapse into complete silhouettes in another'.[23] *Osaka Elegy* ends at night with Ayako upon the new Ebisu Bridge, symbolising her choices between two worlds, the traditional and the modern. She tosses away an empty cigarette packet into the polluted, garbage-ridden waters, emblematic of her being tossed out into a tainted world. The family doctor approaches her and inquires about her health, implying that respectable women would not be out at that time. In *kansai ben*, the dialect of the Osaka region, Ayako claims to be *nora inu* ('a stray dog') who now suffers from the incurable sickness of delinquency. The word delinquency (*furyo*) extends to meanings of 'useless', 'inferior', 'damaged', all of which apply to Ayako's now outcast status. Her 'illness' sardonically sums up her new-found hard-boiled attitude. She walks away into the night, the final shot being her resolute face filling the screen. With her final cynical and determined resolution, she accepts that she is a 'stray dog'.

New feminine noirs developed in response to the transformation of urban Japanese women, particularly with the advent of the new women (*atarashii onna*) of the 1920s. Lascivious behaviour, loose morals and even sexual depravity characterised the public imagination of *moga* (modern girls) throughout the 1920s, so much so that by the latter years of the decade, Tokyo police investigated the sexual freedom of *moga*, habituées of cafés, dance halls and cinemas. Popular fiction of the era often described *moga* as 'decadent, hedonistic, and superficial.' [24] Causes for non-traditional behaviour of *moga* were Western styles, dress and mannerisms, often depicted in Hollywood films of the Pre-Code period, which increased in popularity throughout the late 1920s. Outrageous, flamboyant fashions and hairstyles, *à la* flappers, were common among *moga*, primarily working women in the major urban centres such as Tokyo and Osaka. *Moga* were eroticised in the public imagination, especially as hostesses and waitresses, who were not exactly prostitutes but expected to be flirtatious and forward with male patrons. Governmental officials, the press and moral reformers were concerned by the growing numbers of independent women in Japan: 'In 1929, the number of café waitresses nationwide passed 50,000, exceeding licensed prostitutes. By 1936, the police counted over 111,000 waitresses'.[25] Types of female occupations associated by police authorities with lascivious conduct, even crimes, included '*geisha*, restaurant maid (*jochu*), entertainer (*geigi*), bar girl (*shakufu*), mistress (*mekake*), prostitute (*shofu*), café waitress (*café no jokyu*) and escort (*koto inbai*)'.[26] While the Depression era witnessed a decrease in the fictional representations of *moga*, films still portrayed both the desires and perils of *moga*, albeit in a newer context of urban economic and moral decline.

Mizoguchi's realism is quite political in thematic content, especially considering the militarism and masculine depictions of imperial Japan. *Osaka Elegy* focuses exclusively upon a *moga* who, for most of the 1936 audience, would represent modern decadence 'associated with that period and generically called *ero guro nansensu*' (erotic, grotesque and nonsense).[27] Mizoguchi, however, transforms the mass cultural symbolism of the *moga* into a melodramatic figure who is caught between two worlds, traditional and modern, neither of which holds a refuge for her. Ayako loses all connections to traditional Japanese social structure: loss of employment, loss of face for being arrested, loss of a fiancé, being disowned by her family. At the conclusion of *Osaka Elegy*, Ayako's cynical resolve defiantly contradicts these roles and suggests that she will make her own way in the world, now that she has been forsaken by her family and potential husband. Shooting her transformation along the mid-1920s bridge at night and illuminated only by harsh streetlamps confirms both the effects of modernisation upon the *moga* and also her entry into the shadow world. Her resolve, however, stands against both Japanese traditional masculine and contemporary fascist views of women. In the end, she becomes an independent woman, which is Mizoguchi's political commentary on the dilemma facing contemporary Japanese women who reject the obsequious roles of wife and mother as reinforced by fascist propaganda.

Japanese fascism represented the feminine in two contradictory images, as mother of the homeland and as foreign other. Alan Tansman offers an intriguing reading of fascist and imperialism in both thematic and visual modes, particularly the relationship of the Emperor to the communal fetishising of the mother. As a descendant of the Shinto Sun goddess *Amaterasu-omikami*, the Emperor's relationship to his people was one of a mother to children, which was to be replicated by women serving the nation as they served their families. For imperial military propaganda, Japanese gender roles were to reflect nationalism in the form of restricted female sexuality at home, while simultaneously extolling male aggression, especially sexual aggression, in the conquered regions of Asia. In Japanese fascist films, China was often made feminine, while Japan was hyper-masculine in these propaganda films. This gender representation is crucial to the radical social commentary of early noirs in Japan. Japanese women, according to imperial rhetoric, were far too vulnerable to deviant Western customs, as evidenced by the rise of *moga* the decade before.

Clearly, proto-noir experiments produced not so much *femmes fatales*, but rather *femmes vitales*, women essential for counter-propaganda in Japan. Those Western critics suffering from eternal presentism so often miss the radical political and feminist nature of these films. Significantly, counter-fascist, proto-noirs in Japan represented women outside the strictures of family and nation. Moreover, these films call into question the hidden presence of the Emperor and imperial fascism, especially with the liberating force of the modern woman. These feminine pariahs are the embodiment of a radicalised social commentary against 'a sentimental and kitschy fascist aesthetic' of woman.[28] The shift from artificial mannequins to live models produced new modern urban women, accentuated woman as object and promoted the male fetishising of the woman's body. By the 1930s, new women were stigmatised and set apart from traditional Japanese roles imposed upon women in families and society. In the imperial and public imagination, these feminine figures of modernity were susceptible to foreign cultural contagion, overly independent and sexually adventurous.

By the late 1930s, the Home Ministry was regulating and censoring the content, themes and depictions in women's magazines in order to ensure nationalist propaganda, as Barak Kushner has documented:

> Along with strengthening regulations against novels about sex and stories that could erode the morals of 'virginal girls,' authorities called for increasing controls of pictures published in popular magazines. Risqué article titles such as 'Anxious Over Not Achieving Satisfaction', 'The

Difference between Virgins and Nonvirgins', 'Methods for Dealing with Sexual Desire,' 'The New Wife's Secret Consultations on Hygiene', and other suggestive phraseology worried regulators that such consumerism would arouse unnecessary desire for sex.[29]

Chastity was a virtue only available to a fictional caste of unmarried women in Japan. *Shashin shosetsu* (picture or photographic fiction) which flooded the marketplace in the 1920s, then grew in popularity throughout the 1930s and into the 1940s and the postwar era; they presented a series of movie-like photographic stills accompanying short script-like plots involving idolised accounts of women's lives. Sarah Frederick points out how this mixed image/text fiction illustrated melodramatic aspects of women's lives, especially betrothal and the state of being newly married: 'in it, the women saw lifestyles that may have conflicted with their own experiences of gender and class expectations, or of their own cultural identities'.[30] Even though war propaganda versions tried to present a unified Japan and a hope-filled future, there was a dissociation between this image and the reality for Japanese women. Quite obviously, Mizoguchi's feminine noirs respond not only to this cultural dissociation, but also to prevailing fascist ideological constructions of gender.

Mark Driscoll makes shrewd connections between Japanese military imperialism and gendered hierarchies, which also recur in the male-dominated attacks on the feminisation of Japanese society. Japanese imperialism in Korea and Manchuria was accompanied by its own brand of psycho-social analysis of the sexually independent femmes fatales (*kidai dokufu*). Driscoll reveals how the colonial sexology became a domestic concern by the 1920s, especially in the works of Tanaka Kogai, especially his popular *Sex Maniacs* (*Aiyoku ni kuru chijin*, 1925). He calculated that 30 per cent of sex workers were suffering from pathological (*byoteki*) nymphomania and hysteria, although Tanaka did admit that prostitutes began their trade for economic reasons: 'Modern capitalism causes huge discrepancies in wealth and poor families often have no other option than to send one of their daughters off to work in a brothel'.[31] Of course, in *Osaka Elegy*, the familial-economic motivation for becoming a businessman's mistress is viewed with utter disdain by Ayako's family members. *Osaka Elegy*, then, examines the darker side to female sex workers, which Mizoguchi continued to explore in his *geisha* and prostitute films.

Set in the famous *geisha* district of Kyoto, *Sisters of Gion* (*Gion no shimai*, 1936), like so many Japanese proto-noirs, cannot be evaluated solely according to Western filmic standards. Mizoguchi's experimentations with interior shot static composition, often with a fixed camera placement, also include evocative lighting and shifting patterns of revealed and concealed spaces and emotions. Nearly completely blackened *geisha* alleyways of night-time Gion reinforce the desperation facing the sisters. *Sisters of Gion* narrates the social conflicts for women between past traditions and present-day modernity, as represented by Umekichi (Umemura Yoko), the mistress of a bankrupt businessman and long-time patron, Furusawa (Shiganoya Benkei), and Omocha (Yamada Isuzu), her new woman of the pleasure world. Umekichi represents the woman of convention, ritual and resignation to social and gender restrictions placed upon her profession. Omocha, unlike her sister, often sports modern fashions, views the world of men as self-interested corruption and seeks to acquire as much money and possessions from men as possible. The sisters also represent two sides of modern economic theory, static compliance to class conditions and entrepreneurial capitalist self-assertion, both modern conditions being detrimental for Japanese women. Mizoguchi often chooses standard framing shots for Umekichi, but more expressive noir angles and lighting for Omocha, particularly in their scenes with men.

Annoyed by Furusawa's invasion of their residence, after taking him home in a taxi, Omocha proposes a tryst with her sister to a drunken business colleague of Furusawa, Jurakudo (Fumio Okura). Omocha uses Jurakudo's money to push Furusawa out the door; however, when Umekichi learns that Furusawa has been reduced to a baby sister, she searches for him in order to live with him again. Meanwhile, Omocha has a liaison with a clerk, Kimura (Fukami Taizo), in order to acquire an elegant kimono for Umekichi. Kimura's boss, Kudo (Shindo Eitaro), ends the liaison abruptly in order to secure Omocha for himself. Kimura informs Kudo's wife (Iwama Shakurako) and then he kidnaps Omocha by car. The night-time trip across Kyoto, both through the windscreen and as mobile street shots, conveys locale shooting, cityscape lighting and adumbrated spaces, and an urban realism recognisable in later noirs. Both the taxi ride and its subsequent crash symbolise Omocha's precarious journey through the labyrinthine urban world. In a hospital bed, Omocha bewails the plight of women to her attending sister, Umekichi, who has lost Furusawa to his new job and his return to his wife. In the end, both sisters are reduced to a state of social, economic and emotional instability at the hands of men.

Expanding upon his earlier Expressionist, neo-noir cinematography, Mizoguchi alternates between a New Realist photography and a stylised theatrical setting. The urban drama of economic and social depravity is played out in coarse, almost hyper-real shots of postwar ruined cityscape. Set in postwar Osaka, *Women of the Night* (*Yoru no onnatachi*, 1948) focuses upon Fusako (Tanaka Kinuyo), a war widow struggling financially for her son's health. She lives with her husband's family, with cinematic attention given to her mother-in-law and especially her teenage sister-in-law, Kumiko (Tsunoda Tomie). Learning of her plight, company president Kuriyama (Nagata Mitsuo) obligingly, though tersely, offers financial assistance. Fusako works as Kuriyama's secretary, but she also serves as his mistress. In the city, Fusako accidentally meets her sister, Natusko (Takasugi Sanae), who is a dance hall girl. Fusako in traditional dress and Natusko in modern clothes represent the Mizoguchi visual convention of past and present dilemmas for women. Realising that both she and her sister are mistresses to the corrupt Kuriyama, Fusako seeks out the only recourse for her shame, a life of prostitution.

The narrative structure of *Women of the Night* is as unconventional as it is uncompromising. While the lapses in temporal sequences do not afford explanations for the hardened transformations of the sisters, Mizoguchi has created a new style of storytelling, one that corresponds to the noir fragmented flashback and to the montage jump cut of later New Wave films. Here, the jump narrative effects a shock to film conventions, one that matches the moral distress of such radical changes in women's characters.

Kumiko has run away from home to Osaka station, seeking the pleasures and independence of the modern urban world. Instead, in a very noir sequence she is lured into a dark back-alley bar/bordello where she is first raped and then set upon by the street trollops, who beat her until she submits to becoming a prostitute. A continual dollying shot lasting ninety seconds follows a left-to-right movement of the whores as they push Kumiko deeper into the urban rubble; there, the whores throw Kumiko down, rip off her clothes, toss her only sandals and deliver an ultimatum: either join them or go home. Now, reversing the dollying right to left, Mizoguchi focuses upon the now hopeless Kumiko following the whores, her face both stricken and hardened by the choice, before the symbolic fade to black.

Natsuko tries to retrieve Fusako from the world of street whores, but ends up arrested and sent to a hospital venereal disease ward for prostitutes. There, she discovers Fusako, now a cynical, thoroughly street-hardened prostitute. Natsuko learns that she is both pregnant and infected with syphilis. Fusako rejects Natsuko's pleas to quit the street life and escapes the hospital, traversing a wall lined with barbed wire, in Mizoguchi's parody of a prison film. Later, Fusako returns to their apartment to discover the released Natsuko drunk and ready to give birth. Fusako takes her to the House of Light, 'open to any woman without friends or a home', where she delivers a stillborn infant. The doctor advises Fusako not to ruin herself completely, even if she is already defiled, thus imposing the male view of the economically and socially lost women of postwar Japan. Reversing tropes for the contemporary image of the 1920s modern woman (*moga*), an attendant concurs with the physician and tells the sisters that they can now become new women (*atarashii onna*), representing 'all women' in a world where their 'virtue and freedom can be protected'. Fusako immediately rejects this naive male sentiment and leaves for the world of whores.

Later, Fusako comes upon a girl gang viciously beating Kumiko, a girl walking their territory without permission. Like the initial beating of Kumiko, the ruined, postwar urban environment is a wild place of feminine brutality, not the newly envisaged world of virtue and freedom of the *House of Light*. Again, Mizoguchi uses a long dolly shot to reveal the grim world and bestial conditions for contemporary women. Fusako intercedes and discovers Kumiko to be the intruding prostitute, but Kumiko, dishevelled and filthy, rejects her help, adopting the tough attitude of a streetwise whore. Then, in an overly emotional, melodramatic shift, Fusako attacks Kumiko, raining blows down on her as she shouts out the inevitable outcomes of syphilis as she ruins 'all the men in Japan and all the women'. Resolved to leave the world of prostitution, now Fusako must face the vicious onslaught of fists and flogging from the whores.

All of this abuse takes place within the bombed-out shell of a former Catholic church. The Madonna and child in stained glass is an ironic conclusion, since the women are left with yet another impossible choice. Formerly, they could not survive in the traditional male world demanding virginity nor could they survive the diseased life of prostitution. Now, under American Occupation, the transcendent role of Virgin Mother only reinforces the abjectness and despair of their plight. While *Women of the Night* concludes with Fusako and Kumiko departing, the discordant sounds of jazz horns and drums as the camera dollies back comments ironically upon the ruined church and ruined women. No refuge exists in this bleak world of male occupation for modern women of the night.

Street of Shame (*Akasen chitai*, 1956), Mizoguchi's final film, follows the interactions of five prostitutes of Dreamland, a brothel in Tokyo's Yoshiwara district, the same setting as *Crossroads*. The film begins and ends with the house manager of the prostitutes extolling the social virtues of the profession in the face of the Diet enacting laws against it. The political commentary of whoredom and financial corruption pervade this film. While often discussed as socially relevant for the passage in the Japanese Diet of the Prostitute Prevention Act of 1957, this film provides insight into the relationship of women to money in reconstruction Japan. Each of the prostitutes represents an economic condition facing modern Japanese women: Mickey (Kyo Machiko) is a frivolous modern girl, whose relationship with money is escapism; Hanae (Kogure Michiyo) works to support her unemployed husband and child; Yorie (Machida Hiroko) has become the object of a man's affection and marital plans; Yumeko, the only widow, devotes her life to the welfare of her son; and Yasumi (Wakao Ayako) successfully saves her earnings in order to pay off her debts and become independent. Yasumi is the most fascinating figure, since she treats economic conditions without emotion; she is a usurer to her fellow prostitutes and a user of her clients, whose money only pays for a transaction, nothing more. The selling of the body, the transaction, the contractual obligation of the female body – all are discussed in this film in terms of prostitution, obligation to family and marriage.

Street of Shame, while sustaining Mizoguchi's noir view of the contemporary society for women, also comments upon the social problems inflicted upon postwar Japan, not by Americans, but by the Japanese themselves. Anti-American views had held sway for several decades in pre- and postwar Japan. By the 1930s, Hollywood film had gained a market control in much of Asia, which the Japanese government viewed as a threat to be countered with 'nationalistic language that justified its actions as necessary to protect or liberate Asia from Western domination'.[32] By 1939, Hollywood studios had witnessed a radical decrease of more than half the number of American films imported into Japan. A form of marketplace extortion was the result, with Hollywood studios threatening to produce anti-Japanese films and then distribute them throughout Asia. This film war set the ideological stage for great competition and eventual war in the Pacific. The result was not only greater isolation in world market distribution, but also a loss in its own national box office, a condition that would last until the end of the US Occupation in 1952.

The end of World War II brought American Occupational culture to Japan, including once-banned Hollywood films. From the autumn of 1945, postwar Japan's film industry was under the supervision of the Supreme Commander of Allied Powers (SCAP), whose Occupation bureaucracy and censorship banned specific themes and subject matter, which included:

> anything infused with militarism, revenge, nationalism, or anti-foreignism; distortion of history; approval of religious or racial discrimination; favoring or approving feudal loyalty or treating human life lightly; direct or indirect approval of suicide; approval of the oppression or degradation of wives; admiration of cruelty or unjust violence; anti-democratic opinion; exploitation of children; and opposition to the Potsdam Declaration or any SCAP order.[33]

The Occupation, while it attempted to stop productions of period films which were so popular during the war years, lifted the fascist ban on crime films (*hanzai eiga*) and gangster films (*gyangu eiga*). US censorship of feudal period films and its all but tacit approval of crime and *yakuza* films meant that Japanese filmmakers could bring a new realism to the screen. The Occupation restrictions on the once male-dominated period films now had a new male-dominated genre to explore.

Yakuza subject matter was not entirely an invention of the postwar era, although what audience recognise today as *yakuza-eiga* began during the Occupation. The typical narrative structure of late 1920s *jidai-geki* (period film genre) films relied upon Tokugama *yakuza*-gamblers (*bakuto yakuza*), who possessed *jingi* (a code of honour) that developed from the internalised tension between 'opposing values of *giri* (social obligation) and *ninjo* (personal inclination)', with the typical hero as an itinerant outsider who combats a ruthless feudal magistrate as 'a kind of Robin Hood among *yakuza* bosses', such as *Chuji's Travel Diary* (*Chuji tabi nikki*, 1927).[34] By the 1950s, the shift from feudal to modern versions of the *yakuza* correspond to the economic transformations of postwar Japan.

Of course, other films also have representative *yakuza* figures or sub-plots. These films, especially Kurosawa Akira's early postwar films, indicate a different response to the encroaching world of the modern *yakuza*. Kurosawa's crime figure is not celebrated, but is seen as a both unsavoury product of and malicious predator upon unstable socio-economic conditions. These films, then, take on a realistic noir world-view and differ drastically from the 1950s films celebrating a formidable, charismatic boss who comes to the aid of oppressed people. One element, then, of Japanese noir remains its counter-stance to and opposing commentary on contemporary film narratives as they seek to depict modernity and its various ills.

In *Drunken Angel* (*Yoidore tenshi*, 1948), set in a postwar slum in Tokyo, an alcoholic physician, Sanda (Shimura Takashi), battles against the hypocritical code of the *yakuza* for the conscience of a young, tuberculosis-infected gangster, Matsunaga (Mifune Toshiro). Kurosawa's varies light and shadow for both worlds in order to mirror their inconsistent views of modern urban existence. Shifting patterns of darkness indicate that both physician and *yakuza* suffer from misplaced codes of honour. Sanda's physical and social cure, based upon willpower, is hypocritically applied only to his patients and not himself, and yet Sanda rightly condemns Matsunaga for the absurd feudal code of *yakuza* misplaced loyalty. In addition to underworld patients, Sanda also tends to a young female high school patient (Kuga Yoshiko) who is steadily being cured of TB by following his abstemious orders. She symbolises the potential future for a stricken postwar Japan of corruption. Matsunaga, however, refuses to give up any of the deviant profligate excesses of alcohol and women. Disease permeates the film as it does post-surrender Tokyo. Most of the characters suffer from social illnesses of fear, greed and unreasoned conformity.

Kurosawa's first noir critiques both US Occupation and the burgeoning *yakuza* rapacious attempts to control urban commerce. SCAP viewed *Drunken Angel* as a success because it misread 'reorientation' of death of the *yakuza* hoodlum.[35] Satirical commentary on American cultural decadence is evident in the men's gangster-style clothes, American jazz music, particularly the rendition of 'Jungle Boogie', and the prostitutes and taxi dancers in modern dress. Still, much of Kurosawa's social commentary is reserved for the rapacity of Japanese culture. The return from prison of the former head of the *yakuza* gang, Okada (Yamamoto Reizaburo), displaces Matsunaga in the organisation's hierarchy, sexually symbolised by Okada's taking of Matsunaga's dance hall moll, Nanae (Kogure Michiyo). Okada represents insatiate avarice and consumption. Sanda's assistant, Miyo (Nakakita Chieko), was once the abused mistress of the sadistic Okada, who now desires to have Miyo under his control once again. In order to save Miyo, and by extension the Sanda, Matsunaga attempts to assassinate Okada. Their death match plays out as an exhausting and thoroughly dishonourable battle first inside Nanae's bedroom, then outside in the corridor where the combatants slide, almost comically, through spilled cans of white paint. It concludes with Okada viciously stabbing to death Matsunaga, who is covered head-to-toe in white paint.

The central figure of this early postwar noir is neither the drunken angel physician nor the drunken reformed *yakuza* angel, but rather the polluted pond that serves as the boundary between their two worlds. The credit sequence is superimposed over the methane bubbling sump. As the film begins, around this foetid pool, bar hostesses in American-style clothes head back to work, while a lone guitar player picks a melancholy tune underneath a single incandescent streetlight. The camera pans from the guitar player across the polluted pool filled with the discarded debris of traditional and modern Japanese culture: a broken-down bicycle, old *tatami*, unravelled hemp rope, broken porcelain jars and forgotten tins, paper and vegetable matter. Throughout this pan, the ramshackle houses are darkly reflected in the pool. As a recurrent image that punctuates segments of the film's narrative, this typhus-infested cesspool not only reflects 'the inner psychological states of the principal characters', but also the social milieu of Occupation Japan.[36] This bog of contagion retains discarded objects of modernity as a mirror of its devastating waste of human life.

Kurosawa's noir vision culminates in a relationship of mirroring images: the initial mirroring of social conditions in the polluted swamp and the tripartite reflection of Matsunaga about to kill his *yakuza* boss. Still, Kurosawa incorporates a thematic mirroring of the blackened pool with the white paint spattering the killing scene. That scene commences in Nanae's bedroom with Okada playing on the guitar the same tune that opens the film, an eerie echoing. The fight between the *yakuza* rivals moves out into an empty white hallway with noir lattice shadows on the walls. This white emptiness is the obverse reflection of black sump; and yet both images comment upon the void of a postsurrender life of materiality. Moreover, Kurosawa's mirroring of black and white self-reflectively comments upon his own noir sensibility. The excessive delineation of space, light and form reflect a new cinematic realism, one expressing psycho-social conflicts through the medium of noir commentary.

With *Stray Dog* (*Nora inu*, 1949), Kurosawa takes a new noir direction in this police procedural set during a sweltering summer among the ruins of postwar Tokyo. The film pairs an old veteran robbery detective, Sato (Shimura Takashi), with an up-and-coming homicide rookie, Murakami (Mifune

EARLY JAPANESE NOIR

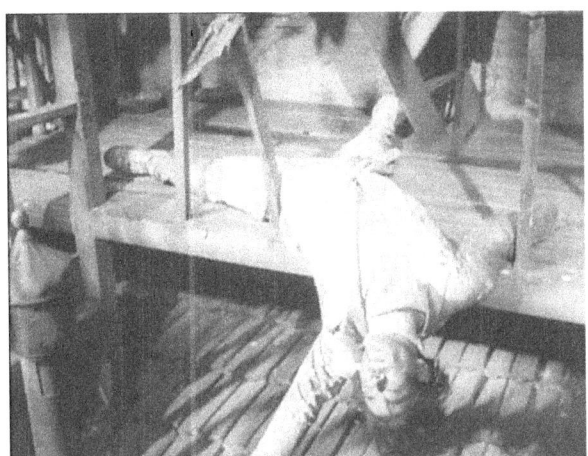

Figure 4.2   Mifune's death in *Drunken Angel*.

Toshiro). It begins with the theft of Murakami's Colt pistol, a symbolic representation of American cultural occupation, by a pickpocket. Of course, few guns are more iconically American than a Colt pistol. Still, Kurosawa trains his eye upon Japanese postwar corruption. Much of the film relies upon noir narrative and visual conventions, such as the use of striated shadows upon the walls to indicate psychological entrapment as well as prophetic imagery for the postwar world.

Donning his undercover disguise as former soldier, Murakami, in a montage sequence of urban neo-realism, moves through back alleys and black markets in search of the leads to the illicit gun trade. His soldier's uniform in the markets comments ironically on the rise of the *yakuza*, many of whom were displaced former soldiers in postwar Occupation Japan. This montage sequence is a mini-epic of postwar Tokyo culture, effectively relying upon noir techniques, as Stephen Prince points out:

> Kurosawa's tendency to handle narrative transitions as moments of formal excess reaches something of a climax in this film, where a single montage showing Murakami's search through the districts of Asakusa and Ueno last an amazing eight minutes and 35 seconds. During this sequence, the narrative completely halts while Kurosawa explores the purely visual properties of wipes, dissolves, superimpositions, and shot articulating moment from right, left, diagonally, and horizontally.[37]

The silence dominating this tour of the Tokyo underworld recalls several photorealist, street-level scenes of New York's Lower East Side in Dassin's *The Naked City* of the previous year.

Murakami and Sato trail a gun dealer, Hondo (Yamamoto Reisaburo), to a baseball game, America's pastime, who directs them to Yusa (Kimura Isao), a war veteran now turned *yakuza*. Complications arise with Yusa's hostess/showgirl mistress Namiki (Awaji Keiko), who, after Sato is shot by Yusa and hospitalised, informs Murakami of their scheduled rendezvous at the train station. There, Murakami finds Yusa, chases him through a forest and is wounded in the arm before capturing the *yakuza*. The final scene in the hospital involves Murakami reflecting upon the similarities between Yusa and him, which Sato dismisses so that Murakami can focus upon the future. Murakami's overly emotional reaction to the corruption and duplicity of the new Japan also associates him with the unruly postwar world. The *kanji* for stray dog means 'field dog' or 'rural dog', but suggests 'savage', 'barbaric' or 'wild' dog. The disturbing image of the panting dog of the opening credit sequence symbolically represents the social malaise and moral fatigue of occupation Japan.

While Peter A. Yacavone admits that both *Stray Dog* and *Drunken Angel* share noir tendencies, he undercuts that reading by emphasising the fact that Kurosawa addresses a social message and the morality of the characters. Moreover, Yacavone defines film noir in odd terms, missing the Japanese social context of many films, especially *Naked City*, which is a double for *Stray Dog*:

> Film noir is dependent on the *isolation* and *crystallization* of certain aspects of modern social experience (at least as Hollywood sees it) at the expense of other aspects, which must be *removed*. In order for moods such as alienation, anxiety and loneliness to come to the forefront, the sort of sentimentality found in *Stray Dog* must be suppressed.[38]

Of course, such a restriction misses the point, since the Japanese were developing their own cultural brand of film noir.

Throughout the 1950s, Kurosawa continued to employ innovative noir techniques. For *Scandal* (*Shubun*, 1950), Kurosawa focused upon confined space, urban decay and disease to reveal postwar hypocrisy in Japanese popular media and the legal system. In *Rashomon* (1950), he relied upon expressive lighting, plays of shadows, and multiple oblique angles, such as the self-referential shifts of camera angles for the woodcutter's discovery of the crime, to convey the narrative's multiple perspectives and interpretations. In *The Lower Depths* (*Donzoko*, 1957), an adaptation of Maxim Gorky's play, Kurosawa combined the stark setting, the filth and squalor of deprivation and oblique angles to transform theatrical conventions by means of contemporary noir sensibilities. Of course, *Yojimbo* (1961) began a new approach to both *samurai* and period films (*jidaigeki*), but also to Japanese noir, as well as influencing American and European filmmaking. Based loosely upon Dashiell Hammett's *Red Harvest*

(1929), *Yojimbo* parodies the lone, itinerant *yakuza* films of the late 1920s and 1930s, while simultaneously establishing the *ronin* figure as a kind of lone gunslinger *à la* American westerns. *Yojimbo* would influence directly spaghetti westerns and much of the narratives that form Clint Eastwood's film portrayals. Such mixed genre elements were already apparent in the transitional period from the Occupation to the New Wave in Japan. With underworld and *yakuza* films by Imamura Shoehei, Suzuki Seijun and Nikkatsu Studio, the late 1950s to the 1960s would usher in new directors and new versions of noir.

The post-Occupational period of the late 1950s, however, does end with a representative noir that bridges the postwar experiments and the new gangland films of the 1960s. Masaki Kobayashi's *Black River* (*Kuroi kawa*, 1957) focuses upon the kinds of social diseases afflicting Japan in the postwar period. The narrative's action occurs between an American airbase and a squalid, *yakuza*-controlled pleasure district and surrounding slum. Occupation policies did not prevent American abuses against the Japanese, especially women. For example, *Black Spring* (*Kuroi Haru*), published in 1953, included 'a number of first-hand testimonies of victims of sexual violence' committed by Occupation American soldiers.[39] Kobayashi critiques the crisis confronting the post-Occupation Japanese Self by pointing his gaze, as Kurosawa had done, at the Japanese themselves. The narrative develops through the interrelated stories of a group of lower-class tenants of a dilapidated, bleakly lit warehouse and the black world of *yakuza*-run bars and brothels servicing the US Naval airbase. Their conniving landlady plans to evict the residents so that she can build, with the help of *yakuza* muscle, a bathhouse on the site. All of the tenants suffer from economic deprivation that leads them to ethical depravity, such as drunkenness, sexually licentious behaviour and a general lack of empathy. So debased financially are the tenants that they quarrel over the removal, use and ownership of their excrement. Economics, therefore, besmirches ethical conduct. The base, amoral *yakuza* world represents Japan's new economy, a limited, corrupt market of extortion, abuses, and rapine and destructive self-interest.

Connecting the two social divisions is the love interest between a naive student, Nishida (Watanabe Fumio), who moves into the tenement and Shizuko (Arima Ineko), a young woman whose white parasol is a traditional emblem of virginal purity. In this bleak noir world, both are destined to be forcibly corrupted. In a rigged psycho-drama of rape, 'Killer' Jo (Nakadai Tatsuya) saves the helpless Shizuko from his own thugs, but then rapes her himself. This scene of sexual aggression, assaulted feminine virtue and predatory male behaviour is played out at night along the symbolic black river. After the rape, Jo relates his conquest to his drunken *yakuza* henchmen, all the while playing with Shizuko's stolen parasol, now the symbol of her loss of face and her continual shame. Jo turns Shizuko from a café waitress into his *yakuza* mistress, a pattern of moral descent similar to that predicted for the *moga* (modern girl) of twenty years prior.

Neither Nishida nor Jo can give up Shizuko: one from a misplaced sense of devotion; the other from monomaniacal need for possession. Their inevitable conflict occurs during a night of *yakuza* revelry, a hedonistic celebration of Jo's birthday, during which both Nishida and, later, the compromised Shizuko seek revenge. Initially, Nishida confronts Jo with the fraudulent removal of the tenants, but that changes when Shizuko arrives and engages in a forced embrace and kiss with Jo. In order to spare Nishida from Jo's thugs, his former moll (Awaji Keiko) takes him as her lover for the night. To Nishida's mounting anger, Shizuko effects flagrant sexual desires for Jo, all the more feigned when she discovers her missing parasol in the *yakuza* den. As Shizuko secretly plies Jo with more and more saké, Nishida's jealousy increases until he explodes. In their phallic bar duel, Nishida draws Jo's knife while Jo slashes with Shizuko's parasol. The women stop the fight as the men head outside to the newly rain-soaked, blackened, dimly illuminated street, lined with signs of commerce and the continual traffic of military vehicles. As Shizuko leads the besotted Jo along the bridge over the black river, Nishida follows with Jo's inebriated moll, who calls out insulting epithets against Shizuko's supposed innocence.

In a series of low-angle long shots on the bridge, Kobayashi frames Shizuko and the stumbling Jo, who still holds the white parasol, in front of oncoming roaring military trucks, whose headlights reflect off the wet pavement. As a cacophonous jazz score plays, the film cuts between the two couples, now representative of Japanese culture's precarious situational ethics. As Shizuko turns her head as distant headlights appear, Nishida too notices them and runs towards her, in full knowledge of her murderous intent. As the military

Figure 4.3   Conclusion image from *Black River*.

truck passes him, the film cuts to Jo trying to kiss Shizuko, who pushes him out of frame as the truck, seeming to be within the same shot, roars by over his body. *Black River* concludes with a shot of Shizuko's parasol open and upturned upon the black pavement as she runs off, her ever-receding white figure engulfed by the night. With *Black River*, the elements that forged early Japanese noir – *moga* and *yakuza* – craft a hopeless allegory of Japanese modernity as bleak as any American noir ending.

The milieu and mindset of *Black River* and subsequent noirs reflect the postwar period's amorality. Imposing a purely American conceit about early Japanese noir misses the social and philosophical fascination with crime in postwar Japan. As Douglas N. Slaymaker has admirably pointed out, Sakaguchi Ango's essay '*Darakuron*' ('On decadence') of 1946 endorses it as the purest form of existence, since it does not rely upon state-imposed or modern doctrinaire ideals of progress and striving to move culture forward. Instead, Ango asserts that such conformist authoritarian concepts impose a negation upon the basic, foundational humanity, which is decadence, 'a falling', 'a defection from reigning morals and societal strictures':

> What prevents us from being fully human is ideology, he claims: the various, capricious, and self-serving societal structures arbitrarily put into place by politicians and other authorities, the ethical systems enforced by tradition and society, urging people upward and forward to some 'ideal'.[40]

To such an end, Ango views the illegal activities of the early postwar era, especially black marketeering, as a vision of the new world to come. Obviously, black marketeering and *yakuza* are in the backdrop of *daraku*, with its view of criminals acting out of a survival mode of necessity. Ango's reduction to nothingness, to a non-future, reveals a world not dependent on the bankrupt ideology and social structure of the past and a world not seeking progress as the outcome of modernity, but rather a world of a constant restructuring and re-evaluating of the meaning of values, ethics and morality. Such re-evaluative critiques are evident in *Dragnet Girl*, *Drunken Angel* and *Stray Dog*.

In so many ways, Ango's description of the new woman's body represents the predicament of women in Japanese noir, who find 'no pleasure in sex. Living as an entertainer, a prostitute, she survives by providing physical pleasure with her body ... She lives by treating her body as a commodity, a mechanical toy'.[41] The *moga* and modern Japanese noir woman often display a lack of emotion in love and forced sexual relationships, remaining alienated as though she were an object, a mannequin. Here is the essence of the Japanese noir modern woman: a liminal figure outside the conventions and traditions of marriage and the family, on the margins of society and its mores, and expressing her individuality and independence by means of self-imposed isolation, both a resignation to and reliance upon decadence and delinquency. This pattern of existence is evident in *Osaka Elegy*, *The Sisters of Gion*, *Street of Shame* and, especially, in *Black River*. To this extent, Ango's 'On decadence' provides a prophetic glimpse into the pathology of Japanese homogeneity and militarism as it offers a reflection of the social changes occurring immediately following the Japanese surrender. This new postwar world is empty, corrupt, bleak and, ultimately, so very noir.

Notes

1. Marius R. Jansen, *The Making of Modern Japan* (Cambridge, MA: Harvard University Press, 2000), p. 277. See also note 28, p. 812, which explains that the 'black ships' were designated to distinguish them from the 'white ships' from China.
2. Karen M. Gerhart, *The Material Culture of Death in Medieval Japan* (Honolulu, HI: University of Hawai'i Press, 2009), p. 84.
3. Sharalyn Orbaugh, *Japanese Fictions of the Allied Occupation: Vision, Embodiment, Identity* (Leiden: Brill, 2007), p. 403.
4. Peter B. E. Hill, *The Japanese Mafia: Yakuza, Law, and the State* (Oxford: Oxford University Press, 2003), pp. 42–5.
5. David E. Kaplan and Alec Dubro, *Yakuza: Japan's Criminal Underworld* (Berkeley, CA: University of California Press, 2003), p. 84.
6. Aaron Gerow, *Visions of Japanese Modernity: Articulations of Cinema, Nation, and Spectatorship, 1895–1925* (Berkeley, CA: University of California Press, 2010), p. 63.
7. Joanne Bernardi, *Writing in Light: The Silent Scenario and the Japanese Pure Film Movement* (Detroit, MI: Wayne State University Press, 2001), p. 29. This is an essential work for any scholar pursuing the history, culture and influences upon early Japanese filmmaking.
8. Joseph L. Anderson and Donald Richie, *The Japanese Film: Art and Industry* (expanded edition) (Princeton, NJ: Princeton University Press, 1982), p. 37.
9. Bernardi, pp. 303–4.
10. Daisuke Miyao, *The Aesthetics of Shadow: Lighting and Japanese Cinema* (Durham, NC: Duke University Press, 2013), p. 204.
11. Yuko Itatsu, 'Japan's Hollywood boycott movement of 1924', *Historical Journal of Film, Radio and Television* 28(3) (August 2008), 363.
12. William O. Gardner, 'New perceptions: Kinugasa Teinosuke's films and Japanese modernism', *Cinema Journal* 43(3) (spring 2004), 63.
13. Andrew Gerow, 'The word before the image: Criticism, the screenplay, and the regulation of meaning in prewar Japanese film culture', in Dennis Washburn and Carole Cavanaugh (eds), *Word and Image in Japanese Cinema* (Cambridge: Cambridge University Press, 2001), p. 23.
14. Noël Burch, *To the Distant Observer: Form and Meaning in the Japanese Cinema* (Berkeley, CA: University of California Press, 1979), p. 128.
15. Miyao, *The Aesthetics of Shadow*, p. 132.
16. R. A. Rajakaruna (trans.), *Kinugasa Teinosuke's A Crazy Page and Crossroads* (Colombo: Godage International Publishers, 2010), p. 63.
17. Mitsuyo Wada-Marciano, *Nippon Modern: Japanese Cinema of the 1920s and 1930s* (Honolulu, HI: University of Hawai'i Press, 2008), p. 33.

18. Kawabata Yasunari, *The Scarlet Gang of Asakusa*, trans. Alisa Freedman (Berkeley, CA: University of California Press, 2005), p. 30.
19. Seiji M. Lippit, *Topographies of Japanese Modernism* (New York: Columbia University Press, 2002), p. 130.
20. Ibid., p. 126.
21. *Modern Photography in Japan, 1915–1940* (San Francisco, CA: The Friends of Photography, 2001) (no page numbers for plates).
22. David Bordwell, *Ozu and the Poetics of Cinema* (Princeton, NJ: Princeton University Press, 1988), p. 245.
23. Donald Kirihara, *Patterns of Time: Mizoguchi and the 1930s* (Madison, WI: University of Wisconsin Press, 1992), p. 114.
24. Barbara Sato, *The New Japanese Women: Modernity, Media, and Women in Interwar Japan* (Durham, NC: Duke University Press, 2003), p. 65.
25. Andrew Gordon, *A Modern History of Japan from Tokugawa Times to the Present* (Cambridge, MA: Harvard University Press, 2003), p. 185.
26. Christine L. Marran, *Poison Woman: Figuring Female Transgression in Modern Japanese Culture* (Minneapolis, MN: University of Minnesota Press, 2007), pp. 109–10.
27. Mori Toshie, 'All for money: Mizoguchi Kenji's *Osaka Elegy* (1936)', in Alastair Phillips and Julian Stringer (eds), *Japanese Cinema: Texts and Contexts* (London: Routledge, 2007), p. 41.
28. Alan Tansman, *The Aesthetics of Japanese Fascism* (Berkeley, CA: University of California Press, 2009), p. 193.
29. Barak Kushner, *The Thought War: Japanese Imperial Propaganda* (Honolulu, HI: University of Hawai'i Press, 2006), p. 62.
30. Sarah Frederick, '"Novels to see/movies to read": Photographic fiction in Japanese women's magazines', *positions* 18(3) (2010), 765.
31. Mark Driscoll, *Absolute Erotic, Absolute Grotesque: The Living, Dead, and Undead in Japan's Imperialism, 1895–1945* (Durham, NC: Duke University Press, 2010), p. 98.
32. Michael Baskett, *The Attractive Empire: Transnational Film Culture in Imperial Japan* (Honolulu, HI: University of Hawai'i Press, 2008), p. 108.
33. Anderson and Ritchie, *The Japanese Film*, p. 160.
34. Keiko Iwai McDonald, 'The Yakuza film: An introduction', in Arthur Nolletti, Jr and David Desser (eds), *Reframing Japanese Cinema: Authorship, Genre, History* (Bloomington, IN: Indiana University Press, 1992), p. 167.
35. Hiroshi Kitamura, *Screening Enlightenment: Hollywood and the Cultural Reconstruction of Defeated Japan* (Ithaca, NY: Cornell University Press, 2010), p. 53.
36. Mitsuhiro Yoshimoto, *Kurosawa: Film Studies and Japanese Cinema* (Durham, NC: Duke University Press, 2000), p. 138.
37. Stephen Prince, *The Warrior's Cinema: The Cinema of Akira Kurosawa* (Princeton, NJ: Princeton University Press, 1991), p. 91.
38. Peter A. Yacavone, 'Shinoda's *Pale Flower* as a Japanese film noir', *Journal of Japanese and Korean Cinema* 3(1) (2011), 24.
39. Yuki Tanaka, *Japan's Comfort Women: Sexual Slavery and Prostitution during World War II and the US Occupation* (London: Routledge, 2002), p. 127.
40. Douglas N. Slaymaker, *The Body in Postwar Japanese Fiction* (London: Routledge, 2004), p. 104.
41. Ibid., p. 113.

5. THE GUNMAN AND THE GUN: JAPANESE FILM NOIR SINCE THE LATE 1950s

David Desser

'Nikkatsu Noir' – there is something very provocative about this: the alliteration, the double consonants in 'Nikkatsu' and the invocation of 'noir', certainly the most evocative of all genre names. In packaging its Eclipse Series 17, for the first time Criterion – the estimable company that has revolutionised the field of DVD–Blu-ray distribution with its combination of scholarly subtance and first-rate transfers of usually non-mainstream movies – did not group the films by director. From Japan, Criterion had previously released 'Late Ozu', 'Postwar Kurosawa', 'Silent Ozu', 'Kenji Mizoguchi's Fallen Women' and 'Travels with Hiroshi Shimizu'. But 'Nikkatsu Noir' was something different: not just the release of a group of little-known films, but a kind of invention of a genre. It would be churlish to claim that the films – *I am Waiting* (*Ore wa matteiru ze*, Kurahara Kureyoshi, 1957); *Rusty Knife* (*Sabita knife*, Masuda Toshio, 1958); *Take Aim at the Police Van* (*Sono gosôsha wo nerae: 'Jûsangô taihisen' yori*, Suzuki Seijun, 1960); *Cruel Gun Story* (*Kenju zankoku monogatari*, Furukawa Takumi, 1964); and *A Colt is My Passport* (*Colt wa ore no passport*, Nomura Takashi, 1967) – are not noir. That the films were not originally imagined as noir would not, of course, disqualify them from being noir. There was no imagination of 'noir' as such in classic Hollywood in the postwar era and no discourse of noir. There was a cycle of films with enough similarities to strike critics, first in France in 1955, as a kind of genre, movement or mode. Only when named and when this name entered more popular discourse did 'noir' take on the kind of generic cachet it has today. While noir had little cachet in the late 1950s for the Japanese, by the turn of the new century it certainly would.

After listing many of his influences, Joe Shishido (Shishido Jo) is asked if film noir is one of his influences on *Rusty Knife* and films of that era. He answers with a brief, 'Yes, that was an influence, on everyone from the director to the actors. I was the one who knew that genre best'.[1] Maybe so, but what did he know and when did he know it? Noir classics like *Out of the Past*, *The Lady from Shanghai* and *In a Lonely Place* had not played in Japan. The 1946 version of *The Postman Always Rings Twice* did not show until 1979. Other films played some years after their US release though Kubrick's *The Killing* and Orson Welles' late-classic noir *Touch of Evil* played around the time of their American distribution. Virtually none of these noirs made the prestigious *Kinema Junpo* 'Best' list, often consisting of as many as twenty or thirty films per year. This does not mean that these noirs did not have decent distribution, but it does mean that noir was not yet the prestige genre it would later come to be. (Welles' *Touch of Evil* was only twenty-third in 1958.) The questioners do not pursue the issue with Joe – what films had he seen and where had he seen them? And what is the significance of Joe having known the genre best? What influence did he have on the films: their script, direction, style and themes? Joe made over thirty films between 1958 and 1968, which reveals the speed with which Nikkatsu made these films and therefore the unlikelihood that he would have had much influence upon them, save for his performances. Clearly, however, noir had penetrated Japan. As Daisuke Miyao reminds us, in a café scene in Ozu's 1957 *Tokyo Twilight* (*Tokyo boshoku*; his last black-and-white film) we see a poster of Robert Mitchum, iconic actor of film noir, on the wall.[2] Of course, Ozu had a penchant for intertexual references to Hollywood via dialogue, music or, in this case, a poster, but the choice of Mitchum does seem telling. Similarly, Miyao insists that the art film *Conflagration* (*Enjo*, Ichikawa Kon, 1958) is often considered a film noir, a crime film that relies on flashbacks and high-contrast black-and-white cinematography.[3] Whether or not we consider either *Tokyo Twilight* or *Conflagration* to fit within or nearby the canon of noir, it is clear that it had made its way into the consciousness of filmmakers as diverse as Ozu and Ichikawa. Alternatively, however, Foster Hirsch maintains that in America, at least, the label 'noir' 'did not gain a foothold . . . until the late 1960s and early 1970s'.[4] The filmmakers may have known the films, but not their collective name. Meanwhile, in the late 1950s, Nikkatsu hit upon a generalised formula to make 'borderless' (*mukokuseki*) action films. They thus scrupulously avoided the kinds of images and sounds associated with classical Japanese cinema, such as picturesque *ryokan* (Japanese-style inn), *izakaya* (Japanese pub), Zen gardens, Tokyo's broad and leafy postwar streets, Kyoto's unspoiled temples and the like. Instead, in situating their films in the back alleys of Tokyo (as Ozu did in *Tokyo Twilight*), the docks of Yokohama and the wide-open spaces of Hokkaido, they imagined they would attract American and European audiences, especially with influences from both classic and younger arty, edgy non-Japanese directors. This strategy did not work; instead Euro-American audiences continued to appreciate the 'films for export' model established earlier in the decade by Daiei, films that participated in the postwar movement of 'art' cinema in ways that the genre-oriented action films did not – and did not intend to. But whereas these borderless action films found little play overseas at the time, they turned out to be huge hits in Japan.

The biggest star of these films was Ishihara Yujiro, who had made his mark in the exciting and influential *Crazed Fruit* (*Kurutta kajitsu*, Nakahira Ko, 1956). As successful as it was, the 'sun tribe' (*taiyo-zoku*) films were short lived, mostly because of public outrage, so Ishihara and the studio moved to the *mukokuseki* action genre, including, in 1957, *I Am Waiting* and *The Guy Who Started a Storm* (*Arashi o yobu otoko*, Inoue Umetsugu).[5] The latter film, a huge hit, utilised modern, Westernised locations and imagery such as the Ginza at night and its nightclubs, pop music and a violent ex-con seeking to go straight as a drummer.[6] These invocations of noir would combine with the conscious attempts at borderlessness in *Red Quay* (*Akai hatoba*, Masuda Toshio, 1958). Despite its title, the film was in black and white (Nikkatsu was split between colour and black and white in this period, though Eastmancolor would win out for the majority of their productions soon after), which Schilling claims is a 'reworking' of *Pépé le Moko* (Julien Duvivier, 1937).[7] It is the very setting along the 'quay' (*hatoba*) that invokes a liminal space or borderlessness and perhaps also calls to mind *Le Quai des brumes* (*Port of Shadows*, Marcel Carne, 1938) – the two French films essentially containing the essence of noir. Ishihara, himself, contained something of borderlessness about him – his long legs made him seem somehow un-Japanese and the way he walked was closer to John Wayne than to any Japanese star.[8]

The influence of both French and Hollywood cinema would continue to be apparent in Nikkatsu Action. Following in the footsteps of Ishihara Yujiro came Kobayashi Akira, three years Ishihara's junior (both actors made their film debuts in 1956, but Ishihara was an immediate star). It was in 1959 that Kobayashi made his breakthrough out of a combination of Nikkatsu genre and Hollywood themes. Inoue Umetsugu's *The Friendship that Started a Storm* (*Arashi o yobu yujo*) was clearly a reference to Ishihara's 1957 hit as was the film's setting in Tokyo's burgeoning jazz milieu. Saito Buichi's *Farewell to Southern Tosa* (*Nangoku Tosa o ato ni shite*) was another of those tales about the ex-con who is trying to go straight but is pulled back into his old life. It, too, was a smash.[9]

Kobayashi made numerous films every year in typical Nikkatsu business mode. Yet the films were hardly thoughtless; they may have been churned out, but they had things in mind. The *mukokuseki* ideal was at the top of the list. The paradigmatic borderless films were to be the *wataridori* series inaugurated by Saito's *The Rambling Guitarist* (*Guitar o motta wataridori*, 1959). These were modelled on Hollywood westerns and today films in this series have come to be understood as part of a subgenre known as the Asian western. Over half a dozen instalments of the series testify to their popularity and to the star's appeal

With Ishihara and Kobayashi churning out action films (with a touch of romance – Kitahara Mie for Ishihara, Asaoka Ruriko for Kobayashi) Nikkatsu made sure to find more dynamic young male stars and did so in the appealing forms of Wada Koji and Akagi Keiichiro, forming the 'Diamond Line'. In the early 1960s, Joe Shishido joined the line as he became a leading man, if a decidedly unromantic one. And romance was certainly important. Kitahara and Asaoka became big stars, but not as action heroines. That was left to Kaji Meiko, who found her niche in action films in 1970 with *Stray Cat Rock: Delinquent Girl Boss* (*Nora-neko rock: onna bancho*, Hasebe Yasuharu) and extending through four more films, the most famous of which is *Stray Cat Rock: Sex Hunter* (*Nora-neko rock: sex hunter*, Hasebe). The introduction of the issue of race into the film brings a social consciousness to the cycle. Here the figures of half-black-half-Japanese teenagers bring forth a host of underlying tensions, including mixed race vs Japanese purity; the social inferiority of Africa and African-Americans in the Japanese mind; and the reminder of Japanese defeat in the war and the continuing presence of American soldiers on Japanese soil. Shot near the US naval base in Yokosuka, the film manages to balance its exploitation elements with its social concerns.

Kaji continued her career and achieved even greater cult fame at Toei with the 'Female Convict 701: Scorpion' (*Joshuu 70-1-go: Sasori*, Ito Shunya) series beginning in 1972. The noir elements are even stronger here than in her previous series, as Kaji's character Nami is set up by her corrupt police officer boyfriend to take the fall for his crimes. Her attempt to stab him lands her in prison and we have, then, also a Women-in-Prison film replete with all the rape, torture, beatings and other excuses for nudity typical of the form (which began in 1971 with Roger Corman's *The Big Doll House* and *Women in Cages*). Sequels inevitably followed, of course, though the third, *Female Convict Scorpion: Beast Stable* (*Joshuu sasori: Kemono-beya*, Ito, 1973), finds Nami/Sasori out of prison and trying to go straight. As in classic Japanese noir, she is inevitably drawn into the dark world of the city, the world of *yakuza*, prostitutes, vengeful cops and a touch of incest. Exploitation, perhaps, but the noir world gives such exploitation every excuse to thrive.

Back at Nikkatsu at the turn of the 1960s, the '*Kenjū*', or 'Tales of a Gunman' film cycle, all films of which were made in 1960 and directed by Noguchi Hiroshi – *Ryuji the Gun Slinger* (*Kenjû buraichô: Nukiuchi no Ryû*); *Man in Lightning* (*Kenjû buraichô: Denko sekka no otoko*); *Man With a Hollow Laugh* (*Kenjû buraichô: Futeki ni warau otoko*); *Man Without Tomorrow* (*Kenjû buraichô: Asunaki otoko*) – mark an important transition to noir. These films star Akagi Keiichiro and Joe Shishido as rival gunmen, hired killers, who end up working together. Mark Schilling describes their dominant tone as 'noirish'.[10] Akagi died in a car accident on the Nikkatsu lot in 1961; his last film was another story of a hitman, *Crimson Pistol* (*Kurenai no kenju*, Ushihara Yoichi, 1961).

As the early 1960s gave way to the mid-1960s, Nikkatsu's stars, directors and audiences aged, as will inevitably happen. One could say, too, that borderless action suffered the inevitable decline of all genres – over-exposure and over-familiarity. The films of the mid-60s began to take on a darker tone and more adult themes. Films from this period, especially those of Ishihara Yujiro, came to be called 'mood action' and, as Schilling puts it, 'the mood was usually down'.[11] It was during this period, beginning in 1963 with *Youth of the Beast* (*Yaju no seishun*) under the increasingly inventive direction of Suzuki Seijun, that Joe Shishido became a star and, later, a cult figure. Schilling claims that his films at this time – *A Colt is My Passport*, *Branded to Kill* (*Koroshi no rakuin*) and *Slaughter Gun* (*Minagoroshi no kenju*, Hasebe Yasuharu) – began to allow him to venture into the dark underside of contemporary Japanese life.[12]

Watari Tetsuya represented the last of Nikkatsu's attempts to bring back the glory days of the 'Diamond Line'. He first made two films with Ishihara Yujiro in 1965–6, and starred in remakes of four of his older colleague's films, including *Velvet Hustler* (*Kurenai no nagareboshi*, 1967), Masuda Toshio's loose remake of *Red Quay*. Schilling notes that the hitman played by Watari was modelled on Jean-Paul Belmondo's character in *Breathless*.[13]

It is *Branded to Kill*, Suzuki's wildly incoherent and hilarious look at a hitman with some interesting psycho-sexual proclivities, the film for which he was notoriously fired in 1968, that has best come to represent the 'Nikkatsu Noir' mode. The use of black and white as late as 1967 is one reason for its paradigmatic status. But, as Miyao reminds us,

> The dark surfaces of film noir . . . came about as a result of the financial limitations imposed upon B pictures. In order to hide their cheap sets, lighting was used in such movies in a very sparse and economical manner. *Branded* was eventually shot in black and white even though it was planned as a color film from the very beginning.[14]

The studio was experiencing a severe economic downturn at this time and so the black and white might have been one concession to budgets. We note that *A Colt is My Passport* also boasts monochrome cinematography. Putting the two films side by side, so to speak, reveals interesting similarities, including that of style as well as the presence of Joe Shishido. Though perhaps less 'delirious' than Suzuki's film, *Colt*, under the direction of Nomura Takashi, does some interestingly avant-garde things.[15] A Nikkatsu contract director like Suzuki,

Nomura had previously directed *The Quick Draw Kid* (*Hayauchi yaro*, 1961), another perfect paradigm of the borderless action movie, where its hero, Ace no Joe (Shishido), outwits and outshoots 'the bad guys in a Japanese "Wild East" town the likes of which could only have existed in a Japanese studio'.[16] *Colt* differs from *Branded* only in degree, not in kind. The climactic shoot-out features a segment of shot-reverse shot with takes of around one second each. Nor is the script particularly tight: a subplot involving the waitress at the hotel where the hitman and his driver hide out never really pays off in terms of narrative or emotional closure.

What we must take away here is that a dual fascination had developed in Japan in the 1960s, culminating in these two odd films: the hitman and the gun. We have already seen the popularity of *kenju* (gun) in the 'Tales of a Gunman' series and we should note now the numerous other films that use *kenju* in their title, as listed above. These films combine the gun with the gunman, typically a hitman. We might well wonder which of these linked icons – the gunman and the gun – give rise to the other. Guns are, in Japan, the province of criminals and policemen. Japan has extremely tough and restrictive gun-control laws; only shotguns and air rifles are legal and even they are difficult to acquire, made onerous by various levels of state control. What is forbidden in life may be fascinating on screen, and the man (or woman) who possesses a gun, who is skilled in its use and knowledgeable of its properties, perhaps becomes doubly fascinating. The figure of the hitman, though often employed by a criminal organisation, is in stark contrast to the *yakuza* of the *ninkyo* films popularised by Toei Studios in the postwar era through the 1970s and made by Nikkatsu too in the mid-1960s.

Ninkyo-eiga is the term used in Japan to describe a specific variation of what is more generally called the *yakuza* film (*yakuza-eiga*). The *ninkyo-eiga*, or chivalry film, featured stories focusing on garishly tattooed gangsters attached to warring gangs in the early part of the twentieth century. Nikkatsu utilised young star Takahashi Hideki in their variation of the form, particularly the *Otoko no monsho* (Symbol of a Man) series beginning in 1963. Of these roles, he is best known for *Tattooed Life* (*Irezumi ichidai*, 1965), a relatively straightforward film considering it was made by Suzuki Seijun. But it is the Toei films that best reveal the distinction between the *ninkyo yakuza* and the hitman variation. In lieu of a gun, the favoured weapon of the *yakuza* is a sword (a shorter version of the samurai *katana*, kept in a plain wooden scabbard); instead of a suit the *yakuza* wears a plain kimono that, when he prepares for a fight, is pulled down to reveal the complex interweaving of tattoos on his back. Concepts of *giri/ninjo*, loyalty to the *oyabun* (gang boss) and to the *yakuza* brotherhood are central, as are various rituals that make for exciting cinema, especially the infamous *yubitsume* (slicing off the tip of the left little finger). The use of a modified samurai sword and the practice of *yubitsume* (a derivation of *seppuku*, presumably) link the *yakuza* to the samurai tradition and thus place the individual *yakuza* within a strong social context. Invariably there is betrayal, divided loyalties, perhaps a romance (though what is now called a 'bromance' is a stronger thematic), and a violent, cathartic climax that usually sees the hero dead. The hitman, with his techno-weaponry, expensive suit and fast cars, is also a loner, a figure of modernity and not of tradition. This is what makes the gun and the gunman films far closer to noir than the *yakuza* film – which is often a variation of the *jidai-geki* (especially as the films are set in the past, albeit the more recent past) – with its values and weaponry. Betrayal, shifting loyalties, a romance and a bromance are not uncommon, but the world in which the hitman lives is an isolated and atomised one.

Writing about Kurosawa Akira's noir, Dolores Martinez, adapting my own ideas about Kurosawa's portrayal of modernity and the problem of heroism, notes that for Japan and the US, 'the struggle to be a good man in uncertain times is central to the film noir narrative ... Both postwar Japan and the USA, despite their different societies, shared this modern predicament, born within the very conditions that would produce a sense of postmodernity'.[17] While this is undeniably true of the Kurosawa films, it is far less true of Nikkatsu noir. Although the times are indeed uncertain, seen in the constant betrayals that characterise the films, the hero is not necessarily a good man, except in relative terms. The ex-con trying to go straight is the closest these films come to that trope, wherein the hero used to be a bad guy and now is trying to be a good guy. The gunman movies insist that the hero is a killer. Yet by circumscribing the world in which he operates, the films remove the greater society and leave only the *yakuza* world and its related locales: the restaurants, bars, nightclubs, docks, fleabag hotels and so on (what in Chinese is poetically called the *jianghu* – literally rivers and lakes, but referring to the world of martial artists and the people with whom they typically interact). This separation from society, the closed-in world of the *jianghu* of gangsters, low-level criminals, hitmen, bar hostesses or waitresses, may be a dark mirror of Japanese society if one wishes to see it that way, but it seems clearer that the separation from *sarariman* reality is what is at stake. In fact, the Toei *ninkyo yakuza* films had an overwhelmingly working-class male audience, just as the Nikkatsu Noir appealed to educated youngsters: the former alienated from mainstream middle-class society; the latter resisting inclusion therein.

The bankruptcy of Nikkatsu and their resurrection as the purveyor of porn (*roman poruno* was the brand name for their films – a categorisation which would spread across the output of other studios, essentially replacing the previous term 'pink' film) had strong implications across the genre spectrum of Japanese cinema of the 1970s. The action woman first appeared at Toei in the 1970s with Sugimoto Miki and Ike Reiko in soft-core porn/hardcore action films featuring girl gangs. The 'girl boss' (*sukeban*) series, part of Toei's 'pinky violence' brand, got things started in 1972 under the direction of respected pink film director Suzuki Norifumi. *Girl Boss Guerilla* (*Sukeban: Gerira*) was followed six months later by *Girl Boss Revenge: Sukeban* (*Sukeban*, 1973). The mantle of pinky sex and violence was taken up a few months later by Nakajima Sadao with *Girl Boss: Escape from Reform School* (*Sukeban: Kankain dasso*, 1973). Sugimoto Miki would continue for a few more years in the noirish sex-and-violence mode, morphing her image from criminal to cop in the especially violent and perhaps disturbing *Zero Woman: Red Handcuffs* (*Zeroka no onna: Akai wappa*, 1974). Sugimoto would retire in 1977; Ike Reiko, after some offscreen troubles, would retire in 1980. The genre of pinky violence would also come to its end and Japanese noir would go on hiatus for some few years, resurrected in the 1980s by the singular talent and genre referentiality of Hayashi Kaizo.

A period of quiescence seemed to unleash a torrent of neo-noir in the 1990s. This was presaged in 1989 with the exciting directorial debut of Kitano Takeshi. Taking over the directorial reins from stylish veteran *yakuza* director Fukasaku Kinji, who had taken ill, Kitano made *Violent Cop* (*Sono otoko, kyobo ni tsuki*). Though the image of Clint Eastwood's Dirty Harry is often invoked to describe the violent cop of the title, the film is far darker than anything the San Francisco cop had to confront – inside or out. Corrupt cops; powerful *yakuza*; drug dealing and addiction; the endangerment of his disturbed sister – the film has all the elements of Japanese noir with new levels of violence. Kitano, unquestionably the most important of post-1980s Japanese directors, has long been associated with the crime film, especially his works in the noir-filled 90s.

Much of the noir of the 1990s can be classified as neo-noir as the films betray a certain knowingness in their evocations of the genre. Few, however, are as knowingly winking as in the case of Hayashi Kaizo's *The Most Terrible Time in My Life* (*Waga jinsei saikaku no toki*, 1994). As in his first and still best-known film, *To Sleep so as to Dream* (*Yume miru yoni nemuritai*, 1986), the film is as much a meditation on cinema as it is an examination of character and setting. The earlier film was a lovely and loving tribute to the particularities of the Japanese silent cinema, done largely in the form of a silent film. Its plot revolves around a private eye and his search for an aging actress's kidnapped daughter. We can easily get lost in the silent-film stylings, especially the use of a *benshi*, played by one of the last of the great *benshi*, Matsuda Shunsui (who died shortly after the release of this film), and his disciple, the inestimable Sawato Midori. Similarly, we may admire the recreation of a *jidaigeki* (period film) from 1915 (though we could quibble and note that Hayashi's film-within-the-film is far more 'advanced' than a film of the era). But in so doing we miss something important here, that in the use of a private eye searching for a missing girl, who finds himself lost amidst a confusing swirl of clues, characters and conundrums, we have entered the world of noir. The framing story – the hiring of the private eye – is set in the 1950s, which is to say at the height of classic film noir, at a time when the genre had been named as such and when genuine auteurs like Welles, Wilder and Aldrich were demonstrating both the essential characteristics of noir and its stylistic flexibility. There is, for instance, something of *Sunset Blvd* (1950) in the use of a fading actress who sends the protagonist on his journey, along with the invocation of the silent cinema; and when the private eye and his sidekick find themselves in 1915 Asakusa (suggested more than recreated with brief glimpses of elements of the famed entertainment area of Tokyo in the teens) are we that far from Welles' famous funhouse hall of mirrors in *The Lady from Shanghai*?

The Most Terrible Time of My Life uses the figure of the private eye in a deliberate nod to the Hollywood figure of the hard-boiled detective. Called 'Hama Mike' (i.e. Mike Hammer and Mike Yokohama at the same time), it is hard to miss the reference to the late-classic noir. Hama's office is inside a cinema, its marquee outside boasting 'CinemaScope', yet the film being shown at that time is *The Best Years of Our Lives*, which, in the title sequence, becomes the title of the film we are watching, i.e. *The Most Terrible Time of My Life*. These jokey allusions (*The Best Years of Our Lives* was made half a dozen years before the introduction of CinemaScope; few of the classic noirs, even those made after 1952, were in 'Scope) are part of an intertextual chain extending from American noir, the French New Wave and Nikkatsu Action. Joe Shishido himself makes a longish cameo appearance as a mentor to Mike.[18]

Two direct sequels quickly followed: *The Stairway to the Distant Past* (*Harukana jidai no kaidan o*, 1995), which abandons its black-and-white look, and *The Trap* (*Wana*, 1996), also in colour. The films were made in CinemaScope and all feature cult favourite Nagase Masatoshi in the leading role. And all were directed by Hayashi. The third and final one is of particular interest for the way in which it gets at the dark heart of noir – the unstable hero who has lived by the code of being a good man, but who cannot be trusted, even by himself.[19]

The private eye, the PI, is another figure of alienation. Like the hitman, he works alone (private) or with a partner, taking cases that somehow appeal to him or out of a sense of obligation. Yet the PI is an uncommon figure in Japanese noir. Whereas Hollywood films are positively bursting at the seams with private eyes, in Japan that is entirely not the case. Perhaps the PI, a popular figure in American literature as well, appeals to American audiences as a liminal figure, somewhere between the law and the outlaw. The kind of in-betweenness represented by the PI may be linked to issues of social mobility or the possession of multiple identities. We might say that in Japan it remains more difficult to be in-between. One can lose social status, experience a shift in circumstances, but perhaps the ability to move between social classes is more

Figure 5.1 Theatre front in *The Most Terrible Time in My Life*.

difficult. Think of the tragic figure of the ronin – he is more than an unemployed samurai. Though today the term 'ronin' is sometimes used for a salaryman who is between jobs, more typically ronin is used to describe a teenager who has failed to win a place at a prestigious college or university and is taking classes in order to resit the exam. This is a form of social alienation or even disgrace, not a liminal figure moving between realms with one foot in each and a self-satisfied sense of being a loner.

One can think of no such PI figure in classical Japanese noir. It would take the 1990s to introduce him, especially in anime. *Case Closed* (*Meitantei Conan*, aka *Detective Conan*), is a very popular manga series that began in 1994, with televisual anime beginning in 1996, followed by feature anime, OVA (original video animation), video games and live-action television specials. A typically bizarre world is created – a teenage boy is subjected to a poison intended to kill him, but instead transforms him into a child who calls himself Conan Edogawa (a variation on famed pseudonymous Japanese mystery author Edogawa Rampo; i.e. Edgar Allan Poe). He seeks to destroy the dastardly Black Organisation, whose members take the *nom de guerre* of alcoholic beverages, with Gin, Vodka and Vermouth the major antagonists. An earlier PI series was *Goku Midnight Eye* (Kawajiri Yoshiaki, 1989), released as two OAVs, which concerns a dogged police officer who, while investigating a series of police suicides, is warned off the case. When he refuses he is almost killed, his left eye gouged out. He is then rescued by a mysterious scientist who implants a cybernetic eye in place of his missing one. His cybernetic eye can connect with any computer in the world. He becomes a PI in this generally futuristic, adult-oriented manga and anime.

Most manga and/or anime featuring private detectives are closer to the mystery genre than the tough-guy detective story. In addition, *Goku Midnight Eye* is one of the few with an adult protagonist; the others use children detectives – no surprise given the primary demographic of manga and anime. Of equal import, however, is that anime is often intended for a global market, being the new, successful version of the old Nikkatsu *mukokuseki* ideal. Thus, in creating detectives and private eyes, Japanese anime is relying on the global penetration of such figures and not necessarily any particular Japanese dimension. To be sure, *Detective Conan* was wildly successful, but one might attribute that to its sci-fi setting and the transformation of its teenage protagonist into a child as much as any detecting.

The mid-90s through the rest of the decade was clearly a golden age of neo-noir. A wonderful retro/neo-noir is to be found in the form of *Another Lonely Hitman* (*Shin Kanashiku Hitman*, Mochizuki Rokuro, 1995). Rarely has colour cinematography looked and felt so much like black and white. Sparse settings, minimal dialogue, a genuinely troubled tough-guy protagonist (portrayed by up-and-coming star Ishibashi Ryo) and a dark world of betrayal and disillusionment characterise this post-Nikkatsu neo-noir. Ishibashi portrays Tachibana, a *yakuza* hitman newly released after ten years in prison. He is clearly out of step from the moment he steps out of prison. The world has changed and the *yakuza* have changed with it. At first, however, his old gang is welcoming, presenting him with a gift of cash, the aid of an admiring factotum and a cute call girl for the evening. Tachibana, for all his skill at violence, is sexually impotent. However, he begins a relationship with the call girl, Yuki, after he beats her pimp for beating her. But that is when he learns the first of many hard lessons, that the pimp is connected with another *yakuza* family, a more powerful one – in fact the very family whose boss he killed (along with crippling the boss's daughter). He is dismayed when he sees that money is the foundation of *yakuza* life now; violence is frowned upon when dealing with other gangsters, but loyalty is becoming in short supply. Tachibana, a former junkie, is also dismayed to see that drug pushing has become a lucrative *yakuza* enterprise. He helps Yuki kick her habit.

Gang member Mizohashi is the most significant figure with whom Tachibana must contend. He continually reminds him that money greases all wheels and that conflict amongst *yakuza* families is to be avoided. Yet he plays all sides in his role as go-between, with a lucrative side angle in heroin. He feels the big money is in the building of a golf course and has worked hard (and behind the scenes in secret) to acquire the land. This idea of heroin funding a golf course is not just the perfect metaphor for the changes in *yakuza* life that alienate Tachibana from his former gang family (his real family, his ex-wife and his mother have completely renounced him, keeping him estranged from his daughter and his sister), but is also a deft swipe at middle-class striving for the attributes of wealth, golf and golf courses being extraordinarily expensive in Japan.

Director Mochizuki, who got his start making *roman poruno* at Nikkatsu, keeps the sex and nudity to an almost bare minimum. Eschewing *roman poruno* for the most part (a rather odd scene of Yuki peeing her pants perhaps being the only nod to the sometimes-perverse sexuality of the genre), and keeping the violence from becoming overwhelming, the films is a character study of a man out of sorts with the changing times. The most he can accomplish is the redemption of one young prostitute. Otherwise, all is noir.

If the violence of *Another Lonely Hitman* is understated, the same cannot be said of the almost indescribable films of Miike Takashi. A major contributor to the neo-noir cycle in the 90s, especially with his 'Black Society' trilogy, *Shinjuku Triad Society* (*Shinjuku Kuroshakai: Chaina Mafia Senso*, 1995), *Rainy Dog* (*Gokudo Kuroshakai*, 1997) and *Ley Lines* (*Nihon Kuroshakai*, 1999), Miike brought a new level of violence and cultural critique to the genre. Miike is enamoured of Shinjuku, especially its notorious Kabukicho section – Tokyo's official (as well as unofficial) red-light district. If Kurosawa saw parts of Tokyo becoming headquarters for hedonism in *Stray Dog* and *Ikiru*, Kabukicho is the nightmare vision of this image. Miike is equally fascinated by the intermingling of Chinese gangs and Japanese criminals in Shinjuku's warren of alleyways, nightclubs, brothels and love hotels. Miike's sense of 'intermingling' extends to images of mixed-race characters, including the corrupt-cop protagonist of *Shinjuku Triad Society* (the Triads are Chinese gangsters so the very title indicates the mixing of Japanese and Chinese).

Shot on film and released theatrically, *Shinjuku Triad Society* features the exploits of driven cop Tatsuhito, the half-Chinese/half-Japanese officer assigned to take down the Chinese mafia in Shinjuku. Tatsuhito discovers his younger brother is the Triad lawyer. His anger and resentment at this is part of the powder keg the film sets alight. The perversions that were humorously handled in Nikkatsu Noir become a staple of Miike's cinema, except that his humour is questionable. Mafia chief Wang is a homosexual exhibitionist and sadist. Tatsuhito is unafraid to resort to rape and violence to get what he wants. This is to say that the line between good and evil, right and wrong, is a bit murkier than in the past. Miike's cops are corrupt, but his bad guys perhaps even more so. The film brings together some of the favoured Miike and neo-noir stars-in-the-making: Osugi Ren as the Japanese *yakuza* leader; Sabu (Hiroyuki Tanaka) as Tatushito's partner; Taguchi Tomorowo as the Taiwanese Triad lesader, Wang; and Shiina Kippei as Tatsuhito. The main one missing from this list is Aikawa Sho.

Miike would rectify that by starring Aikawa in the second film of the (very loose) 'Black Society' trilogy as a *yakuza* exiled to Taiwan. This enables Miike both to explore one of his favoured themes, that of racial-ethnic intermixing, and to continue the tradition of noir and neo-noir with its alienated heroes, loners in a society that makes such a state both difficult and tragic. There is also the reversal of the image of the first-world Japanese and the third-world Taiwanese, or the coloniser vs the colonised, in that the hero, Yuji, has no passport and is thus an illegal alien in Taiwan, the reversal of the Chinese

Figure 5.2   Alienated figures of *Rainy Dog*.

Triad members in the earlier film. He works in a slaughterhouse and also takes assignments as a hitman from a Taiwanese crime boss. He is also being pursued by a Japanese man who is most likely a hitman from a rival *yakuza* gang. His life becomes infinitely more complicated still when a former one-night stand leaves a mute youngster with him, claiming it is his son. Tom Mes notes the resemblance to Luc Besson's *Léon* (1994) only to note also the vast difference in style, temperament and execution.[20] Interestingly, Mes calls Yuji 'the lonely hitman', an unintentional but revealing link to films like Mochizuki's discussed above.[21] And, like Mochizuki's earlier film, escape from the life is possible only by death.

Ley Lines, the third film in the Black Society trilogy, is called by Tom Mes 'the quintessential Miike film'.[22] With a completely different plot and set of characters than the earlier Japan-set film, many of the same actors appear: Osugi Ren, Taguchi Tomorowo and Takeshi Caesar, along with now-regular Aikawa Sho. Again, the uneasy presence of Chinese in Japan is highlighted, this time through the use of characters born in Japan of Chinese parents; they speak Japanese fluently and are completely acculturated to Japan, but are still barely accepted as Japanese. Three boys flee their rural hometown and light out for the dark world of Shinjuku. Once there they are scammed by a Chinese prostitute, but when they later discover her bruised and beaten by her pimp, they realise their solidarity as outsiders, not just as Chinese in xenophobic Japan, but as marginalised workers living on the fringes. Mes even notes that when they become low-level drug dealers, the drug they sell on the streets is toluene: 'They are such outcast [sic] that they aren't even allowed to sell a decent drug'.[23] (Toluene is methylbenzene, a solvent as well as an octane booster for petrol that can be used as an inhalant to get high, but only at the risk of neurological damage.) Their outcast status forces them into a life of crime which inevitably leads to death, at least for some, and an ambiguous end for others.

In the mid-1990s, films about female assassins/hitmen (hitwomen) combined a decidedly noir sensibility with an overtly sexualised image of the leading lady. *Beautiful Beast* (XX: *Utsukushiki kemono*, Ikeda Toshiharu, 1995) was a direct-to-video feature starring Shimamura Kaori. Typically such films as this are B films (shot in high-def video), in terms of budget and stars, along with running time, but there is less stigma attached to this distribution pattern than there is in the US. This is a common practice in anime, for instance, and was part-and-parcel of the career trajectory of Miike Takashi. Director Ikeda is best known for his cult horror hit *Evil Dead Trap* (*Shiryo no wana*, 1988) and the connections between a film like that and *Beautiful Beast* tell us something of the underlying darkness in these films. However, the link between sex and violence is of greater import in this and other hitwomen films. *Beautiful Killing Machine* (XX: *Utsukushiki kino*, Hara Takahito, 1996) starring Natsume Rei, a model who eventually made only three films, features a female bodyguard up against the top hitman in the business in order to protect her client. A third 'Beautiful' (*utsukushiki*) film was quickly turned out by Ikeda, also in 1996. *XX: Beautiful Prey* (XX: *utsukushiki emono*) was the rare noir to utilise a policewoman for its tormented protagonist, here caught up in a web of S&M sex in her search for a rapist-murderer. Though the 'Zero Woman' series (1995–7, inspired by the original *Zero Woman* and the success of Luc Besson's *Nikita*, 1990, and its American remake, *The Point of No Return*, John Badham, 1993) also focused on a policewoman, and it relies on copious amounts of nudity as all these films do, the films draw strict lines between good and evil and allow its protagonist to be free of self-doubt and torment.

Perhaps the most noir-like of any of these 'girls with guns' films (this seems to be the transnational genre into which such films are categorised) is *Black Angel* (*Kuro no tenshi* Vol. 1, Ishii Takashi, 1997). Filled with sex and violence, the film manages, under the direction of the skilled Ishii Takashi – best known for two entries in the controversial 'Angel Guts' series – to create the appropriate noir atmosphere out of Tokyo's neon-lit nights along with the aura of corruption on the mean streets. The second entry in the series is less noir and more action. Indeed by the late 90s the 'action' film would become more of a global genre, and would capture the imagination of the likes of Miike and dilute the noir elements in favour of spectacle.

The 1990s, especially the last half of the decade, was, as we have seen, a mini-Golden Age of neo-noir. It is easy to draw a connection between the cultural context and the rise of the cycle. It seems clear that neo-noir was very much attuned to the so-called 'lost decade' of the Japanese economy (*ushinawareta junen*, or 'lost ten years'). Whereas classic noir was a response to the Japanese economic miracle, the downturn in the economy led to a myriad of societal problems. Overrated land and real-estate prices in the 1980s combined with low interest rates led to massive borrowing and heavy investment in the stock market. A rise in interest rates to counteract the bubble made it burst and the stock market crashed. A debt crisis followed. Japan's famed lifetime employment system was said to have collapsed as one result of the stagnant economy that followed during this lost ten years. While that is something of a myth – long-term employment increased during the 90s and the changing of jobs was only negligibly more noticeable – over the course of the decade and thereafter the nature of the Japanese workforce changed as did the impression of lifetime work.[24] Perhaps even more importantly, the nature of work did change for Japanese youth. High school and university graduates of the 1990s came to be called the lost generation. The smooth transition from school to work and the lifetime employment that could be expected had broken down for many young people. Here came the problem of 'freeters' and 'NEETs'. The former refers to workers employed in temporary or part-time work, originally by choice in the 1980s when the term was coined, but later in the 90s due to the economic downturn. The term is a neologism derived from the English 'free' and the German *Arbeit* (work). The latter is an acronym meaning 'not in education, employment or training'. This is a social problem among the 18–34 year old demographic, the same as that which makes up the major audience for the film.

Though we wish to see cultural connections to cycles of noir, there are other compelling factors to consider. If we think of the Mike Hama trilogy as retronoir, we should certainly think of the noir films of Sabu (Tanaka Hiroyuki) as neo-noir with a decidedly postmodern, hip twist. His early films, like the hilarious *Dangan Runner* (1996), *Postman Blues* (1997) and *Drive* (2002), belong less to any sense of lost-generation disillusionment and depression in Japan than to the rush to imitate the early films of Quentin Tarantino – themselves imitations of earlier films.[25]

Dangan Runner is the obvious forerunner to Tom Tykwer's frenetic *Run Lola Run* (*Lola Rennt*, 1998), though it lacks the narrative repetitions/variation. It belongs to that category of films that grow out of the surrealism of city life with its odd coincidences and juxtapositions. *Pulp Fiction* (1994) is the model here, with its fragmented, disjointed narrative presentation. More comedy than noir, though it eventually evolves into a dark comedy, *Dangan Runner* concerns a two-bit would-be criminal (played by Miike favourite Taguchi Tomorowo) who angers a convenience-store clerk with his attempt to steal a gauze mask (in order to rob a bank). The clerk chases him with an unending sense of purpose. In turn, the clerk, a strung-out former rock musician (played by real-life rocker Diamond Yukai), is being pursued by his drug dealer (TV actor Tsutsumi Shin'ichi working his way into films), a low-level *yakuza*. The three run with the stamina of Lola, maintaining a consistent distance apart as they wend their way through the city. One particularly piquant moment occurs when the three young men run past an attractive woman. The small-time crook imagines making love to her in a gentle, romantic fashion; the rock star fantasises a slightly more kinky encounter; the *yakuza* envisages raping her. As they run the film flashes back to their stories. The chase is occasionally interrupted by the discussions between two *yakuza* (one played by Osugi Ren, one of his ten film roles in 1996) about the *yakuza* code of honour and its concomitant willingness to die for one's *oyabun*. There is even a fantasy sequence done in classic *yakuza-eiga* style from their point of view.

Tsutsumi Shin'ichi and Osugi Ren return in *Postman Blues*. Again, the figure of the hitman recurs, especially in the tragic image of the terminally ill Joe (Osugi) whose name might be a nod to the figure of the American loner or perhaps to Joe Shishido. The dark humour here occurs when postman Sawaki (Tsutsumi) runs into his old schoolmate, now a low-level *yakuza* who has just performed the ritual of *yubitsume*. Unbeknownst to either man, the fingertip has rolled off the table and into Sawaki's mailbag. From there on in, Sawaki is mistaken for a vicious *yakuza* killer and drug-dealer by the clueless, frightened police.

Chance encounter plays a significant role in *Drive*, Sabu's third film, involving kinder, gentler versions of the *yakuza*. Tsutsumi Shin'ichi and Osugi Ren are joined in this film by Terajima Susumu. This film is even lighter than the others as a young man and woman are kidnapped after a botched mission by completely incompetent *yakuza*. What could have been a tense ride through the *yakuza* underworld is instead a bemused and amused look at the reality behind the poseurs of gangland Japan.

Tsukamoto Shinya, already a cult favourite with his 'Tetsuo films' (1989, 1992), resisted the urge for postmodern pastiche or even the retro-noir of the alienated hitman. Taking seriously not the figure of the gunman, but that of the gun, *Bullet Ballet* (1998) is an intense psychological drama about a man traumatised by his girlfriend's suicide by gunshot. Initially he seems less interested in why she killed herself and more in the gun she used: what kind of gun was it and how did she get it? He determines to acquire a gun just like hers. Given the difficulty of getting a gun in Japan, Goda (played by Tsukamoto himself) searches through the Tokyo underworld, the black-and-white cinematography (as he had used in *Tetsuo, the Iron Man*) emphasising the noir world he now moves through. Of course we understand that his quest to get a gun represents a displacement of his sense of failure in his relationship, his emasculation. That is an obvious reading, but for all that an important one. In his quest Goda also acquires a secondary mission, that of saving Chisato from her self-destructive ways as part of a small-time criminal gang. Goto's downward spiral is inevitable and Tsukamoto captures it with jagged editing and sometimes dizzying camerawork, a melding of theme and style that makes this a quintessential neo-noir without the po-mo irony behind it.

Either the end of the 90s or the start of the new millennium, depending on your perspective, saw the intriguingly titled *Film Noir* (*Koroshi*, 2000, Kobayashi Masahiro). Though the Japanese title means 'killer' and not 'film noir', given its subject matter – an ordinary man becomes a hitman – the English title seems appropriate enough. With its dedication to French noir auteur Jean-Pierre Melville, it is hard not to place this film in its proper generic context. *Another Lonely Hitman*'s Ishibashi Ryo stars as a salaryman who has lost his job but is afraid to tell his harridan wife. So he trudges off to 'work' each morning, but goes instead to the next town to hang out at a pachinko parlour. He and his wife continue to send money overseas to their daughter in school in the States, so he knows his money supply is dwindling. One day he is approached by a man, played by 80s cult favourite Ogata Ken, who offers him a job as a contract killer. Needing the money, he eventually agrees. Soon he finds the work satisfying as he equally finds sex with his wife satisfying.

The cultural chords here are plentiful. As a salaryman, Yuji would once have lived with the expectation of lifetime employment. But the lost decade of the 90s cost him his job. His daughter at school in the States represents another status indicator in contemporary Japan. But mostly the wicked humour of equating work as a salaryman with work as a hitman is the film's most challenging idea. The setting in rural, wintry Hokkaido seems anathema to noir – white snow vs neon lights; cold vs hot (it rains in noir, but it never snows); small town vs big city. Yet in its focus on a man betrayed by his society, emasculated by his job and his wife, who is regenerated through violence, the film works as neo-noir. And as the man known only as the Client, Ogata Ken brings to the role the necessary sense of mystery, arbitrariness and even absurdity. Why these particular people need to be killed is never explained and only when Yuji is assigned to kill someone he knows does he come up short in his blithe killing spree.

The hitman figure continues to recur in neo-noir of the new millennium. One interesting example brings back the hitwoman/assassin cycle of the mid-1990s. Model-turned-actress Yonekura Ryoko stars in *Gun Crazy: A Woman from Nowhere* (2002), directed by Muroga Atsushi. Its success inspired not a series of sequels, but a series of episodes, not much longer than an hour, featuring different casts, all released as direct-to-video. *Gun Crazy* is a competent, if ultimately uninvolving amalgam of *Yojimbo/A Fistful of Dollars, Once Upon a Time in the West* with a soupçon of *The Good, the Bad and the Ugly* thrown in. Given its contemporary setting – although in a fictional town – replete with motorcycles, cars, trucks, swimming pools and big guns, it is closer in tone to the original source for Kurosawa's influential samurai film, Dashiell Hammett's *Red Harvest*. Crucially, however, it does not feature the lone gunfighter offering his services to two competing cartels. Instead, it is a story of vengeance as if paring down *Once Upon a Time in the West* just to the Harmonica/Frank story.

If *Yojimbo*, as Dolores Martinez argues, is film noir, then this low-budget adaptation of it also must be noir.[26] Despite the loose definition of noir and its permutations across global cinema, I cannot accept *Yojimbo* as noir despite my admiration for the arguments made in support of this case by Martinez. If noir is primarily a style, as Nikkatsu Noir demonstrates, then *Yojimbo* fails that test (compare the look of *Yojimbo* to *Stray Dog* and *High and Low* and you will see that Kurosawa understood noir just fine). If the noir protagonist, especially in Japan, is a damaged hero, then Kurosawa has created his darkest character in the figure of the Yojimbo. As a consequence of this darkness of character, Kurosawa has directed his lightest film – light meant in two ways. First, the film takes place almost entirely in daylight. Only the beating the bodyguard receives and his subsequent escape from town as the Seibe clan is destroyed takes place at night. And, second, the film is, despite its violence, light in its theme. The jaunty music, Yojimbo's swaggering walk, the cheerful nihilism of the ending all contribute to a film that works to overcome the potential darkness of the character – a ronin, a loner, a man of violence, but with a good heart, roaming through an increasingly amoral, materialistic world.

When Kurosawa wants to confront the dark side, the underbelly, of life he does so forthrightly as in his best noir (and one of his best films): *High and Low*. The utter depravity of the kidnapper almost brings Gondo Kingu to ruin and certainly exposes him to a side of life he barely knew existed. Though Gondo has worked his way up by his bootstraps, so to speak (he is a shoe manufacturer), he now lives high above a world of poverty, of squalor, that seems drawn from imagery of postwar destruction, right down to a foetid lake that itself recalls the offending mosquito-infected sump of *Ikiru* (1952). But Gondo is spared the worst of it. The police detectives stake out the kidnapper in Tokyo's dark passageways and back-alley nightclubs, working their way through a veritable throng of drug addicts with their avid eyes and Noh-like complexions. This is a world Gondo never sees, but we do; a shocking world behind the placid and agreeable image of irenic Japan. Kurosawa even uses the opening scenes of the film, the steps Gondo takes to secure control of his company and the machinations of his partners to wrest control away from him, to suggest the kind of noir world he had presented in *The Bad Sleep Well*. There his concern was with corporate corruption and the excesses of the new materialism, couched in the guise of a reworking of *Hamlet*. The crosses and double-crosses in the smoke-filled back rooms of corporate Japan are as cynical as any noir and, with the death of its protagonist before he achieves his revenge, almost nihilistic in its conclusion. Much of this film, unlike *Yojimbo*, takes place at night and the shadows and light-bars that characterise noir are used in abundance. Nishi, the protagonist (played by Mifune Toshiro, who appears in all of Kurosawa's noirs), is no hero like the playfully nihilistic but ultimately romantic Yojimbo or the earnest, forthright businessman Gondo.

He is a morally ambiguous hero as virtually all commentators on the film note. His death is retribution for his sins, but at least his mission will, to a certain extent, be carried to its conclusion. The comic violence Kurosawa would portray in *Yojimbo* is a far cry from the vicious and cynical violence wielded by corrupt corporate and government officials remaking the new Japan, perhaps in the image of the old.

Given *Gun Crazy*'s contemporary setting and its nihilistic attitude, along with the heroine's physical and psychological wounds, we do have the depiction of 'a damaged hero resorting to a liberating violence that is not sanctioned in mainstream Japan' – one of Martinez's central tenets of the noir worldview.[27] In this case, our protagonist and the film that contains her are figures outside of the Japanese norm – a vengeance-driven hitwoman in a direct-to-video B film. The influence of Miike Takashi is even greater than that of Kurosawa, from whom director Muroga takes virtually nothing stylistically or morally. When, at the end, Saki confronts the villain he shoots off her artificial leg. While drawing a bead on her to finish her off, she picks up the leg which transforms, we see for the first time, into a bazooka. Needless to say, he is no more. Since we had no idea that her leg was also a weapon, let alone that she had an artificial limb (she walks with a pronounced limp and does have hardware connecting her thigh to her shin, but it could as easily be a leg brace as a prosthesis), comes as a surprise that makes us laugh with its excess, and not revel in its poetic justice. The idea of a beautiful young woman having a prosthesis due to the cruelty of the villain – we see in flashback how her father died and she was injured – is an interesting twist on the emasculated noir hero of the postwar era. And we could slot in the use of the American presence to continue to place us in Japan's long postwar period. Perhaps surprisingly the film features a number of American soldiers working for the villain, whose name, all too symbolically, is Tojo. A number of these soldiers are killed in their roles as bad guys in the villain's employ. One significant motif in the film is the recurring shots of American fighter jets roaring across the sky. Tojo is said to live within the confines of an American military base, thus putting him off limits to Japanese authorities. These clear indices of the American military presence aligned with Japanese gangsters certainly speak to post-1970s revelations of political and corporate corruption. That they have emasculated the hero(ine), and wounded her in body and soul, gives the film a richer dimension that is belied by its Miike-derived violence and by-the-numbers plotting despite its derivations from *Yojimbo*.

In fact, the entire 'Gun Crazy' series is given over to explorations of corruption. The corruption of the justice system by organised crime is the subject of *Gun Crazy: Episode 2: Beyond the Law* (Muroga, 2002). TV star Kikukawa Rei is featured in a story of a female lawyer who takes to the way of the gun and becomes an assassin. *Gun Crazy Episode 3: Traitor's Rhapsody* (Muroga,

JAPANESE FILM NOIR SINCE THE LATE 1950s

Figure 5.3   Stray Cat from *Pistol Opera*.

2003) features a rookie policewoman who, against orders, decides to take down the terrorists who killed her partner. *Gun Crazy Episode 4: Requiem for a Bodyguard* (2003) is the story of a kidnapped corporate executive's daughter rescued by a childhood friend.

Suzuki Seijun also took a gander to the distaff side of the world of assassins with *Pistol Opera* (2001). Starring leggy beauty Esumi Makiko, the film is essentially a colour and colourful reworking of *Branded to Kill*. If, as Daisuke Miyao has it, *Branded* is partially an avant-garde film, then *Pistol Opera* takes the 'avant' even further.[28] Each scene is staged on its own terms and can stand alone as a short film about killing.

Each of the assassins the hitwoman Stray Cat must kill to complete her assignment (calling her Stray Cat must be a subtle nod to Kaji Meiko, queen of the tough-chick flick) is given an outrageous personality and MO. There is the teacher, confined to a wheelchair but still ready for revenge upon the woman who put him there; Painless Surgeon is a foreigner with a particular love of Japanese theatre and Japanese women who, as his name indicates, favours scalpels and other surgical equipment – but 'painless' does not refer to his assassination methods, but rather to his own inability to feel pain; and there is Dark Horse, so named for his black cloak, though the blonde wig doesn't quite complete the ensemble that his name implies – his killing is precise, the laser scope of his pistol always aimed at the juncture where the brain stem meets the spinal cord. With minimal connections between scenes, the narrative is almost impenetrable which, combined with its theatricalised and stylised staging, makes this perhaps more avant-garde than noir. But the sense of paranoia and the odd psycho-sexual perversions of the hitmen are clearly extensions – humorous exaggerations to be precise – of classic Nikkatsu Noir. It is as if Suzuki is returning to the scene of the crime, remaking the film that got him fired, only this time studio president Hori Kyusaku was long gone, having passed away in 1974.

The year 2001 also saw the increasingly outrageous Miike Takashi make *Ichi the Killer* (*Koroshiya 1*). Along with the horror film *Audition* (1999), *Ichi* remains Miike's signature film for both cultists and general audiences. Certainly its most memorable element is the extremity of its violence. While *Audition* climaxes with horrifying torture-porn, *Ichi* confronts the audience with ever-increasing ways to maim, hurt, injure, wound, mutilate, mangle, disfigure and deform a human body. A quartet of cult favourites, including Asano Tadanobu, Terajima Susumu, Sabu and Tsukamoto Shinya, head the cast of this blood-drenched gore-fest. Yet at its basic level this is a noir set in the *yakuza* underworld, whose protagonist, Kakihara, is a loyal lieutenant to gangland boss Anjo. When his boss disappears (he has been murdered, but Kakihara wants to believe he is missing), Kakihara seeks him out, literally cutting a swathe through the *yakuza* underworld. The psycho-sexual perversity of the noir hero, pioneered by Joe Shishido in *Branded to Kill*, is taken to a dimension even beyond Suzuki's avant-garde imaginings. Kakihara is a masochist, his face a nightmare of scars and piercings. Crime boss Anjo was the only one who could satisfy his masochistic urges. Thus the *yakuza* theme of loyalty to one's *oyabun* combines with the noir motif of sexual desire that is somehow perverted. With the clandestine machinations of Jiji, both Kakihara and Ichi (the latter a victim of hypnosis and false memories) find ever-new and unpleasant ways to torture and slaughter. But at its (admittedly difficult to find) heart, the film is really a search for family and fulfilment. Ichi craves sexual normality; Kakihara a suitable sadist; young Takeshi a sense of safety; his disgraced ex-cop father a sense of belonging. Miike's films may lack clarity and coherence, but certainly they continue to participate in the Japanese neo-noir where being an outsider, alienated and alone, is the most frightening thing of all.

Perhaps appropriately, the master manipulator that was Jiji in *Ichi the Killer* is played by Tsukamoto Shinya. The director of *Bullet Ballet*, one of the cycle of neo-noir not concerned with cops or killers, contributed to post-millennial neo-noir with another psycho-sexual exploration, *A Snake of June* (*Rokugatsu no hebi*, 2002). As the marriage of a middle-class couple deteriorates, the younger wife is blackmailed into performing ever-more socially dangerous acts of a sexual nature. She, however, finds these liberating and soon her husband is drawn into the erotic regeneration. The figure of the mysterious photographer, who has power over her – the power to blackmail her, the power to control the gaze, but also the power to know her better than she does herself – is precisely the neo-noir vision of the sexual pervert, the dangers of the city and the fear of social ostracism. Hand-held camera work, jagged editing and the rain-slicked city streets also contribute to the noirish atmosphere.

Like *A Snake of June*, *Villain* (*Akunin*, Lee Sang-il), the *Kinema Junpo* Best

One Award winner of 2010, avoids both the gunman and the gun tropes. We have here the stuff of melodrama, perhaps, or a throwback to the *taiyo-zoku* (sun tribe) films of the 1950s or a neo-noir in the spirit of the Coen brothers. With issues of social class, self-hatred, anger and alienation, Zainichi Korean director Lee Sang-il has crafted a penetrating look at the lingering effects of discrimination across a variety of characteristics in contemporary Japan. Sexual desire, violence, betrayal and the possibility of redemption structure the film in archetypal neo-noir fashion despite the lack of the familiar characters we have seen since the 1950s.

Nevertheless, the familiar icons of the gunman and the gun have ruled the roost of Japanese noir and neo-noir for over forty-five years, testimony to the hold these images have on the Japanese imaginary. Whereas the American hitman, the assassin, is prized for being a loner, a variation on the gunfighter of many a Hollywood western, a skilled craftsman of killing, the Japanese find such a figure to be a tragic one. To be alienated and alone, adrift from family and friends, is a fate worse than death, though death tends to be his ultimate fate.

Bibliography

Croce, Fernando F. (2009), 'Eclipse Series 17: Nikkatsu Noir', online at www.slant-magazine.com/dvd/review/eclipse-series-17-nikkatsu-noir (accessed 30 June 2013).

Desser, David (1992), '*Ikiru*: Narration as a moral act', in Arthur Nolletti, Jr and David Desser (eds), *Reframing Japanese Cinema: Authorship, Genre, History*, Bloomington, IN: Indiana University Press, pp. 56–68.

——.(2003), 'Global noir: Genre film in the age of transnationalism', in Barry K. Grant (ed.), *Film Genre Reader III*, Austin, TX: University of Texas Press, pp. 516–36.

Field, Simon and Tony Rayns (1994), *Branded to Thrill: The Delirious Cinema of Suzuki Seijun*, London: Institute of Contemporary Arts.

Geller, Theresa L. (2008), 'Transnational noir: Style and substance in Hayashi Kaizo's *The Most Terrible Time in My Life*', in Leon Hunt and Leung Wing-fai (eds), *East Asian Cinemas: Exploring Transnational Connection on Film*, London: I. B. Tauris, pp. 172–87.

Gerow, Aaron (1995), 'When the East fails to meet the West', *Daily Yomiuri*, 8 August 1995, online at http://pears.lib.ohio-state.edu/Markus/Review/Films95/East.html (accessed 6 January 2014).

Iles, Timothy (2009), 'Noir's dark heart: Hayashi Kaizo's *Hama Maiku* trilogy', online at www.japanesestudies.org.uk/reviews/filmreviews/2009/Iles1.html (accessed 10 January 2014).

Martinez, Dolores (2014), 'Kurosawa's noir quartet: Cinematic musings on how to be a tough man', in Chi-Yun Shin and Mark Gallagher (eds), *East Asian Film Noir: Transnational Encounters and Intercultural Dialogue*, London: I. B. Tauris, pp. 1–21.

Mes, Tom (2003), *Agitator: The Cinema of Miike Takashi*, Goldaming: FAB Press.

Miyao, Daisuke (2007), 'Dark visions of Japanese noir: Suzuki Seijun's *Branded to Kill* (1967), in Alastair Phillips and Julian Stringers (eds), *Japanese Cinema: Texts and Contexts*, London: Routledge, pp. 193–204.

———.(2014), 'Out of the past: Film noir, whiteness and the end of the monochrome era in Japanese cinema', in Shin and Gallagher (eds), *East Asian Film Noir*, pp. 27–47.

Okamoto, Daisuke (2011), 'Revisiting Japanese lifetime employment system: Financial performance analysis using artificial neural networks', *Keio Business Review*, 46: 1–23.

Raine, Michael (2001), 'Ishihara Yujiro: Youth, celebrity and the male body in late 1950s Japan', in Dennis Washburn and Carole Cavanaugh (eds), *Word and Image in Japanese Cinema*, New York: Cambridge University Press, pp. 202–25.

Rich, Jamie S. (2012), 'A Colt is my passport – Eclipse Series 17', online at www.criterionconfessions.com/2012/03/nikkatsu-noir-cold-is-my-passport.html (accessed 30 June 2013).

Schilling, Mark (2007), *No Borders, No Limits: Nikkastsu Action Cinema*, Godalming: FAB Press.

Stephens, Chuck (2009), 'Eclipse Series 17: Nikkatsu Noir', online at www.criterion.com/current/posts/1216-eclipse-series-17-nikkatsu-noir (accessed 3 January 2014).

Yaju no webpage (n.d.), online at http://shishido0.tripod.com/shishido.html (accessed 3 January 2014).

Zipangu Fest (2012), 'To sleep so as to dream', online at http://zipangufest.com/films/2012/to-sleep-so-as-to-dream (accessed 30 June 2013).

Notes

1. Mark Schilling, *No Borders, No Limits: Nikkastsu Action Cinema* (Godalming: FAB Press, 2007), p. 87.
2. Daisuke Miyao, 'Out of the past: Film noir, whiteness and the end of the monochrome era in Japanese cinema', in Chi-Yun Shin and Mark Gallagher (eds), *East Asian Film Noir: Transnational Encounters and Intercultural Dialogue* (London: I. B. Tauris, 2014), p. 30.
3. Ibid., p. 39.
4. Foster Hirsch, *Detours and Lost Highways: A Map of Neo-Noir* (New York: Limelight Editions, 1999), p. 2.
5. Schilling, *No Borders, No Limits*, p. 14.
6. Ibid., p. 15.
7. Ibid., p. 15.
8. Michael Raine, 'Ishihara Yujiro: Youth, celebrity and the male body in late 1950s Japan', in Dennis Washburn and Carole Cavanaugh (eds), *Word and Image in Japanese Cinema* (New York: Cambridge University Press, 2001), pp. 207–9.
9. Schilling, *No Borders, No Limits*, p. 15.
10. Ibid., p. 50.
11. Ibid, p. 7.
12. Ibid., p. 22.
13. Ibid. p. 23.
14. Daisuke Miyao, 'Dark visions of Japanese noir: Suzuki Seijun's *Branded to Kill* (1967)', in Alastair Phillips and Julian Stringers (eds), *Japanese Cinema: Texts and Contexts* (London: Routledge, 2007), pp. 196–7.
15. See Miyao, 'Dark visions', for a discussion of *Branded to Kill* as an avant-garde film. For the notion that Suzuki's cinema is 'delirious', see Simon Field and Tony Rayns, *Branded to Thrill: The Delirious Cinema of Suzuki Seijun* (London: Institute of Contemporary Arts, 1994).
16. Aaron Gerow, 'When the East fails to meet the West', *Daily Yomiuri*, 8 August

1995, online at http://pears.lib.ohio-state.edu/Markus/Review/Films95/East.html (accessed 6 January 2014).
17. David Desser, 'Ikiru: Narration as a moral act', in Arthur Nolletti, Jr and David Desser (eds), *Reframing Japanese Cinema: Authorship, Genre, History* (Bloomington, IN: Indiana University Press, 1992), pp. 56–68; Dolores Martinez, 'Kurosawa's noir quartet: Cinematic musings on how to be a tough man', in Chi-Yun Shin and Mark Gallagher (eds), *East Asian Film Noir: Transnational Encounters and Intercultural Dialogue* (London: I. B. Tauris, 2014), p. 8.
18. For an in-depth discussion of this film with particular emphasis on how it harkens back to postwar anxieties and also how it deals with Japan's former colonisation of Taiwan, see Theresa L. Geller, 'Transnational noir: Style and substance in Hayashi Kaizo's *The Most Terrible Time in My Life*', in Leon Hunt and Leung Wing-fai (eds), *East Asian Cinemas: Exploring Transnational Connection on Film* (London: I. B. Tauris, 2008), pp. 172–87.
19. Timothy Iles, 'Noir's dark heart: Hayashi Kaizo's *Hama Maiku* trilogy', online at www.japanesestudies.org.uk/reviews/filmreviews/2009/Iles1.html (accessed 10 January 2014).
20. Tom Mes, *Agitator: The Cinema of Miike Takashi* (Goldaming: FAB Press, 2003), p. 115.
21. Ibid., p. 115.
22. Ibid., p. 154.
23. Ibid., p. 156.
24. Daisuke Okamoto, 'Revisiting Japanese lifetime employment system: Financial performance analysis using artificial neural networks', *Keio Business Review* 46 (2011), 21.
25. See David Desser, 'Global noir: Genre film in the age of transnationalism', in Barry K. Grant (ed.), *Film Genre Reader III* (Austin, TX: University of Texas Press, 2003), pp. 516–36.
26. Martinez, 'Kurosawa's noir quartet', pp. 9–13.
27. Ibid., p. 16.
28. Miyao, 'Dark visions', p. 200.

6. DARKER THAN DARK: FILM NOIR IN ITS ASIAN CONTEXTS

Stephen Teo

Chinese and Korean Noir

This chapter focuses on film noir in the contexts of the Hong Kong and South Korean cinemas, two Asian film industries that have produced some of the most remarkable films noirs of the contemporary era. If Asian noir is seen as a later phenomenon in the development of film noir in world cinema, South Korean cinema has produced some of the most striking examples of neo-noir in the past ten years or so and it may be argued that South Korean filmmakers have inherited a wider tradition of noir cinema in the world and simply perpetuated it within their own industry. However, from an Asian cinema perspective, the South Korean films are part of a tradition that arguably stretched back to the Hong Kong cinema's New Wave which materialised in 1979 through the first feature films of Ann Hui (*The Secret*), Tsui Hark (*The Butterfly Murders*), Alex Cheung (*Cops and Robbers*) and Peter Yung (*The System*). All of these are films noirs in their conscious conveyance of a 'new mood of cynicism, pessimism, and darkness', as Paul Schrader has defined noir in his seminal article 'Notes on film noir'.[1] The Hong Kong New Wave simply infused this mood into the Asian cinema mainstream which at the time was mostly dominated by Hong Kong martial arts pictures, comedies and romantic melodramas. So pervasive was the noir sensibility in the Hong Kong New Wave films that it was not so much a New Wave as a Noir Wave. The New Wave generation of directors sought to suture the tone and sensibility of noir into the body fabric of Hong Kong cinema as a kind of collective mood-motif which had not really been present before. Noir's manifestation in Hong Kong cinema can be attributed to the fact that many of the New Wave directors were educated in the West and had brought back with them Western influences. The 1970s was a time of transition in which the dawn of the New Wave marked a modernist phase of development in Hong Kong cinema which had, after all, patterned itself after Hollywood. As noir took critical hold in the American critical discourse during the 1970s (Paul Schrader's 'Notes on film noir' was first published in 1972), Hong Kong was affected one way or another. Noir was a 'kind of modernism in the popular cinema' that could spread across 'virtually every national boundary and every form of communication', as James Naremore tells us,[2] and the Hollywood film noir, symbolised in the 1970s by Polanski's very influential *Chinatown* (1974) and Scorsese's equally influential *Taxi Driver* (1976), 'is both a type of modernism and a type of commercial melodrama'[3] which may best describe the kind of new paradigmatic formula that the Hong Kong New Wave filmmakers sought to introduce into their own highly commercial industry.

Yim Ho's *Happenings* (1980), Tsui Hark's *Dangerous Encounters of the First Kind* (1980), Alex Cheung's *Man on the Brink* (1980) and Patrick Tam's *Love, Massacre* (1980) were just the kind of challenging works of the Hong Kong Noir Wave, suggesting a consolidation of noir sensibility in the industry as these young directors went about tackling sensitive material in a social if not political fashion by injecting an even deeper feeling of black funk into the system. This darker-than-dark sensibility went on to fructify around the specific genre of the *jingfei pian* (or 'cops and robbers' films) which mostly centred on the conflict between Triad gangsters and the Hong Kong police force. Johnny Mak's *Long Arm of the Law* (1984) established the black-realist conditions of the confrontation between Triad gangsters and the police in the Hong Kong crime genre,[4] but the latter films of John Woo and Johnnie To went on to develop the more abstract 'cops and robbers' strain of noir which Naremore has rather shrewdly observed is 'inflected by the French New Wave's fascination with noir'.[5] Indeed, it is this very strain that is now the most closely identified with Hong Kong cinema's noir sensibility. Johnnie To is the one director who has done most to engender the neo-noir sensibility in the Hong Kong-style *jingfei* genre. In fact, To has been the most distinctively creative of the *jingfei* directors, and his films of the last ten years or so constitute some of the foremost neo-noir works of Asian cinema. They include *PTU* (2003), *Breaking News* (2004), *Election* (2005), *Triad Election* (2006), *Exiled* (2006), *Mad Detective* (2007), *Sparrow* (2008), *Vengeance* (2009), *Life without Principles* (2011) and *Drug War* (2012). In addition, To's work has influenced a whole series of Hong Kong *jingfei* films including the *Infernal Affairs* trilogy (2002–3), *One Night in Mongkok* (2004), *Confession of Pain* (2006), *The Detective* (2007), *Protégé* (2007), *Shinjuku Incident* (2009),

Overheard (2009), *Accident* (2009), *Punished* (2011), *Overheard 2* (2011), *The Detective 2* (2011), *Nightfall* (2012) and *Cold War* (2012). The Hong Kong films noirs are overwhelmingly concentrated on the *jingfei* genre to the point that the whole recognition of Hong Kong noir depends on this one specific genre, although it is possible to detect the noir sensibility in other Hong Kong-style genres.[6]

In South Korean cinema, the neo-noir sensibility was inducted into the mainstream industry through two milestone works in the late 1990s, Lee Myung-se's *Nowhere to Hide* (1999), which is today regarded as a cult masterpiece, a more stylish variation of the typical Hong Kong-style *jingfei* genre, and Jung Ji-woo's *Happy End* (1999), a blackly realist *ménage à trois* melodrama that helped to establish the violent persona of its male lead, Choi Min-shik, who later evolved into one of the nastiest of noir monster-protagonists in world cinema. Throughout the first decade of the twenty-first century, South Korean cinema has produced a steady stream of compelling, if also highly disquieting, neo-noir works including Park Chan-wook's 'Vengeance' trilogy – *Sympathy for Mr Vengeance* (2002), *Oldboy* (2003) and *Sympathy for Lady Vengeance* (2005) – and Bong Joon-ho's superior *Memories of Murder* (2003). These films are the more internationally known works of the South Korean neo-noir cycle which has otherwise developed in a more local fashion, demonstrating itself as a powerful, obsessive and unremittingly violent energy field through a brilliantly sustained series of works: *Bad Guy* (2001), *Public Enemy* (2002), *A Tale of Two Sisters* (2003), *Hypnotized* (2004), *Spider Forest* (2004), *The Scarlet Letter* (2004), *A Bittersweet Life* (2005), *Bystanders* (2005), *A Dirty Carnival* (2006), *Puzzle* (2006), *Voice of a Murderer* (2007), *Black House* (2007), *A Love* (2007), *Seven Days* (2007), *The Chaser* (2008), *Handphone* (2009), *Breathless* (2009), *Mother* (2009), *Secret* (2009), *No Mercy* (2010), *Secret Reunion* (2010), *Parallel Life* (2010), *Bedevilled* (2010), *The Man from Nowhere* (2010), *I Saw the Devil* (2010), *Enemy at the Dead End* (2010), *Yeouido Island* (2010), *The Yellow Sea* (2010), *Hindsight* (2011), *Silenced* (2011), *Nameless Gangster* (2012), *Helpless* (2012), *The Thieves* (2012), *Pieta* (2012), *Confession of Murder* (2012) and *New World* (2013).

The Korean noir cycle is more varied than the Hong Kong cycle in the genres represented: many belong to the cops and robbers category or the gangster genre (*A Dirty Carnival, Breathless, Nameless Gangster, New World*) but quite a few are gothic, psychotic thrillers (*A Tale of Two Sisters, Spider Forest, Black House, The Chaser, I Saw the Devil*) with a subset that also contains a supernatural theme (*A Tale of Two Sisters, Hypnotized, Spider Forest, Yeouido Island*); some are social-critical in intent (*Breathless, Silenced, Nameless Gangster*) while others contain a mixture of dark social realism and pure action melodrama (*A Bittersweet Life, The Yellow Sea, The Man from Nowhere*). There is a psychiatric strain (*Hypnotized, Spider Forest, Black*

House), and one involving femmes fatales (*Hypnotized, The Scarlet Letter, Sympathy for Lady Vengeance, Black House, Helpless*). Films like *Bystanders, Seven Days, Mother, Secret* and *Pieta* portray the femme fatale as subtle modulations of the Korean mother and wife, subverting the traditional roles of the female in South Korean's male-dominated and largely misogynistic society. Then, there is the long line of serial killer noirs which the South Koreans have made into a quite singular form all their own (*Public Enemy, Memories of Murder, Sympathy for Lady Vengeance, Bystanders, Black House, The Chaser, I Saw the Devil, Helpless, Confession of Murder*).

The quantitative mass of South Korean and Hong Kong films noirs represents a late-capitalist surge of industrial and creative energy, and one that virtually cries out for critical attention. This Asian noir outburst demonstrates the transgeneric sensibility of noir with both cinemas sharing the striking qualities of unrelenting violence and a deep, unrelieved pessimism. The theme of this chapter is to try to work out how Asian films noirs are distinctive while fulfilling the generic notions and conditions of noir as an international style. The present South Korean cycle seen *in toto* is possibly the darkest and most disturbing of all the noir films produced in Asia – and the Hong Kong films are not far behind. The fact that Asian films noirs are darker than most noir films produced internationally seems to mark them out as unique but how does one explain this uniqueness? Hyangjin Lee has stated that Asian films noirs 'combine transnational flows with national attributes, localising the regional and global genre'.[7] I do not wish in this chapter to delve into national psyches and the dark recesses of the socio-political environments of both the South Korean and Hong Kong contexts to explain the reasons why Asian films noir are darker than dark. What I intend to do in the short space of this chapter is to place Asian films noirs in the generic context of international noir while also gradually trying to define what is distinctive about the Asian variation.

Fundamentally, the thesis here is to discuss film noir in its Asian contexts as late reactions to the noir traditions of Hollywood, or as a cycle of films relating to the international contexts of noir or neo-noir. In its essence, to discuss noir is to put it into its contexts, following the subtitle of James Naremore's book-length study *More Than Night: Film Noir in Its Contexts*. While Naremore's main title *More Than Night* suggests a fairly amorphous kind of contextual setting – an imaginary or subconscious formless field or domain in which noir fiction operates – the book does attempt to locate noir firmly in its cinematic milieu and to come to terms with noir's paradoxical nature. Naremore tells us that film noir has 'no essential characteristics'[8] but is rather 'a critical tendency within the popular cinema – an antigenre that reveals the dark side of savage capitalism'.[9] That noir has no essential characteristics I take to imply that noir is not a genre – it does not fulfil the conditions outlined by Rick Altman that genre films should 'have clear, stable identities and borders'[10] and share 'certain fundamental characteristics'.[11] Without any essential characteristics, noir has nevertheless become so identified with specific genres, namely the detective thriller, the gangster movie or the generic crime movie, that the characteristics of these genres are usually seen as belonging to noir and, in this way, noir attains recognition as a genre (I will however see it as a tendency or sensibility and not a genre). The noir contexts are therefore the contexts of the genres that have been referred to – these being the chief ones where the noir sensibility is most infusive. As far as Asian films noirs are concerned, noir contexts can be clearly identified as that of the genres already mentioned as belonging to noir: the *jingfei* genre, with its variations of lone assassins, serial killers, femmes fatales, gangster types and detectives of all kinds including private and public. The contexts of these genres chime with the contexts of the Hollywood equivalents and it is this contextuality of the first instance that I will be most concerned with.

Naremore's book and most of the literature that has been published around the subject of noir has yielded the critical revelation that noir relies on the need to study the contexts of its settings and the locations if not so much its themes and conceits – rather the themes flow out of the contexts. One of the effects therefore of Naremore's book as well as others that have followed in Naremore's wake is clearly to push scholarship on noir towards an imperative of contextuality, which has both temporal and locational elements. Given this contextual need, what then are the contexts of the Asian films noirs? Asking such a question is to acknowledge that contexts are not just different one from the other but are also overdetermined inasmuch as noir 'is almost entirely a creation of postmodern culture'.[12] Postmodernism, then, suggests much slippage and equivocality from one context to another. Yet contextuality may seem to anchor the films in distinct spaces and places, indicating that noir has cultural and national moorings rather than an abstract global fathomlessness. However, it is beyond the scope of this chapter to fully deal with the Asian cultural and national norms and conditions that may distinguish Asian films noirs. Rather, the task of this chapter is to address the way in which Asian films noirs can be seen as alternative reactions to the American contexts of noir criticism.

Film Noir and American Centricity

Historically speaking, the American context of noir has always been central and continues to be so in the literature. Though the whole critical undertaking of appreciating noir, and the term itself, is inherited from the French, it appears that even the French had always applied it to American films. Naremore's book gives us this historical context and the author goes on to discuss the films as fundamentally American films, even though some of the contexts have shifted: for example, Naremore addresses noir in an Asian context but primarily discusses American films with an Asian theme.[13] Naremore tells us that the French 'invented the American film noir'[14] even if 'it is not a specifically American form'.[15] Marc Vernet had earlier asserted much the same thing in his essay '*Film noir* on the edge of doom'[16] and had provided a good contextual background of how the French invented film noir. Robin Buss avows that the term 'had a special relevance to the French context',[17] and wrote a whole book on French film noir as if noir was contextually native to French cinema.

However, while the French may have instituted the critical study of film noir, the literature on noir has overwhelmingly concentrated on the films produced by the classical Hollywood studio system which established the kinds of genres (the detective film, the gangster film or the crime film) that came under the noir rubric. The literature on noir has solidified around this American contextual link. The editors of *Film Noir: The Encyclopedia* claim that film noir is 'an indigenous American form'.[18] In the wake of Naremore's book, Paula Rabinowitz's *Black & White & Noir: America's Pulp Modernism* is premised on a view of film noir 'as the context (in which) its plot structure and visual iconography make sense of America's landscape and history'.[19] Edward Dimendberg's book *Film Noir and the Spaces of Modernity* examines American cities as the storehouse of noir forces. He makes no distinction between 'content and context',[20] showing that American cities are the spatial context in which the content of noir takes shape. To Dimendberg, postwar American cities and landmarks are 'the very cultural force that legitimated scholarship on film noir'.[21] Ken Hillis's article 'Film noir and the American dream: The dark side of enlightenment' submits that film noir 'is central to understanding the formulations of postwar American identity and its relationship to the meaning of citizenship'.[22] Donald Pease makes the point that 'the conventional wisdom concerning the film noir (is) namely, that film noir emplots within its narrative the ideological contradictions and social antagonisms intrinsic to the U.S. social order'.[23] Charles Scruggs argues that 'film noir is American to the core, having its source not only in post-World War II paranoia but also in American literary Gothicism'.[24] And so on it goes: the overwhelming evidentiary track of research in noir is its reliance on, or indeed its complete identification with, the American context.

Against the fact of American centricity, it is pertinent to ask whether Asian films noirs suggest some kind of misplacement of a style from the West to the East, or whether they are completely distinctive in their own right? If noir is a transnational style and mood, it stands to reason that it can spring out of a particular cinema's own conventions and genres, and it seems unnecessary to connect it to a prior cinema with its own noir tradition. For example, the Hong Kong *jingfei* genre is sometimes known as *heibang* ('black gang') or *heidao* ('black path' or 'black force'). Blackness is intrinsic to the Hong Kong or Chinese concept of crime, signifying a path that is corrupt and deviant from that of the white, which stands for righteousness and justice. The black and white paths (*heidao* and *baidao*) are tropes that are consistent with the cops and robbers genre (they also apply to other genres, such as the martial arts *wuxia* and kung fu movies), referring to the moral implications of good (white) and evil (black). Gangsters are said to have chosen the black path, while a copper has chosen the white one and a kind of counter-balancing between the two paths is operative, with both sides dependent on each other for their existence. Hong Kong noir cinema is intrinsically a native black cinema, with all the concomitant sensibilities of angst, violence and moral perversity. There is, however, no recognition of a 'white cinema' or *baidao* film; any film with cops as protagonists seems automatically to be black.

The blackness of the *heidao* invests Hong Kong cinema with its own conceptual (and moral) framework of blackness. In order to address the Asian noir contexts of the Hong Kong and South Korean films under discussion in this chapter, it is appropriate, for my purposes, to connect to the whole noir tradition of the American context, which, while not the only context available for reference, is by far the most representative. Asian films noirs are usually referred to as a later movement or a late style in the currents of world cinema, which suggests that it was influenced by more dominant cinemas and had inherited the style from a much later tradition in the dominant cinemas. Indeed, most critics refer to the Hong Kong and South Korean films noirs as a movement that essentially began from the 1990s onwards (though, as I have suggested, it began much earlier in the case of Hong Kong), which is the period in which traditional noir morphed into 'neo-noir' in its original American historical context. Noir had already fundamentally changed according to consumer tastes in America in the 1990s, as Norman M. Klein has intimated in his essay entitled 'Staging murders: The social imaginary, film, and the city'.

Klein's short essay places neo-noir in a poststructuralist age which 'reflects the perversities of consumer panic as a way to hide urban realities'.[25] From Klein's perspective, noir films take place in a range of American cities that are decaying, overrun by gangster warlords who deal in drugs, prostitution and murders. They are also populated by ethnic communities, and one of the key films in this regard is Polanski's *Chinatown* (1974), which evokes an ethnic noir community even though the film itself has substantially nothing to do with this community. Chinatown as a notion is enough to evoke the mystery and dread of ethnicity in the American context, marking a mode of perception of the noir detective portrayed by Jack Nicholson, and indeed of the whole noir universe, 'as Western, white, and male', as Philip Novak has put it.[26] Novak echoes James Naremore who has described this ethnic trait of noir as one that involves 'white characters who cross borders to visit Latin America, Chinatown, or the "wrong" parts of the city'.[27] Naremore's description (which covers a greater geographic scope) appears also to fall smack into the lap of Klein's reading of noir (or contemporary noir) as 'delusional journeys into panic and conservative white flight' which ultimately help to 'sell gated communities, and "friendly" surveillance systems' in America.[28]

Klein sees noir as a consequence of contemporary urban existence in the United States, but also something of an allegory of American life in the city, albeit a limited form of allegory since, for Klein, noir shows 'very little of the totality of urban experience'.[29] What it shows are imaginary but specific locations where murders are staged: 'perhaps only twenty minutes out of a day, usually the ten minutes before and after a murder'.[30] While noir might have begun as social critique, contemporary noir 'has just the right tropes for promoting shopping malls ... and has become even more purely a variation of tourism; it belongs more at an Urban Outfitters than on a city street'.[31]

Klein tends to reduce noir in its contemporary form to being a logistical kind of film method, in which 'staging murders' and its locational 'requirements' are really the primary obsessions. Their effect is to reinforce 'a Victorian panic about ethnicity and class' as well as to reinforce 'illusions about where crime-ridden cities end and safe suburbs begin'.[32] Klein's article, as with all the literature cited above, reinforces the America-centric view of film noir. In this American centricity lies a sense that noir's attraction to critics and scholars is its very attachment to the American context. As noir shifts to other contexts, we need to consider the nature of the American context and what exactly it is that makes it American. Americans themselves may take their contextuality for granted and may be hard put to tell how it is that noir contexts are exactly American. The critics I have cited above show that noir is intimately bound up with an American localism and such is the key to understanding American contextuality. Klein's view of contemporary noir or neo-noir is perhaps more local than most, since his points of reference are essentially specific parts of the city of Los Angeles.

Klein's view boils down to locational scenes of murder and crime as if such locations were essential to noir, which of course they are, without losing sight of their social contexts (in fact, Klein is lamenting neo-noir's tendency to create visual shorthands instead of concentrating more on the social context of its locations). It may be instructive to follow Klein's local instinct here, since he presents us with some possible analytical tools to understand Asian films noirs and their contexts. Klein refers to noir in the contexts of the 'urban "requirements" for a location where a murder should take place'.[33] He speaks of murder where others might speak of some crime or violence taking place in a location, and it is the location that is vital to shape our response to noir (one can think of the streets, the alleys, as well as the placement of buildings and the type of neighborhoods). Vivian Sobchack has provided other characteristic settings: 'the cocktail lounge, the nightclub, the bar, the hotel room, the boarding-house, the diner, the dance hall, the roadside café, the bus and train station, and the wayside motel'.[34] Edward Dimendberg mentions 'the skyscraper, the jazz nightclub, the magazine or newspaper office, the bus terminal, the diner, the automobile, the traffic-congested street, and the highway' as the 'characteristic twentieth-century spaces' of film noir.[35] As noir has morphed into neo-noir, there is a fascination with urban decay, and Klein calls this 'the American obsession'.[36] R. Barton Palmer suggests that noir films portray 'a version of contemporary urban America that also contains its nightmarish mirror image'.[37] 'This negativity customarily assumes textual solidity through the dark city, a site of transgressive modernity whose most characteristic figure is the alienated individual'.[38] In the context of the dark city, 'conservative white flight' seems like a natural psychological disposition. There is, of course, a racial dimension to film noir's American context. In his article 'Film noir and the racial unconscious', Julian Murphet asserts that 'any reference (no matter how veiled) to blackness in US culture instantly evokes the entire history of race relations in US politics and everyday life'.[39] In the Asian context, blackness evokes gangsterism and the forces of evil (as I have explained above in connection with the concept of *heidao*) and there is a more metaphorical dimension to the idea of blackness, which is not to say that there is absolutely no racial issue in Asian films noirs. The notion of white flight can be seen in the light of the notions of the *heidao* and the *baidao* (the black and the white paths or forces inherent in Asian noir) and thus be applied as a dialectical response to the concept of *heidao*. In other words, Klein's evocation of white flight could be used as a critical method – in completely metaphorical terms. Klein, then, actually offers us a useful trope that allows us to expand the horizons of noir as an international form.

Asian Noir and Local Contexts

Joelle Collier has given us an abstract of Asian noir, which she dubs 'Noir East', noting certain 'discrepancies' between 'Asian noirs and their American predecessors'.[40] Basically, Collier notes one chief discrepancy which concerns the portrayal of the femme fatale, who is more often than not absent in Asian films (Collier was referring in her article to Hong Kong films mainly), and 'where she exists at all in Noir East, turns out to be a decoy'.[41] The real monster in Noir East, according to Collier, is the patriarch or 'the monstrous father'.[42] Thus,

> while classic American *films noir* allude to the threat to male authority (in the figure of the femme fatale), Noir East films depict the stranglehold patriarchy still has on Asian society. What is new in Noir East is the rendering of Confucian patriarchy in such an extreme form, which in and of itself suggests a challenge to it.[43]

In this respect, Collier suggests that 'instead of applying a formula mechanically', Hong Kong filmmakers had 'transformed the genre's conventions to meet their own cultural needs'.[44] In other words, the Hong Kong filmmakers had simply put noir into the context of the Confucian patriarchy, which may then be seen as the social and cultural context of 'Noir East'. This seems to me a feasible kind of context in which to place Asian films noirs, but I will not retread this same ground even if it needs more elaboration and theorising. I am interested to consider the contexts of locality and the way in which these locales bear on the psyches of the characters. One aspect of context which is not often examined in the literature is localism. Norman Klein's understanding of neo-noir is based on the city spaces of Los Angeles, a local space. This kind of localism is a contextual space that can just as easily be transmitted as any other. American local contexts can be transmuted to being Asian local contexts, as I will seek to demonstrate. However, the question is whether one can note discrepancies of space between Asian films noirs and their American predecessors. Geographic locality may already imply a degree of discrepancy as the noir sensibility shifts from West to East. However, in Asian films noirs, the 'requirements' of location in a crime scene may comply with the same kind of spatial requirements of American films noirs. What, then, precisely is the difference?

The imperative of context as a method of exploring and discussing the substance of noir, I suggest, can be both misleading and useful – misleading because the noir context begins from its American antecedence while it also implies a far wider scope of coverage. In this paradoxical way, it becomes useful to our discussion of Asian films noirs. What this chapter might show is that Asian films noirs are contextualised within both an American frame and their own Asian frame. Asian noir cannot really be divorced from the American context and what matters most in this is the dynamism of noir's interaction and ultimate transmutation from one context to the other. That there is such dynamism (of influence and exchange, of mutability and transmutability) between Hollywood and Asian cinemas is often taken for granted but not much examined in the literature. Rather, following Collier, it is the discrepancies that are more often highlighted. On the other hand, as a result of the America-centric literature on noir, Asian films noirs are utterly sidelined and marginalised, functioning perhaps on the symbolic level of *Chinatown* – as part of a syndrome, as films of mystery and ultra-violence and ultimately inscrutable. From such a perspective, Asian films noirs are ethnic noir films, *Chinatown* writ large. It goes without saying that such a perspective needs to be challenged. The interrelationship of Hollywood and Asian cinemas is usually paid lip service to, but scholarship in this research area is not exactly thriving, and therefore the process of dynamism in this interrelationship and its movement towards change or transmutation merits more examination and discussion. It is necessary to carry out more comparative ways to judge how Asian films noirs complement the American noir experience and how this extends into the depths of Asian noir cinema.

Let us briefly examine Oxide Pang's *The Detective* (2007). Seen from both the American and Asian contexts, it is a typical noir film, but from the Hong Kong cinema context, it is a rather unusual Hong Kong detective film in that it is actually set in the Chinatown of Bangkok (Pang is a Hong Kong director whose career began in Thailand and he has worked there consistently; in *The Detective*, he fluidly integrates his seemingly Hong Kong-type characters into Bangkok's seedy Chinatown setting). The Bangkok location has the effect of rendering the film even more noir, by its sense of a renewed atmospheric charge into the Chinatown setting (if it were set in Hong Kong, sometimes called the world's biggest Chinatown, the setting would be merely banal). In Bangkok, Chinatown gains more mystery and a depraved kind of seediness. Indeed, it is something of a hell on earth, which it is intended to convey, as the investigation of the detective will gradually show, and as the story reveals a supernatural twist in which the detective encounters the ghost of the woman he is hired to find. The Bangkok Chinatown setting also defines the performance of Aaron Kwok's detective of the title. Kwok gives a likable but quirky performance that is hard to describe perhaps because it is a performance that is perfectly synchronised with its milieu. In another sense he personifies the indefinable dynamism of the interrelationship between American and Hong Kong (or Asian) noir and something extra – the inter-Asian relationship between Hong Kong and Thai cultures. Chinatown links Bangkok with Hong Kong, and it also links the film with its American predecessor, Roman Polanski's *Chinatown*.

The Detective engages with *Chinatown* and essentially performs a dialectical exchange of ideas and elements familiarised by Polanski's film. The Chinatown location evokes Kwok's detective as an Asian Jake Gittes (the detective played by Jack Nicholson). Gittes exhibits the sleazy self-confidence of the American detective, and Kwok's Chan Tam is a more amateurish version of this detective. Both detectives are essentially faux-cool, somewhat impoverished in terms of intellectual savviness, but they are dogged and determined investigators and they both operate in Chinatown. As it relates to Gittes, however, Chinatown is a syndrome, following Phillip Novak's examination of Polanski's film. The syndrome results from Gittes' sensibility and his attitudes, which we might call local or even parochial. Part of the complexity of the plot of *Chinatown* actually lies in its local contextuality, which most likely will baffle non-American audiences; and therefore part of the problematic nature of the character of Jake Gittes is also due to this localism-cum-parochialism. What *Chinatown* shows us – and this is generally true of detective fiction – is that detectives investigate local contexts and very rarely operate out of these contexts. Murder and crime take place in local places (the very streets and alleys of 'staged murders' which Norman Klein ruminates about) and it is up to local detectives to solve the crimes. Part of the fascination of detective fiction lies in its empiricism and proceduralism, which are methods based entirely on local, native contexts. In this way, Gittes is very much a local detective, with a parochial sense of identity. It is with this in mind that we should understand Phillip Novak's claim that Gittes is 'a negative example',[45] whose view of the world is clearly coloured by the prejudices arising out of his community and its contexts (prejudices which he no doubt shares and which ultimately brand him). Novak goes on to dissect Gittes' character as a negative example of the conventional American detective, focusing on his misogyny and latent racism. 'The movie is about him,' Novak writes, 'about his way of seeing things: his way of conceiving the world, himself, and others'.[46]

Chan Tam mirrors Gittes in that he is a Chinese variation of the American detective, with some differences in character – and the differences may be attributed to the differences of their local contexts. As an Asian detective, Chan Tam is no longer 'a negative example' of a noir stereotype. If anything, he may be seen as a positive example, even though he does share with Gittes some traits of flawed character. The movie is also about him and his way of seeing things. In fact, Chan Tam is equally obsessive as a detective and what essentially drives him is his need to find out about his long-missing parents since the time of his childhood, both of whom he discovers at the end of the film have been murdered. Chan, then, is perhaps the prototypical Asian filial detective, and the noir contexts of his locality involve what might be called Asian variations of Polanski's *Chinatown*, or, indeed, the Chinatown syndrome of Novak's analysis. These variations turn the syndrome into a supernatural set of variables. It turns out that the woman whom Chan Tam was hired to find was in fact a murdered woman whose ghost had instigated the whole investigation and had helped the detective to discover the corpses of his parents as well as to uncover the mystery of her own real murderer.

The supernatural elements of this noir mystery are a surprising and effective twist. They are somehow in tune with the underworld dimensions of the Bangkok Chinatown setting and make its seediness and even its foul smells completely perceptible. Chinatown, it might be said, is a syndrome of the spirit in which a symptom is a sense of white flight – whiteness here representing spirits and ghosts, or in fact representing one's spirit and the implicit emptiness of character following spiritual flight. Pang's film very cleverly exploits noir mood and the expectations of the detective genre from Polanski's *Chinatown* and transposes them into an Asian Chinatown setting, in the process transmuting the detective genre into the supernatural ghost genre. The sense of white flight is that of ghosts fleeing (or seeking to escape) from the blackness of the world. Chinatown represents the Chinese sense of blackness, marked by criminality, murder and violence, and it is this world that Chan Tam continues to reside in and the blackness of which he must learn to deal with.

White flight is a palpable conceit in Johnnie To's *Drug War* which deserves some attention here because it is the most recent outstanding film of its director, a noir stalwart whose work bridges the Asian and the international contexts of noir. His films are highly regarded by local critics in Hong Kong and have gone down well particularly in France if not so much in America. The film is notable for being To's 'first-ever full-fledged mainland Chinese production',[47] and, as such, it marks To's (and Hong Kong cinema's) attempt to implant Hong Kong-style noir into mainland Chinese cinema. To subverts the clear demarcations of black and white (an imposition of the Chinese censors) by making the Chinese police protagonists (who represent the *baidao* or the white force) a mobile group which easily blends into the *heidao* (the black force) they are pursuing (the plot concerns the efforts of Chinese drug enforcers to capture drug runners from China and Hong Kong who are trafficking illicit products from the south to the main northern port city of Tianjin from where the drugs can be transported elsewhere into Asia). The methods used by the Chinese police involve underhand means of subterfuge, disguise, role-playing and entrapment. We might see this as a case of the forces of white retreating into blackness, even if temporarily. The film maintains the theme of flight – the black, of course, fleeing from the white (a foregone conclusion), but the white itself fleeing from its own whiteness, and this is To's most subversive touch in his first mainland Chinese production where he had to grapple with the censorious hand of the Chinese authorities (particularly over the depictions of the Chinese police). At the end, To shows us a remarkable dénouement in which both the white and the black are seemingly converging in a violent resolution and there appears to be no difference between them. Death combines the white and the black. Perhaps everything, then, is black, in the blackest of all possible worlds – and it is worthwhile remembering that in Hong Kong cinema, there is really no recognition of a white cinema. Asian films, then, show the blackest of all possible worlds in the noir community, and there is no white world in the sense of a happy ending (there are, of course, exceptions to the rule, but such films tend to be the weakest and least convincing of Asian noirs). White flight can only lead to a bad end. Such a resolution is quite typical of Johnnie To's noir films and it is the kind of tradition that seems now to be closely identified with Asian films noirs, as in the South Korean cycle which is possibly the blackest in the world of contemporary noir. I come back, finally, to the question of why this is the case and how it may possibly be seen as a unique Asian trait of noir.

One might see Asian films noirs as a psychoanalytical complex of fantasmatic blackness and violence, its characters being Asian 'noir subjects' following Slavoj Žižek's '"The thing that thinks": The Kantian background of the noir subject'. The violence and utter blackness of Korean films noir suggest

Figure 6.1 Mirroring of black and white forces in *Drug War*.

the line of Žižek's analysis that noir involves a shift 'from logic-and-deduction narrative (as in the classical detective film) into noir narrative . . . the shift of *desire* into *drive*'.[48]

> Desire is that very force that compels us to progress infinitely from one signifier to another in the hope of attaining the ultimate signifier that would fix the meaning of the preceding chain. In opposition to desire, drive is not 'progressive' but rather 'regressive', bound to circulate endlessly around some fixed point of attraction, immobilized by its power of fascination.[49]

In a sense, the South Korean films noirs exemplify the drive of an entire industry in late-capitalist mode, translating its libidinal desire of fantasies and dreams into a plausible and credible cinema with an explicit drive to offer alternative variations or reactions to the dominant cinema that is Hollywood. Korean noirs have attained their deepest degree of blackness because they are fundamentally negative copies of the American classical noirs and neo-noirs. Violence is that fixed point of attraction around which Korean cinema has crystallised its power: violence as a regressive hence more powerful mode vis-à-vis the Hollywood model. Such engagement with Hollywood makes the Korean films noirs a cutting-edge form of filmmaking in international cinema today. Christina Klein's article 'Why American Studies needs to think about Korean cinema, or, transnational genres in the films of Bong Joon-ho' has made the case clear that South Korean filmmakers have an ambivalent relationship with Hollywood, and that a filmmaker like Bong Joon-ho (the director of *Memories of Murder*, perhaps the best of the South Korean noirs) has appropriated the American crime film and reworked its genre conventions:

> Bong thus occupies a middle ground in his relationship with Hollywood, neither blindly emulating its conventions for the sake of profit nor wholly

rejecting them in favor of some notion of cultural authenticity or art. He engages Hollywood and uses it for his own aesthetic, critical, and commercial purposes.[50]

This is generally the reason for the appeal of South Korean film culture at the present moment, but the violence in Korean noir is a challenging and provocative strain of international noir. The Koreans have demonstrated that noir is an object of baroque cruelty, in essence a harsh, critical form transmitting just the kind of warning 'about the disastrous social issue of a felt mutation in the structures of power' that Joan Copjec proclaims in her Introduction to *Shades of Noir*.[51] If the Korean noirs are an appealing kind of cinema, it is as a cinema of fatal attraction. *Oldboy*, *A Bittersweet Life*, *Black House*, *The Chaser*, *Handphone*, *The Yellow Sea*, *The Man from Nowhere* and *I Saw the Devil* are some of the most violent films ever made in world cinema today and there is a sense of more to come from the South Korean film industry – so conscious are the South Korean filmmakers of their historical moment. In her discussion of the discrepancies between 'Noir East' and American noirs, Joelle Collier has made the point that in American noirs, 'violence is more potential than actual' and that 'the threat of violence is constant, but its realisation infrequent'.[52] In Asian noirs, the violence is 'orgasmic' and 'prolonged' and it is the killing that is prolonged, not the dying.[53] In this one discrepancy, we may discern how in fact South Korean cinema has pushed the envelope on violence in noir; and this achievement has generally been recognised as a kind of Asian 'extreme cinema', following the UK Tartan DVD 'Asia Extreme' label;[54] but such a label may be misleading as labels often are, taking no account of the subtleties of character behaviour as well as the social contexts of violence. Korean noirs such as *Memories of Murder*, *Spider Forest*, *The Scarlet Letter* and *A Tale of Two Sisters* are violent in a less gratuitous way than may be perceived by the 'extreme' label, and they perhaps show film noir at its darkest best, reaching heights of Gothic poetry in their psychological sensitivity and intense characterisations. The films are also striking contemplations on memory and identity.

Memories of Murder has a political critique to boot which increases the depth of its contextuality. As Christina Klein has pointed out, the true subject of the film is 'daily life in the late 1980s – that is, during the darkest years of Korea's military dictatorship'.[55] The film may have won international recognition, but like Polanski's *Chinatown*, it is essentially a high-context film which presupposes a high knowledge of Korean politics and recent history, as well as the ambivalent relationship between South Korea and the United States. In a sense, the surface features of noir (the darkness, depravity and despair) may overshadow and hide the depths and degree of the local contexts of the narratives in films noirs. On the other hand, it could also be argued that it is

Figure 6.2 Rural police, innocent suspect and cultural violence in *Memories of Murder*.

precisely such surface features that make the film more accessible to audiences everywhere, whereby we should then refocus our attention to the function of contextuality and ask the question, what is noir without contextuality?

The contexts of South Korean society and its social problems are manifest in all the Korean noirs. Issues touched upon include corruption in the police, the justice system, business and politics, prostitution, drugs, organ-peddling, gangsterism, loan-sharking, kidnapping and, above all, violence against women and children, against one's own parents and against migrants (including Chinese citizens of Korean descent). These social contexts serve to identify and define the noir sensibility in Korean terms. Noir may be a transcribed, transliterated and transmuted form but once its Korean contexts kick in, it assumes a certain urgency towards a new epistemological cognition of film noir all over again. The locational imperatives are just as striking as in the American contexts: the streets and alleys, the highways, the roads, the skyscrapers, the bars and nightclubs, and the decaying warehouses of Seoul and Busan (these cities being the main locations featured in Korean noir) satisfy the urban requirements of noir, although a film like *Memories of Murder* is actually set in the rice-growing countryside and a small town – which makes it even more special as a film noir in the Asian context. Most Korean noirs may ultimately also reflect 'the perversities of consumer panic as a way to hide urban realities'[56] and therefore induce a sense of white flight into inner sanctuaries (films like *Secret Reunion*, *Hindsight* and *The Thieves* fall more aptly into this category, and all of them have happy endings that seem to go against the grain of Korean noir). White flight as a motif is present in the violent reactions of the mostly male protagonists of Korean noirs. This is the spiritual whiteness of terror and nihilism, which, to the credit of the Korean filmmakers, is laid bare for all to see. The imperative of contexuality in noir suggests that the violence of Korean noir be seen and understood in the context of this spiritual white flight motif.

Conclusion

The ever-increasing volumes of scholarship on noir predicated on American contextual studies can in effect be subjected to a hegemonic impulse marginalising the achievements of Asian films noirs. This chapter offers some preliminary arguments for a greater scope in the study of noir as it moves into its Asian contexts. It adopts the methodology of comparative engagements of Asian films noirs with their American predecessors in an effort to demonstrate how the contexts of Asian films noirs can transmute the contexts of American noirs. The American centricity of noir drives the contextual tool of analysis, as the literature on noir suggests, but contextuality itself suggests that a topic of research must be covered in greater range and depth which thus compels the need to examine noir in other national or continental contexts. This chapter has not covered the social, political, historical, cultural and nationalist dimensions of film noir in its Asian contexts and I leave these areas of research for future scholars to pursue. I have attempted to place Asian films noirs in relation to the American readings of noir scholarship. Asian films noirs are seen as correlative and interactive reactions to the American form and their contexts change and adjust according to Asian circumstances in their respective national contexts (here the focus is on Hong Kong and South Korean noirs).

The intense violence of Korean films noirs is a response both to the social and political contexts of the South Korean milieu and to the American tendency of film noir as a global movement. Against the American contextual hegemony, the South Korean films noirs attain a cutting edge particularly in the depictions of violence. Korean films noirs contain their own contextual vibrations and social and political readings but in their violence, they approach a unique kind of cinema. Violence also marks Hong Kong cinema's contribution to the noir sensibility. Why is it, then, that as film noir shifts from the American to the Asian contexts, the whole sensibility becomes darker, much more violent, belligerent and psychotic? This demands more, not less, study of the contexts of Asian noir in order to further understand not so much the nature of violence as the nature of noir cinema itself and its contexts. Suffice it for now to conclude that the violence of Asian noir is an unrepressed expressiveness in the function of the cinema of attractions, an industrial response to the institutional weight and hegemony of the Hollywood machine, and to the overwhelming American-centricity of the discourse on noir. Asian noir is significant for its receptivity to the American context and, even if purely for this reason, it deserves to be integrated into the discourse, following Marc Vernet's declaration that noir 'belongs as a notion to the history of film criticism'.[57]

Asian noir should be widely discussed within this ultimate context, so that noir may deservedly be recognised as an international tendency.

NOTES

1. Paul Schrader, 'Notes on film noir', in R. Barton Palmer (ed.), *Perspectives on Film Noir* (New York: G.K. Hall, 1996), pp. 99–109, at p. 99.
2. James Naremore, *More Than Night: Film Noir in Its Contexts*, Berkeley, CA: University of California Press, 1998, p. 38.
3. Ibid., p. 48.
4. Raymond Durgnat had observed that 'black realism' had evolved out of the crime thriller. See Raymond Durgnat, 'Paint it black: The family tree of film noir', in Palmer (ed.), *Perspectives on Film Noir*, pp. 83–98, at p. 83.
5. Naremore, *More Than Night*, p. 228.
6. For example, the martial arts film, as in Tsui Hark's *Detective Dee and the Mystery of the Phantom Flame* (2010) and Wong Kar-wai's *The Grandmaster* (2013).
7. Hyangjin Lee, 'The shadow of outlaws in Asian Noir: Hiroshima, Hong Kong, and Seoul', in Mark Bould, Kathrina Glitre and Greg Tuck (eds), *Neo-Noir*, London: Wallflower, 2009, pp. 118–35, at p. 121.
8. Naremore, *More Than Night*, p. 5.
9. Ibid., p. 22.
10. Rick Altman, *Film/Genre* (London: British Film Institute, 1999), p. 16.
11. Ibid., p. 24.
12. Naremore, *More Than Night*, p. 10.
13. Ibid., pp. 225–9.
14. Ibid., p. 13.
15. Ibid., p. 5.
16. Marc Vernet, '*Film Noir* on the edge of doom', in Joan Copjec (ed.), *Shades of Noir* (London and New York: Verso, 1993), pp. 1–31, at p. 8.
17. Robin Buss, *French Film Noir* (New York: Marion Boyars, 1994), p. 13.
18. Alain Silver, Elizabeth Ward and James Ursini (eds), *Film Noir, The Encyclopedia* (New York and London: Overlook Duckworth, 2010), p. 15.
19. Paula Rabinowitz, *Black & White & Noir: America's Pulp Modernism* (New York: Columbia University Press, 2002), p. 14.
20. Edmund Dimendberg, *Film Noir and the Spaces of Modernity* (Cambridge, MA: Harvard University Press, 2004), p. 7.
21. Ibid., p. 3.
22. Ken Hillis, 'Film noir and the American dream: The dark side of enlightenment', *The Velvet Light Trap* 55 (spring 2005), 3–18, at 3.
23. Donald E. Pease, 'Borderline justice/states of emergency: Orson Welles' *Touch of Evil*', *CR: The New Centennial Review* 1(1) (spring 2001), 75–105, at 80.
24. Charles Scruggs, '"The power of blackness": Film noir and its critics', *American Literary History* 16(4) (winter 2004), 675–87, at 675.
25. Norman Klein, 'Staging murders: The social imaginary, film, and the city', *Wide Angle* 20(3) (1998), 85–96, at 91.
26. Phillip Novak, 'The Chinatown Syndrome', *Criticism* 49(3) (summer 2007), 255–83, at 276.
27. Naremore, *More Than Night*, p. 13.
28. Norman Klein, 'Staging murders', p. 89.
29. Ibid., p. 89.
30. Ibid., p. 89.

31. Ibid., p. 89.
32. Ibid., p. 88.
33. Ibid., p. 86.
34. Quoted in R. Barton Palmer, 'The divided self and the dark city: Film noir and liminality', *symploke* 15(1–2) (2007), 66–79, at 73.
35. Dimendberg, *Film Noir and the Spaces of Modernity*, p. 25.
36. Klein, 'Staging murders', p. 87.
37. Palmer, 'The divided self and the dark city', 69.
38. Ibid., 69.
39. Julian Murphet, 'Film noir and the racial unconscious', *Screen* 39(1) (spring 1998), 22–35, at 22.
40. Joelle Collier, 'The Noir East: Hong Kong filmmakers' transmutation of a Hollywood genre?', in Gina Marchetti and Tan See Kam (eds), *Hong Kong Film, Hollywood, and the New Global Cinema* (New York: Routledge, 2007), pp. 137–58, at p. 145.
41. Ibid., p. 148.
42. Ibid., p. 148.
43. Ibid., pp. 149–50.
44. Ibid., p. 149.
45. Phillip Novak, 'The Chinatown Syndrome', 257.
46. Ibid., 276.
47. Clarence Tsui, 'Cannes: Johnnie To on the "anxiety" of censors, challenges of making a film in mainland China', *Hollywood Reporter* (May 2013), online at www.hollywoodreporter.com/news/cannes-johnnie-anxiety-censors-challenges-523270 (accessed 15 May 2013).
48. Slavoj Žižek, '"The thing that thinks": The Kantian background of the noir subject', in Joan Copjec (ed.), *Shades of Noir* (London and New York: Verso, 1993), pp. 199–226, at p. 222.
49. Ibid., p. 222.
50. Christina Klein, 'Why American Studies needs to think about Korean cinema, or, transnational genres in the films of Bong Joon-ho', *American Quarterly* 60(4) (December 2008), 871–98, at 873.
51. Joan Copjec, 'Introduction', in Copjec (ed.), *Shades of Noir*, pp. vii–xii and x–xi.
52. Collier, 'The Noir East', p. 150.
53. Ibid., p. 150.
54. Chi-Yun Shin, 'Art of branding: Tartan "Asia Extreme" films', *Jump Cut* 50 (spring 2008), online at www.ejumpcut.org/archive/jc50.2008/TartanDist/text.html (accessed 5 June 2013).
55. Christina Klein, 'Why American Studies', 882.
56. Norman Klein, 'Staging murders', p. 91.
57. Marc Vernet, '*Film Noir* on the edge of doom', p. 26.

7. NORDIC NOIR AND NEO-NOIR: THE HUMAN CRIMINAL

Andrew Nestingen

In the closing scene of Niels Arden Oplev's *Män som hatar kvinnor* (*The Girl with the Dragon Tattoo*, 2009), the film's principal female character, Lisbeth Salander (Noomi Rapace), steps from a limousine onto a seaside promenade. She walks down the promenade, away from the camera. The scene depicts Salander as a femme fatale through cinematography and costuming. As the scene begins, the camera is positioned on the passenger side of the car; the driver-side door opens and the chauffeur rises and steps back to open the door for his passenger. The camera moves to the driver's side, tilting down to ground level, then rising from Salander's stiletto heel, over the car door to her face, shielded by large sunglasses. The camera movement from her legs to her face recalls the angular cinematography of film noir. It also works to lay stress on her costume of stiletto heels, black stockings, business suit, heavy make-up and platinum blonde wig – a costume that differs from her appearance in the rest of the film. The scene then moves to a medium shot of Salander paying the chauffer, then to a final long shot of her walking down the promenade, refusing to yield the pavement to conversing businessmen. Salander got the money, and got away with it. Does her costume in the concluding scene reveal what Salander has always been, a femme fatale? Or is it a 'costume', which dissimulates, obscuring another identity? Why does the film close on a citation of the noir repertoire? Such questions presume more fundamental ones. What is the genealogy of film noir in Nordic cinema? Where does the femme fatale fit into Nordic cinema? These questions take on special interest because the term 'Nordic noir' has gained currency as the catch-all term for crime fiction on page, screen and television from Denmark, Finland, Iceland, Norway and Sweden.[1]

While film noir is a minor tradition in Nordic cinema, neo-noir has come to figure prominently, as we see in *The Girl with the Dragon Tattoo*. All the Nordic cinemas (except that of Iceland) produced films during the 1940s and 1950s, which scholars and critics would later come to see as films noirs. Since the 1990s, neo-noir has dominated much of Nordic cinema, often as part of films inspired by, or adapted from, Nordic crime fiction. Nordic crime fiction itself has come to be known as 'Nordic noir', particularly in UK usage. (To avoid confusion over these terms, this article uses the term 'Nordic noir' and 'classical film noir' to speak of the period of production during the 1940s and 1950s, during which films now called noir were produced. I use the term 'Nordic neo-noir' to speak of films produced since the 1970s.) The tradition of film noir in the Nordic countries on the whole, including both noir and neo-noir, is distinct in the broader film noir tradition for its characterisation of noir's criminal perspective. In the Nordic noir universe, criminals tend to be humanised, and often childhood experience or a traumatic event is used to gloss their criminality. The doomed characters of Nordic noir thus have their fates shaped by social forces, in a way somewhat reminiscent of the characters in the French poetic realist films of the 1930s.[2] Their fates are not a matter of chance, pathology or pursuit of anti-social pleasure. Such a world-view also resonates with the social-democratic outlook, which dominated political life in the Nordic countries from the 1930s to the 1980s, with the exception of the war years. The noir legacy is also relevant for its impact on auteur filmmakers, notably Lars von Trier and Aki Kaurismäki, who draw on classical noir, as well as the poetic realist films, to give their films a sometimes overt, sometimes subtle, neo-noir quality.

Classic Noir

An account of film noir in the Nordic countries is inseparable from the conceptual problems that figure in the historiography of film noir. As is well known, the term was first used by French critics writing about American films of the 1940s. Since the 1970s, English-language critics have disagreed about noir: genre, style, mode, historical period, family concept, American or international? French critics writing in the 1940s connected the pessimistic, high-contrast American crime films made during the war years to French poetic realism of the mid-1930s. James Naremore reminds us that 'the term film noir had in fact been employed by French writers of the late 1930s in discussions of poetic realism'.[3] What is relevant in the genealogy of noir to an account of Nordic film noir is its bifurcated source; filmmakers in the Nordic countries who made what we now call film noir often found their inspiration in French poetic realism. And critics in the Nordic countries at the time noticed the French connection. At the same time, canonical accounts of domestic noir in the film histories of the Nordic countries have tended to use the term 'film noir' in relation to Hollywood production history, emphasising the relationship between noir in the Nordic countries and the emergence of Hollywood noir. Yet the noir films in Nordic cinema of the 1940s and 1950s are arguably more melodramatic than the Hollywood noirs, as well as more interested in the causes of their characters' amorality and criminality. The distinction has to do with the Nordic films' adherence to a notion of moral foundation: whereas the Hollywood productions are cynical, tending to the nihilistic, the Nordic films are more melodramatic in tending to affirm a notion of redemption – their narrative worlds rest upon a moral foundation. These features are related to Nordic noir's connection to poetic realism, as well as to the impact of cultural radicalism and social democracy on Nordic popular culture.

The issues that arise from the relationship between the French and American notions of noir are evident in the historiography of film noir in Finland, for example. In a 2005 article titled 'On film noir in Finland', critic Rami Nummi argues that twenty-three noir films were made in Finland during the 1940s and 1950s.[4] They were crime films set in the city, shot in low-key lighting with strong contrasts. The films used the crime story to depict social conflicts and the psychic trauma of the war experience and postwar malaise in a changing social situation.[5]

Nummi's notion of noir echoes Paul Schrader's point about noir as a reflection of postwar American malaise. 'The disillusionment many soldiers, small businessmen, housewife/factory employees felt in returning to a peacetime economy was directly mirrored in the sordidness of the urban crime film'.[6] It is notable, however, that whereas Schrader emphasises realism in his argument, Nummi emphasises melodrama. A number of the films he discusses find redemption and hope (and even comedy) in their stories, despite the pessimism. Such films require the moral registers of melodrama. This melodrama leads Nummi to suggest that Finland's noir films combined influences of Hollywood's noir and poetic realism.

Nummi argues that the most significant director of noir in Finland was the studio filmmaker Matti Kassila. For example, he lists his film *Radio tekee murron* (*The Radio Breaks In*, 1951) as an important noir, although many critics at the time wrote of the film as a comedy, praising it for the 'subtle spicing of its parody'.[7] The film depicts a radio reporter whose ever more daring reportage pieces end up entangling him in a museum robbery, which he must then investigate. He discovers a criminal gang committed the robbery and sought to pin it on him. The film is constructed around the point of view of the fall guy, in noir style, yet some cheerful comedy minimises the sense of doom typical of noir. The film ends happily.[8]

Another key figure for Nummi is Teuvo Tulio, a Latvian émigré who made his career in Finland. Tulio is mainly known as a melodramatist. Such films as *Sellaisena kuin sinä minut halusit* (*Just as You Wanted Me*, 1944), *Rikollinen nainen* (*A Criminal Woman*, 1952) and *Olet mennyt vereeni* (*You've Gotten Into My Blood*, 1956) include many noir elements, such as the sinful, criminalised city and the femme fatale figure. And yet the films' confusions of identity, love triangles and sentimental relationships are also typical melodramatic features.

What we see in Finnish noir is how the noir definition can give us a broader international history of the form – a set of Finnish noir films – but how such a broad definition causes us to perhaps force into the category of noir film forms that were part of a broad popular response to the trauma, pessimism and malaise of the early postwar period, but whose fit with noir is problematic. Nevertheless, critics of the time recognised the universality of these dark stories. Tulio's films were often praised for their international style, a point also made about *The Radio Breaks In*. Nordic noirs were often praised in the Nordic countries for their artistic ambition and international style.

The same issues arise in Norwegian cinema too, although Norwegian noir also has a distinctive genealogy. This has been established by Audun Engelstad in his richly researched study, *Losing Streak Stories: Mapping Norwegian Film Noir*.[9] Again, French poetic realism is an important source of inspiration. Engelstad notes that between 1936 and 1940 'more than one hundred French films had theatrical release in Oslo, among them films by Marcel Carné, Jean Renoir, Julien Duvivier, [and] Pierre Chanal'.[10] The definitive films of French poetic realism received enthusiastic critical attention. Engelstad writes that 'when the first Norwegian film noir was made, Edith Carlmar's *Døden er et kjærtegen* (*Death is a Caress*, 1949), it was the influence from French film that was noticed', even though the films the French critics called film noir – *Double Indemnity* (1944), *Murder, My Sweet* (1944), *The Blue Dahlia* (1946) and *The Postman Always Rings Twice* (1946) – also screened in Oslo in 1947 and 1948, only a year after they had screened in Paris.[11]

Norwegian culture has some other sources for noir in the literary and visual arts, in particular in the work of Edvard Munch. Engelstad reminds us that Munch was a key source for German expressionism, as Paul Schrader has emphasised.[12] Engelstad points out that the expressionist staging of some of Henrik Ibsen's plays in Germany drew on Munch's work, or involved commissions for Munch to do the set design.[13] 'Despair, anxiety, jealousy, and loneliness are recurring themes in [Munch's] paintings, just as they are in film noir,' writes Engelstad.[14] Munch's work also recurrently features the femme fatale figure, for example in *Vampyr* and *Dødskys* (*Kiss of Death*).[15]

Munch was also an interest of the novelist and art critic Arve Moen, whose novel *Death is a Caress* was adapted for Edith Carlmar's film of the same title.

Indeed, in a different book on Munch's work entitled *Kvinnen og eros* (*Woman and Eros*), Moen underscores the noir themes in his own novel, writing: 'love and desire, devotion and sexual impulse fight for mastery. When harmony appears to have been achieved, the restraint it imposes appears unbearably irksome, for in his heart Man is lonely'.[16] Moen could have been writing about his own novels, or about those of James M. Cain. Yet it is also worth noting a stoicism in his views which differs from the bleakness of American film noir. For example, in *Death is a Caress*, the couple Erik and Sonja accept their lousy marriage and unhappiness; the novel and film narrate their attempt to live in their marriage and maintain a balanced passivity that stills the forces roiling beneath them. By contrast, Cain's Frank and Cora choose to murder, and their choice is depicted as their attempt to shape their fate. The former is stoic, the latter nihilistic and bleak.[17]

Moen's interest in the themes and motifs of noir indeed carried him to James M. Cain, and *The Postman Always Rings Twice*.[18] Engelstad notes many similarities between *Death is a Caress* and Cain's *The Postman Always Rings Twice*, differences notwithstanding. They are both written in the first person in the then fashionable terse style. In both texts, the protagonists are car mechanics who fall in love with women frustrated in their marriages. In both Cain and Moen, passion leads to murder. Film historian Gunnar Iversen lays stress on the many similarities between *Death is a Caress* and American film noir, including its expression of male melancholia, its retrospective narrative structure, the angular framing in its visual style and its chiaroscuro lighting.[19] Finally, though, *Death is a Caress* takes a different course than American noir, for the protagonist Erik needs only to divorce his first wife to marry his lover, the older, upper-class Sonja, whereas Frank and Cora must murder Nick in order to marry one another.[20] Also, in *Death is a Caress*, Erik murders Sonja, but the murder occurs in a fit of passion when he learns that she has had an abortion because she viewed their marriage as unsustainable. 'There is a significant element of loss at play in this, not only of the offspring, but of everything it came to signify: trust, love, hope ... Murder becomes an unavoidable conclusion to their love affair', as Engelstad writes.[21] Moen's novel and Carlmar's film entail a different notion of fate and doom than in the world of American noir.

The sense of fatalism and doom in *Death is a Caress* is typical of the other Norwegian noirs discussed by Engelstad, including Tancred Ibsen's *To mistenklige personer* (*Two Suspicious Characters*, 1950), a film banned by the Norwegian courts.[22] The fatalism differs from that of American noir, which has its root in the total criminalisation of society, to take Raymond Chandler's view of it. In Chandler's famously long list of such criminal features, he writes that interwar and wartime American society was a world in which 'gangsters can rule nations, and almost rule cities ... where no man can walk down a dark street in safety because law and order are things we talk about but refrain from practicing'.[23] By contrast, the Norwegian noirs emphasise weakness and fate as the source of murder, rather than venality and monstrosity. In this, they resonate with the modernist logic of the rising social-democratic worldview, whose key principles include the notion that social ills have their root in poverty and neglect, and that rational legislation and policy by the state can ameliorate these problems. As a result, the figures tend to be rounded characters, who are let down by society and whose lives are thus negatively impacted by social forces; this characterisation prompts a sympathetic response from readers and viewers.[24]

A similar point could be made about the few Swedish noirs that have been analysed by scholars. The most important study of the history of Swedish crime films has been written by Daniel Brodén.[25] Brodén argues that only a few films were produced in Sweden during the classic noir period of the 1940s and 1950s which could be seen as noirs, including Alf Sjöberg's *Hets* (*Torment*, 1944) – the screenplay for which was written by Ingmar Bergman – and Hasse Ekman's *Flicka och hyacinter* (*Girl and Hyacinths*, 1950). Brodén's study encompasses the corpus of Swedish crime films, seeking to theorise the cultural politics of subgenres of crime film. He writes about the whodunnit, the psychological thriller, the gangster film, the police procedural and the political thriller, claiming that noir is not a relevant category, although he draws to some extent on Dudley Andrew's study of French poetic realism, *Mists of Regret*[26] and James Naremore's study of noir, *More Than Night*, to develop his argument about other subgenres of crime film. Brodén ultimately argues that the crime film works out an ambivalent relationship to the Swedish welfare state, tending to criticise and affirm culturally dominant notions about its historical phases, whether the class solidarity of the 1950s or the individualistic neo-liberalism since the 1990s.

Girl and Hyacinths has been held as the chief example of noir in Sweden. Mia Krokstäde observes that the director of the film, Hasse Ekman, spent six months in Hollywood during the late 1940s observing production practices at the studios; he sought to imitate what he learned when he returned to Sweden.[27] *Girl and Hyacinths* tells the story of the investigation into the suicide of Dagmar Brink (Eva Henning). Puzzled by her death, her neighbours the Wikners seek to find out why the promising woman killed herself. The film recounts their investigation, revealing a love triangle. But the object of Dagmar's love is finally revealed not to be the involved man, but the mysterious Alex (Anne-Marie Brunish), a lover who Dagmar met in Paris. Alex is also depicted as a femme fatale in a world of sexual decadence.[28] The love triangle encodes the doom of noir in a way reminiscent of the Norwegian noirs, suggests Krokstäde, for Dagmar's fate is to be queer under the regime of the 'postwar years' ideals of family unity and conformity'.[29] In this way, Dagmar

Figure 7.1   Eva Henning in *Girl with Hyacinths*.

is a round, sympathetic figure, rather than a tough or criminal one. To be sure, the queer character is punished, doomed to suicide. Yet, suggests Krokstäde, her fate highlights the significance of individual difference in a context of conformist sexual norms.[30] It is also worth noting that such a valorisation of queer sexuality stands in contrast to a more conventional American noir alignment of homosexuality with the upper classes, often a target of populist critique, as evident in the character of Jules Amthor (Otto Kruger) in *Murder, My Sweet* or Waldo Lydecker (Clifton Webb) in *Laura* (1944). Writing about the latter, James Naremore notes 'a covert homophobia is linked with a populist attitude toward social class: the villainous Lydecker is depicted as a parasitic dandy, in contrast to the more proletarian tough guy hero', even if such characters can carry significant complexity, as he also points out.[31] Still, the subversive quality of Ekman's *Girl and Hyacinths* is worth noting.

Film noir in Denmark has been the object of a number of studies, including a chapter in Ib Bondebjerg's *Filmen og det moderne*, a discussion by Eva Jørholt on noir in *100-års dansk film* and Rune Christensen's *Local Inflections of*

Darkness, as well as other studies discussed by Christensen.³² Danish commentators count some six to ten films produced during the 1940s and 1950s. As Jørholt suggests, while these films have some similarities to American noir of the same period, their settings are more provincial, and they are more sympathetic to their characters, at the same time as they share the misanthropy, fatalism and visual style of American noir. Examples include such films as *Mordets melodi* (*Melody of Murder*, 1944) and *Besættelse* (*Obsession*, 1944).³³ In contrast to Jørholt's emphasis on the American connection, Bondebjerg links Danish film noir to French poetic realism.³⁴ This source tends to make the Danish noir films more melodramatic and also more quotidian, he suggests; the criminal underworld and the private investigator do not play a role. Rather, Danish noir is 'an expressive subcategory of the erotic and social melodrama where the sudden appearance of desire and sexuality has a disturbing effect on the everyday universe'.³⁵ This notion of noir calls to mind Engelstad's point about the Norwegian noir films; like the Norwegian films, the Danish films noirs contextualise and humanise (and, one might add, melodramatically inflect) the actions of their characters in ways that make them more sympathetic. Christensen argues that three central Danish noirs, *En forbryder* (*A Criminal*, 1941), *Jeg mødte en morder* (*I Met a Murderer*, 1943) and *John og Irene* (*John and Irene*, 1949) have their roots in the Danish cultural radicalism movement, which dates to work of eminent literary and cultural critic Georg Brandes' lectures and writings of the 1870s. The freethinking (*frisind*) and cultural radicalism movements of the 1920s and 1930s attacked the conservatism, sexism and classism of the establishment.³⁶ This places the films in the lineage of nineteenth-century naturalism, familiar from the work of Émile Zola, as well as from dramas of Henrik Ibsen and August Strindberg, such as *A Doll House* (1879) and *Miss Julie* (1888). The first Danish noir, *A Criminal*, for instance, is an adaptation of Sven Lange's 1902 play of the same name. Lange was a 'great admirer of Brandes, and this particular play echoes the naturalistic reformist ideals that Brandes promoted'.³⁷ Christensen writes that this source helps explain the emphasis on everyday experience and the fate of common people, and their fateful betrayal by a system benefiting the upper classes. We don't find the focus on exceptional acts and persons typical of American noir.³⁸ Driven to desperation by the system, characters become doomed criminals, leaving audiences with the question of what causes the desperation in the first place. The social-democratic dimension of this world-view arises from the implicit remedy of rational, systemic reform to benefit the working classes. Notions of fate and doom thus shift from having their source in the laws of the criminal underworld to having them in the moral conflicts of everyday life. This tendency persists in the neo-noir of Nordic cinema, as we will also see.

Nordic films noirs show a strong connection to French poetic realism, in their pessimism and bleak view of human fates but also in their melodrama and cultural politics; similarities of visual style also connect them to American noir. In their similarity to French poetic realism, classic Nordic noir's characters' criminality and amorality is often explained by way of social conditions, a character's past or a traumatic experience. This aligns the films with the universalism of the Social Democratic or Labour parties, which dominated postwar politics in Denmark, Norway and Sweden. They sought to build a system that provided resources and security to all, as a means of making the population productive and minimising social ills. The Nordic noir films seek out these social ills in everyday life, but tend to suggest that those touched by such ills are affected for a reason. Pathological criminals such as Moose Malloy and spider women such as Phyllis Dietrichson are not the model.

Sources of Nordic Neo-noir and Crime Fiction

Neo-noir has thrived in Nordic popular cinema since the 1990s. Many domestic blockbusters have been neo-noirs or featured prominent noir elements, including *Nattevagten* (*Nightwatch*, 1994), *Pusher* (1996), *Pusher 2* (2004), *Pusher 3* (2005), *Insomnia* (1997), *Raid* (2003), *Smala Sussie* (*Slim Susie*, 2003), *Vares* (*Vares: Private Eye*, 2004), *V2: Jäätynyt enkeli* (*V2: Dead Angel*, 2007), *Flammen og citronen* (*Flame and Citron*, 2008), *Reykjavik-Rotterdam* (2008), *Snabba Cash* (*Easy Money*, 2011) and *Hodejegerne* (*Headhunters*, 2011), among others. What is more, television crime serials with strong noir elements, Danish ones in particular, have attracted huge audiences, including such series as *Rejseholdet* (*Unit One*, 2000–4), *Forbrydelsen* (*The Killing*, 2007–12), *Ørnen: En krimi-odyssé* (*The Eagle*, 2004–6) and *Bron* (*The Bridge*, 2011–). While these last are also police procedurals, they nevertheless overlap with the noir repertoire in world-view and visual style. The flourishing of neo-noir can be explained in part by increases in the number, quality and variety of films produced since the 1990s, as well as the resources devoted to popular cinema, brought about by institutional changes in the Nordic national film institutes. As popular cinema has received increased support from state-funded film institutes, filmmakers have produced more quality neo-noir films.

The film institutes were established during the 1960s and 1970s to support the production of the art film and auteur filmmakers, when film came to be viewed as an art form, and the old national studios such as Nordisk (DK), Svensk filmindustri (S), Suomi-filmi (SF), Norsk Film (N) and some others cut significantly or stopped film production altogether. Since then, almost all films that make it into production in the Nordic countries have been underwritten by the national film institutes as well as by national television stations. Yet, with important exceptions, such films did not fill theatre seats from the 1960s to the 1980s. Domestic audiences attended farces and comedies, if they went to domestic films at all. Hollywood imports accounted for 70 to 90 per cent of admissions. In response to this ongoing 'crisis', the film institutes began to support popular film more fully, beginning in the late 1980s. An indicative change for the Nordic region is the 1989 amendment to the Danish Film Law, which introduced the so-called 50/50 system. When a producer raised 50 per cent of a film's budget, the film institute guaranteed it would provide the remaining 50 per cent. In Denmark, this system supplemented a consultant system, in which film institute appointed consultants awarded funding on a project-by-project basis. By contrast, in Sweden and Finland, applications went to a committee of film professionals. The success of Danish cinema since the mid-1990s can be traced to institutional changes, such as the 50/50 scheme, as well as to a variety of other factors, including changes at the Danish film school, changes in creative and business practice, and technological changes such as digitalisation.[39] These changes have continued apace since the late 1990s. Similar changes have occurred in the other Nordic countries, including the regionalisation of film production in Sweden; reorganisation of the film institute system, establishment of a new film school and large budget increases for film production in Norway; and institutional reorganisation and identification of new funding priorities in Finland.[40]

What is clear, at least, is that all of the Nordic countries have seen an increase in the vitality of domestic film industries and a rise in the popularity of domestic cinema, as reflected in the number of films being made, their variety, perceived quality and the audiences they are attracting domestically and internationally. Domestic productions have accounted for 25 to 40 per cent of all film admissions in the best years since the mid-1990s, while in the 1970s and 1980s attendance at domestically produced films often accounted for only 5 to 10 per cent of total film attendance. The changes in question have thus facilitated the production and favour of popular cinema, including neo-noir.

Another reason for a neo-noir cycle in Nordic cinema is the popularity of Nordic crime fiction, that is to say, we are dealing with a cycle in popular culture production, not just film. International and domestic crime fiction, and the whodunnit in particular, have been popular in the Nordic countries since the late nineteenth century.[41] Contemporary Nordic crime fiction and its predominant subgenre, the socially critical police procedural, date to 1965. In that year, Maj Sjöwall and Per Wahlöö published the first of a ten-novel series about Inspector Martin Beck and his group of investigators in Stockholm, with the subtitle *Roman om ett brott* (*Story of a Crime*). Sjöwall and Wahlöö used the crime novel to critique the Swedish welfare state from the left, depicting the predominant Social Democratic party as favouring the economic interests of Sweden's capitalist class to cement their party's hold on political power.

The Sjöwall-Wahlöö tradition continued when a new generation of socially critical writers embraced their legacy during the 1990s, albeit with a twist.

Rather than attacking the welfare state from the left, as Sjöwall and Wahlöö had done, these writers defended the welfare state from its left flank, affirming social-democratic political solidarity against neo-liberalism, retrenchment and economic globalisation. The most prominent exemplar of this crime fiction is Henning Mankell and his Kurt Wallander series of the 1990s. Mankell's critique echoes in the careers of other key writers in the Nordic countries, for example in the feminist hard-boiled crime fiction of Leena Lehtolainen and the social criticism of Danes Agnete Friis and Lene Kaaberbøl, as well as in the novels of Jussi Adler-Olsen. It can also be found to some degree in the hard-boiled texts of Jo Nesbø and in the police procedurals of Icelander Arnaldur Indridason. It is arguably present in such television shows as *Unit One*, *The Killing* and *The Bridge* too. Capitalising on the popularity of these popular texts, film producers have adapted scores of crime novels, making the boom in Nordic crime fiction a source for Nordic neo-noir film and television.

Since the Sjöwall-Wahlöö novels of the 1960s and 70s, fiction connected to crime, whether on page or screen, has enjoyed consistent attention, which has only increased since the 1990s. For some commentators, it has been too popular. A recurrent argument has been that audience enthusiasm for such popular crime stories crowds out and attenuates serious high culture.[42] Moreover, in keeping with the tradition of the socially critical Nordic crime story, crime novels and neo-noir films have tended towards social criticism, making them ubiquitous and culturally salient. In this way, they are instances of middlebrow popular culture, embracing entertainment values while also seeking to be prominent and influential in public debate. Finally, the commercial success of the crime novels and cinematic neo-noirs have attracted large domestic and international audiences, and created a brand identity, 'Nordic noir', resulting in the production of more of the same, not least high-concept neo-noir adaptations of crime fiction[43] – for example Stieg Larsson's *Millennium* trilogy, Jo Nesbø vehicles such as *Headhunters* or the *Vares* adaptations of Reijo Mäki's novels in Finland. What we find, though, is that in their embrace of social criticism, the neo-noir films continue to contextualise and humanise their doomed criminal protagonists, in ways that call to mind some of the examples from the classical noir period in Nordic cinema.

Form and Epistemology in Nordic Neo-noir

It is no great discovery to observe that Nordic neo-noir films and crime fiction hold a dystopian outlook. Does it have distinct elements that characterise it? This question in some ways presupposes the already mentioned problem of noir scholarship, the question, 'What is it?' a genre, a style, a historical movement, a cycle, an attitude, a national or international category?[44] While the same definitional problem applies to neo-noir, both intrinsically and in relation to film noir, here we can skirt such debate about the status of the object of analysis and instead treat neo-noir as part of a discourse and critical practice, as James Naremore suggests.[45] Naremore's response to the definitional problem also helps make clear the importance of connecting film and popular literature, an important connection for Nordic neo-noir. Naremore's 'loose, evolving system of arguments and readings that helps to shape commercial strategies and aesthetic ideologies' in noir also overlaps with a similar discourse concerning crime fiction.[46] Bringing these discourses and critical practices together can help us develop an account of a broad notion of Nordic neo-noir by identifying some recurrent debates in the discourse that help situate the objects of study more richly.

Two related distinctions are relevant, a formal one and an epistemological one. The formal point can be drawn from Nino Frank's essay on film noir, in which he writes that in noir 'the essential question no longer has to do with who committed the crime, but with how the protagonist handles himself'.[47] To make sense of Frank's point as a formal principle, it is helpful to recall Tzevtan Todorov's observation that crime fiction always includes two stories, the story of the crime and the story of the investigation.[48] While Frank is not writing about crime fiction, one can make a useful point about noir by reading Frank through Todorov. What noir does, according to Frank, is diminish or eliminate the formal significance of the story of the investigation. As a result, the formal interest in noir resides in what Todorov calls the crime story. The noir texts make this clear by often aligning the viewer with a criminal protagonist's perspective, making his or her moves structure the narrative; it is not the structure of the investigation the shapes the narrative, as in crime fiction.[49] The formal organisation of the narrative thus concerns the organisation of a series of encounters with characters, problems and settings, rather than the assembly of an investigation working towards answering the question, 'whodunnit?' This is important for Nordic neo-noir, because these films tend to structure their protagonist's narrative in a broad way, which accommodates the contextualisation and humanisation we have traced.

The second distinction concerns Joan Copjec's argument about the self in noir, which I read as an epistemological point about what the viewer can know about the criminal perspective of the protagonist. Copjec's point also relates to Frank's observation. Copjec maintains that the classical detective story and noir invoke different notions of the self. In crime fiction, the self is imagined to be bounded, containing an interiority; in noir, the self is boundless and without interiority, continually being remade through symbolic associations.[50] Crime fiction's interest lies in the investigation that prises criminal secrets from the private self, which identify the criminal. The notion is that the investigation can come to know the perpetrator's motive, that it can match a theory developed through investigation to the interior world of the perpetrator's private self. By contrast, argues Copjec, in noir divulging secrets is not the point, because the self is epistemologically different. The noir self is continually shaped through chains of signification within the surrounding social world, she argues. One might call this a Lacanian reading of Frank, for what Copjec is saying is that the protagonist's handling of him- or herself occurs through signifying chains. The viewer thus asks about what leads the protagonist to behave the way he or she does, but noir does not offer the assurance of motive available in crime fiction. What is of interest, then, is how the protagonist is made and remade in different contexts. This epistemological point helps us see the extent to which Nordic neo-noir invites viewers to seek to understand how the protagonist is shaped, even if, as Copjec suggests, noir is not premised on an idea that we can understand such shaping.

Using these formal and epistemological points about neo-noir can help us see some important features of neo-noir in Nordic cinema which also connect it to the films of the classical noir period discussed above.

NEO-NOIR AND THE FAMILY

A prominent element of Nordic neo-noir films, as well as Nordic crime fiction, is an obsession with children as criminals and as victims of violence, or sometimes both. This recurrent theme recalls the cultural radicalism and social-democratic ethos of the classic Danish films noirs mentioned by Christensen. It recurs in recent neo-noir films in Nordic cinema. Audun Engelstad writes about early neo-noir films in Norway during the 1970s – *Bortreist på ubestemt tid* (*Away for an Indefinite Period*, 1974) and *Angst* (1976) – that they display an interest in 'showing the criminal as a human, not a monster, and by so doing making the audience invest their sympathy in him'.[51] While he is careful to qualify this point (for example, he argues for the influence of Claude Chabrol on these films), Nordic neo-noir often seeks to contextualise and make sense of social forces that generate criminality, rather than depicting the criminal as pathological, inexplicable, monstrous or nihilistic.

The obsession with children is a means of humanising criminality. The navigation of the social world involves children and childhood memories, and yet the meaning of children and childhood memories and experiences often remains mysterious. Many examples can be mentioned, both in crime fiction and neo-noir cinema. The neo-noir films often foreground children and families: *Insomnia* concerns the murder of a fifteen year old, ostensibly by a peer. Stieg Larsson's *Millennium* trilogy is a cardinal example of violence and abuse aimed at young people, including not only the fate of Harriet Vanger in the first novel of the trilogy, but the abuse suffered by her brother Martin, as well as Lisbeth Salander's suffering of childhood abuse.[52] Although children do not figure in *Headhunters*, the film is obsessed with family; its resolution turns on the decision by the protagonist and his partner to have children. In *Easy Money*, many of the characters have children on their mind or in tow, as they conspire and then execute violent crimes. *Slim Susie* is about adolescents trapped in a provincial, neo-noir world. In one of Swedish crime writer Henning Mankell's best-known novels, *Villospår* (*Sidetracked*), adapted both for Swedish television and by the BBC, an abused teenage boy murders a number of men who have victimised underage prostitutes, of which the boy's sister is one.[53] Norwegian Karin Fossum's novels recurrently deal with young people who commit crimes against other young people, for example *Svarte sekunder* (*Black Seconds*) and *Varsleren* (*The Caller*).[54] Finnish crime writer Leena Lehtolainen's novels and their television adaptations often deal with the murder or abuse of children, for example *Kuolemanspiraali* (*Death Spiral*).[55] In contrast, children are absent from the classical noir films of the Nordic cinemas during the 1940s and 1950s, just as they are absent from auteur Nordic neo-noir.

One of the most striking aspects of the ubiquity of children is their relative absence from classic film noir, as has been noted by such scholars as Vivian Sobchack. She argues that such absence implicitly naturalises the isolation of noir's characters. She writes: 'hotel rooms, cocktail lounges, bars, roadside diners and even the cold interiors of the houses of the rich and corrupt . . . all refuse individual subjectivity and intimacy (as they encourage individual isolation and secrecy)'.[56]

Even when noir enters the domestic sphere, it finds itself in a space of inhumane and ill-gotten 'cold glitter'.[57] Sobchack argues that in these settings we have a Bakhtinian chronotope of what she calls lounge time, a textual space and time in which certain events and characters recur:

> The spatiotemporal structures and smaller chronotopic units (or motifs) like the cocktail lounge or the hotel room that structure lounge time emerge in their historical coherence as a threats to traditional function, continuity, contiguity, and security of domestic space and time . . . Children do not normally (or normatively) find their way into these spaces . . . Women at home in these spaces are rarely mothers . . . nor are men fathers. No familial connection and intimacy can be eventful in lounge time.[58]

One dimension of Sobchack's argument is the idea that noir is a world of stranger sociality characterised by distrust. Such a world entails complex and potentially dangerous navigational challenges, and hence formal complexity and narrative pleasure. At the same time, this world of stranger sociality's lack of intimacy means knowledge of others, and of one's relationship to them, will always remain cloudy, calling Copjec's point to mind.

Sobchack's view resembles the argument made by Sylvia Harvey about the family in noir. Harvey argues that

> it is the representation of the institution of the family, which in so many films serves as the mechanism whereby desire is fulfilled, or at least ideological equilibrium is established, that in film noir serves as vehicle for the expression of frustration.[59]

For Harvey, Sobchack's lounge time is a narrative world of ideological imbalance and blocked desire, where frustration predominates. Hence the family is absent, or depicted in dystopian terms if present.

The Nordic neo-noirs take advantage of these dimensions of lounge time, while notably inserting children into the chronotope, to use Sobchack's theoretical framework. Take, for example, the Swedish neo-noir *Easy Money*. The film is an adaptation of the first novel in Jens Lapidus's *Stockholm noir* trilogy.[60] It tells the story of JW (Joel Kinnaman), for whom driving an illegal taxi is a gateway job into a narcotics and money-laundering conspiracy. For JW, the 'easy money' on offer is appealing as a means of class mobility. He comes from a working-class family in northern Sweden, but hangs out and studies with the well-heeled children of Sweden's old noble families at the Stockholm School of Economics. JW believes if he can make a big illicit score, he can establish himself with his friends and win the love of a woman, whose family belongs to the Swedish elite. He is obsessed with family background, then, his own and that of his friends. Needless to say, he fails; yet this is a twofold invocation of family, which calls to mind Sobchack and Harvey's points. In the first place, the invocation of family expresses JW's frustration, for he is ideologically blocked by the persistence of Sweden's class system. Yet, at the same time, the persistence of this class system and its investment in the family as its indispensible 'mechanism' of control is represented in dystopian terms. Family and children are present only to show the dystopian depth of the world JW inhabits.

The men in the criminal part of JW's life are also obsessed with family and children, and they are ethnic Others in Sweden as well, of Chilean, Serbian and Lebanese origin. Of these men, three are fathers or surrogate fathers who become increasingly focused on their relationship with their children. The enforcer Mrado (Dragomir Mrsic) is forced take over the care of his seven-year-old daughter from her addled mother. The organised crime leader Radovan (Dejan Kukic) makes his son witness to a drug war he prosecutes against a rival gang. And the middleman Jorge (Matias Varela) becomes preoccupied with his sister's pregnancy and delivery, after escaping from prison and helping orchestrate the enormous drug deal, of which JW is also part. A fourth figure, the drug dealer Abdulkarim (Mahmut Suvakci), recurrently appears in

Figure 7.2 Swedish-style neo-noir, *Easy Money*.

his family's apartment. These men spend a lot of time in the bars and hotels mentioned by Sobchack, but they also spend a lot of time at home with their children, and each of them (except Abdulkarim) speaks of changing his child's life as a means of erasing the abuse he suffered at the hands of his father. When they bring children into lounge time, the characters are depicted as having a past and a life outside of the lounge, which works to humanise them.

JW's painfully obscure family connections, and the disappearance of his sister at a young age, also humanise and motivate his character. At the same time, the dystopian representation of families makes the characters' desires for their children appear ironically misguided and impossible, an expression of the frustration identified by Harvey.[61]

On another view, a historicist reading of the figure of the child and family in Nordic neo-noir leads us to link these films to the cultural politics of the welfare state. In this way, humanising the criminal character by depicting his or her relationship to children and to an emptied ideology of the family also works to create a dystopian image of the state. The figure of the child underscores the criminality of the social world of neo-noir. For any social milieu that allows, or even encourages, the abuse, degradation and destruction of children goes against social norms in all of the Nordic countries, each of which maintains an 'Ombudsman for Children', who guides and monitors each state's compliance with the rights of the child, outlined in the UN Convention on the Rights of the Child.[62] The Ombudsman office dates to the early 1990s. The convention holds that 'every child has certain basic rights, including the right to life, his or her own name and identity, to be raised by his or her parents within a family or cultural grouping'.[63] Sweden made corporal punishment of children a crime in 1979, and many of the universal benefits of the welfare state are aimed at children, including free health care, free education, exceptionally generous parental leave polices, subsidised daycare and a monthly child subsidy paid to mothers. To be sure, one can see the operation of Foucaudian bio-power in such a state apparatus, but that doesn't change the fact that in historicist terms the child is a societal canary in the coalmine.[64] Depicting abuse of children and their suffering is a means both of social critique and of depicting ostensibly authentic yet human and understandable criminality.

Social criticism is also relevant to the question about the femme fatale, with which the chapter began. Salander is an interesting figure in this regard, as she commits many crimes, uses sex to get what she needs and uses her appearance to manipulate men and women around her. At the same time, her figure visually and narratively disrupts any attempt to be defined sexually or otherwise in relation to men, the salient crime of the femme fatale in Janey Place's account.[65] Salander could be said to invert the conventions of the femme fatale, a victim who refuses her victimisation, a sexualised character who has sex mostly with women but suffers male attacks, abuse and rape, against which she retaliates. She is also a victim of systematic familial and institutional abuse, which has been aided, abetted and even carried out by the Swedish state. This traumatic background works as a means both of characterisation and of undermining the femme fatale reading of her character, which is surely one of the reasons the femme fatale has not received attention in studies of Stieg Larsson's *Millennium* trilogy.[66]

Still, Salander's childhood abuse, rape and suffering work both to make her character complete and to critique the Swedish welfare state and Western modernity as a patriarchal, misogynist dystopia. Such a characterisation can easily be seen as a clichéd use of trauma. Its centrality is clear, as is evident in David Fincher's adaptation of *The Girl with the Dragon Tattoo*. His film visually depicts Salander's identity as the anti-femme fatale in the conclusion of the film, sticking close to Larsson's novel. Where Niels Arden Oplev uses security footage to show Salander in costume, Fincher depicts her purchasing a femme fatale disguise, then donning it 'backstage' in her hotel room and finally disposing of it after she has stolen a fortune from the accounts of the Bernie Madoff figure in the text, financier Hans Erik Wennerström. In so doing, Fincher underscores that Salander is not a femme fatale, by showing her putting on and taking off that stereotype. In this way, her identity remains enigmatic, again recalling Copjec.

In Nordic neo-noir's tendency toward social criticism, we arguably see a continuation of the contextualisation and humanisation of the criminal which figured in the Nordic noir films. At the same time, however, the individualism evident in such films as *Easy Money* and the *Millennium* trilogy also differs from the emphasis on the collective in the postwar period. Still, the human criminal remains a definitive feature of Nordic noir and neo-noir.

Auteur Neo-noir

The films of Aki Kaurismäki and Lars von Trier also affirm the noir legacy, but do so at least in part as a way of rejecting the political filmmaking of the 1970s, scorning social-democratic consensus and affirming their own cinematic identity. As Peter Schepelern points out,

> Kaurismäki and Trier can be seen as parallel Nordic auteurs with hardly any connection ... Both Kaurismäki and Trier emerged in the era in which postmodernism predominated in the international art film. On the agenda were aesthetic experiments with the music video genre, the postmodern genre par excellence, and, most important, the ironic play with genres and clichés, which often connected high and low culture.[67]

Such self-aware use of genres and clichés helps makes evident a cinephilic relationship to the history of cinema, which shows up in the filmmakers' use of noir. Von Trier's debut feature film, *The Element of Crime* (1984), has been received as a neo-noir, and the director himself has remarked that the 'film relates to and makes use of certain film noir clichés'.[68] In its cinephilic way, *The Element of Crime* uses 'the Tarkovskian theme of the incursion of nature within a "world of decay" as perceived through the detritus of memory', as Linda Badley writes, pulling together the film's doomsday rejection of politics, its affirmation of aestheticism and its love of the cinematic past.[69] His third feature, *Europa* (1991), though not stylised as a neo-noir in such a pronounced way, also includes noir elements. In both films, the Euro-American hybridity of film noir is foregrounded. Aki Kaurismäki's films of the 1980s are also visually and thematically within the noir tradition. These films include *Rikos ja rangaistus* (*Crime and Punishment*, 1983), *Calamari Unioni* (*Calamari Union*, 1985), *Varjoja paratiisissa* (*Shadows in Paradise*, 1986), *Ariel* (1988) and *Tulitikkutehtaan tyttö* (*The Match-Factory Girl*, 1990). Among Kaurismäki's later films, *Laitakaupungin valot* (*Lights in the Dusk*, 2006) is overtly neo-noir in visual style and narrative. Kaurismäki and von Trier's films display a self-reflexive relationship to cinematic history, and this dimension makes their films noteworthy examples of neo-noir. Mark Bould, Kathrina Glitre and Greg Tuck underscore self-reflexivity as a definitive characteristic of neo-noir:

> While many of the makers of film noir would have been conscious of the work of their contemporaries and predecessors, none of them would have set out to make something called 'film noir' ... The concept and category simply did not exist for them. Neo-noir is made and watched by people familiar with the concept of film noir.[70]

What do these filmmakers do with the noir repertoire, then? What might explain their engagement with neo-noir? At least a part of the answer has to do with both filmmakers' affirmation of noir as a dialectical rejection of the social realism that dominated 1970s Nordic cinema. In furnishing a world of isolated individuals, doomed fates and a cinematic toy box of visual style choices, the noir repertoire provide these filmmakers with a means of opting out of the previous generation's collective emphasis, utopian aspirations and earnest realism, while embracing a filmmaking that gave voice to impulses of the 1970s and 1980s.

Both von Trier's and Kaurismäki's first films were praised as generational films which gave voice to the emergent punk ethos. In his book on von Trier, journalist Nils Thorsen writes about that ethos of the late 1970s and 1980s: 'Youth culture had been shaped by humanistic, leftist thought. When punk broke in, that was the end of writing *love* on one's forehead ... The new slogan was *no future*!'[71] Doom, pessimism and decadence featured in the antisocial attitudes of punk, its DIY rejection of the mainstream and its search for an alternative pared-down musical language and culture. These attitudes found cinematic expression in a self-aware aestheticism, which differed from the realism of the 1970s. This aestheticism is evident in both filmmakers' early experiments with noir: *Element of Crime*'s sepia lighting, shooting locations in the sewers of Copenhagen, its intertexts with Welles, Dreyer, Lang, Scorsese and Tarkovsky, and hypnotic voiceover give it an arch-noir quality. Kaurismäki's early films are instances of film noir seen through the lens of the French New Wave, and its fixation on Hollywood noirs, among other films. In *Calamari Union*, for example, the twelve Franks (and one Pekka) who make up the cast face their doomed fates coolly, in black and white, wearing suits, fedoras and trenchcoats. The majority of actors in the films were musicians, a number of whom played in bands that created a period-defining Finnicised version of punk, for example the emblematic band Eppu Normaali. The same turn to aestheticism and punk is also evident in Kaurismäki's casting. Regular actors in his early films – Matti Pellonpää, Kari Väänänen, Vesa Vierikko – were participants in a definitive 1978 production of the play *The Death of a Tightrope Walker, or How Pete Q. Got Wings (Nuorallatanssijan kuolema eli kuinka Pete Q sai siivet)*, a mystical story about artistic inspiration in conflict with political dogma, which affirmed art as a kind of anarchic, antiauthoritarian moral act.[72] The aestheticism, as in von Trier, was a means of defining a new cinematic direction.

Von Trier's experimentation with genres continued in diverse directions, but Kaurismäki continued to come back to the noir sources. For example, the lighting, the clipped dialogue of his films (rendered in strange, 'book' Finnish that eschews everyday dialects but calls to mind the terse language of noir) and the doomed fates of his characters show his debt to noir. At the same time, many commentators have observed that the hint of optimism and redemption in his films cause them to differ from noir, and link them to the French poetic realist films. Those films were associated with the leftist Popular Front, one of whose anthems was the optimistic song, 'Les temps des cerises', a song associated with the French Left since the Paris Commune of 1871. That song features in a late poetic realist film Kaurismäki has called one of his all-time favourites, *Casque d'or* (*Golden Marie*, 1954), as well as in Kaurismäki's own *Juha* (1999) and *Le Havre* (2012). The latter film is set in the French port city, which is also associated with poetic realism because it was a key setting in such films as *La Bête humaine* (*The Human Beast*, 1938) and *Le Quai des brumes* (*Port of Shadows*, 1938).

If the early use of noir by von Trier and Kaurismäki can be seen as an affirmation of cinematic aesthetics that rejected a reigning style and the politics that underpinned it, Kaurismäki's 2006 *Lights in the Dusk* marks an interesting shift. The film tells the story of Koistinen (Janne Hyytiäinen), a hapless security guard working for a large Helsinki security firm. Koistinen's occupation is a noteworthy metonymy for the 'night-watchman state' – the neo-liberal view that the state should provide a modicum of security, and no more. Such ideas have led to policies like that in Helsinki, where the municipality has subcontracted out significant parts of its policing, for example maintenance of law and order in the public transportation system. Koistinen is targeted by an organised crime group, whose boss Lindholm (Ilkka Koivula) dispatches his girlfriend, the femme fatale Mirja (Maria Järvenhelmi), to seduce Koistinen and steal his security codes in order to rob a jewellery shop. Koistinen takes the fall, protects Mirja and is aggressively prosecuted by state officials, who tacitly work on behalf of the kingpin Lindholm. Koistinen loses everything, goes to prison and continues to be persecuted after his release.

In *Lights in the Dusk*, Kaurismäki returns to neo-noir. Yet rather than an embrace of noir as an affirmation of anarchy and an aesthetic rejection of a reigning style, neo-noir becomes a vehicle for affirming social-democratic solidarity with the average worker, who is portrayed as being exploited by bold and aggressive criminals and abused by supine state authorities. The pessimism of film noir and poetic realism is palpable here, only in this film it is used to depict the globalised, deregulated Nordic welfare state as a dystopia. Notably absent from Kaurismäki's film, however, are the children and memories

Figure 7.3   Finnish-style neo-noir, *Lights in the Dusk*.

of popular neo-noir. In this way, the film gives voice to a nostalgia for the classical period of American film noir, which is an element of Kaurismäki's auteurism – just as it was for one of his idols, Jean-Luc Godard.

Nordic Noir and the Human Criminal

Film noir and neo-noir in Nordic cinema draw on Hollywood noir and French poetic realism, in particular, but in so doing contextualise and humanise their criminal characters. These characters' doomed fates are born of societal failure and untrammelled social forces, which many of the films implicitly criticise. There are exceptions, such as the aestheticism and anti-conformism present in the early films of von Trier and Kaurismäki. Still, the noir tradition remains relatively minor on the whole in Nordic cinema, although the popularity of neo-noir and crime fiction since the 1990s is arguably changing the place of the crime story in the history of the Nordic cinemas. Noir is also noteworthy in the Nordic cinemas for being a form that connects these somewhat insular cinemas to the international history of film. As such, the noir tradition provides a means of more fully grasping the connections between Nordic cinema and European and American cinema, as well as showing the way these cinemas differ from that tradition, not least in their affirmation of the human criminal.

Acknowledgements

Thanks to Rune Christensen, Audun Engelstad, Maaret Koskinen, Anders Marklund, Kerstin Bergman and Eric Ames.

Bibliography

Ahonen, Kimmo, Janne Rosenquist, Juha Rosenquist and Päivi Valotie (eds) (2003), *Taju kankaalle: Uutta suomalaista elokuvaa paikantamassa*, Turku: Kirja-Aurora.

Andrew, Dudley (1995), *Mists of Regret: Culture and Sensibility in Classic French Film*, Princeton, NJ: Princeton University Press.

Arvas, Paula and Andrew Nestingen (2011), 'Introduction: Contemporary Scandinavian crime fiction', in Andrew Nestingen and Paula Arvas (eds), *Scandinavian Crime Fiction*, Cardiff: University of Wales Press, pp. 1–17.

Badley, Linda (2009), *Lars von Trier*, Urbana, IL: University of Illinois Press.

Bainbridge, Caroline (2007), *The Cinema of Lars von Trier: Authenticity and Artifice*, London: Wallflower.

Bould, Mark, Kathrina Glitre and Greg Tuck (2009), 'Parallax views: An introduction', in Mark Bould, Kathrina Glitre and Greg Tuck (eds), *Neo-Noir*, New York: Wallflower, pp. 1–10.

Brodén, Daniel (2008), *Folkhemmets skuggbilder: En kulturanalytisk genrestudie I svensk kriminalfiktion i film och TV*, Stockholm: Ekholm & Tegebjer.

Chandler, Raymond (1995), 'The simple art of murder', in *Raymond Chandler: Later Novels and Other Writings*, ed. Frank McShane, New York: Library of America, pp. 977–92 [1945].

Christensen, Rune (2009), 'Local inflections of darkness: Danish film noir during the classical noir cycle', unpublished dissertation, University of California, Davis.
Copjec, Joan (1993), 'The phenomenal and nonphenomenal: Private space in *Film Noir*', in Joan Copjec (ed.), *Shades of Noir: A Reader*, New York: Verso, pp. 167–98.
Eisner, Lotte (1969), *The Haunted Screen*, Berkeley, CA: University of California Press.
Engelstad, Audun (2006), *Losing Streak Stories: Mapping Norwegian Film Noir*, Oslo: Faculty of Humanities, University of Oslo.
——.(2011), 'Dealing with crime: Cyclic changes in Norwegian crime films', *Journal of Scandinavian Cinema* 1(2), 205-21.
Forshaw, Barry (2012), *Death in a Cold Climate: A Guide to Scandinavian Crime Fiction*, New York: Palgrave Macmillan.
——.(2013), *Nordic Noir: The Pocket Essential Guide to Scandinavian Crime Fiction, Film & TV*, London: Oldcastle Books.
Fossum, Karin (2002), *Svarte sekunder*, Oslo: Cappelen.
——.(2009), *Varsleren*, Oslo: Cappelen.
Frank, Nino (1996), 'The crime adventure story: A new kind of detective film', in R. Barton Palmer (ed.), *Perspectives on Film Noir*, New York: G. K. Hall, pp. 21–4 [1946].
Hedling, Erik and Ann-Kristin Wallengren (eds) (2006), *Solskenslandet: Svensk film på 2000-talet*, Stockholm: Atlantis.
Hjort, Mette (2005), *Small Nation, Global Cinema: The New Danish Cinema*, Minneapolis, MN: University of Minnesota Press, 2005.
Iversen, Gunnar (2011), *Norsk filmhistorie: spillefilmen 1911-2011*, Oslo: Universitetsforlag.
Krokstäde, Mia (2010), 'Little Miss Lonely: Style and sexuality in *Flicka och hyacinter*', in Anders Marklund and Mariah Larsson (eds), *Swedish Film: An Introduction and Reader*, Lund: Nordic Academic Press, pp. 161-8.
Kulick, Don (2005), 'Four hundred thousand Swedish perverts', *GLQ: A Journal of Lesbian and Gay Studies* 11(2), 205-35.
Lapidus, Jens (2008), *Snabba Cash: Hatet, rivet, jakten*, Stockholm: Månpocket [2006].
——.(2008), *Aldrig fucka upp*, Stockholm: Wahlström & Widstrand.
——.(2011), *Livet deluxe*, Stockholm: Wahlström & Widstrand.
Larsen, Jan Kornum (2003), 'A conversation between Jan Kornum Larsen and Lars von Trier', in Jan Lumholdt (ed.), *Lars von Trier: Interviews*, Jackson, MS: University of Mississippi Press, pp. 32–46.
Larsson, Stieg (2005), *Män som hatar kvinnor* [*The Girl with the Dragon Tattoo*], Stockholm: Norstedts.
——.(2006), *Flickan som lekte med elden* [*The Girl who Played with Fire*], Stockholm: Norstedts.
——.(2007) *Luftslottet som sprängdes* [*The Girl who Kicked the Hornets' Nest*], Stockholm: Norstedts.
Lehtolainen, Leena (1997), *Kuolemanspiraali*, Helsinki: Tammi.
Luhr, William (2012), *Film Noir*, Malden, MA: Wiley-Blackwell.
Mankell, Henning (1995), *Villospår*, Stockholm: Ordfront.
Moen, Arve (1957), *Woman and Eros*, trans. Christopher Norman, Oslo: Forlage Norsk Kunstreproduksjon [1947].
Naremore, James (2008), *More Than Night: Film Noir in Contexts*, revised edition, Berkeley, CA: University of California Press.
Nestingen, Andrew (2013), *The Cinema of Aki Kaurismäki: Contrarian Stories*, New York: Columbia University Press.
Nestingen, Andrew and Paula Arvas (eds) (2011), *Scandinavian Crime Fiction*, Cardiff: University of Wales Press.

Nummi, Rami (2005), 'Film noirista Suomessa', *Filmihullu* 3, 26–31.
Peacock, Steven (ed.) (2013), *Stieg Larsson's Millennium Trilogy: Interdisciplinary Approaches to Nordic Noir on Page and Screen*, New York: Palgrave Macmillan.
Persson, Magnus (2011), 'High crime in contemporary Scandinavian literature: The case of *Miss Smilla's Feeling for Snow*', in Nestingen and Arvas (eds), *Scandinavian Crime Fiction*, pp. 148–58.
Pfeil, Fred (1992), 'Home fires burning: Family noir in *Blue Velvet* and *Terminator 2*', in Joan Copjec (ed.), *Shades of Noir: A Reader*, New York: Verso, pp. 227–60.
Place, Janey (1998), 'Women in film noir', in E. Ann Kaplan (ed.), *Women in Film Noir*, London: British Film Institute, pp. 47–68.
Redvall, Eva (2010), 'Teaching screenwriting in a time of storytelling blindness: The meeting of the auteur and the screenwriting tradition in Danish film-making', *Journal of Screenwriting* 1(1), 59–81.
Schepelern, Peter (2001), 'And the winner is ...: 1980–89', in Peter Schepelern (ed.),*100- års dansk film*, Copenhagen: Rosinante, pp. 279–304.
——.(2010), 'The element of crime and punishment: Aki Kaurismäki, Lars von Trier, and the traditions of Nordic cinema', *Journal of Scandinavian Cinema* 1(1), 87–103.
Schrader, Paul (1996), 'Notes on film noir', in Alain Silver and James Ursini (eds), *Film Noir Reader*, New York: Limelight Editions, pp. 53–64 [1972].
Smith, Carrie Lee and Donna King (eds) (2012), *Men Who Hate Women and Women Who Kick Their Asses: Stieg Larsson's Millennium Trilogy in Feminist Perspective*, Nashville, TN: Vanderbilt University Press.
Sobchack, Vivian (1998), '"Lounge time": Postwar crises and the chronotope of film noir', in Nick Browne (ed.), *Refiguring American Film Genres: History and Theory*, Berkeley, CA: University of California Press, pp. 129–70.
Thorsen, Nils (2010), *Geniet: Lars von Triers liv, film og fobier*, Copenhagen: Politiken forlag.
Todorov, Tzvetan (1981), *The Poetics of Prose*, trans. Richard Howard, Ithaca, NY: Cornell University Press.
UNICEF (2013), 'Convention on the rights of the child', online at www.unicef.org/crc (accessed 30 July 2013).
Vernet, Marc (1993), 'Film noir on the edge of doom', in Copjec (ed.), *Shades of Noir*, pp. 1–32.

FILMOGRAPHY

Angst (Oddvar Bul Tuhus, N, 1976, *Anguish*)
Ariel (Aki Kaurismäki, SF, 1988)
Besættelse (Bodil Ipsen, DK, 1944, *Obsession*)
Bortreist på ubestemt tid (Pål Bang Hansen, N, 1974, *Away For an Indefinite Period*)
Bron (Måns Mårlind, Hans Rosenfeldt, Nikolaj Scherfig, DK, TV series, 2011–, *The Bridge*)
Calamari Unioni (Aki Kaurismäki, SF, 1985, *Calamari Union*)
Casque d'or (Jacques Becker, F, 1952, *Golden Marie*)
Døden er et kjærtegen (Edith Carlmar, N, 1949, *Death is a Caress*)
Double Indemnity (Billy Wilder, US, 1944)
En forbryder (Arne Weel, DK, 1941, *A Criminal*)
Europa (Lars von Trier, DK, 1991)
Flammen og citronen (Ole Christian Madsen, DK, 2008, *Flame and Citron*)
Flicka och hyacinter (Hasse Ekman, S, 1950, *Girl and Hyacinths*)
Forbrydelsen (Søren Sveistrup, DK, TV series, 2007–12, *The Killing*)

Hets (Alf Sjöberg, S, 1944, *Torment*)
Hodejegerne (Morten Tyldum, N, 2011, *Headhunters*)
Insomnia (Erik Skjoldbjærg, N, 1997)
Jeg mødte en morder (Lau Lauritzen, DK, 1943, *I Met a Murderer*)
John og Irene (Asbjørn Andersen, Anker Sørensen, DK, 1949, *John and Irene*)
Juha (Aki Kaurismäki, SF, 1999)
La Bête humaine (Jean Renoir, F, 1938, *The Human Beast*)
Laitakaupungin valot (Aki Kaurismäki, SF, 2006, *Lights in the Dusk*)
Laura (Otto Preminger, US, 1944)
Le Havre (Aki Kaurismäki, SF, 2012)
Le Quai des brumes (Marcel Carné, F, 1938, *Port of Shadows*)
Män som hatar kvinnor (Niels Arden Oplev, S, 2009, *The Girl with the Dragon Tattoo*)
Mordets melodi (Bodil Ipsen, DK, 1944, *Melody of Murder*)
Murder, My Sweet (Edward Dmytryk, US, 1944)
Nattevagten (Ole Bornedal, DK, 1994, *Nightwatch*)
Olet mennyt vereeni (Teuvo Tulio, SF, 1956, *You've Gotten Into my Blood*)
Ørnen: En krimi-odyssé (Mai Brøstrøm, Peter Thorsboe, DK, TV series, 2004–6, *The Eagle*)
Pusher (Nicholas Winding Refn, DK, 1996)
Pusher 2 (Nicholas Winding Refn, DK, 2004)
Pusher 3 (Nicholas Winding Refn, DK, 2005)
Radio tekee murron (1951, SF, Matti Kassila, *The Radio Breaks In*)
Raid (Tapio Piirainen, SF, 2003)
Rejseholdet (Søren Sveistrup, Mai Brøstrøm, Peter Thorsboe, DK, TV series, 2000–4, *Unit One*)
Reykjavik-Rotterdam (Baltasar Koramakur, I, 2008)
Rikollinen nainen (Teuvo Tulio, SF, 1952, *A Criminal Woman*)
Rikos ja rangaistus (Aki Kuarismäki, SF, 1983, *Crime and Punishment*)
Sellaisena kuin sinä minut halusit (Teuvo Tulio, SF, 1944, *Just as You Wanted Me*)
Smala Sussie (Ulf Malmros, S, 2003, *Slim Susie*)
Snabba Cash (Daniel Espinosa, S, 2011, *Easy Money*)
The Blue Dahlia (George Marshall, US, 1946)
The Element of Crime (Lars von Trier, DK, 1984)
The Postman Always Rings Twice (Tay Garnett, US, 1946)
To mistenklige personer (Tancred Ibsen, N, 1950, *Two Suspicious Characters*)
Tulitikkutehtaan tyttö (Aki Kaurismäki, SF, 1990, *The Match-Factory Girl*)
Vares: Yksityisetsivä (Aleksi Mäkelä, SF, 2004, *Vares: Private Eye*)
Varjoja paratiisissa (Aki Kaurismäki, SF, 1986, *Shadows in Paradise*)
V2: Jäätynyt enkeli (Aleksi Mäkelä, SF, 2007, *V2: Dead Angel*)

Notes

1. Barry Forshaw, *Nordic Noir: The Pocket Essential Guide to Scandinavian Crime Fiction, Film & TV* (London: Oldcastle Books, 2013).
2. Naturalism here means the literary and philosophical movements of the 1870s and 1880s. Its promulgators included, among others, Hyppolyte Taine, Émile Zola, Georg Brandes, August Strindberg and Henrik Ibsen, the last speaking to the impact of naturalism on Scandinavian culture through the so-called Modern Breakthrough of the 1870s.
3. James Naremore, *More Than Night: Film Noir in Contexts*, revised edition (Berkeley, CA: University of California Press, 2008), p. 15.

4. Rami Nummi, 'Film noirista Suomessa', *Filmihullu* 3 (2005), 26–31.
5. All translations are mine, unless otherwise noted. Nummi, 'Film noirista Suomessa', 25.
6. Paul Schrader (1996), 'Notes on film noir', in Alain Silver and James Ursini (eds), *Film Noir Reader*, New York: Limelight Editions, p. 55 [1972].
7. Elonet, Finnish Audiovisual Archive, 'Radio tekee murron', online at www.elonet.fi/fi/elokuva/112912 (accessed 6 August, 2013).
8. A noteworthy point of connection to international film noir in the case of *The Radio Breaks In* might be the radio drama or the 'radio aesthetic' of film noir. See Neil Verma, 'Radio, film noir and the aesthetics of auditory spectacle', in Robert Miklitsch (ed.), *Kiss the Blood off My Hands: Re-Screening Classic Film Noir* (Urbana, IL: University of Illinois Press, forthcoming).
9. Audun Engelstad, *Losing Streak Stories: Mapping Norwegian Film Noir* (Oslo: Faculty of Humanities, University of Oslo, 2006).
10. Ibid., p. 42.
11. Ibid., p. 43.
12. Schrader, 'Notes on film noir', pp. 55–7.
13. Engelstad, *Losing Streak Stories*, p. 37; also see Lotte Eisner, *The Haunted Screen* (Berkeley, CA: University of California Press, 1969).
14. Ibid., p. 37.
15. Ibid., p. 37.
16. Arvid Moen Moen, *Woman and Eros*, trans. Christopher Norman (Oslo: Forlage Norsk Kunstreproduksjon, 1957), p. 8 [1947]. Quoted in Engelstad, *Losing Streak Stories*, p. 61.
17. The Cain connection in *Death is a Caress* provides an interesting twist on Jennifer Fay and Justus Nielead's argument that the circulation of noir provides a form for articulating local anxieties in an international style. Jennifer Fay and Justus Nieland, *Film Noir: Hard-Boiled Modernity and the Cultures of Globalization* (New York: Routledge, 2010), p. xi.
18. Engelstad, *Losing Streak Stories*, p. 58.
19. Gunnar Iversen, *Norsk filmhistorie: Spillefilmen 1911–2011* (Oslo: Universitetsforlag, 2011), p. 166.
20. Ibid., pp. 59–61.
21. Engelstad, *Losing Streak Stories*, p. 85.
22. Ibid., p. 85.
23. Raymond Chandler, 'The simple art of murder', in *Raymond Chandler: Later Novels and Other Writings*, ed. Frank McShane (New York: Library of America, 1995), p. 991.
24. Engelstad, *Losing Streak Stories*, pp. 85–8.
25. Daniel Brodén, *Folkhemmets skuggbilder: En kulturanalytisk genrestudie i svensk kriminalfiktion i film och TV* (Stockholm: Ekholm & Tegebjer, 2008). The title translates as 'Dark Shadows Over the People's Home: A Culture Genre History of Crime Fiction in Swedish Film and Television'.
26. Dudley Andrew, *Mists of Regret: Culture and Sensibility in Classic French Film* (Princeton, NJ: Princeton University Press, 1995).
27. Mia Krokstäde, 'Little Miss Lonely: Style and sexuality in *Flicka och hyacinter*', in Anders Marklund and Mariah Larsson (eds), *Swedish Film: An Introduction and Reader* (Lund: Nordic Academic Press), p. 162.
28. Ibid., pp. 165–6.
29. Ibid., p. 167.
30. Ibid., p. 167.
31. Naremore, *More Than Night*, p. 222.

32. Ib Bondebjerg, *Filmen og det moderne* (Copenhagen: Gyldendal, 2005); Eva Jørholt, 'Voksen, følsom og elegant', in Peter Schepelern (ed.), *100-års dansk film* (Copenhagen: Rosinante, 2001), pp. 121–64; Rune Christensen, 'Local inflections of darkness: Danish film noir during the classical noir cycle (unpublished dissertation, University of California, Davis, 2009), pp. 10–15.
33. Jørholt, 'Voksom, følsom og elegant', pp. 131–2.
34. Bondebjerg, *Filmen og det moderne*, p. 274.
35. Christensen's translation of Bondebjerg, *Filmen og det moderne*, p. 274, quoted in Christensen, *Local Inflections of Darkness*, p. 13.
36. Christensen, *Local Inflections of Darkness*, p. 25.
37. Ibid., p. 39.
38. Ibid., p. 25.
39. Mette Hjort, *Small Nation, Global Cinema: The New Danish Cinema* (Minneapolis, MN: University of Minnesota Press, 2005); Eva Novrup Redvall, 'Teaching screenwriting in a time of storytelling blindness: The meeting of the auteur and the screenwriting tradition in Danish film-making', *Journal of Screenwriting* 1(1) (2010), 59–81.
40. Iversen, *Norsk filmhistorie*; Audun Engelstad, 'Dealing with crime: Cyclic changes in Norwegian crime films', *Journal of Scandinavian Cinema* 1(2) (2011), 205–10; Kimmo Ahonen, Janne Rosenquist, Juha Rosenquist and Päivi Valotie (eds), *Taju kankaalle: Uutta suomalaista elokuvaa paikantamassa* (Turku: Kirja-Aurora, 2003); Erik Hedling and Ann-Kristin Wallengren (eds), *Solskenslandet: Svensk film på 2000-talet* (Stockholm: Atlantis, 2006).
41. Paula Arvas and Andrew Nestingen, 'Introduction: Contemporary Scandinavian crime fiction', in Andrew Nestingen and Paula Arvas (eds), *Scandinavian Crime Fiction* (Cardiff: University of Wales Press), pp. 1–17.
42. Magnus Persson, 'High crime in contemporary Scandinavian literature: The case of *Miss Smilla's Feeling for Snow*', in Nestingen and Arvas (eds), *Scandinavian Crime Fiction*, pp. 148–58.
43. Barry Foreshaw, *Nordic Noir: The Pocket Essential Guide to Scandinavian Crime Fiction, Film & TV* (London: Oldcastle Books, 2013).
44. Naremore, *More than Night*, pp. 9–11; Marc Vernet, 'Film noir on the edge of doom', in Joan Copjec (ed.), *Shades of Noir: A Reader* (New York: Verso, 1993), p. 2; Fred Pfeil, 'Home fires burning: Family noir in *Blue Velvet* and *Terminator 2*', in Copjec (ed.), *Shades of Noir*, pp. 227–8.
45. Mark Bould, Kathrina Glitre and Greg Tuck, 'Parallax views: An introduction', in Mark Bould, Kathrina Glitre and Greg Tuck (eds), *Neo-Noir* (New York: Wallflower, 2009), pp. 4–5); Naremore, *More than Night*, p. 11.
46. Naremore, *More than Night*, p. 11.
47. Nino Frank, 'The crime adventure story: A new kind of detective film', in R. Barton Palmer (ed.), *Perspectives on Film Noir* (New York: G.K. Hall, 1996), p. 22 [1946]; quoted in Christensen, *Local Inflections of Darkness*, p. 16.
48. Tzvetan Todorov, *The Poetics of Prose*, trans. Richard Howard (Ithaca, NY: Cornell University Press, 1981), p. 44.
49. William Luhr, *Film Noir* (Malden, MA: Wiley-Blackwell, 2012), pp. 4–5.
50. Joan Copjec, 'The phenomenal and nonphenomenal: Private space in *film noir*', in Copjec (ed.), *Shades of Noir*, p. 194.
51. Engelstad, *Losing Streak Stories*, p. 121.
52. Stieg Larsson, *Män som hatar kvinnor* [*The Girl with the Dragon Tattoo*] (Stockholm: Norstedts, 2005); Stieg Larsson, *Flickan som lekte med elden* [*The Girl who Played with Fire*] (Stockholm: Norstedts, 2006); Stieg Larsson, *Luftslottet som sprängdes* [*The Girl who Kicked the Hornets' Nest*] (Stockholm: Norstedts, 2007).

53. Henning Mankell, *Villospår [Sidetracked]* (Stockholm: Ordfront, 1995).
54. Karin Fossum, *Svarte sekunder* (Oslo: Cappelen, 2002); Karin Fossum, *Varsleren* (Oslo: Cappelen, 2009).
55. Leena Lehtolainen, *Kuolemanspiraali* (Helsinki: Tammi, 1997).
56. Vivian Sobchack, '"Lounge time": Postwar crises and the chronotope of film noir', in Nick Browne (ed.), *Refiguring American Film Genres: History and Theory*, (Berkeley, CA: University of California Press, 1998), p. 143.
57. Ibid., p. 144.
58. Ibid., pp. 157–8.
59. Sylvia Harvey, 'Woman's place: The absent family of film noir', in E. Ann Kaplan (ed.), *Women in Film Noir* (London: British Film Institute, 1998), p. 36.
60. Jens Lapidus, *Snabba Cash: Hatet, Rivet, Jakten* (Stockholm: Månpocket, 2008); Jens Lapidus, *Aldrig fucka upp* (Stockholm: Wahlström & Widstrand, 2008); Jens Lapidus, *Livet deluxe* (Stockholm: Wahlström & Widstrand, 2011).
61. Harvey, 'Woman's place', pp. 36–9.
62. UNICEF (2013), 'Convention on the rights of the child,' online at www.unicef.org/crc (accessed 30 July 2013).
63. Ibid.
64. Don Kulick,'Four hundred thousand Swedish perverts', *GLQ: A Journal of Lesbian and Gay Studies* 11(2) (2005), 205–35.
65. Janey Place, 'Women in film noir', in Kaplan (ed.), *Women in Film Noir*, pp. 47–68.
66. Carrie Lee Smith and Donna King (eds), *Men Who Hate Women and Women Who Kick Their Asses: Stieg Larsson's Millennium Trilogy in Feminist Perspective* (Nashville, TN: Vanderbilt University Press, 2012); Barry Forshaw, *Death in a Cold Climate: A Guide to Scandinavian Crime Fiction* (New York: Palgrave Macmillan, 2012); Steven Peacock (ed.), *Stieg Larsson's Millennium Trilogy: Interdisciplinary Approaches to Nordic Noir on Page and Screen* (New York: Palgrave Macmillan, 2013); Forshaw, *Nordic Noir*; Nestingen and Arvas (eds), *Scandinavian Crime Fiction*.
67. Peter Schepelern, 'The element of crime and punishment: Aki Kaurismäki, Lars von Trier, and the traditions of Nordic Cinema', *Journal of Scandinavian Cinema* 1(1) (2011), 91.
68. Jan Kornum Larsen, 'A conversation between Jan Kornum Larsen and Lars von Trier', in Jan Lumholdt (ed.), *Lars von Trier: Interviews* (Jackson, MS: University of Mississippi Press, 2003) p. 43.
69. Linda Badley, *Lars von Trier* (Urbana, IL: University of Illinois Press, 2009), p. 23; also see Caroline Bainbridge, *The Cinema of Lars von Trier: Authenticity and Artifice* (London: Wallflower, 2007), pp. 26–32.
70. Bould, Glitre and Tuck, 'Parallax views', p. 5.
71. Nils Thorsen, *Geniet: Lars von Triers liv, film og fobier* (Copenhagen: Politiken forlag, 2009), p. 176. My translation; italics in original. The words 'love' and 'no future' are in English in the original.
72. Andrew Nestingen, *The Cinema of Aki Kaurismäki: Contrarian Stories* (New York: Columbia University Press, 2013), p. 68.

8. INDIAN FILM NOIR

Corey K. Creekmur

Has the Indian film industry – often identified as the world's largest – produced film noir? Pursuing an answer to this seemingly straightforward question may require, like the tangled plots of many noir films, tracing a forward path through a series of flashbacks and unexpected detours. Most claims for the existence of non-Hollywood film noir are relatively recent, reinforcing the fundamental historical circumstance succinctly emphasised by Tom Gunning: 'Film noir may be the great achievement of film studies'.[1] Indeed, any attempt to expand the international purview of film noir, once viewed as distinctly and exclusively American (despite recognisable European roots), cannot ignore the nagging reminder that film noir was discovered – if not wholly invented – by film critics rather than the Hollywood studio filmmakers making movies they and their initial audiences would have readily identified as thrillers, detective stories or mysteries, among other more familiar genre terms.[2] As has been the case elsewhere, the designation or categorisation of a group of films as 'Indian film noir' is emphatically retroactive, a critical act of explicit historical reclassification that may ultimately be as misleading as illuminating. In fact, as Nikki J. Y. Lee and Julian Stringer have warned, the larger, now commonly invoked category of 'Asian noir' may be no more than a 'dubiously unifying concept', 'a mere category of convenience behind which lurk a range of more stubbornly complex stories concerning the historically specific characteristics of multiple regional film industries'.[3] If we belatedly locate examples of Indian film noir, we must also acknowledge the historical and cultural conditions that now allow us to do so, decades after the films we seek to make comprehensible through this category were made and enjoyed: in short, any responsible claim for the existence of Indian film noir must waver with critical uncertainty.

Nevertheless, while crime stories, as elsewhere, have been an unsurprisingly common component of Indian popular cinema, contemporary critics have, if only in passing, increasingly attributed a 'darker' aspect to a portion of India's vast corpus of films, thereby affiliating these recently retrieved examples with Hollywood and other commercial national cinemas, in effect constructing a comparative perspective that retrospectively 'corrects' the absence of popular Indian cinema from most historical accounts of world cinema until the 1990s. Now that popular Indian cinema has secured a place in this expanded history, perhaps, it appears, there once was Indian film noir too. For instance, in the groundbreaking *Encyclopedia of Indian Cinema* (first published in 1994, and revised in 1999), the Hindi film *Baazi* (*Wager*, Guru Dutt, 1951) is described as 'a confident assimilation of the Warner Bros. noir style, esp. in the lighting, the camera placements and the editing'.[4] Elsewhere, the *Encyclopedia* says, of *Bambai Ka Babu* (*Gentleman from Bombay*, Raj Khosla, 1960), 'After the film's noirish beginning, as in so many Dev Anand starrers, it turns into a romance'.[5] Such claims are infrequent and notably hesitant assertions of the approximation of film noir in Indian cinema, allowing at most 'noirish assimilation' rather than the real thing. Similarly tentative claims can be found throughout the first wave of serious scholarship on Indian popular film, which was simultaneously attentive to a large body of previously neglected examples while in dialogue with the Western cinephilia that had canonised film noir in the development of the discipline of film studies. Thus Ravi Vasudevan, emphasising the symbolic function of the city street in 1950s Hindi cinema 'as the space of the dissolution of social identity', links key Indian examples of what he labels 'crime melodramas' to 'the glistening rain-drenched streets so familiar from the American *film noir*'.[6] Jyotika Virdi is similarly circumspect when noting 'noir lighting' in Bimal Roy's *Madhumati* (1958),[7] or when she claims that Raj Khosla's *C.I.D.* (1956) is 'fashioned after noir thrillers both in form and content' and 'visibly influenced by noir films'.[8] Such claims are telling in their willingness to acknowledge the evident influence of film noir on Hindi cinema, but they also stop short of declaring as film noir these specific Indian films.

More recently, however, as the possibility of viewing film noir as a genuinely transnational phenomenon has been more widely asserted and accepted, it seems that such hesitation is fading. For instance, in a recent book centred upon Mumbai's history as a prominent film location, Ranjani Mazumdar briefly cites a few historical precursors from the 1940s and 1950s featuring 'the expressionistic lighting common to noir', before crediting a cycle of contemporary (post-1989) Hindi crime and gangster films with instantiating 'Mumbai Noir', a term that, she notes, 'only gained currency in the 1990s after the release of a few landmark films that directly drew on the stories of the underworld'.[9] (I, perhaps pedantically, think these films may more accurately be identified as 'neo-noir', and will discuss them as such later in this chapter.) Another recent volume, the lavishly illustrated *Bollywood Posters*, with commentary by the prominent Indian film journalist Jerry Pinto, contains a section on crime films, among other prominent genres. After summarising earlier Indian sound films as 'morality plays' that 'gave cinematic expression to the idea of the struggle between good and evil', Pinto boldly announces: 'When film noir arrived, things began to change somewhat'. After citing *Kismet* (1943), an important and wildly popular pre-independence crime film, as a prototype, Pinto asserts that 'It was only in the 1950s that Bollywood began to develop the outlines of its own version of noir'.[10] In these more recent examples of criticism, Indian film noir is more confidently asserted than hesitantly pondered, ostensibly confirming what others have wondered: whether film noir, even in its early, 'classical' phase (roughly 1941–58), was already a transnational cultural phenomenon, extending not only to somewhat expected locations like France, Great Britain and Germany but even to South Asia. Whether earlier, in the Indian film industry, or only lately, in Indian film criticism, film noir appears to have finally 'arrived'.

However, perhaps the sort of caution glimpsed in earlier criticism is still warranted: to simply, belatedly affirm the existence of Indian film noir too easily avoids implicit and crucial questions regarding the ways we understand the cultural functions of film styles or genres, the shaping role of film criticism upon film history and especially the ideological implications of locating transnational film genres within the larger bodies of national cinemas, with the latter an especially complex category in relation to India, which has produced both art and popular cinema from its multiple regions and in multiple languages, both under colonial rule and, since 1947, as an independent nation.[11] What conceptual negotiations are involved in at last locating a form of popular American cinema first identified by French critics within South Asian cinema, otherwise marked by distinct cultural traditions and stylistic conventions? Claims for non-Hollywood film noir tend to challenge older models of cultural imperialism that viewed the international circulation and impact of Hollywood cinema as unidirectional and simply oppressive: rather, as Andrew Spicer writes with reference to European cinemas, 'although European film noirs have characteristics that are specific to their national cultural formation, each has been profoundly affected, in various ways, by American noir, in a complex, two-way process that ranges from imitation to radical originality via all shades of hybridity'.[12] Similarly, Jennifer Fay and Justus Nieland argue 'that film noir is best appreciated as an always international phenomenon concerned with the local effects of globalization and the threats to national urban culture it seeks to herald'.[13] If (to raise the persistent question) film noir is a genre, and an international or transnational genre at that, then how does it intersect with the 'local' genres most often associated with popular Indian cinema, especially the 'social', the broad category for films concerned with the problems of contemporary life (as opposed to the 'historical', centred on the past, or the 'mythological', depicting the 'eternal' stories of Hindu gods and goddesses)? If it is no longer common to view film noir as fundamentally or exclusively an American genre, the specific characteristics of an Indian strain of film noir remain rather elusive.

Film Noir in Bombay

At first glance, the most obvious evidence for a 'vernacular' Indian film noir would seem to rest with a number of films themselves, produced simultaneously with the later phase of Hollywood film noir, during the period now mythologised as the 'golden age' of Hindi cinema. A cycle of popular Hindi films, almost all set in (then) contemporary Bombay, regularly featured many of the characteristic elements of Hollywood film noir, including heroes (most consistently embodied throughout the period by the suave star Dev Anand) who skirt the border of legal and illegal activity; like their counterparts in American film noir, these are men who are streetwise but can confidentially negotiate swanky nightclubs featuring alluring femmes fatales (often explicitly Westernised through signifiers such as clothing, smoking and the use of English) as well as the semi-illicit temptations of alcohol and gambling. Such films often take the time to foreground the luxury objects that signalled cosmopolitanism and (Western-style) sophistication in the decade following independence, including telephones, whisky, cars and Western fashion. Perhaps even more significantly, a large number of these films employ many of the stylistic elements associated with noir, such as location shooting (with prominent Bombay icons featured), chiaroscuro lighting producing expressive shadows, unusual camera angles and tangled plots that rely upon narrative devices such as flashbacks and dream sequences (often in the form of the elaborate song sequences, or 'picturisations', that became a defining feature of popular Indian cinema, across all genres, with the arrival of sound). Simply put, a significant number of popular Hindi films from the Bombay industry in the first decade or so following independence look a lot like the distinctive American examples that motivated French critics to isolate film noir as a distinctive type of movie.

Indeed, as in Hollywood cinema, even Hindi films preceding and those most readily aligned with American film noir suggest precedents and 'family resemblances' rather than a complete overlap with the genre: producer-director-actor Raj Kapoor, the key figure of post-independence Hindi cinema, launched his successful career as a director with a series of films – *Aag* (*Fire*, 1948), *Barsaat* (*Rain*, 1949) and *Awara* (*The Vagabond*, 1951) – that rely extensively on moody, expressionistic black-and-white cinematography, even if their narrative elements don't suggest film noir as much as its close Hollywood relatives, the Gothic romance or melodrama. The slightly later, now-classic films of producer-director-star Guru Dutt, especially *Pyaasa* (*Thirst*, 1957) and *Kaagaz Ke Phool* (*Paper Flowers*, 1959), also rely extensively on 'noirish' dramatic high-contrast lighting and expressionistic camerawork, as well as elaborate flashback structures, but again do not otherwise evoke the familiar content of film noir, although the intensely self-reflexive *Kaagaz Ke Phool*, the story of a film director's rise and fall, suggests a Bombay variation on self-reflexive and cynical Hollywood-centred film noir such as Billy Wilder's *Sunset Blvd.* (1950).

More direct support for identifying a cycle of Hindi film noir arrives on the heels of Raj Kapoor's first films, with prominent examples like *Baazi* (*Wager*, 1951), Guru Dutt's debut as a director for the production company Navketan, launched in 1949 by brothers Chetan Anand and Dev Anand as the latter was developing a screen persona that offered Bombay's closest equivalent to the image of Humphrey Bogart. Like Bogart, Dev Anand often portrayed a loner without evident family ties – almost unthinkable for previous Indian heroes – whose moral compass was allowed to waver and even step outside the law if social justice could not be served otherwise. *Baazi* opens with a deck of cards being cut and dealt in a seedy gambling den, but quickly elevates its lucky hero Madan (Dev Anand) into a more elegant – but still dimly lit – nightclub run by a mysterious 'Boss' who (like Dr Mabuse) remains obscured in deep shadow for most of the film. Cars, cigarettes, Western clothing and a singing vamp (Geeta Bali) who literally ensnares the hero in her web are all prominently displayed within the first few minutes of the film, providing an aura of both unsavoury urban decadence and titillating, illicit pleasures.

Figure 8.1   Dev Anand listens to Geeta Bali play in *Baazi*.

Eventually, Madan will be falsely accused of the murder of the sympathetic vamp, and the identity of the 'Boss' will be exposed in a surprising revelation that will allow Madan's courtship of a beautiful doctor after he serves a short prison sentence for his minor transgressions. In effect, *Baazi*, like many other films to follow, resembles Hollywood film noir on its surface but not at its heart (*dil*, a key term in Hindi cinema): for reasons that will be touched upon shortly, the grim and cynical plots and shockingly 'unhappy endings' that often made Hollywood film noir appear to violate the conventions of the very system that produced it remain generally inconceivable in post-independence India. The goals of creating rather than destroying the romantic couple, and restoring rather than undermining social order drive films like *Baazi*, even if they revel in the dangers of modern urban India along the way.

Following *Baazi*, the crime film become a speciality at Navketan, whose titles throughout the 1950s – *Taxi Driver* (Chetan Anand, 1954), *House No. 44* (M. K. Burman, 1955), *Kala Pani* (*Black Water*, Raj Khosla, 1958), and *Kala Bazar* (*Black Market*, Vijay Anand, 1960) – solidified the banner's association with stories set in stylish urban settings. Other notable 'noirish' crime films from other production houses during the period include *C.I.D.* (Raj Khosla, 1956), *Howrah Bridge* (Shakti Samanta, 1958), *Post Box 999* (Ravindra Dave, 1958), *Guest House* (Ravindra Dave, 1959), *Bambai Ka Babu* (*Gentleman from Bombay*, Raj Khosla, 1960), *Jaali Note* (*Counterfeit Bill*, Shakti Samantha, 1960) and *China Town* (Shakti Samanta, 1962). As M. K. Ragavendra notes, the 'strange fascination' with the city central to all of these films 'is also evidenced by the numerous films of the period that proclaim themselves through English titles, terms with urban associations'.[14] Indeed, the persistent, even fetishised urban setting of such films is arguably the element that links them most significantly to the transnational tradition of film noir: their regular location in Bombay (with some exceptions, including Calcutta) might even justify the specification of 'Bombay film noir' as a more accurate term than a broader 'Indian' film noir. Again, frequent location shooting or at least inserted documentary footage (often used explicitly to introduce the location) of prominent Bombay landmarks is a common attraction. As Raghavendra emphasises, this love-hate relationship with the city of Bombay both relies upon and challenges the common assumption that 'authentic' Indian tradition and identity are associated with the village, not the city where, again, English often marks the space as 'foreign'. Although a vision of the future Indian city was central to Prime Minister Jawaharlal Nehru's ambitious plans for the modernisation of the newly independent nation, Bombay retained an aura of worldly decadence and inevitable corruption that could be exploited by filmmakers throughout the 'Nehruvian' period. Movement from the village to the city frequently serves as a moral test for characters in Indian cinema of the period, with the typical film hero carefully balanced between the 'timeless', traditional values of the village and the undeniably attractive modern style of the city – much like the position of cinema itself in its frequent attempt to invoke authentic 'Indian' narratives within a medium and technology that was inevitably modern, urban and Western.

If the regular focus on Bombay grounds Indian gestures towards film noir, the postwar ennui that underlies the darkest Hollywood film noir (so often noted by scholars attempting to explain the genre's social origins) and the semi-official, nationalist optimism of India in the wake of independence under the influence of Nehruvian progress are starkly opposed. Whereas Hollywood film noir is often striking in its rejection of Hollywood's penchant for happy endings that join (rather than destroy) romantic couples, Hindi cinema produced in the same era cannot so readily displace optimism with cynicism. More often than not in popular Indian cinema of the period, heroes triumph and couples overcome the obstacles that have prevented their happiness until the final reel. The corruption that is often revealed at the heart of the city is exposed and presumably vanquished for a brighter future. In this regard, the assimilation of film noir in 1950s Hindi cinema arguably reaches its ideological limit and inevitably appears naive when placed against Hollywood's increasingly brutal products.

There is also, perhaps, another important way in which the darkest moods of Hollywood film noir could not be wholly imported into popular Indian cinema: in summarising the early sequences of *Baazi* earlier, I neglected to add that, a short while into the narrative, a wholly expected thing in popular Indian cinema happens: the gambler hero of the film sings a song. (More accurately, the hero mimics a song performed by an unseen but more often than not famous 'playback singer', a formal arrangement known to all Indian audiences, in contrast to Hollywood's rigorous obscuring of the traces of such dubbing practices.) Moreover, he sings a song about money while wandering among the city's sleeping pavement-dwellers, a 'realistic' element indicative of modern urban life that provides a vivid contrast to the choreographed stylisation of the performed musical number. Among the most important and lasting conventions of Indian popular cinema, the organisation of film narratives around a series of choreographed song sequences disallows any straightforward transposition of Hollywood genre categories to Indian film. Films that might otherwise be identified as socials, historicals or mythologicals, or via Western terms such as thrillers, romances or comedies, all contain songs (a 'requirement' that moreover renders any distinct genre of the musical unnecessary in India). While song performances are, in fact, fairly common in Hollywood film noir, they are usually reserved for 'realistic' locations like nightclubs, and are rarely featured more than once in a film. Whereas Indian viewers expect songs in virtually all popular films as a primary attraction, many Western viewers are startled to encounter, for instance, singing and dancing detectives or gangsters in Indian crime films. However, if the inclusion of song sequences can be reconciled with crime narratives, one recognises that Indian filmmakers often approached this apparent discordant mix with wit and ingenuity (as well as more formulaic sequences, of course). Indeed, 1950s Indian crime films provided some of the era's most popular hit songs: if film noir can be located in India, it is song-filled. If a song-filled movie cannot be acknowledged as film noir, then, once again, the claim of Indian film noir may be untenable.

Mumbai Neo-noir

If the status of film noir in the 'golden age' of Hindi cinema necessarily remains unstable, confirming the active presence of neo-noir in contemporary Indian film seems secure. India's increasingly globalised media landscape and relatively easy access to diverse examples of international cinema (whether legal or not) via a range of video formats has permitted Indian filmmakers as well as their audiences to view many of the American, East Asian and European crime films critics have identified as neo-noir.[15] (Among other things, Indian cinema paralleled most of the rest of the world by making the virtually complete shift from black-and-white to colour film stock by the end of the 1960s.) Even somewhat earlier, since the mid-1970s, representations of Bombay's criminal underworld and the glamorous if doomed lives of gangland 'dons' and '*goondas*' (gangsters) had become staples of Hindi cinema.[16] The latter half of the decade was especially dominated by a series of films featuring superstar Amitabh Bachchan in his wildly popular 'angry young man' persona. Although a populist anti-hero and even a sympathetic criminal in most of his key films, his breakthrough role was as a wronged police inspector in *Zanjeer* (*Chains*, Prakash Mehra, 1973), while he was unambiguously a gangster in *Deewar* (*The Wall*, Yash Chopra, 1975) and a petty thief in *Sholay* (*Flames*, Ramesh Sippy, 1975), among the most successful and influential films in the history of Hindi cinema. However, even Bachchan films set more directly in the underworld, such as *Don* (1978), where he plays the double role (an Indian film tradition) of a crime lord and his innocent doppelganger, seem only vaguely affiliated with the stylistic elements of film noir that can be located in earlier Hindi cinema: indeed, the Bachchan vehicles of the 1970s are a reminder that the gangster film, in India and elsewhere, has typically been viewed as a distinct genre, lacking many of the elements associated with film noir despite their shared basis in crime stories. The 'Bachchan phenomenon' – the virtual domination of the cinema by the star during an especially volatile period in Indian history, most notably Prime Minister Indira Gandhi's 'Emergency' from 1975 to 1977, when elections and civil liberties were suspended – has received extensive commentary within Indian film studies, but seems on the whole a tangential link to any 'tradition' of Indian film noir.[17] Rather, after decades of popular romantic films featuring female leads, the massive success of his films seems to have solidified the centrality of the male star in action-driven films, often but not necessarily built around crime elements, in the last decades of twentieth-century popular Indian cinema.

Neo-noir thus arrives in India more fully following the period of Bachchan's dominance, through a remarkable series of gangster films that re-energised the genre in India. Beginning with director Mani Ratnam's influential Tamil film *Nayakan* (*Hero*, 1987), starring South Indian superstar Kamal Hassan and partially inspired by *The Godfather* (1972), and followed by Vidhu Vinod Chopra's *Parinda* (*Bird*, 1989), the contemporary gangster film signalled by these examples immediately appeared more realistic and more brutal than its predecessors. Soon thereafter, a loose trilogy of stylishly directed films by Ram Gopal Varma – *Satya* (1998), *Company* (2002) and the less successful *D* (2005) – were built upon their audience's knowledge that the characters and events onscreen closely resembled the well-publicised and notorious offscreen gangsters and crimes that had in some cases infiltrated the film world: among other self-reflexive moments, *Satya* features a shooting at a crowded cinema and *Company* depicts an assassination on a film set. Whereas the gangsters in *Satya* are on the lower or perhaps middle rungs of the underworld hierarchy (albeit with links to powerful political figures), *Company* and *D* (named after the infamous D-Company led by actual crime boss Dawood Ibrahim, the model for a number of recent cinematic interpretations) are more 'globalised', as dangerous for the killings they arrange via their mobile phones as with guns. (*Satya* is the film often cited as the first example of 'Mumbai noir'. Once again, I am arguing that the historical specificity of the now widespread term 'neo-noir' is more appropriate for such post-classical examples.) Again, as in critical discussions of the Hollywood cinema that has sometimes inspired such films – both *Parinda* and Ram Gopal Varma's *Sarkar* (2005) and its sequel *Sarkar Raj* (2008) borrow rather obviously, if often inventively, from *The Godfather* – the gangster film might be distinguished from most examples of film noir, despite family resemblances. Amidst this revival of the Hindi gangster film, among the more inventive recent examples is a pair adapted from Shakespeare: Vishal Bharadwaj transforms *Macbeth* into *Maqbool* (2004) and *Othello* into *Omkara* (2006), with surprisingly effective connections between the original characters and their contemporary underworld avatars. Other contemporary Hindi neo-noir films typically rely on less elevated and more recent sources: the heist film *Kaante* (*Thorns*, 2002), directed by Sanjay Gupta and shot entirely in Los Angeles with a cast of prominent male stars, draws rather obviously upon Quentin Tarantino's *Reservoir Dogs* (1992), Bryan Singer's *The Usual Suspects* (1995) and Michael Mann's *Heat* (1995) to construct its convoluted bank robbery plot: such 'borrowing', which often skirts the legal niceties of an official remake, has become common in contemporary Hindi cinema, and is often cited by critics to decry the industry's lack of originality: in other cases, the act of 'translation' results in witty and perceptive hybrids. Perhaps the full arrival of an arguably more creative, highly self-reflexive, postmodernist variation on neo-noir is best represented by *Johnny Gaddaar* (*Johnny Traitor*, 2007), directed by Sriram Raghavan.[18] The flamboyantly stylised film, organised in an intricate but playful flashback structure, is packed with allusions to both Hindi cinema – the title invokes Vijay Anand's *Johny Mera Naam* (*My Name is Johnny*, 1970) – as well as Hollywood film noir, including Stanley Kubrick's *The Killing* (1956). Much like Quentin Tarantino's collage-like neo-noir films, *Johnny Gaddaar* presumes an increasingly cine-literate viewer, not only familiar with the 'classics' it quotes relentlessly, but equally attentive to the hyperkinetic and foregrounded formal techniques in the film. Most significantly, the film assumes viewers whose cinephilia is global as well as 'local', as adept at catching a witty reference to Brian De Palma's *Scarface* (1983) or Orson Welles' *Citizen Kane* (1941) as to Jyoti Swaroop's Hindi thriller *Parwana* (*Moth*, 1971), which featured Amitabh Bachchan in one of his first villain roles. Such films, increasingly common from younger Indian filmmakers, increasingly take for granted that their audiences (at home and abroad) are savvy consumers of a wide range of global media, rather than the mass audience which filmmakers once seemed to treat as naive spectators of the exotic, unattainable world on Indian screens.

Notes

1. Tom Gunning, 'More than night: Film noir in its contexts' (book review), *Modernism/modernity* 6(3) (1999), 151.
2. The argument for identifying non-Hollywood film noir (and neo-noir) in five European countries is outlined carefully in the editor's 'Introduction' to Andrew Spicer (ed.), *European Film Noir* (Manchester: Manchester University Press, 2007), while Jennifer Fay and Justus Nieland, *Film Noir: Hard-Boiled Modernity and the Cultures of Globalization* (New York: Routledge, 2010) centres on 'film noir as an always international phenomenon concerned with the local effects of globalization and the threats to national urban culture it seems to herald' (p. ix). Their study locates examples of film noir in the United States, Europe, Asia (including India, via a single film) and Latin America. On the other hand, Spencer Selby, *The Worldwide Film Noir Tradition* (Ames, IA: Sink Press, 2013) lists films from almost two dozen countries (including India, with six titles) as examples of film noir, but provides virtually no critical justification for its selections.
3. Nikki J. Y. Lee and Julian Stringer, 'Film noir in Asia: Historicizing South Korean crime thrillers', in Andrew Spicer and Helen Hanson (eds), *Companion to Film Noir* (New York: Wiley-Blackwell, 2013), p. 502. In the same volume, Lalitha Gopalan's illuminating essay on what she terms 'Bombay Noir' begins with an even more bold warning: 'Looking for film noir in India is to miss the point of Indian cinema altogether'. See Lalitha Gopalan, 'Bombay Noir', p. 518.
4. Ashish Rajadhyaksha and Paul Willemen (eds), *Encyclopedia of Indian Cinema: New Revised Edition* (London: British Film Institute, 1999), p. 322.
5. Ibid., p. 362.

6. Ravi S. Vasudevan, 'Shifting codes, dissolving identities: The Hindi social film of the 1950s as popular culture', in Ravi S. Vasudevan (ed.), *Making Meaning in Indian Cinema* (New Delhi: Oxford University Press, 2000), p. 110.
7. Jyotika Virdi, *The Cinematic ImagiNation: Indian Popular Films as Social History* (New Brunswick: Rutgers University Press, 2003), p. 51.
8. Ibid., pp. 100–1. Virdi mistakenly identifies producer Guru Dutt rather than Raj Khosla as the director of *C.I.D.*, although claiming Dutt's influence on the style of the film seems reasonable.
9. Ranjani Mazumdar, 'Mumbai Noir: An uncanny present', in Helio San Miguel (ed.), *World Film Locations: Mumbai* (New York: Intellect, 2012), p. 68.
10. Jerry Pinto and Sheena Sippy, *Bollywood Posters* (Mumbai: India Book House, 2008), pp. 60–1. As has become common in writing on Hindi cinema, Pinto retroactively names the earlier film industry 'Bollywood', a practice I and other critics find historically misleading.
11. This essay concentrates on the large popular Hindi-language cinema produced in Bombay (now Mumbai), now commonly and somewhat controversially identified as 'Bollywood'. (The retroactive designation of earlier Hindi cinema as 'Bollywood' cinema is an especially misleading historical inaccuracy.) I also refer to Bombay for the period before 1995, when the name of the city was officially changed to Mumbai, although the older name remains in common use. Increased critical attention is now being paid to India's many so-called 'regional' cinemas, including the Tamil and Telugu industries, which are often as large as the Hindi cinema: whether early examples from these cinemas might be reasonably associated with film noir remains to be argued.
12. Andrew Spicer, *European Film Noir*, p. 1.
13. Jennifer Fay and Justus Nieland, *Film Noir*, p. ix.
14. M. K. Raghavendra, *Seduced by the Familiar: Narration and Meaning in Indian Popular Cinema* (New Delhi: Oxford University Press, 2008), p. 134.
15. On neo-noir as an international phenomenon, see David Desser, 'Global noir: Genre film in the age of transnationalism', in Barry Keith Grant (ed.), *Film Genre Reader IV* (Austin, TX: University of Texas Press), pp. 628–48, and a number of the essays in Mark Bould, Kathrina Glitre and Greg Tuck (eds), *Neo-Noir* (London: Wallflower, 2009). Neither of these texts includes examples from Indian cinema.
16. I discuss contemporary Hindi gangster films in Corey K. Creekmur, 'Bombay Bhai: The gangster in and behind popular Hindi cinema', in Corey K. Creekmur and Mark Sidel (eds), *Cinema, Law, and the State in Asia* (New York: Palgrave Macmillan, 2007), pp. 29–43. For illuminating analyses of *Nayakan* and *Parinda*, see the full chapters devoted to each film in Lalitha Gopalan, *Cinema of Interruptions: Action Genres in Contemporary Indian Cinema* (London: British Film Institute, 2002). Also see Ranjani Mazumdar, *Bombay Cinema: An Archive of the City* (Minneapolis, MN: University of Minnesota Press, 2007), especially Chapter 5, 'Gangland Bombay', pp. 149–96, and Ranjani Mazumdar, 'Friction, collision, and the grotesque: The dystopic fragments of Bombay cinema', in Gyan Prakash (ed.), *Noir Urbanisms: Dystopic Images of the Modern City* (Princeton, NJ: Princeton University Press, 2010), pp. 150–84.
17. Among many treatments of Amitabh Bachchan's significance in the 1970s, see the chapter in Vijay Mishra, *Bollywood Cinema: Temples of Desire* (New York: Routledge, 2001), pp. 125–56.
18. For an ingenious and detailed analysis of *Johnny Gaddaar*, see Gopalan, 'Bombay Noir', pp. 504–10.

9. THE NEW SINCERITY OF NEO-NOIR

R. Barton Palmer

Noir and New Noir

If one truth has emerged from the intense scholarly debate during the last two decades over the nature of Old Hollywood, it is that the writing of American film history must avoid the essentialist trap of considering the so-called 'classical text' of that era as a relatively undifferentiated flow of product whose watchwords were sameness and conformity. A correlative of this truth is that New Hollywood filmmaking, even with its emphasis on package production (with each film in some sense a unique entity unto itself), still offers regular forms of textuality that differ from those of the studio era only in subtle, not in fundamental, ways. Thus the two distinct periods of Hollywood history are characterised by complex forms of continuity and discontinuity, as exemplified by the film noir phenomenon, whose two periods (classic and neo-noir) mirror larger changes in the industry even as they bespeak underlying continuities in the national cinema and the public taste it strives to satisfy.

This chapter is devoted to the neo-noir phenomenon in Hollywood, and it bears remarking that a similar renovating secondariness manifests itself as well in some other national cinemas, whose post-classical noir traditions are dealt with in other chapters in this volume. Beginning with the genre revisionist work of noted Hollywood Renaissance auteurs in the early 1970s, American neo-noir is much too extensive, having endured now for more than four decades, more than twice the temporal reach of the original series, to be surveyed adequately in a brief essay. Instead, my hope here is to trace some of the general features of the phenomenon through a sustained focus on two noteworthy and exemplary releases, *Body Heat* (Lawrence Kasdan, 1980) and *The Man Who Wasn't There* (Joel and Ethan Coen, 2001), which bookend the period of neo-noir's greatest popularity. Both of these films connect, if in radically different ways, to James M. Cain's novels *Double Indemnity* and *The Postman Always Rings Twice* (both 1936), as well as to the Old Hollywood film versions (Billy Wilder, 1944 and Tay Garnett, 1946 respectively). These films are foundational early entries in the classic noir series and are discussed at length in earlier chapters of the companion volume to this one. The neo-noir Cain revivals, if we may call them that, speak eloquently about the urge to begin again with materials and visual styles initially developed and popularised about fifty years earlier. They are exemplary in illustrating both the artistic quality of much neo-noir filmmaking and also its creative re-use of time-honoured conventions.

The approach to neo-noir adopted here has two advantages. First, it demonstrates even for recently produced noirs the continuing importance of *série noire* fiction from the 1930s, 40s and 50s; like classical film noir, the neo period is heavily dependent on literary adaptation, with some underexploited earlier writers – such as Patricia Highsmith, Jim Thompson and David Goodis – even finding greater interest from film producers. Any account of neo-noir must acknowledge the perdurable relevance of characters, themes and plots whose literary sources are pulp crime fiction writers from the period, particularly the imposing figure of Cain and, to an important if still lesser degree, Raymond Chandler. In an interesting twist of critical fortunes, this fictional tradition today is widely read and admired by literati, precisely the upscale *cognoscenti* whose knowing tastes neo-noirs are particularly intended to satisfy. Neo-noir viewership, at least of the culturally informed variety, is also a readership interested in and intrigued by contemporary crime writers whose work deliberately evokes the *série noire* tradition (including James Ellroy, Elmore Leonard, Michael Connelly and Lawrence Block, all of whom can claim Cain as a formative influence).

Body Heat and *The Man Who Wasn't There* can be appreciated without reference to the Cain novels in either their fictional or cinematic form, and the marketing campaigns for the two films did not emphasise the extent to which the culturally aware viewer would instantly recognise them as interesting recyclings and recontextualisations. Viewing the two films, many undoubtedly remained unaware that they are appropriations of the novels and their original screen versions. Both films, however, abound with Cainian allusions and echoes, intertexts that provide both intellectual and aesthetic pleasures for viewers with the cultural capital to 'get it'. For example, secondary characters in *Man* bear the unusual surnames (Nirdlinger, Diedrickson) by which *Double Indemnity*'s notorious femme fatale is known in the book and original screen versions of the story. These gestures, or allusions if you like, are metafictional in the sense that they take the viewer outside the film to its intellectual and textual sources, marking it out as overtly secondary. It is revealed as an appropriation of the already written and the already filmed, underlining the 'neo' in 'neo-noir', a term that was already well established in critical usage by the time that the Coens set about recreating the cinematic and literary past. Such allusions, of course, play with the temporality of the film, showing for those in the know that it refers to a cultural (also cinematic and literary) 'then' that is summoned up for, and aligned with, a textual 'now'. The affect they create so doing is nostalgia, which is, as many have noted, especially Fredric Jameson, a key element in the postmodernism that constitutes the larger aesthetic context of the neo-noir movement.[1]

Exemplifying processes at work more generally in New Hollywood, *Body Heat* and *The Man Who Wasn't There* conjure up a past that is usable in two senses – first, as the pleasurable object of an informed yearning (or a pleasurably poignant contemplation of its absence); and, second, as an extensive body of conventions with proven appeal upon which a new production might easily and profitably draw. It is this basic form of re-use (characteristic of commercial cinema's conservation of popular material in general) that largely accounts for *Body Heat*'s noirness. And yet some neo-noirs, and here *The Man Who Wasn't There* is a useful example, break decisively from the models of the Hollywood past by probing deeply the social and cultural history of the early postwar years. Such retro productions acknowledge their deep connection to a bygone cinematic era, interestingly mirroring the way in which noir protagonists often find themselves confronting something that comes out of the past, destabilising the present. Neo-noirs of this type also self-reflexively explore understandings of wartime and postwar culture developed during the last half century in a film culture that has become increasingly fascinated by noirness, for which no one at the time of its flourishing in America had a name. Retro neo-noirs thus 'know' a tradition (not just the texts themselves but their contexts of production and reception) that could not know itself. In pretending to this awareness, they are thoroughly New Hollywood, of which more below. With Peter Brooker, we may well see older styles and artistic movements as anything but extinct, as making available in fact a different form of newness that might result from 'the practice of an imaginative remaking which edits, echoes, borrows from, recomposes and "refunctions" existing narratives or images'. Suitably transformed, what has been borrowed can then 'work in a different medium with an invigorated social and artistic purpose'.[2]

Hollywood Old and New

The functionalist analysis offered in the much-cited and controversial study *The Classical Hollywood Cinema* offers powerful evidence and compelling argument that supports the emergence of a group style in the American film industry during the first half of the twentieth century. This was, in sum, an aesthetic that developed inevitably from standardised modes of production at all levels within Hollywood and served well the assembly-line aspects of studio work.[3] Yet such centripetal tendencies towards identity and regularity (natural enough forces in a business based on the efficient, rapid manufacture of product that needed to fit the stabilised needs of the exhibition sector) were from the outset necessarily balanced by an equally strong commitment to difference and diversification. Studio-era productions, to put it simply, needed at a fairly general level to be as interchangeable as practically possible (in order to take advantage of economies of scale and to keep the exhibition sector running smoothly), but, in terms of specific appeals to the audience, Hollywood's releases had to be seen as interestingly and significantly different from one another.

The essential fact about Hollywood is that it was simultaneously 'industrial' in the modern sense (and thus could profit from such business practices as elaborate production schema and specialised long-term contract labour arrangements) but also 'artisanal', that is, absolutely dependent in the final analysis on the flexible and ever-evolving talents of craftsmen. Classical Hollywood filmmaking was necessarily supervised by businessmen committed to providing a predictably profitable service, even as creative personnel, however Taylorised their eventual contributions might in some sense become, still played an indispensable role because they bent or violated industry rules, often pursuing an agenda of creativity rather than simply following established procedures. In this way, Hollywood's craftsmen became the guarantors of novelty, as well as powerful sources of irregularity and often disruption. Yet such unpredictability, we might say, was something that studio executives counted on to be predictable.

These aspects of the Hollywood system reflected the inalterable reality that consumption was modulated by a dialectic of identity and non-identity. Audiences went to the cinema week in and week out to have essentially the same experience (popularly conceived as 'going to the movies'), but each time with a never-before-seen film. As Murray Smith points out, moreover, filmgoers needed to be encouraged in their attendance habit not so much by singular, but by multiple (and constantly shifting) appeals to their interests of the moment: 'The variety of genres and the range of stars testified to and catered for a range of different audience tastes; and . . . the individual film is distinctive to a degree that most mass-produced commodities are not'.[4] We might in fact go further and say that the individual studio-era film, in terms of its claims to uniqueness, was absolutely dissimilar to all other mass-produced commodities and therefore better suited than were they in appealing to ever-protean popular tastes. Henry Ford achieved his early success by selling only the Model-T (with black the sole colour 'option'), but Hollywood offered its customers something new and appealing more than twice a week for decades, collectively producing more films than even diehard fans could see in the course of a year.

Forces of divergence were in this way matched by equally powerful forces of convergence during the studio era. And yet, as Michael Storper has convincingly shown, the pre-1948 Hollywood industry (that is, commercial filmmaking before the end of vertical integration) was essentially Fordist, that is, catering in terms of product, pricing and service to a mass public largely conceived as undifferentiated.[5] Classical Hollywood was certainly not post-Fordist in the sense of providing specialised products for a cluster of divergent markets.[6] Whether the New Hollywood of the last three decades is thoroughly post-Fordist is currently much debated. Blockbusters, a central element of New Hollywood textuality, are arguably Fordist in their calculated appeal to huge mass audiences. In any event, it is undeniable that the American industry, at least in part, now seeks to develop and control profitable niches in the exhibition sector through the production of radically different kinds of films.[7] This post-classical strategy is perhaps most visible in the New Hollywood treatment of what might be called the genre repertoire, an essential element of classical Hollywood filmmaking that provided producers and filmgoers alike with set of easily readable signs allowing them to negotiate effectively the dialectic of similarity and difference.

In the studio era, genre films were defined by a shared identity: that is, their claims to uniqueness, established by the fashion in which they inevitably modified the conventions of the genre, were simultaneously compromised, as those same conventions were referenced and perpetuated by the very act of redefinition. During the studio period, individual genres (musicals, detective stories, women's pictures and so forth) might be more attractive to some (theoretically) identifiable element of the mass audience, but, and this was crucial, every genre was thought to have some appeal to all filmgoers. This was, of course, true also for the film type (or genre or cycle or series or discursive formation) that we retrospectively identify as film noir, whose emergence and (always limited and minoritarian) success with audiences of the time had its sources in the 'irregular' or 'creative' permeability of Hollywood to an unlimited number of literary, cinematic and cultural influences. The stylistic, thematic and narrative difference that so marks these films for scholars today should thus be understood as a predictably unpredictable divergence from the template that was the 'classical text'. Never produced for or marketed to an identified niche, film noir was 'for everyone', even if these dark tales of urban malaise, which offered versions of the contemporary national experience that challenged the optimism that was then more generally a feature of Hollywood films, did not suit every taste every time.

In contrast, film noir's contemporary reflex is not 'for everyone'. This change in the nature of the noir phenomenon has everything to do with the conditions now prevailing in the American industry. A singular quality of New Hollywood production is that there has been, as Smith puts it, 'a return to genre filmmaking' after the brief period in the late 1960s and early 1970s when an American art cinema held sway. This return to genre establishes a continuity with the studio past, but with the crucial difference that this production strategy is, as Smith observes, 'now marked by greater self-consciousness'.[8] In part, this self-consciousness manifests itself in a rhetoric of metagenericism; genre is referenced in these films so as to comment pleasurably on genre. Genre, instead of simply informing and shaping the viewer's experience, is foregrounded as theme and as textuality, in gestures of self-reflexivity not unknown to classic Hollywood films, though much more common and forcefully present since the 1980s. More important, however, self-consciousness today manifests itself also in product differentiation; in other words, genre is inflected diversely in the films designed for separate niche markets.

Thus New Hollywood metagenericism becomes a key element, on the one hand, in the deliberate playfulness and 'knowing' escapism of such B-movie extravaganzas as the *Jurassic Park* or *Indiana Jones* or *Harry Potter* franchises, and, on the other, in the intellectually compelling contemplation of the workings of intertextuality, including generic conventions, that is such an attractive feature in commercial/independent productions such as Todd Haynes' *Far From Heaven* (2002), which resuscitates in an exaggerated yet 'realistic' fashion the 1950s melodramas of Douglas Sirk in order to dissect and correct their gender, sexual and racial politics; or Steven Soderbergh's *Side Effects* (2013), which updates the Hitchcockian 'wrong man' thriller by providing it with a richly detailed contemporary metrosexual setting, even while invoking Production Code era theories of poetic justice in an interesting retro gesture. Today's 'event' franchises are also connected to readily identifiable genres (among other aspects of popular culture such as comic books or graphic novels), built on special effects and designed to hasten the flow of adrenaline for huge audiences of largely youthful filmgoers. These films constitute the essential first and profitable steps taken towards creating after-markets of huge earnings potential. The event film finds its other in the commercial/independent production in its several, constantly evolving industrial forms, films put together on a modest budget and marketed to a relatively small coterie of *cognoscenti* and media buffs, whose expected pleasures are more dependent upon notions of difference, artistry, style, wit and intellectually engaging themes.

These tastes are especially catered to by many neo-noir productions, those which not only recycle studio-era conventions, but take the idea of classical film noir (as inferred from valued texts and critical works) as their subject matter, thus solidifying the claims of those films to be a genre (and, more broadly speaking, something like a world-view that critics have been accustomed to term 'noirness'). Richard Martin has aptly characterised this central aspect of the transition to neo-noir: 'The industrial assimilation of the term film noir . . . has contributed to its establishment as a contemporary Hollywood genre irrespective of how one is inclined to define the generic status of the classic films of the forties and fifties'.[9] I would add only that this assimilation, like many of the texts it generates, is thoroughly self-conscious, a studied and deliberate return to a classical type that has become, through the attention first paid to it by French New Wave innovators such as François Truffaut and Jean-Luc Godard, and then soon afterwards by Hollywood Renaissance directors, perhaps especially Martin Scorsese and Robert Altman, whose cinematic renovations have been much valued in the more sophisticated areas of film culture.

Noir is an element of contemporary filmmaking and consumption comparable in some ways to auteurism (which seems now to have entered a self-conscious 'neo' phase as well), for it connects complexly to particular forms of viewer taste that we can legitimately label as highbrow. Noting the growing popularity of neo-noir in the early 1990s, James Naremore opines that 'the dark past keeps returning'.[10] Or, to put it a bit differently, New Hollywood filmmakers keep returning to the dark past, if for different reasons than their Old Hollywood predecessors. Nowhere, in fact, on the current American scene are the complex workings of the generic self-consciousness that now characterises production as a whole more central than in what is called neo-noir. In its representation of the indissoluble connection of the studio past to the contemporary scene, this term, in fact, perfectly describes its object. But what is that indissoluble connection? How, in short, is the co-presence of the past and present to be described? Most studies of neo-noir make an issue out of the genre's definition (including its historical reach), suggesting that scholars must choose between two different alternatives.[11] Are neo-noir films a continuation of classic film noir, which, in that case, did not end with the *fin de siècle*-like meditation on its themes and style offered by Orson Welles in his notorious *Touch of Evil* (1958), but was, instead, kept alive by maverick filmmakers like Sam Fuller and John Boorman during the 1960s, only to re-emerge to prominence during the Hollywood Renaissance of the next decade, with such notable (neoclassical?) works as Martin Scorsese's *Taxi Driver* (1976) and Arthur Penn's *Night Moves* (1975)? Or did film noir, after reaching baroqueness with Welles in the late 1950s, end, as Paul Schrader suggests, because it was 'a movement, and therefore restricted in time and place'?[12] Such an understanding of classic noir means that neo-noir must essentially be, as Silver and Ward put it, a revival that aims to 'recreate the noir mood, whether in remakes or new narratives . . . undertaken by filmmakers cognizant of a heritage and intent on placing their own interpretation of it'.[13] This scholarly argument, it is easy to see, replicates *in parvo* the larger question of the relationship of the 'old' to the 'new' Hollywood, importantly engaging the vexed concept of 'continuity'. Questions difficult or, perhaps, impossible to answer inevitably arise. How do we account for the persistence of foundational institutional elements in the face of inevitable historical evolution or change? What exactly would it mean for film noir to 'end' so that it could be revived? And so forth.

But perhaps periodising (and, to be sure, essentialising) speculations of this kind are all ultimately beside the point, especially if film noir is, as I think, like all other generic or classificatory categories (at least from a critical point of view) no more and no less than a heuristic enabling discussion of some body of films selected for critical discussion, a concept useful, then, only insofar as it advances rather than retards their collective analysis. As Naremore wisely points out, in fact, 'there is no transcendent reason why we should have a noir category at all'.[14] Indeed. But, of course, as he goes on to affirm, this is not a question left entirely up to the discretion of critics since genres are not simply 'categories' that the academy finds useful or not; they are also part of a broad film culture in which the notion of noir has become truly global, as this volume demonstrates through its anatomising of noirness in regional or national cinemas. The variety and abundance of international noir films therein anatomised are likely to surprise even the most informed cinephile. Film noir, Naremore persuasively argues, is fundamentally a discursive category, a way of talking about selected Hollywood productions and similar releases from other film traditions. But within contemporary film culture, film noir has also become a set of conventions, values and ideas that govern production even as they decisively inform and shape consumption for certain niche viewers around the world. The globalness of the noir phenomenon thus owes much to what Richard Martin has termed the 'industrial assimilation' of what was originally simply a critical label.

Metagenericism, the self-conscious and critical return to the cinematic past, is one of the most important of the features of contemporary American noir, and it marks this stage of the phenomenon as radically different from its classical phase. These earlier films exist within the boundaries of an emerging, if unorganised, group practice; neo-noir films, more often than not, take that practice as their subject matter, as the 'meaning' they intend to express and deconstruct for a narrowly defined audience knowledgeable about, and fascinated by, Hollywood history, which such filmgoers are eager to see recognised and commented upon. This is one of the differences between modernist and postmodernist versions of cultural production, or between Fordist and post-Fordist senses of product.[15]

As one might expect, given the general appeal to cinematic 'knowingness' of New Hollywood production, neo-noirs self-consciously reflect a central thematic preoccupation of the genre: the domination of the present by the past (put another way, the failure of a future for the characters to emerge from the machinations of the plot). This domination by the past is figured in different ways in the two Cain appropriations discussed here. If classic noir heroes, like Jeff Bailey in *Out of the Past* (Jacques Tourneur, 1947), are abruptly (and, as it were, as a result of bad luck) recalled from their plans to make new lives and forced to resume a discarded self, usually with disastrous consequences, neo-noir films draw representational and thematic strength from cinematic and literary history, which, in the spirit of a creative archaeology, they re-construct, revise and always, in one way or another, celebrate. Such metagenericism demands to be carefully anatomised; it reflects complex, even contradictory cultural currents.

The New Sincerity

Cultural critic Jim Collins has interestingly pointed out that New Hollywood production, especially in the 1980s and 1990s (the era of neo-noir's greatest flourishing, as it now seems), emphasises two distinct kinds of genre films that hardly fit into the category of 'blank parody', Fredric Jameson's dismissive description of the postmodern resuscitation of once-vital, but now exhausted cultural forms. On the one hand, genre hybrids such as *Back to the Future III* (1990), which are 'hyperconsciously intertextual', play their knowingness of forms like the western and the science fiction film for laughs. Their 'eclectic irony' exploits the 'dissonance' produced by the unpredictable yoking together of disparate, irreconcilable elements, which are drawn not from the 'real', but from the ready-mades of the cultural past. This is the effect that Collins describes as 'John Ford meets Jules Vernes and H. G. Wells', and it is usefully exemplified in the Robert Zemeckis film by the sequence in which Marty (Michael J. Fox) and Doc (Christopher Lloyd) find themselves transported back not to the Old West, but to the Old West of Hollywood film.[16] For neo-noir, we could point to the very similarly constructed *Dead Men Don't Wear Plaid* (Carl Reiner, 1982), in which Steve Martin plays a hard-boiled detective whose case consists almost entirely of a number of clips from classic noir films into which his image is inserted. *Back to the Future*, as its title indicates, engages even more directly with the idea of a history that can be re-entered and, if only accidentally, even subverted. At one point, the DeLorean 'time machine' of the two protagonists is hauled across Monument Valley like a buckboard, an incongruous (and, of course, anti-realist) invocation of many John Ford movies, most notably *Stagecoach* (1939). On the other hand, 'new sincere' explorations of classic genres aim at conveying some kind of 'missing harmony', some transcendent significance that the celebrated exemplars of the genre allude to but never fully express or properly configure, perhaps because they do not fully know themselves. Thus the western, as in *Dances with Wolves* (Kevin Costner, 1990) and *Unforgiven* (Clint Eastwood, 1992), can be reshaped through an engagement with 'real' as opposed to 'cinematic' American history, revealing what, for either ideological or institutional reasons, has hitherto been confined to its margins or simply unexpressed. The new western can occupy itself with the struggle for control over the land between native peoples, who, no longer demonised as Indians, emerge as representatives of a natural, self-sustaining and peaceful society. Opposed to them are the rapacious white settlers bent on extracting wealth from the land through its mindless destruction. Or, to take a more recent example, Michael Mann's *Public Enemies* (2009), the 'authentic' political atmosphere of Prohibition-era, crime-wave America can be revealed, even as the 'true' personality of John Dillinger, especially his romantic attachment to Billie Frechette (Marion Cotillard), can be anatomised. That this kind of cultural archaeology had already been notoriously and successfully performed during the Hollywood Renaissance in Arthur Penn's *Bonnie and Clyde* (1967) does not matter. However anticipated and repetitive, the revealing gesture towards new sincerity in the Mann unmasking is all.

Collins concludes that these two types of genre film 'represent contradictory perspectives on "media culture": an ironic eclecticism that attempts to master the array through techno-sophistication; and a new sincerity that seeks to escape it through a fantasy technophobia'.[17] We might add to his analysis that, at least in his two examples, eclectic irony and the new sincerity are both deployed with a view towards recovering valued pasts (the end of the frontier, the advent and flourishing of teen culture in the 1950s, an era of romantically admired public enemies), imagined as distinct from the flat and unsignifying present, as, in fact, vanished realms of plentitude (however problematic that richness might eventually be seen to be as it suffers the 'fall' into being narrativised and represented). Perhaps the unrealisable aims of recovering the unmediated truth of history and defying the omnipresent regime of representations through an ironic probing of their depth in time, if strategies opposed in their stance toward 'media culture', equally reflect what many have identified as a central theme of postmodernism: its archaeological fascination with resurrecting a past that is always already seen nostalgically, that is, as impossibly beyond the irresistible urge toward its reconstitution. Here is a form of pleasure that neo-noir is ideally positioned to engage, what with its connection both to bygone forms of representation (cinematic, televisual and literary) and culture (the fashions and mores of America in the 1930s, 40s and early 50s, the period whose most meaningful meta-event is 'the War', and which now seems to many as a kind of golden age of the national experience).

It is difficult to overestimate the importance of Roman Polanski's *Chinatown* (1974, from a script by Robert Towne) in engaging and popularising this desire for cultural revivification, here tied to the screenwriter's urge to dramatise the municipal politics of the era, especially the struggles over water rights and oil leasing (this latter issue is explored in the Towne-scripted sequel, *The*

Two Jakes [Jack Nicholson, 1990]). This Chandleresque detective narrative ends with a moral and epistemological ambivalence reminiscent of such classic noirs as the Chandler adaptation *Murder, My Sweet* (1944), as the detective is reduced to impotence (and in some sense blindness), even as the revealing of the truth of the case – his traditional, empowering function – is displaced onto other characters. Poetic justice emerges through a complex interplay of circumstance and intention in *Murder*, as the murderous malefactor is delivered to an appropriate retribution despite the protagonist's inability to settle accounts. In *Chinatown*, however, the system fails to apprehend and punish the powerful man responsible for subverting the communal good, murdering those standing in his way and sexually abusing his daughter and granddaughter. The rejection of a more conventional ending (which was arrived at by the filmmakers only after much dispute) speaks a less pleasant truth, fills in a painful blank in the history of Los Angeles, revealing a past of which Chandler's own texts, and the films made from them, were notoriously silent.

Not all neo-noir films, of course, manifest this historically revisionist new sincerity. In his account of postclassical noir filmmaking, Richard Martin observes that 'by the early seventies . . . there was in coexistence two distinctive neo-noir traditions, the revisionist and the formulaic'. The formulaic, as the label implies, is the least interesting of these, 'a manifestation of renewed cinematic interest in a popular narrative pattern that had temporarily [in the late 1950s and throughout the 1960s] been relegated to the small screen and other art forms'.[18] This series represents a continuation of classical film noir more or less as such, that is, unselfconsciously, as customary narrative patterns and themes are updated, occasionally even provided with a contemporary twist, but not connected to the understanding of noirness that has been emerging in American film culture since the 1960s. The noir redivivus category even includes remakes of well-known noir releases that avoid any reference to the original film, postwar culture or noir visual style, costuming and art design; the trend is exemplified by *Night and the City* (1950/1992), *Kiss of Death* (1947/1995), *Out of the Past/Against All Odds* (1947/1984) and numerous other classical/neo-noir pairings.[19] For Martin, revisionist neo-noirs, in contrast, are 'inspired by the *nouvelle vague*'s experimental/investigative approach to film',[20] an aesthetic energised by a pronounced *nostalgie* for the recent Hollywood past, which is resurrected with both wit and reverence in key New Wave films such as Godard's *À bout de souffle* (*Breathless*, 1959). The American revisionist neo-noir films 'self-consciously investigate the generic traditions [they] invoke' and, often, 'eschew postmodern pastiche for a more integrated, if no less self-conscious, use of generic convention, with *a return to textual depth instead of just a play of surfaces*' (my emphasis).[21]

Martin finds in neo-noir a somewhat different contrast than does Collins between two types of New Hollywood genre productions: not the eclectic irony of postmodern pastiche, but a straightforward refitting of classical conventions, on the one hand; and, on the other, instead of an attempted escape from generic boundaries in the spirit of the new sincerity, an integrated investigation of those traditions, whose 'truths' are deepened rather than discarded. The revisionist recyclings, though not defined by the 'new sincerity' in the same sense that *Dances with Wolves* can be said to be, however, are exactly what we should expect in the particular case of neo-noir, which, unlike the western (which aims in some sense to signify the American west), has no world as such to demystify and authenticate. Instead, neo-noir's restorative objective is a complex nexus of representations, primarily literary and cinematic, that cluster around a modern *idée fixe*: the dark, threatening city. In the revisionist neo-noir tradition, then, integration creates textual depth through the self-conscious turn of investigative gestures, invoking the 'real' of postwar culture through a re-embodying and historicising of noir conventions, which are not discarded but rather fulfilled, that is, provided with contextual depth. The end result is that the revisionist neo-noir offers the nostalgic spectator something along the lines of what Collins calls 'missing harmony', with noir conventions (and, especially, intertextual references) now thoroughly naturalised and authenticated through their deep grounding in cultural themes.

The difference between what Martin calls 'formulaic' and 'revisionist' neo-noir can be readily seen in the two Cain appropriations that will be analysed here in some detail: *Body Heat* and *The Man Who Wasn't There*.[22] Like most of the films of the early stages of the noir revival in the 1980s, *Body Heat* updates classic conventions but does not attempt to identify the 'truth' of the genre by giving expression to what it should have said but never could; with its contemporary setting, the film also offers little more than superficial references to the cultural and representational past, especially the sordid world of plotting, betrayal and ironic reversal limned in both *Double Indemnity* and *Postman*.

The Man Who Wasn't There: Noir After Existentialism

The Man Who Wasn't There deploys its Cainian allusions as a framework upon which, in the spirit of the new sincerity to reconstruct the noir universe – or, perhaps more accurately, to attempt to produce for the first time its 'true' version. Cain's two novels unfold in the early years of the Depression and reflect that era of social breakdown and economic scarcity. But the original Hollywood versions (Billy Wilder's *Double Indemnity* [1944] and Tay Garnett's *The Postman Always Rings Twice* [1946]) are set in a vaguely contemporary America; neither film attempts to update Cain's narratives in order to explore deeper currents within then contemporary culture, including and especially the profound changes being brought about by the war.

THE NEW SINCERITY OF NEO-NOIR

The Man Who Wasn't There, in contrast, offers a deeply particularised context, with 'textual depth' created by pervasive and connected thematic references, closely linking a resurrected noir narrative *à la* Cain to the era that shaped it and thus making present the cultural history hitherto mostly unexpressed in the genre. *The Man Who Wasn't There* is set in 1949, as the revelation that the Russians now possess the atomic bomb began to mark profoundly what in retrospect seems truly 'the age of doubt', as the historian William Graebner terms it. This was a time that, in his formulation, was strongly coloured by 'the anxiety of the lonely, fragmented individual', of which the Coens' protagonist is a striking example.[23] Unlike Cain's scheming adulterers, who are trapped by limited economic horizons and oppressive institutions, especially marriage and social class, all the characters in *The Man Who Wasn't There* suffer from a vaguer but perhaps deadlier malaise, the deep feeling of the age that, as described in Graebner's apt account, 'like life itself, values seemed to come and go, without pattern or reason'.[24] This anomie produces a strong sense of disconnection, even absence, to which they react in various ways, seeking either to 'make it big' in the tradition of the American dream or to withdraw from the struggle by numbing themselves with alcohol or music. They settle in the end for neither success nor escape, but for death, which haunts and frustrates all their aspirations, yet paradoxically offers as well the opportunity for transcendence.

The film's main character is Ed Crane (Billy Bob Thornton), a barber *malgré lui* who, looking to escape his 'condition', is frustrated in his plans to make it big in the dry-cleaning business, and who comes to see life as a series of sudden, inexplicable and irretrievable losses. In particular, Crane's thoughts are haunted by the memory of the thousands of 'Nips vaporised at Nagasaki'.[25] His boss's wife is haunted by an even more bizarre and gloomier 'metaphysics', her belief that she and her husband were briefly abducted by aliens, an incident they report to the proper authorities, only to be persecuted, she thinks, by the government, which for reasons unknown is reluctant to admit the truth – all this an evocation of the mass paranoia that gripped America in the course of the great UFO panic, which began in 1949 and extended throughout the next decade.

Printed (but not filmed) in a flat black and white that avoids all forms of glamorising, including, save for a couple of key sequences, the stylings that have been in the last four decades as 'noir' (including low-key lighting, pronounced chiaroscuro effects, disjointed editing, a mise-en-scène as well as camera framings that suggest entrapment and so forth), *The Man Who Wasn't There* offers itself more as a rich period piece.

Here is a 'new sincere' version of film noir in which Cain's explorations of lust and greed, the discontents of violation and the ironic, horrifying ends towards which criminality relentlessly drives the characters all yield a meaning

Figure 9.1   Barber shop in *The Man Who Wasn't There*.

that is perhaps closer to the everyday 'truth' of noirness, this *Weltanschauung*'s evocation of the uncertainty of human life, its fascination with the loathing, disgust and horror of the abject that haunts everyday experience. Cain's materials are deliberately 'existentialised', accommodated to Camusian absurdism and Sartrean nausea, in a thematic move that reflects the way in which scholarly discussions of film noir have intellectualised the phenomenon by providing it with philosophical underpinnings. This existentialising, we might add, is also yet another way to deepen the context of the story by locating it within forms of thought popular in the postwar era. In fact, unlike classic noir, the focus of the film is not the identification of, and then a bare escape from, the threat to orders both sexual and cultural posed by an underworld of temptation and rapacious criminality. *The Man Who Wasn't There* is actually more about the hope for spiritual growth, the leap of faith made possible by the embrace of meaninglessness, a concept for which the Coens also discover a 'historical' explanation in the spirit of the new sincerity.

In a Cainian tangle of illegitimate motives and ironic misconnections, Ed, in self-defence, kills his wife's employer and lover, Big Dave (James Gandolfini), whom he had blackmailed in order to get the money necessary to get started in the dry-cleaning business; he escapes the scene undetected. Doris (Frances McDormand) is mistakenly put on trial for the crime (which she had plausible reasons to commit), and Ed half-heartedly confesses his culpability to her hot-shot attorney, Riedenschneider (Tony Shalhoub), who does not think that the jury will believe him. As the lawyer explains it, the legal system, though officially committed with its seemingly forensic proceedings to the discovery of the truth, is really concerned only with credibility, the issue at the thematic centre of the film. Doris's fate hangs upon what the jurors and judge can be made to believe or, rather, what they can be persuaded not to believe through the evocation of 'reasonable doubt'. 'There's a guy in Germany,' the lawyer says, 'who maintains that when you want to understand something scientifically you have to look at it, but your looking changes it'. Applied to human affairs, this means that you can never truly know 'the reality of what happened' as you explore actions and motivations. Thus Riedenschneider places his concern about alibis and workable defences (a motif derived directly from *The Postman Always Rings Twice*) within a broader context of ideas through these meditations on the Heisenberg Uncertainty Principle (which is never named as such). For it no longer seems the case that lawyers like Riedenschneider are simply being cynical when they ignore getting at the 'truth' of the case as they search for an explanation that will work rhetorically, as it were, to convince jurors that they in fact do not know what happened.

Viewed from the perspective of universal and inescapable uncertainty, reasonable doubt is no more than the admission that provisional certainty (a certainty subject to only minimal doubt) is often a mirage. In the courtroom, the provisional certainty needed to convict is easily undermined by the demonstration that there is a plausible alternative, some other way of construing the facts. This plausible alternative, however, does not require absolute and detailed proof; it does not require, in fact, provisional certainty. It must point only towards the improbability of knowing for sure. Thus Riedenschneider's profession, as he explains, occupies itself with the serial demonstration of a central epistemological axiom, of whose ineluctability he must persuade jurors. As he puts it, 'there is no what happened', and the ironic correlative of this postulate is that 'the more you look, the less you know'. An inescapable paradox rules human affairs; the 'only fact', the only certainty, is uncertainty. Not only does uncertainty undermine the all-too-human search after determinate knowledge. It also reveals an unknowability that deepens as the desire to know and thereby master experience grows stronger.

The lawyer understands, if in a partial and self-serving fashion, some of the larger implications of Heisenberg's theorising (whose ultimate point is quite the opposite of what he maintains, it being to identify a provisional form of certainty, the relative probabilities in the tracking of the position and momentum of subatomic particles). But Riedenschneider deceives himself that the Uncertainty Principle offers him mastery over Doris's plight. And this is because he falls victim to another paradox, his own certainty about uncertainty, the mistaken notion that the chain of 'unknowing' must end somewhere in an unshakable predictability of which he may take advantage, that, in short, there are no surprises in store. Riedenschneider's detective has discovered what the lawyer thinks is the key to the successful defence of Doris. Big Dave, it turns out, was not the war hero he always bragged of being; though drafted, he never left the United States. Dave's fabrications provide the blackmailer that Doris said approached her lover (it was, of course, Ed) with an exploitable weakness. Big Dave would have been easy prey to anyone learning the truth of his service record, which would not have been hard to do. And, as Riedenscheider points out, the fact that Big Dave had lied to the very people sitting on the hometown jury means that they would be more likely to see such a blackmailer as a real possibility. He exults that the jurors will feel reasonable doubt about the state's version of Dave's death. Doris will thus be acquitted.

And yet it is not to be. We should not forget that 'the more you look, the less you see'. Big Dave's continual self-revelation, his incessant bragging, actually conceal unexpected secrets. But the exposure of these lies offers only a slim point of certainty with regard to him. And, most important, that Dave has been unmasked does not mean that either Doris or Ed is now knowable. Riedenschneider, as it turns out, hasn't even learned all that there is to know about Dave. But knowledge, even the immediate kind that flows from one's own experience, is of dubious value. The knowledge that the lawyer thought would assure his client's deliverance actually drives her to suicide, making any question of legal proceedings irrelevant. Riedenscheider never takes the trouble to determine if Doris and Dave were actually having an affair, even though Ed's 'confession' offers his jealousy about their relationship as his motive, which Doris never disputes. Thus the revelation about Big Dave's past has an effect on Doris that Riedenschneider in no way foresees. Doris's attraction to her lover, as Ed had earlier surmised, was based on, first, the he-man image he presented to the world (so much of a contrast to slightly built, unassuming and depressive Ed, who proved unfit for war service because of fallen arches); and, second, the promise Dave offered her of a deliverance from economic marginality and sexual boredom. Dave was going to expand his department store operation by building an 'annex' where Doris would be comptroller. The blackmailer deprived them of this hope by taking the money Dave needed for the new enterprise and put them in jeopardy by forcing Doris, who was the bookkeeper, to betray her profession and embezzle money ('my books were always perfect'). Then, in an ironic turning borrowed straight from Cain, Doris, who had sacrificed herself to save him, stands accused of his murder.

But the revelation that Dave's 'bigness' was in the final analysis only a mirage proves too much for her to bear. She commits suicide in her cell the night before the trial can begin. Shocked, Riedenschneider still fails to understand, thinking that Doris had despaired of his ability to get her off. Because he does not even consider the truth of Ed's revelation that Dave and Doris were having an affair, the lawyer never thinks that 'getting off' might no longer matter to her once she has learned the truth about him. Sometimes knowledge is indeed a curse, a truism that echoes interestingly throughout the remainder of a narrative built upon misunderstanding, misdirection, misreading and misconnection.

The Man Who Wasn't There offers a series of variations on the uncertainty principle ('there is no what happened') and its twin, though opposed, correlatives: unknowability ('the more you look, the less you know') and the discontents of knowing ('sometimes knowledge is a curse'). What animates the characters' experience with uncertainty and (un)knowing is a vague, numbing dissatisfaction with the absurdity of things that gives rise to an inchoate malaise and, finally, a desperate desire for change (or, perhaps better, self-refashioning). Doris, Ed, and Big Dave all regret their too easily granted acquiescence to mediocrity and ordinariness. And yet, true to the noir vision of human experience, they prove unable to change their circumstances. Only *in extremis* does Ed feel the desire for spiritual transcendence, as, about to be executed not for killing Big Dave but for killing his erstwhile business partner (whom Big Dave had actually murdered, in yet another ironic turning), he admits that 'seeing it whole gives you some peace', offering yet another parallel to Camus's stranger, Meursault, who likewise experiences a profound pre-execution *éclaircissement* (as, of course, does Frank in the original film version of *Postman*).

In the spirit of the 'new sincerity', *The Man Who Wasn't There* resuscitates generic conventions (the narrative of get-rich schemes, sexual misadventure and fateful coincidences popularised by Cain and the film adaptations of his novels). These elements are only occasionally identified as borrowings, to be ironised or celebrated as forms of representation; instead they are more often naturalised (invoked more or less 'realistically') even as they are provided with depth and context, including both an appropriate intellectual schema (the meditations on uncertainty) and an authentic historical context (the great UFO scare, anxiety about the atomic bomb, the secular musings of Heisenberg on human curiosity and its inevitable weakness, as well as the postwar imperative to make it big in an era of expanding opportunity).

The Cainian influence, of course, is meant to be 'obscure' yet also palpably 'there' in order to appeal to the knowingness of the well-informed noir aficionado, who would naturally not fail to see it clearly, enjoying how the Coens have reworked (and in some ways much improved upon) what they have appropriated. *The Man Who Wasn't There*, however, is not at all, properly speaking, a remake or adaptation; it is structured by no rhetoric of identity despite its hauntingly referenced sources. But these occulted quotations are more than a form of flattering puzzle meant to be decoded by those well-versed enough in matters cinematic and literary. Contextualised, integrated and provided with depth, this network of intertextual references offers a resurrected and a now fully represented world, a version of the American structure of feeling of the late 1940s, an element of that era's ideology only hinted at (or, perhaps better, 'referenced') by classic film noir.

This is not to say that the Coens' film rejects entirely an ironic view of the cinematic past. In a scene once again derived from Cain (Frank Chambers on the eve of his execution for a crime he did not commit, contemplating the meaning of his life with the prison chaplain in Garnett's *Postman*), the anticipated last moments of Ed's life 'play' out in an execution chamber whose abstract, minimalist design comes right from German Expressionism as Walt Disney might have imagined it. As a whole, however, the film eschews such eclecticism (carried to a humorous extreme in that ingenious pastiche, *Dead Men Don't Wear Plaid*, in which a character from 'now' speaks, through the magic of special effects, to filmic counterparts from 'then', who can be manipulated to make it seem as if they were present rather than 'filmed'). The resurrected, confected nature of the revitalisation, of course, is always already present. In contrast, *The Man Who Wasn't There* attempts to locate the 'missing harmony' of classic noir, that structure of feeling that in some sense animates the earlier movement, never hitherto fully evoked, it being the result, properly speaking, of the objectifying intellectualisation to which the cinematic past has been subject.

Identifying a spiritual malaise rather than, in the classic noir tradition, the criminality of the dark city, the film's title refers to Ed Crane, whose lack of passion makes him absently present. Like Camus's Meursault, he is a man both alienated and anomic, but he becomes, at least retrospectively, self-analytical, the possessor of knowledge that separates him from others, who live happily unenlightened about life's bitter ironies and impenetrable strangeness. At first saying not 'yes' but only 'all right' to life and, afterwards, refusing to reconnect with the epistemological limitations of his fellows, Crane is never fully 'there', and this alienation sets him both apart from and over others. After his encounter with the absurd (the chain of events that 'lead' him involuntarily to kill Big Dave and bring about the deaths of Doris and his erstwhile business partner), Ed refuses the easy embrace of unreflective meaninglessness that full immersion into everydayness brings. But the title can also be taken as usefully characterising the film's cultural archaeology: the attempt of the Coens to bring to life the noir protagonist such as he never was, but in some sense should have been (or, rather, is now for us, corresponding to our desire for complexifying reconfiguration).

The Coens, it must be said, not only re-inscribe but also revise the tradition upon which they so deeply depend. Cain's heroes never manage the escape from solipsism Ed Crane haltingly manages. They are never free from the powerful desires that move them, never manage to move 'outside' the entanglements caused by their transgressiveness and scheming. Ed's sudden movement of consciousness owes more to Camus. As he dramatises in *The Stranger* (and discusses at more length in his 1942 essay *The Myth of Sisyphus*), the realisation of death's inevitability and arbitrariness strips the world of obfuscating romanticisms, revealing it to be foreign, strange and inhuman, indifferent to human hopes and hardly accommodating of any attempt to endow it with transcendent meaning. Like Ed, the absurdist finds himself living a life parallel to others, inhabiting their world but refusing to share with them the protective mythologies of common sense, of an existence not lived in the continual knowledge of unpredictable, unreasonable and inevitable extinction.

Like Meursault, Ed comes to sense that others are engaged in a struggle (those motions necessary to sustain life) whose true significance – that it has no significance beyond itself – escapes them. But while Meursault is satisfied with being misunderstood by others, as he is during his trial, and actually looks forward to the uncomprehending hatred they will express at his execution, Ed is filled with a desire for human connection in some better world beyond the grave. Cain's two novels, and *The Stranger*, end with their male protagonists desperately disconnected from the world and facing imminent death, while Roquentin in Sartre's *Nausea* moves beyond human contact (dramatised in his final failed attempt to persuade the 'Self-Taught Man' to accept the meaninglessness of existence) towards an artist's self-imposed isolation.

The Man Who Wasn't There, in contrast, concludes with a wish for the restoration of the community whose absence leads to the suicidal war of one against all. This is a political, perhaps moral, point implicit in Cain's analysis of the evident failure of modern society to produce bonds that satisfy and sustain, and one common to the so-called hard-boiled writers in general who portray an America in which, as Sean McCann argues, 'civil society can no longer contain private desire'. This profanation of the liberal ideal could only be healed, McCann suggests, by a reassertion of 'public values over private interests'. But this is a thoroughgoing social reformation whose manner of unfolding the hard-boiled novelists, especially Cain, cannot begin to conceive, as they fail to provide a literary equivalent to the state socialism envisaged by Roosevelt's New Deal.[26] On the contrary, Cain's novels call into existence fictional worlds dominated by those who can imagine bettering themselves only by betraying or destroying those to whom they are joined by bonds of loyalty, service and *communitas*. The concept of the public sphere, at least in the sense of reformable state institutions, has no purchase in his version of America.[27] In the spirit of the new sincerity, expressed by Ed's utopianism, the Coens provide what might be construed as missing from their film's ostentatiously evoked literary sources, and the cinematic tradition of noirness that they in large part inspired.

Body Heat: A CARA Revisioning

Though they achieved a widespread popularity with readers, Cain's novels were initially rejected as source material for commercial screening by the Production Code Administration (PCA), which found the dependence of the narrative in each case on both adultery and conscience-less, profit-oriented homicide to be in violation of the general industry rule that Hollywood films should provide moral uplift by endorsing consensus, and hence morally conservative, values.

With the projects finally getting PCA approval during the war as film culture became somewhat more liberal, the screenplays in each case retained the main outlines of Cain's plotting, massaging the endings to bring them more in line with industry conventions, as the malefactors find themselves not only punished, but appropriately penitent, cognisant of sinfulness and accepting the eminently righteous judgement they had in large part brought upon themselves (as, to be sure, the novelist himself had outlined).[28]

Though adulterous lust, for which the protagonists initially feel no guilt, figures as an important motivation in both novels, Cain was no D. H. Lawrence or Henry Miller; he did not share the interest of literary modernists in pushing the limits of sexual representation. Given the censorship, both formal and informal, that governed literary production in the era, he could not, of course, have offered an account of sexual passion that went beyond euphemistic abstraction. And yet, as Gregory Porter puts it, Cain found sex 'primal, foundational, structurally and ontologically indispensable'.[29] Neither novel offers even a brief description of the sexual passion that so strongly bonds the illicit couple in each case, while Cain's language is never even mildly prurient. What PCA officials, and many readers at the time, found morally problematic was the characters' unpained disregard for hallowed institutions, expressed through an adultery whose logic is that it becomes coldly murderous, concerned with transforming in both cases inconvenient husbands into a financial windfall, into easy money of the most horrific kind. It is hardly surprising, of course, that the initial film versions feature nothing more than brief embraces and kissing that would hardly qualify as 'lustful', which is the kind of physical self-indulgence that would violate the Production Code. In fact, the sexual encounters that are dramatised between Walter and Phyllis in *Double Indemnity* and Frank and Cora in *Postman* are almost chaste, even within the context of Old Hollywood, making it more than a little difficult for viewers to sense properly the irresistibility of the connections that motor these relationships. In promoting the centrality of sexual attraction, Cain's novels speak eloquently to long-established structures of feeling in the national culture, of this there is no doubt for those of us who inhabit a post-Kinsey America. But classic film noir could only hint at the carnality that existed uneasily beneath the surface of conventional living, stipulating but not spectacularising its existence, often displacing it metaphorically. In Henry Hathaway's *Niagara* (1950), for example, which recycles the key elements of *Double Indemnity*'s plot, the marketing copy proclaimed 'Marilyn Monroe and Niagara, a raging torrent of emotion that even nature can't control'. The Falls, and the rushing waters that feed them, stand in for the eroticism that prompts the unfaithful wife's murderous plot and causes the husband, who survives her lover's attack, to then strangle the woman whom, even in death, he cannot cease loving. Undone by passion, he actualises in his dying the film's foundational metaphor, as he is swept over the falls in a boat that, with appropriate irony, has run out of gas.

Changing mores as well as the industry's rapidly evolving relationship to American culture more generally led to the abandonment of the Code in 1968 and the institution of the Classification and Ratings Administration (CARA), which was charged with rating the variable suitability of films for audiences of different ages. In effect, the advent of CARA, and the audience tastes that brought it into existence, made it possible for Hollywood to push the envelope on sexual representation quite far. The American industry, if only for a brief time in the early 1970s, even agreed to major distributors experimenting with making available for adult audiences more generally witty and sophisticated versions of what had hitherto been considered to be hardcore pornography and thus of interest to only a specialised viewership.[30] This moment quickly passed, however, and by the 1980s, film producers had turned instead to stylish softcore productions whose sexual charge was amplified by glamour rather than the all-revealing anatomical realism that was the stock-in-trade of films such as *Deep Throat* (Jerry Gerard) and *Behind the Green Door* (Mitchell Brothers), both released in 1972 as part of what became known as the 'porno chic' movement (*Green Door*, interestingly enough, got a screening at Cannes that year, indexing the changing position within establishment film culture of sexually explicit films). Hardcore films, however sophisticated, proved unworkable for various reasons, mostly legal. Harry Reems, who acted in *Deep Throat*, found himself persecuted by the legal system in New York and Tennessee, and actions were brought in several communities against the filmmakers by state and local attorneys. With self-imposed limits on representation, the softcore approach proved to be more commercially practical, especially since the US Supreme Court determined in Miller v. California (1973) that in order to avoid prosecution for obscenity a film needed to possess *serious* artistic, scientific or social significance. Hollywood-style melodrama, as it turns out, would be serious enough to foreclose any legal difficulties, except in those jurisdictions (notably Fulton County in Atlanta, Georgia) where zealous prosecutors went after even these releases.[31]

Classic noir films, in which lust more than affection figured as the basis of 'romance', were an obvious source for remaking as a new genre, soon christened 'erotic thriller' within the industry, quickly rose to profitable prominence, with such early releases as *Dressed to Kill* (Brian De Palma, 1980), *Cat People* (Paul Schrader, 1982), *Body Double* (Brian De Palma, 1984) and *Fatal Attraction* (Adrian Lyne, 1987). If the retro noirs such as *The Man Who Wasn't There* recontextualise their literary and cinematic sources, adding intellectual complexity for viewers interested in the more intellectual and, especially, existential aspects of the original series, the early erotic thrillers do not eschew obvious connections to the classic period. *Dressed to Kill* and *Body*

Double offer complex homages to Alfred Hitchcock's *Psycho, Rear Window* and *Vertigo*, while *Cat People* is a remake (original version directed by Jacques Tourneur, 1942, as arguably the darkest of a series of noirish horror thrillers produced by Val Lewton). *Fatal Attraction*, while based on an original script, deliberately evokes a series of classic noir 'melodramas of mischance', as critic Foster Hirsch terms them, films such as André de Toth's *Pitfall* (1948), which depicts the deadly consequences of a suburban husband's slip into infidelity.[32] All these films are either noir or noirish, according to critical consensus, as are those of a second wave of productions in the 1990s designed to appeal to women's now-discovered tastes for sexually explicit films began to appear. Productions such as *The Last Seduction* (John Dahl, 1994) exemplified this emerging brand, which prompted a crisis in second wave feminist thinking about pornography.[33]

The most distinctive feature of the erotic thriller is its semi-prurient agenda. Sexual scenes are frequent, featuring full nudity of both partners, though, in the softcore manner, genitalia remain covered. Glamorously styled displays of exuberant passion are presented as the culmination of elaborate seductions (such as the famous initial encounter of the ill-starred lovers in Wilder's *Double Indemnity*), but the resultant sexual encounters are not elided through discreet cutaways or simply 'represented' by implication. In *Body Heat*, it hardly seems coincidental that the female lead, Kathleen Turner, bears more than a passing resemblance to then world-famous Marilyn Chambers, while the film's star is the smooth-bodied and almost pretty William Hurt. Hurt's looks were hardly ruggedly masculine, but certainly suiting the type of male then becoming prominent in Hollywood softcore productions. As is Richard Gere in *American Gigolo* (Paul Schrader, also released in 1980), Hurt is accorded the kind of glamorised focus hitherto accorded mostly to women. One of the film's opening shots memorably catches him from behind, naked from the waist up and enjoying a moment of post-coital contemplation before, his erotic focus returning, he turns one more time to his partner, who has just started to get dressed. Walter Neff in *Double Indemnity* hardly appears without his business suit and tie (the costume that seems to image his status as an ace salesman). However Hurt's character, Ned Racine, spends more time out of his clothes than in them and, so the viewer is made to believe, he is much more talented at lovemaking (if that is the correct term) than at his nominal profession, which is lawyering. He conducts what the narrative quickly reveals to be a none-too-successful individual practice, and his incompetence is known to local judges and his friends on the police force, who show him a condescending affection.

Body Heat updates Cain's story by making Ned more the victim of the woman who becomes his partner in crime, Matty Walker (Turner). She makes him believe that their meeting is accidental. The affair begins, so it seems,

THE NEW SINCERITY OF NEO-NOIR

Figure 9.2 Kathleen Turner.

because he pursues her and she finds him irresistible, even though she is a married woman. Ned thinks it is because they cannot be happy apart that they decide to murder her inconvenient husband Edmund (Richard Crenna), a lawyer turned developer who quickly judges Ned a failure when they meet. The plot goes ahead, and Edmund is defeated in a hand-to-hand struggle that almost turns against Ned, but this takes place without the elaborate staging of Cain's original version, which constitutes the most elaborate proof of Walter's cunning and intrepidness. In Kasdan's rewriting of the novel, the murder is made to seem an implausible accident, and there is no symbolically significant substitution of the murderer for his victim to complete the deception. Ned gradually learns that his plotting is nothing more than a useful illusion, constructed by Matty in order to frame him for Edmund's murder. Looking for a lawyer she could easily hoodwink, Matty had set out to seduce Ned for the purpose. Her attraction to him was feigned, and her cold-bloodedness extended far enough to murdering a lookalike girlfriend, whose identity she had stolen years before, in order to provide a corpse that will fool the police

Figure 9.3 Marilyn Chambers.

into thinking she is dead. Ned winds up in prison, convicted of murder, but only then – much too late for it to make any difference – does he find the evidence that uncovers Matty's scheme. The film ends with a shot of Matty comfortably reclining on a beach chair in some obviously far distant tropical beach, having triumphed over the feckless men she has lured into her life and then destroyed for her own purposes.

In the original film version of *Double Indemnity*, Walter remains firmly in control of the narrative, killing his lover Phyllis after she failed to kill him and revealing the details of their plotting in a confessional Dictaphone recording meant for his boss. Kasdan's sexual politics are quite different, and they constitute, to be sure, a significant updating of Cain's original concept. But, as the title indicates, this is a film about sexuality, pure and simple. Criminality, especially the sociopathy of the two lovers and their quite different levels of self-possession and cunning, only constitutes the requisite plot in which passion and lust find their appropriately extended representation, with Cainian twists and turns providing a strictly subordinate form of pleasure. *Body Heat*, in short, is a kind of anti-romance in which the illicit and murderous plotting of the two lovers legitimates a carnality that had first found much more limited cinematic representation in the two classic noir versions of Cain's fiction. In this film, and in other neo-noir erotic thrillers such as Catherine Hardwicke's recent *Plush* (2013), which also accords full, and often disturbing, representation to the destructive power of sexual compulsion, the 'something missing' of classic noir is both evoked and supplied.

NOTES

1. See, in particular, Jameson's collected essays on the subject, *The Cultural Turn: Selected Writings on the Postmodern* (London: Verso, 1998).
2. Peter Booker, 'Postmodern adaptation: Pastiche, intertextuality and re-functioning', in Deborah Cartmell and Imelda Whelehan, *The Cambridge Companion to Literature on Screen* (Cambridge: Cambridge University Press, 2007), p. 114.
3. David Bordwell, Janet Staiger and Kristin Thompson, *The Classical Hollywood Cinema: Film Style and Mode of Production to 1960* (London: Routledge, 1985). The argument toward aesthetic and production regularity advanced by Bordwell et al. probably goes too far. For a recent partial corrective, see Nick Smedley, *A Divided World: Hollywood Cinema and Émigré Directors in the Era of Roosevelt and Hitler, 1933–1948* (Bristol: Intellect, 2011).
4. Murray Smith, 'Theses on the philosophy of Hollywood history' in Steve Neale and Murray Smith (eds), *Contemporary Hollywood Cinema* (London: Routledge, 1998), p. 8. Further references noted in the text. This point is also made usefully, if in a different way, by Richard Maltby, who argues that 'Hollywood functions according to a commercial aesthetic, one that is essentially opportunist in its economic motivation. The argument that Hollywood movies are determined, in the first instance, by their existence as commercial commodities sits uneasily with ideas of classicism and stylistic determination', in Richard Maltby, *Hollywood Cinema*, second edition (Oxford: Blackwell, 2003), p. 15.
5. Vertical integration of the film industry involved, for the five major studios, the organisation of production, distribution and exhibition activities under the same corporate structure, a powerful business arrangement that was ended by Supreme Court action at the close of the 1940s.
6. Michael Storper, 'The transition to flexible specialisation in the US film industry', in Ash Amin (ed.), *Post-Fordism: A Reader* (Oxford: Blackwell, 1994), see especially pp. 216–17.
7. In addition to the Smith chapter already cited, a useful contribution to this ongoing discussion comes from Richard Maltby, "Nobody knows everything': Post-classical historiographies and consolidated entertainment', in Neale and Smith, *Contemporary Hollywood Cinema*, pp. 21–44.
8. Smith, 'Theses', p. 11.
9. Richard Martin, *Mean Streets and Raging Bulls: The Legacy of Film Noir in Contemporary American Cinema* (Lanham, MD: Scarecrow Press, 1999), p. 5.
10. James Naremore, *More than Night: Film Noir in its Contexts* (Berkeley, CA: University of California Press, 1998), p. 277.
11. See, for example, Martin, *Mean Streets and Raging Bulls*, pp. 11–34; Foster Hirsch, *Detours and Lost Highways: A Map of Neo-Noir* (New York: Limelight Editions, 1999), pp. 1–20; and Alain Silver and Elizabeth Ward (eds), *Film Noir:*

An Encyclopedic Reference to the American Style, third edition (Woodstock, NY: Overlook, 1992), pp. 398–423.
12. Quoted in Hirsch, *Detours and Lost Highways*, p. 2.
13. Silver and Ward, *Film Noir*, p. 398.
14. Naremore, *More than Night*, p. 276.
15. The model developed by French theorist Jean Baudrillard to describe the radical transition from modernity to postmodernity might be usefully invoked to characterise the change from classical to neo-noir. For Baudrillard, the project of modernity is the analysis of cultural phenomena utilising a 'hermeneutics of suspicion' that allows (as in the classic examples of Marx and Freud) undiscovered, 'deep' layers of meaning to be recognised and acknowledged. Postmodernity, in contrast, rejects such sweeping claims for 'meaning' and is occupied with 'playing with the pieces' of a rejected, discredited, yet still fascinating culture. In such a project of restoration lies, in Baudrillard's view, the only hope for cultural rebuilding. See Jean Baudrillard, *Simulations* (New York: Semiotext(e), 1983).
16. Jim Collins, 'Genericity in the nineties: Eclectic irony and the new sincerity', in Jim Collins, Hilary Radner and Ava Preacher Collins (eds), *Film Theory Goes to the Movies* (New York: Routledge, 1993), p. 243.
17. Ibid., p. 262.
18. Martin, *Mean Streets and Raging Bulls*, p. 27.
19. For further discussion, see Constantine Verevis, 'Through the past darkly: Noir remakes of the 1980s', in Alain Silver and James Ursini, eds., *Film Noir Reader 4: The Crucial Themes and Films* (New York: Limelight Editions, 2004), pp. 306–22.
20. Martin, *Mean Streets and Raging Bulls*, p. 27.
21. Ibid., pp. 33, 32.
22. These comments draw on the fuller discussion of the two films in R. Barton Palmer, *Joel and Ethan Coen* (Urbana, IL: University of Illinois Press, 2004), pp. 15–35 and 62–79. I thank the University of Illinois Press for permission to reprint some of the material that first appeared in that book.
23. William Graebner, *The Age of Doubt: American Thought and Culture in the 1940s* (Boston, MA: Twayne, 1991).
24. Ibid., pp. 19–20.
25. *The Man Who Wasn't There*, directed by Joel Coen (Working Title Films, 2001).
26. Sean McCann, *Gumshoe America: Hard-Boiled Crime Fiction and the Rise and Fall of New Deal Liberalism* (Durham, NC: Duke University Press, 2000), pp. 4–5.
27. This is not true of later writers in the tradition, as McCann shows, for example, in the case of Chester Himes, who uses the hard-boiled novel to 'dramatize the intimate relations between racism and American democracy', p. 252.
28. See Sheri Chinen Bisen, *Blackout: World War II and the Origins of Film Noir* (Baltimore, MD: The Johns Hopkins University Press, 2006) for an illuminating discussion of these developments.
29. Gregory Porter, 'Double Cain', *Novel* 29 (1996), 285. Porter explains: 'The Cainian hero, like it or not, cannot not love; despite a casualness that makes it all seem – for the hero, at least – fortuitous, the sheer numerical insurgency of these moments indicates that for Cain there's no imaginable alternative to an originary love-bond that quite literally "makes the world go round"', p. 285.
30. See the detailed account of these developments in Jon Lewis, *Hollywood v Hard Core: How the Struggle Over Censorship Created the Modern Film Industry* (New York: New York University Press, 2000).
31. For a detailed discussion of Fulton County District Attorney Hinson McAuliffe's crusade against Hollywood adult fare, see www.leagle.com/decision/1980196361 0F2d1353_11760 (accessed 6 December, 2013).

32. See Hirsch, *Detours and Lost Highways* for further discussion of this key critical term.
33. Nina K. Martin provides an admirable survey of this debate in her *Sexy Thrills: Undressing the Erotic Thriller* (Urbana, IL: Illinois University Press, 2007), which focuses on direct-to-video releases.

10. POST-NOIR: GETTING BACK TO BUSINESS

Mark Bould

For anyone attempting to periodise a genre, let alone discuss its 'postness', there is a vital lesson in perspective to be learned from Tag Gallagher's critique of evolutionary models of genre. He points out that Robert Warshow, writing in 1954, 'found differences between early-1950s and pre-war westerns almost identical to those which critics like [Thomas] Schatz . . . detect between westerns of the 1970s and early 1950s'.[1] Gallagher attributes this, at least in part, to critics often being 'unsympathetic to the subtleties of "old" movies',[2] perhaps loving them 'for their supposed naïveté' but nonetheless setting them up 'as the "fall guys" for invidious comparisons'[3] which favour recent films that are thus purported to be more 'complex, . . . amoral, and . . . vivid'.[4] Thus it becomes clear that any film that might now seem to be 'post' will inevitably – and soon, perhaps even in the lag between writing and publication – fall back into the mass of genre productions. Whatever distinctiveness and exceptionality was created for it by the sheer contemporaneity of its specific variation upon generic repetitions will be speedily forgotten, levelled out, homogenised into a general pattern. Furthermore, as current understandings of genre suggest, to speak of post-noir is to speak of that which, in an important sense and like all genres, does not, and cannot, exist. It is not a material object, but a contingent and contested discursive construct; it is a claim, an argument, a manoeuvre.

This chapter begins with a reflection on the notions of 'post' and 'postness' and how they function. It indicates the ways in which dominant understandings of noir as primarily a US phenomenon might be challenged and refreshed by a turn towards noir in other national, international and transnational contexts. Finally, inspired by Jennifer Fay and Justus Nieland's treatment of noir 'as an always international phenomenon concerned with the local effects of globalization and the threats to national urban culture it seems to herald',[5] and by one of Richard Dyer's propositions about the consequences of neo-noir pastiche, it considers a range of films which, in the light of their work, can be regarded, at this current conjuncture, as post-noir.

Genre, periodisation, postness, pastiche

Writing at the turn of the millennium, Jack Boozer refers to 'the classic *noir* period', 'the neo-*noir* era of the 1960s and 1970s' and the 'contemporary or post-*noir* films of the 1980s and 1990s',[6] as if this represents a consensus terminology and periodisation. However, in a rather defensive endnote he anxiously hedges his bets and proliferates terms. Neo-noir and post-noir are lumped together as 'post-classic *noir*', although it is unclear if this evocation of 'classic' noir intends a periodisation by mode of production (i.e., classical, that is, Fordist, rather than post-classical or post-Fordist, Hollywood) or whether it is just a journalistic gesture towards a popular noir canon. Boozer describes neo-noir as 'transitional', but it is unclear where this transition leads, since his 'post-*noir* is merely a convenient term to describe the period following Hollywood's transitional or neo-*noir* era'.[7] Furthermore, since his post-noir is 'not meant to suggest specific stylistic changes', the purpose of introducing the term at all remains elusive.[8]

Greg Tuck, writing a decade later about irony and black comedy in neo-noir, moves beyond mere chronology to make subtler use of 'post-noir'. For him, David Lynch 'remains true to the underlying darkness of the original cycle'[9] of US noir, while demonstrating 'the potential for surrealism in this hard-boiled world',[10] and the Coen brothers 'maintain strong links to the ironic anti-sentimental underpinnings of noir' despite parodic 'elements' that 'risk diluting ... it'.[11] However, Quentin Tarantino produces films that are so 'deeply sentimental and ideologically complicit' that 'they are simply not dark; they are not noir'. This 'does not mean that they are not neo-noir' – rather, that Tarantino's 'mode of pastiche' does not regenerate but consumes and negates noir: 'What his films offer us, therefore, is a *post*-noir world where we no longer laugh at the dark and nor are we afraid of it. We have simply been anesthetised against it'.[12] For Tuck, then, describing a film as post-noir is a matter of political and aesthetic judgement. In place of the more-or-less distinct periods/categories proffered by Boozer, he suggests a model of genre that acknowledges its 'combined and uneven development', but without the teleological impulse Trotsky's phrase is sometimes taken to imply.[13]

However, while Tuck's approach to post-noir offers something more flexible than chronology, Chuck Stephens straightforwardly confounds it. In a short piece from 2012 on 'blindingly blonde Fifties no-good-girl Beverly Michaels', he refers to 'her greatest films' as 'post-noir low-rent masterworks'.[14] His description of *The Girl on the Bridge* (Haas, 1951), *Pickup* (Haas, 1951) and *Wicked Woman* (Rouse, 1953) as post-noir might seem so temporally errant as to render the term effectively meaningless – they were, after all, made some years before the original US cycle is usually considered to have come to an end with, say, *Touch of Evil* (Welles, 1958). However, what this actually represents is, like Boozer's and Tuck's usages of 'post-noir', the complex process of negotiation between multiple discursive and material agents, including writers, producers, distributors, marketers, readers, fans, and critics, through which a genre's identity is unendingly formulated and reformulated.[15]

John Rieder makes five key points about current theoretical understandings of genre: any genre is 'historical and mutable'; it has 'no essence, no single unifying characteristic, and no point of origin': it 'is not a set of texts, but rather a way of using texts and of drawing relationships among them'; its 'identity is a differentially articulated position in an historical and mutable field of genres'; and the 'attribution' of a genre 'identity ... to a text constitutes an active intervention in its distribution and reception'.[16] For anyone who has waded through the endless debates about how to define film noir – including the question of whether or not it is 'really' a genre – such principles, which recognise that a genre is not a 'thing'[17] or an 'event'[18] but a complex series of discursive and material structures and processes, should come as both a relief and a release. It should enable us to set aside old questions and generate new and more interesting ones.

However, because this contemporary view of genre is sensitive to both historical mutability and the range of discursive and material actants who use, draw relationships among, differentially articulate, attribute, intervene and so on, it cannot escape the inertia of earlier conceptualisations of genre or of specific genres. For example, in the early 1940s the term 'film noir' was used in France to describe some 1930s French films, but Jean-Pierre Chartier's 1946 suggestion that, in the light of *Double Indemnity* (1944), *Murder, My Sweet* (1944), *The Lost Weekend* (1945) and *The Postman Always Rings Twice* (1946), they no longer deserved the name proved prescient. Films such as *Le Quai des brumes* (1938) and *Hôtel du nord* (1938) are, in Anglophone criticism at least, routinely excluded from the genre and treated, at best, as poetic realist precursors of 'real' (i.e, classical Hollywood) film noir of the 1940s and 1950s. Attempts to recover them as fully fledged films noirs typically end up doing so in relation to 'real' noir, sometimes explicitly – as when Ginette Vincendeau identifies the first forty years' worth of French films noirs in terms of 'a systematically more cynical and morally ambiguous worldview' arising from France's 'different censorship codes' – and sometimes implicitly – as when she foregrounds their representation of women and their 'downplaying of action and plot in favour of atmosphere, self-reflexivity, cinephile citations and stylistic flourishes'.[19]

This example also helps to identify the complex temporalities that generic labelling involves. Film noir is often depicted as peculiar because Anglophones did not start using the term until the 1970s, arguably two decades after the genre came to an end; but all genres are named retrospectively. That is, in an important sense, a genre only comes into being after it has been successfully named. For all that the texts within the genre existed prior to its naming, the naming that produces them as part of the genre simultaneously renders them 'post' – they become, for example, noir only after noir has been named and after they have been named noir. This is evident in the French naming of wartime American films noirs in the immediate postwar years, and again three or more decades later as Anglophone cinephiles, filmmakers and film studies scholars adopted the term. Furthermore, to an extent this adoption came about because of a desire to label certain US films of the late 1960s and 1970s 'neo-noir' – if neo-noir existed, it implied (and thus required and produced) a more or less coherent corpus of 1940s and 1950s US crime movies that contemporary films were seen to revisit and revise. In this way, classical Hollywood film noir, despite its priorness, can also be seen to come after neo-noir. Similarly, attempts to recover the 'priorness' of 1930s French films noirs cannot avoid, despite an obvious appeal to simple chronology, simultaneously situating them 'post' classical Hollywood noir.

This complex, counterintuitive temporality can be understood in terms of the recursivity that marks genre definitions – they all 'infer the defining characteristics of' the specific genre 'from films that are already deemed to belong to [it]' – but it is also a product of the desire to periodise.[20] As Fredric Jameson, writing about modernity, notes, 'We cannot not periodize'.[21] However, we must also recognise that a period is primarily 'a narrative category',[22] 'a useful trope for generating alternate historical narratives'.[23] For example, such common terms as proto-noir, classical noir, neo-noir, modernist noir, postmodernist noir, global noir and post-noir serve not only to constitute classical Hollywood noir as a category but also to tell certain kinds of stories about the genre: primarily, that noir is, first and foremost, a Hollywood product of the 1940s and 1950s, and that there was some kind of historical rupture, after which neo-noir appeared. The 'neo' prefix implies change, and the 'noir' suffix continuity. Some subdivide neo-noir into a modernist phase, usually associated with the Hollywood renaissance of the 1960 and 1970s, and a postmodernist phase, associated with Hollywood in the 1980s and 1990s. Global noir suggests that it is only since the heyday of neo-noir, whenever that might have been, that other cinemas have produced films noirs. And post-noir implies . . . well, what does it mean for something to be 'post'?

Writing in 1992, Anne McClintock argued that a recent proliferation of 'post' terms – 'post-colonialism, post-modernism, post-structuralism, post-Cold-War, post-Marxism, post-apartheid, post-Soviet, post-Ford, post-feminism, post-national, post-historic, even post-contemporary' – indicates 'a wide-spread, epochal crisis in the idea of linear, historical "progress"'. For example, post-colonialism 'marks history as a series of stages along an epochal road from the "pre-colonial" to "the colonial" to "the post-colonial,"' betraying 'an unbidden, if disavowed, commitment to linear time and the idea of "development"'.[24] Furthermore, that postcolonialism is only one among many concurrent 'posts' troubles teleology, perhaps even marks the 'end of history', in the words of neo-liberalism's wishful thinker Francis Fukuyama, and the onset of 'centuries of boredom' as Western-style liberal democracy and its supposed corollary, deregulated capitalism, triumph everywhere.[25] At the same time, as McClintock notes, the prepositionality of 'postness' tends to produce a hierarchical binary in which that which has passed continues to be privileged over that which comes after. Furthermore, such binarism tends to homogenise the phenomena corralled under each term and often leads to a fetishised denial both of distinctions within each phenomenon and of other schemes by which they can be approached, interrogated and understood. Indeed, as Jean-François Lyotard, writing about the 'post' in postmodernism, notes, while 'post' can imply 'a simple succession, a diachronic sequence of periods in which each one is clearly identifiable', the clarity of the distinction between periods implies a radical break, a rupture. However, he adds, 'this "rupture" is in fact a way of forgetting or repressing the past, that is repeating it and not surpassing it'.[26] For him, 'post' 'does not signify a movement of *comeback*, *flashback*, or *feedback*, that is, not a movement of repetition but a procedure in "ana-" : a procedure of analysis, anamnesis, anagogy, and anamorphosis that elaborates an "initial forgetting"'.[27]

Each of these 'ana' terms suggests a creative approach to the past so as to make sense of the present – respectively, the analyst and analysand's cooperative working through of dream images; the recollection of those things that have been forgotten; the interpretation of the 'prior' phenomenon so as to foreground those elements that can be claimed to simultaneously foreshadow and typify the 'post' phenomenon; and the examination from a specific angle so as to uncover the 'natural' appearance of that which was 'distorted' when viewed from a conventional perspective.

In a similar vein, Kwame Anthony Appiah argued in 1991 that the insistence on the 'postness' of postmodern architecture, postmodern literature, postmodern art and so on was a space-clearing exercise, a means by which cultural producers distinguished themselves and their work by constructing and marking differences.[28] He argues that the 'postness' of the postcolonial functions in the same way, and as such is 'not concerned with transcending, with going beyond, coloniality'.[29] Such space-clearing gestures require 'the manufacture of Otherness',[30] and in both cases, 'post' implies a coming-after that also 'challenges earlier legitimating narratives'.[31] Although he strongly identifies such space-clearings with the product differentiation demanded by the ubiquity of capital and capitalist social relations, that does not have to be the only reason for 'posting' a phenomenon.

For example, although Jennifer Fay and Justus Nieland never actually use the term 'post-noir', their focus on the long multinational, international and transnational history of noir 'posts' earlier understandings of the genre as a US, or even Euro-American, undertaking.[32] Such a position opens up discussions of noir in two directions. First, it promotes an understanding of the genre in terms of different national film cultures, and the relationship of the genre and those national cultures to other national and global film cultures. Second, this reframing of the genre enables a better understanding of US film noir by not treating it as synonymous with or definitive of the genre as a whole but as an expression of American experiences, whether of the Depression (Dinerstein), labour history (Broe), the wartime film industry (Biesen), German emigrants in Hollywood (Bahr), US citizenship (Auerbach), the American Dream (Osteen) or music and sound (Butler, Miklitsch).

Evolutionary models typically assert that the contemporary version of the genre is more self-reflexive than earlier versions. Writing about pastiche, Richard Dyer at first seems to accept but ultimately rejects this teleological fallacy. His suggestion that films such as *Body Heat* (Kasdan, US, 1981) affirm 'the existence of a genre by the very fact of being able to imitate it'[33] implies a necessary ordering of noir developments in distinct temporal stages. However, he also suggests that a period in which pastiche is, or at least seems, prominent is one in which there is a broader wave of genre production, 'so that making things noir becomes simply a way of doing things, aware of where the style supposedly comes from but not especially nostalgic or ironic about the fact, not so much neo-noir as just noir now'.[34] Consequently, pastiche, rather than representing some self-reflexive pinnacle, or waning, of a genre's evolution, can 'also be a stage in generic renewal (neo-noir being a step towards normalising contemporary noir production)'.[35] For example, he points to an a cycle – *A Rage in Harlem* (Duke, UK/US, 1991), *Deep Cover* (Duke, US, 1992), *One False Move* (Franklin, US, 1992), *The Glass Shield* (Burnett, France/US, 1994) and *Devil in a Blue Dress* (Franklin, US, 1995) – that moved African Americans 'from the margins of 1940s and 1950s noir' to centre stage.[36]

However, he also acknowledges 'a common model of the history of noir' that identifies pastiche neo-noir as a phenomenon that comes between 1960s and 1970s modernist/revisionist noir and 1990s films that 'either use the genre with a heightened sense of ironic intertextuality, pastiche gone mad', as in *The Two Jakes* (Nicholson, US, 1990), *Reservoir Dogs* (Tarantino, US, 1992) and *Romeo Is Bleeding* (Medak, UK/US, 1994), or that 'have simply got over noir's provenance and distinctiveness and got on with working with its tropes and styles', as in *Someone to Watch Over Me* (Scott, US, 1987), *Red Rock West* (Dahl, US, 1993), *The Last Seduction* (Dahl, UK/US, 1994) and *Bound* (Wachowski and Wachowski, US, 1996).[37] In a footnote, he argues against 'consider[ing] this process only as one phase succeeding another', pointing to the ongoing production of pastiche neo-noir in films such as *Miller's Crossing* (Coen, US, 1990), *Mortal Thoughts* (Rudolph, US, 1991) and *The Man Who Wasn't There* (Coen, US/UK, 2001), as well European films, such as *Shallow Grave* (Boyle, UK, 1994), *The Near Room* (Hayman, UK, 1995) and *Croupier* (Hodges, France/UK/Germany/Ireland, 1998) 'whose geo-cultural difference are liable to lead to the sense of pastiche'.[38] The idea that some contemporary noirs are, thanks to the cycle of pastiches, now able to get back to the business of just being noir is extremely appealing. Indeed, it is largely responsible for the selection of films discussed in the remainder of this chapter. However, the examples of such films that Dyer lists – the wording of his footnote implies that he accepts this description of them – appear, less than a decade later, indistinguishable from those listed as pastiches; and, given the style-consciousness of their directors, Ridley Scott, John Dahl and the Wachowski siblings, it is surprising to find that anyone ever thought otherwise.

Lest I should be charged with committing the very error identified by Gallagher, to which the opening of this chapter referred, they did always seem to me like pastiches. However, this does not necessarily exclude them from the business of noir. To whatever extent Fredric Jameson is correct to describe pastiche as 'speech in a dead language', 'neutral . . . mimicry' and 'blank parody', he is only normalising his own response to textual features.[39] Pastiche can be a major element of a film without being a totalising dominant; and the social relationships within which films are encountered, engaged with and consumed do not produce uniform results. For example, while I personally find nothing of political value in *Someone to Watch Over Me* and *Red Rock West*, there can be no denying the cultural/political impact of *The Last Seduction*'s Bridget (Linda Fiorentino) and *Bound*'s Corky (Gina Gershon) and Violet (Jennifer Tilly) – and the fact that this lesbian couple get away with it – when the films were released, regardless of both films' narrative and visual pastiches of classical Hollywood noir.

Therefore, just as construing noir after the 1980s as necessarily having moved beyond pastiche is problematic, so too is any assumption that because a noir is partly, or even primarily, pastiche it cannot also perform the genre's critical work.

Post-noir: going global, and local, in the era of globalisation

Manuel Castells describes the goals of the capitalist global information network that dominates our world as deepening the capitalist logic of profit-seeking in capital-labor relationships; enhancing the productivity of labor and capital; globalizing production, circulation, and markets, seizing the opportunity of the most advantageous conditions for profit-making everywhere; and marshaling the state's support for productivity gains and competitiveness of national economies, often to the detriment of social protection and public interest regulations.[40]

The imposition, implementation and enforcement of neo-liberal policies worldwide by such institutions as the World Trade Organisation, the International Monetary Fund, the World Bank, the Organisation for Economic Cooperation and Development and the United Nations, and by individual nations, has produced an 'elite specialty labor force' that is highly mobile and 'increasingly globalized', while further constraining the 'bulk of labor' to the 'local'.[41] As Zygmunt Bauman notes, 'the world of the "locally tied", of those barred from moving and thus bound to bear passively whatever change may be visited' upon their locality, 'the real space is fast closing up'.[42] The spaces of these two classes are the spaces of post-noir.

In *The International* (Tykwer, US/Germany/UK, 2009), a rather bedraggled Interpol agent Louis Salinger (Clive Owen) – who was forced out of Scotland Yard several years earlier when a previous investigation into the blandly ominous-sounding International Bank of Business and Credit (IBBC) got too close to uncovering their criminal activities – joins forces with Eleanor Whitman (Naomi Watts), a New York Assistant District Attorney, to pursue evidence that the IBBC is money-laundering for organised crime. Their Europe-wide and Atlantic-hopping investigation uncovers evidence not only of collusion with state agencies and police forces, and of corporate assassination to ease business deals and cover tracks, but also, curiously, that the IBBC wants to buy hundreds of millions of dollars' worth of missile guidance and control systems. When Umberto Calvini (Luca Giorgio Barbareschi), one of only two manufacturers of these systems and possibly Italy's next prime minister, refuses to deal with the IBBC, he is assassinated so that his more pliable sons will take over the business. However, he has already revealed the grander scheme of which the deal is just a small part. The IBCC have bought billions of dollars of Chinese missiles that are inoperable without a particular kind of guidance system. Although they do intend to sell the missiles, the purchase was only a gateway deal in order to secure a future role as the broker for China's international trade in small arms, which plays a major role in global conflicts, especially in the developing world. Whitman assumes the IBCC intends to control conflicts by controlling the flow of weapons. Calvini promptly disabuses her: conflicts create debt, and the IBBC wants control of that debt – banks are only interested in enslaving us all, whether individuals or countries, to debt.

To suggest that the global scope of this international thriller removes it from the purview of noir would be mistaken. Noir always exists in relation to the general filmmaking and cultural norms of its period. For example, classical Hollywood noir typically played out on a smaller scale – a town, a city – without glamorous international locations, and it was frequently driven by dialogue, interspersed with occasional action scenes. However, after the rise of the action movie and in an era of international co-productions, the same anchorings in language and locale need not apply. *Force of Evil* (Polonsky, US, 1948) could establish the parallels between a gangster's attempt to consolidate the numbers racket and the inherent violence of monopoly capitalism, even capturing something of its transformation into finance capitalism, without leaving New York; and both Philip Marlowe and Jake Gittes could map out the operations of capital and its attendant social relationships within and across classes without needing to go much beyond Los Angeles' city limits. But in the time of global digital interconnectedness and neo-liberal hegemony, such restrictions are optional. *The International*'s roaming narrative enables Tykwer to capture, primarily through architecture and design, the interrelatedness of a global capitalist class. There is little to choose between the echoing, tastefully spartan banks, businesses and hotels located in Berlin, Luxembourg or Milan and the Guggenheim in New York, which is at least more distinctive, if equally deracinated. In this visually dark film, which even includes a shot of a window blind's shadow falling across the protagonist, these spaces of the global capital class possess the same kind of sheen as their immaculate limousines. In contrast, the offices of those who seek to police them are cramped, cluttered or both; and the New York of on-the-ground police work resembles the city in *The French Connection* (Friedkin, US, 1971), *Serpico* (Lumet, US, 1973), *The Taking of Pelham 123* (Sargent, US, 1974) or *Dog Day Afternoon* (Lumet, US, 1975), only glossier because that neo-liberal sheen is everywhere and inescapable.

Salinger is a dogged investigator, driven by a somewhat inarticulate code of ethics that seems out of place in this fallen, if glossy, world – 'true-hearted, determined, full of purpose', in the words of William Wexler (Armin Mueller-Stahl), a former Stasi Colonel who is now a senior IBCC counsellor. Whitman possesses similar qualities. When the District Attorney (James Rebhorn) reprimands her for what she defends as her pursuit of 'the truth', he reminds her that 'there's what people want to hear, there's what people want to believe, there's everything else, then there's the truth'. 'And since when is that okay?' she snaps back, adding 'the truth means responsibility'. He agrees: 'Which is why everyone dreads it.' As this exchange suggests, it seems that she will soon, like many a hard-boiled detective before her, be a former employee of the DA.

Wexler acknowledges that, as a young man, he was every bit as upright and purposeful as Salinger, but circumstances overwhelmed him, made him

Figure 10.1 Clive Owen in the Guggenheim Museum in *The International*.

into someone else; on the contrary, Salinger insists, life is always a matter of making choices. Wexler then persuades him that he must choose to step outside the law in order to find justice (in truth, he has already done so multiple times, albeit without realising it). The IBBC cannot be brought down by legal means because the whole system of global capital – multinational corporations, governments, terrorist networks, organised crime – needs banks like the IBCC to exist in order to operate in the grey and black economies that are intertwined with, rather than distinct from, the legal economy. Salinger and Wexler inform the Calvini brothers that the IBBC ordered their father's death, thus forcing the CEO, Jonas Skarssen (Ulrich Thomsen), to buy guidance systems from Ahmet Sunay (Haluk Bilginer) instead. However, Sunay has already sold to Israel countermeasures that will render the missiles ineffective, so all Salinger needs to do is record Skarssen admitting to this knowledge and release the tape to his Syrian and Iranian buyers, who will pull out of the deal and bankrupt the IBBC. This is not defeating the system, but unleashing it upon itself. Of course, in the way of noir, Salinger's plan goes awry, and he finds himself drawing a gun on Skarssen. His big moral dilemma, whether he should shoot or not, is quickly rendered utterly redundant. The Calvinis' hitman steps in from nowhere and kills Skarssen. The system rumbles on.

The end credits display a series of newspapers, moving from front-page coverage of Skarssen's murder to business section accounts of the IBBC's expansion into a third world newly awash in Chinese small arms. The final headline returns us to Whitman, who parted ways with Salinger at his behest when he joined forces with Wexler. She has moved on to bigger and better things, and is now heading an investigation into the money-laundering activities of offshore banks. While it seems like a moment of personal triumph, it is just global capitalism maintaining the façade of legality while ensuring its supposed watchdogs remain powerless to check its lawlessness.

The International does not give any clear view of the primary victims of the IBBC's machinations, reducing them to some briefly glimpsed footage on a peripheral television screen. Although films such as *Perder es cuestión de método/The Art of Losing* (Cabrera, Colombia/Spain, 2004) and *Manorama Six Feet Under* (Navdeep Singh, India, 2007) perhaps prove ultimately less pointed in their critique, they do get us closer to those immiserated and impoverished by globalised capital. In the former, police colonel Moya (Carlos Benjumea) gives Víctor Silanpa (Daniel Giménez Cacho), a middle-aged and rather shabby journalist whose girlfriend has just left him and whose haemorrhoids are playing up, an exclusive to investigate the murder of an unknown man, impaled on a pole, by a lake outside Bogotá. Silanpa gradually uncovers a web of conspiracies and counter-conspiracies concerning the ownership of the lakefront, over which gangsters and other financial speculators are competing since it is ripe for development. In this mildly comical thriller, no layer of society is left untouched by the often-fatal consequences of such dealings, from leading politicians and lawyers to the teenage Quica (Martina García), who pretends to be older than she is in order to work as a prostitute who pretends to be a minor. When Silanpa's findings lead to the arrest of the key conspirators, Moya merely strikes a deal with them that will benefit him financially before releasing them. He concocts a rather implausible story that pins it all on people who are already dead or arrested, and blackmails Silanpa into going along with him. As the theme song tells us, when 'cash is king', when 'politics means theft, millionaires, money and golden papaya', when 'they've bribed us all', then 'nobody's innocent any more' and social relations have dissolved into a war of all against all in which only 'the most violent' will survive.

Manorama, which is modelled after *Chinatown* (Polanski, US, 1974) and full of allusions to *Kiss Me Deadly* (Aldrich, US, 1955), has an even more complicated narrative. It is set in Lakhor, in north-west India, an inconsequential town that makes the news twice a year, once in summer, when about a hundred people die from the heat, and once in winter, when roughly the same number die from the cold. There has been a drought for three years, and construction of the much-hyped Rajasthan Vikas Canal has stopped before it had barely started. Satyaveer Randhawa (Abhay Deol), a junior Public Works Department engineer, has been suspended for accepting a bribe or, rather, for being the one person in a thoroughly corrupt department to get caught doing so. He is also a writer and journalist, the author of *Manorama*, a novel that sold only 200 copies. One night, a woman (Sarika) who claims to be the wife of P. P. Rathore (Kulbhushan Kharbanda), the right-wing Hindu nationalist state minister for irrigation, appears out of the night, in a shot that echoes the first appearance of Kathie (Jane Greer) in *Out of the Past* (Tourneur, US, 1947), to hire Satyaveer. Since she has no access to a private detective, she wants to hire the author of her favourite detective novel to find evidence of the affair she suspects her husband is having; all he manages to photograph, however, is the minister arguing with a young woman. He hands over the undeveloped film, thinking that will be the end of it, but he becomes suspicious after his client, who admits she is not Meenakshi Rathore and that her name is Manorama, apparently commits suicide.

Manorama was actually a social worker and activist opposed to the construction of the canal. Satyaveer tracks down her roommate, Sheetal (Raima Sen) and follows her to the orphanage where she works. It is supported by, and named after, the childless Rathore, whose real wife is confined to a wheelchair. The woman he photographed arguing with the minister turns out to be Sameera (Poonam Gibson), the fiancée of Rathore's personal physician, Anil Poddar (Rajesh M), who also runs the orphanage's clinic. Mistaking Satyaveer for another journalist, she reveals that she is Rathore's illegitimate daughter, and that she needs him to admit to this publicly so that Anil's parents will permit their marriage to go ahead; he refuses to do so because her mother was a Muslim. After witnessing the inflated prices being paid at auction for plots of deserted wasteland that will face onto the canal, if and when it is built, Satyaveer begins to piece the mystery together. He discovers that Sheetal died some time ago and that Neetu, the woman pretending to be her, actually works for Rathore. He is framed for the bloody murder of Sameera and Anil, and while on the run finds the roll of film Manorama shot the night after his failed attempt. It shows Rathore sexually abusing, and accidentally killing, a young girl who had gone missing from the orphanage.[43] Satyaveer concludes Manorama was using it to blackmail Rathore into not restarting construction on the canal. He could not be more wrong.

Manorama worked for Rathore, infiltrating NGOs and protest groups. Anil is her brother, and when they discovered that Sameera was Rathore's daughter, and that Rathore had terminal cancer, they kept the latter a secret from the minister while trying to persuade him to recognise Sameera. Acknowledged as his only child, she would inherit everything, including all the land he owns through and alongside the canal route. They were just in it for his money – the political corruption around the development project, even the decades of child abductions and abuse, which seemed to be the very core of the narrative turn out to have been peripheral to the scheme actually driving the narrative.

It is a clever switch. Early on, posing as a journalist writing an article on an organisation protesting the canal, Satyaveer tries to gather information about Manorama's life and background. He explains to her colleagues that he needs the human interest angle provided by her death to shape a story that will allow him to express their shared 'socio-political views'. In a similar manner, *Manorama* resolves into a melodrama about the conniving of greedy relatives, but not before foregrounding the socio-political backdrop to their actions. After attending the auction, Satyaveer comes across the temporary encampment of some dispossessed peasants, and asks an old man where they are going. He replies:

just moving along. We'll go where our hunger takes us. Our land is gone ... I'm just a peasant, son. All this land belongs to Rathore. Our families worked this land for generations, eked out a living from this dry dirt. But now the canal's coming – the Raja's barren land will yield gold. There's no room for us or our hunger here now. May God have mercy on us.

This cannot help but recall the controversial Narmada dam project,[44] which displaced at least 70,000 people and, while state governments apparently turned a blind eye, failed to comply with almost every mandated environment and health safeguard. Such lucrative development projects, long favoured by the regulatory and directive organisations that work to ensure the extension and perpetuation of the capitalist global economy, are commonplace, as are such consequences.

Despite Hollywood's much commented upon turn to (occasional) narratively complex, broad-tapestry, ensemble-cast, cross-class melodramas in the new millennium, such overt political commentary is relatively rare; John Sayles' semi-independent *Lone Star* (US, 1996) and *Silver City* (US, 2004) are obvious exceptions. Instead, this kind of narrative has found a home in the 'quality' dramas of the TVIII era, most obviously *The Wire* (US, 2002–8), *Forbrydelsen/The Killing* (Denmark/Norway/Sweden/Germany, 2007–12), *Engrenages/Spiral* (France, 2005–) and, in a more fantastical mode, the abruptly cancelled *Day Break* (US, 2006).

In contrast, one particular strength of lower-budget post-noir film lies in its capacity for realist narratives focused on the lives of those Bauman describes as the 'locally tied'.[45] *Frozen River* (Hunt, US, 2008) is set in upstate New York, on the US border with Canada. In the winter, it is difficult to tell the grey sky apart from the snow-covered ground. Ray Eddy (Melissa Leo) lives in a battered old single-wide trailer, with her two sons, fifteen-year-old TJ (Charlie McDermott) and five-year-old Ricky (James Reilly), and a gambling addict husband, Troy, who has just disappeared with their savings – money they need to take delivery of their dream home, a double-wide with three bedrooms and wall-to-wall carpet. She spots Troy's car at the bus stop by the Territorial High Stakes bingo hall on the edge of the reservation, just as it is being stolen by Lila Littlewolf (Misty Upham). When Ray confronts her, the young Mohawk woman tells her where she can sell the car to a smuggler who is always on the lookout for a good car with a button release trunk; however, she goes on to con Ray into crossing the over the frozen river that passes through the reservation, and is thus not patrolled, into Canada in order to smuggle a pair of Chinese workers into the US.[46]

Lila is unpopular with the tribal council, in part because of her husband's death, and is allowed no real contact with her infant son, who was taken away from her and is being raised by her mother-in-law. Ray is reduced to serving her sons popcorn and Tang for two successive meals, and with their television about to be repossessed, she unsuccessfully pleads with her boss at the Yankee Dollar store to put her on full time, as he promised he would after six months when he hired her two years ago. Faced with losing the deposit on the double-wide if she cannot make the balloon payment by Christmas, she sees no way out other than to go into business with Lila; for each person they smuggle into the US, they are paid $1,200.

Despite their initial antagonism, and the particularities of their different situations, Ray and Lila grow to recognise their shared marginalisation and immiseration. A kind of class solidarity emerges between them, affectively figured as a bond shared between mothers whose children have no one else. This is cemented when Ray, who knows she will be treated much more leniently because she is white, gives herself up to the police so that Lila can avoid arrest and expulsion from the reservation. Equally significantly, Ray trusts Lila (who snatches back her own son) to take care of TJ, Ricky and their new home while she serves a couple of months in prison.

As well as capturing the ceaseless, wearying precarity of minimum-wage (and below) workers, *Frozen River* carefully links the constraints on its protagonists to global capital. When Ricky asks his mother what will become of the single-wide when they move into their new home, she explains that it will be flattened, shipped to China, melted down and turned into toys that will be shipped back to the US for her to sell at Yankee Dollar. Although she does not seem to connect this to the Chinese Lila tricked her into smuggling across the border, on their next trip, the first at her own suggestion, the nature of this commerce in people becomes clear. Their cargo have their shoes taken away from them so that, once in the US, they cannot flee; each undocumented worker is destined to indentured servitude to the snakehead gang behind the trafficking operation until they have paid off the cost – some $40,000–$50,000 each – of being brought to the US. On their final trip, Ray even risks her own safety to protect two young women, clearly destined for sex work, from a trafficker's physical abuse. Despite their global movement of such *sans papiers*, they are every bit as locally tied as Ray and Lila.

Mang jing/Blind Shaft (Li, China/Germany/Hong Kong, 2003) is set in Shanxi in northern China, one of the country's poorest provinces. The high, cold, dry plateau often appears like nothing more than a succession of open-cast mines. In this coal-rich region, mine bosses cut corners so as to make their quotas, and with thousands of deaths in the mines every year, they are anxious to avoid investigations. As the opening minutes of the film show us, Song Jinming (Yi Lixiang) and Tang Zhaoyang (Wang Shuangbao), two of China's millions of unemployed and underemployed migrant workers, have found a way to take profitable advantage of this. Having convinced a third man that it is necessary to pose as Tang's brother in order to get a job at this

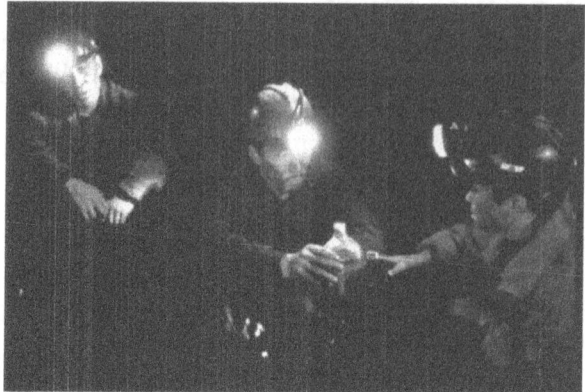

Figure 10.2 Dark prelude to homicide in *Blind Shaft*.

particular mine, they murder him mid-shift then fake his death in a cave-in. So as to contain news of the fatality, the boss orders thugs violently to turn back anyone who tries to leave the mine camp, and then sets about persuading Tang to accept cash compensation for his bereavement in exchange for signing a waiver stating that his brother died from his own carelessness. When a henchman suggests just killing off Tang and Song, the only thing that keeps the boss from doing so is the prospect of the much larger bribe he might have to pay to the police if their deaths are discovered. Once Tang accepts the money, he and Song are fired, which enables them to make their way to a nearby town to remit their earnings to their distant families, and to find another victim for their lethal scam.

Tang is a stone killer, indifferent to everyone except Song and, presumably, the family he supports. Song is more humane, concerned about being able to pay for his son's tuition, and is genuinely reluctant when Tang tricks Yuan Fengming (Wang Baoqiang) into posing as Song's nephew. Yuan is just fifteen, naive and goodhearted. His father left home six months earlier to look for work and has not been heard from since. Yuan left school because he can no longer afford it, and is desperate to earn the money necessary to keep his younger sister in school. He even hopes to find his father while wandering in search of work. When the threesome are eventually hired at a distant mine, they must work a trial period for nothing, and pay for their boots and helmets, before receiving even the meagre pay typical of the industry. Song becomes attached to Yuan, although he denies it, and even wonders whether he is the son of the last man they killed. He cannot bring himself to murder the boy, but one day, after setting blasting charges in the shaft in which they are working, Tang kills their snooping foreman and does not hesitate to strike down Song to get to Yuan. Yuan flees, and Song manages to knock out Tang before collapsing beside him. If either of them is still alive, they are both killed when the charges are ignited. Over his confused protests, Yuan is bullied by the mine boss into accepting compensation for his supposed uncle's death.

Mang jing possesses a kind of grubby, digital documentary realism. It is shot in such a way as to match the footage that was covertly shot on uncontrolled locations, including actual mining camps whose managers Li had to bribe in order to gain access. As with *Frozen River*, affective bonds, albeit considerably more attenuated, are intertwined with recognition of a shared class position. This is apparent in the relationship between Song and Tang, and in the paternal interest Song takes in Yuan, but its most potent and touching expression comes elsewhere. One of the excuses Song concocts to postpone Yuan's murder is that the boy should not die a virgin, so they take him to a brothel in the nearby town and set him up with a young prostitute, Xiao Hong (Jing Ai). She presents herself as a somewhat jaded professional to the older man, but lowers this front a little when alone with Yuan. Some days later, when the men have finally been paid, they return to town, and Yuan is eager to send his wages back home. As he queues up, a rather more conservatively dressed Xiao exits the office where she, too, has been remitting her earnings. He is too shy to respond to her greeting but, as she passes by, she reaches out and squeezes him gently on the shoulder. It is a tiny moment of human empathy, snatched from the cash nexus that otherwise dominates social relations.

Although *Blind Shaft* makes no reference to extensive Western investment and profiteering from China's poorly regulated and extremely dangerous mining industry, the film is careful to signal the global flows of capital through the region. This is signalled by commodities – Song's shoulder bag has a logo saying 'Monterey'; the pornographic images on the walls of the miners' shack and the less explicit ones that decorate Xiao's small room in the brothel are all of Western women – and also by the new lyrics to an old song that the two men are taught by the sex workers in a karaoke bar. It no longer goes

> Long live socialism, long live socialism
> In socialist countries everyone is high status
> Reactionaries overthrown
> Imperialists ran away with their tails behind

but instead

> The reactionaries were never overthrown
> The capitalists came back with their US dollars
> Liberating all of China
> Bringing the sexual climax of socialism

This history has produced a world in which, according to Tang, 'only a mum's feelings for her kids are real'; and Song doubts that even that is true any more.

CONCLUSION

For Lyotard, 'post' represents a discursive strategy, a manner of construing the present so as to shape our understanding of the past. It draws to the surface (or perhaps creates) the latent content of memories. It causes us to remember or, perhaps, creates memories (since, in a sense, that which has been forgotten is not available for recollection). It implies a past that apparently causes, makes necessary, the (construed) present. It normalises the past that can now be seen, freeing it from the distorted view that once concealed it.

In proposing a version of post-noir, one that deliberately marginalises expressionist visual style in favour of realist figuration and critique of capitalism, this chapter is not just an attempt to outline some post-millennial trends in the genre. It also, in a modest way, remembers what noir, the pulp wing of Critical Theory, does when it gets over itself and gets back to business.

BIBLIOGRAPHY

Altman, Rick (1999), *Film/Genre*, London: BFI.
Appiah, Kwame Anthony (1991), 'Is the post- in postmodernism the post- in postcolonial?', *Critical Inquiry* 17(2) (winter), 336–57.
Auerbach, Jonathan (2011), *Dark Borders: Film Noir and American Citizenship*, Durham, NC: Duke University Press.
Bahr, Ehrhard (2007), *Weimar on the Pacific: German Exile Culture in Los Angeles and the Crisis of Modernism*, Berkeley, CA: University of California Press.
Bauman, Zygmunt (1998), *Globalization: The Human Consequences*, Cambridge: Polity.
Biesen, Sheri Chinen (2005), *Blackout: World War II and the Origins of Film Noir*, Baltimore, MD: The Johns Hopkins University Press.
Boozer, Jack (1999/2000), 'The lethal *femme fatale* in the noir tradition', *Journal of Film and Video* 51(3/4), 20–35.
Bould, Mark and Sherryl Vint (2008), 'There is no such thing as science fiction', in James Gunn, Marleen Barr and Matthew Candelaria (eds), *Reading Science Fiction*, New York: Palgrave, pp. 43–51.
Broe, Dennis (2009), *Film Noir, American Workers, and Postwar Hollywood*, Gainesville, FL: University Press of Florida.
Butler, David (2002), *Jazz Noir: Listening to Music from Phantom Lady to The Last Seduction*, Westport, CT: Praeger.
Castells, Manuel (2000), *The Information Age: Economy, Society and Culture, Volume I: The Rise of the Network Society*, 2nd edition, Oxford: Blackwell.
Chartier, Jean-Pierre (1996), 'The Americans are making dark films too', in R. Barton Palmer (trans. and ed.), *Perspectives on Film Noir*, New York: G. K. Hall, pp. 25–7.
Desser, David (2003), 'Global noir: Genre film in the age of transnationalism', in Barry Keith Grant (ed.), *Film Genre Reader III*, Austin, TX: University of Texas Press, pp. 516–36.

Dinerstein, Joel (2008), '"Emergent noir": Film noir and the great depression in *High Sierra* (1941) and *This Gun for Hire* (1942)', *Journal of American Studies* 42(3), 415–48.
Dyer, Richard (2007), *Pastiche*, London: Routledge.
Fay, Jennifer and Justus Nieland (2010), *Film Noir: Hard-Boiled Modernity and the Cultures of Globalization*, London: Routledge.
Frow, John (2007), '"Reproducibles, rubrics, and everything you need": Genre theory today', *PMLA* 122(5), 1626–34.
Fukuyama, Francis (1989), 'The end of history', *The National Interest* (summer), online at http://ps321.community.uaf.edu/files/2012/10/Fukuyama-End-of-history-article.pdf (accessed 18 July 2013).
Gallagher, Tag (1995), 'Shoot-out at the genre corral: Problems in the "evolution" of the western', in Grant (ed.), *Film Genre Reader III*, p. 262–76.
Jameson, Fredric (1991), *Postmodernism or, The Cultural Logic of Late Capitalism*, London: Verso.
——.(2002), *A Singular Modernity: Essay on the Ontology of the Present*, London: Verso.
Lyotard, Jean-François (1993), 'Note on the meaning of "post-"', in Don Barry, Bernadette Maher, Julian Pefanis, Virginia Spate and Morgan Thomas (trans.), *The Postmodern Explained: Correspondences 1982–1985*, Minneapolis, MN: University of Minnesota Press, pp. 75–80.
McClintock, Anne (1994), 'The angel of progress: Pitfalls of the term "postcolonialism"', in Francis Barker, Peter Hulme and Margaret Iversen (eds), *Colonial Discourse/Postcolonial Theory*, Manchester: Manchester University Press, pp. 253–66.
Marcantonio, Carla (2008), 'The transvestite figure and film noir: Pedro Almodóvar's transnational imaginary', in Jay Beck and Vicente Rodríguez Ortega (eds), *Contemporary Spanish Cinema and Genre*, Manchester: Manchester University Press, pp. 157–78.
Miklitsch, Robert (2011), *Siren City: Sound and Source Music in Classic American Film Noir*, New Brunswick, NJ: Rutgers University Press.
Moine, Raphaëlle (2008), *Cinema Genre*, trans. Alistair Fox and Hilary Radner, Oxford: Blackwell.
Osteen, Mark (2012), *Nightmare Alley: Film Noir and the American Dream*, Baltimore, MD: The Johns Hopkins University Press.
Palmer, Lorrie (2012), '*Crank*ed masculinity: Hypermediation in digital action cinema', *Cinema Journal* 51(4), 1–25.
Rieder, John (2010), 'On defining SF, or not: Genre theory, SF, and history', *Science Fiction Studies* 111, 191–209.
Roy, Arundhati (1999), 'The greater common good', in Arundhati Roy, *The Cost of Living*, New York: Modern Library, pp. 1–90.
Shaviro, Steven (2010), *Post-Cinematic Affect*, Winchester: Zero.
Shin, Chi-Yun and Mark Gallagher (eds) (2013), *East Asian Film Noir: Transnational Encounters and Intercultural Dialogue*, London: I. B. Tauris.
Spicer, Andrew (ed.) (2007), *European Film Noir*, Manchester: Manchester University Press.
Stephens, Chuck (2012), 'A face in the crowd: Attack of the 100-foot hotcha. Late-noir firestarter Beverly Michaels's moment in the Hollywood sun', *Film Comment* 48(4), 18.
Tuck, Greg (2009), 'Laughter in the dark: Irony, black comedy and noir in the films of David Lynch, the Coen Brothers, and Quentin Tarantino', in Mark Bould, Kathrina Glitre and Greg Tuck (eds), *Neo-Noir*, London: Wallflower, pp. 152–67.
——.(2007), 'Sex *with* the city: Urban spaces, sexual encounters and erotic spectacle

in Tsukamoto Shinya's *Rokugatsu no Hebi – A Snake of June* (2003)', *Film Studies* 11, 49–60.
Vincendeau, Ginette (2007), 'French film noir', in Spicer (ed.), *European Film Noir*, pp. 23–54.

NOTES

1. Tag Gallagher, 'Shoot-out at the genre corral: Problems in the "evolution" or the western', in Barry Keith Grant (ed.), *Film Genre Reader III* (Austin, TX: University of Texas Press), p. 263.
2. Ibid., p. 268.
3. Ibid., pp. 268–9.
4. Ibid., p. 263.
5. Jennifer Fay and Justus Nieland, *Film Noir: Hard-Boiled Modernity and the Cultures of Globalization* (London: Routledge, 2010), p. ix.
6. Jack Boozer, 'The lethal *femme fatale* in the noir tradition', *Journal of Film and Video* 51(3/4) (1999–2000), 20.
7. Ibid., 33.
8. Ibid., 33.
9. Greg Tuck, 'Laughter in the dark: Irony, black comedy and noir in the films of David Lynch, the Coen Brothers, and Quentin Tarantino', in Mark Bould, Kathrina Glitre and Greg Tuck (eds), *Neo-Noir* (London: Wallflower, 2009), p. 165.
10. Ibid., p. 166.
11. Ibid., p. 166.
12. Ibid., p. 166.
13. On the problems with evolutionary models of genre, see Gallagher, 'Shoot-out at the genre corral'.
14. Chuck Stephens, 'A face in the crowd: Attack of the 100-foot hotcha. Late-noir firestarter Beverly Michaels's moment in the Hollywood sun', *Film Comment* 48(4) (2012), 18. His subtitle adds further confusion by describing Michael as a 'late-noir firestarter'.
15. See Rick Altman, *Film/Genre* (London: British Film Institute, 1999).
16. John Rieder, 'On defining SF, or not: Genre theory, SF, and history', *Science Fiction Studies* 111 (2010), 200.
17. Mark Bould and Sherryl Vint, 'There is no such thing as science fiction', in James Gunn, Marleen Barr and Matthew Candelaria (eds), *Reading Science Fiction* (New York: Palgrave 2008).
18. John Frow, '"Reproducibles, rubrics, and everything you need": Genre theory today', *PMLA* 122(5) (2007), 1630.
19. Ginette Vincendeau, 'French film noir', in Andrew Spicer (ed.), *European Film Noir* (Manchester: Manchester University Press, 2007), p. 45.
20. Raphaëlle Moine, *Cinema Genre*, trans. Alistair Fox and Hilary Radner (Oxford: Blackwell, 2008), p. 60.
21. Fredric Jameson, *Postmodernism or, The Cultural Logic of Late Capitalism* (London: Verso, 1991), p. 5.
22. Ibid., p. 40.
23. Ibid., p. 214.
24. Anne McClintock, 'The angel of progress: Pitfalls of the term "postcolonialism"', in Francis Barker, Peter Hulme and Margaret Iversen (eds), *Colonial Discourse/Postcolonial Theory* (Manchester: Manchester University Press, 2004), p. 254.
25. Francis Fukuyama, 'The end of history', *The National Interest* (summer 1989),

online at http://ps321.community.uaf.edu/files/2012/10/Fukuyama-End-of-history-article.pdf (accessed 18 July 2013).
26. Jean-François Lyotard, 'Note on the meaning of "post-"', in Don Barry, Bernadette Maher, Julian Pefanis, Virginia Spate and Morgan Thomas (trans.), *The Postmodern Explained: Correspondences 1982–1985* (Minneapolis, MN: University of Minnesota Press, 1993), p. 77.
27. Ibid., p. 80.
28. Kwame Anthony Appiah, 'Is the post- in postmodernism the post- in postcolonial?', *Critical Inquiry* 17(2) (winter 1991), 341–2.
29. Ibid., 348.
30. Ibid., 356.
31. Ibid., 353.
32. They are not alone in this drive to treat noir in ways that are not Americo-centric. See, for example, David Desser, 'Global noir: Genre film in the age of transnationalism', in Barry Keith Grant (ed.), *Film Genre Reader III* (Austin, TX: University of Texas Press, 2003), pp. 516–36; Carla Marcantonio, 'The transvestite figure and film noir: Pedro Almodóvar's transnational imaginary', in Jay Beck and Vicente Rodríguez Ortega (eds), *Contemporary Spanish Cinema and Genre* (Manchester: Manchester University Press, 2008) pp. 157–78; Chi-Yun Shin and Mark Gallagher (eds), *East Asian Film Noir: Transnational Encounters and Intercultural Dialogue* (London: I. B. Tauris, 2013); and Andrew Spicer (ed.), *European Film Noir* (Manchester: Manchester University Press, 2007).
33. Richard Dyer, *Pastiche* (London: Routledge, 2007), p. 132.
34. Ibid., p. 129.
35. Ibid., pp. 132–3.
36. Ibid., p. 129.
37. Ibid., p. 129.
38. Ibid, pp. 135–6.
39. Jameson, *Postmodernism*, p. 17.
40. Manuel Castells, *The Information Age: Economy, Society and Culture, Volume I: The Rise of the Network Society*, second edition (Oxford: Blackwell, 2000), p. 19.
41. Ibid., p. 131.
42. Zygmunt Bauman, *Globalization: The Human Consequences* (Cambridge: Polity, 1998), p. 88.
43. Rathore's monstrosity is obviously indebted to *Chinatown*'s Noah Cross (John Huston), himself a Richard Nixon figure. Some European post-noirs, such as *De zaak Alzheimer/The Memory of a Killer* (Van Looy, Belgium/Netherlands, 2003) and *Män som hatar kvinnor/The Girl with the Dragon Tattoo* (Oplev, Sweden/Denmark/Germany/Norway, 2009), emphasise the monstrosity of the capitalist class and its politician-compradors through their paedophilia, incest and other, frequently murderous, sex crimes; others, such as *Intacto* (Fresnadillo, Spain, 2001), *13 Tzameti* (Babluani, France/Georgia, 2005), *Frontière(s)/Frontier(s)* (Gens, France/Switzerland, 2007), *Frygtelig lykkelig/Terribly Happy* (Genz, Denmark, 2008), *Martyrs* (Laugier, France/Canada, 2008) and *Kill List* (Wheatley, UK, 2011), often spill over into fantasy or horror to convey this monstrosity by suggesting the hidden extension into present-day power relations archaic feudal privilege and abuses, often linked to Europe's fascist history and/or the occult. *The International*'s Skarssen is perhaps unusual among such villain figures inasmuch as there is nothing overtly unsavoury about him, although the scenes in which he is seen at home with his young son, teaching him that relationships are instrumental, constantly to be weighed and strategised, do suggest that the sociopathy of

privilege, wealth and control that governs his business dealings – always seemingly rational, but never reasonable – extends into all aspects of his life.
44. Familiar in the West from Arundhati Roy's *The Cost of Living* (1999) and the documentaries *A Narmada Diary* (Dhuru and Patwardhan, India, 1995) and *Drowned Out* (Armstrong, UK, 2002).
45. This emphasis on more overtly realist filmmaking here is not intended to suggest that there is no place in post-noir for what could be broadly described as expressionism. Beyond such oddities as *Revolver* (Ritchie, France/UK, 2005) and *Haywire* (Soderbergh, US/Ireland, 2011) and such genuine one-offs as *Southland Tales* (Kelly, Germany/US/France, 2006), *The Bad Lieutenant: Port of Call – New Orleans* (Herzog, US, 2009) and *Black Swan* (Aronofsky, US, 2010), there are several directors pushing post-noir expressionism in new directions while getting on with the business of noir, including: Tsukamoto Shinya, in *Tokyo Fist* (Japan, 1995), *Bullet Ballet* (Japan, 1998), *Rokugatsu no hebi/A Snake of June* (Japan, 2002); Nicolas Winding Refn, in *Drive* (US, 2011) and *Only God Forgives* (France/Thailand/US/Sweden, 2013) especially, although this tendency has been evident since his earliest films; and Neveldine & Taylor, in *Crank* (US, 2006) and *Crank: High Voltage* (US, 2009), which are frenetic unofficial remakes of *D.O.A.* (Maté, US, 1950) and *Gamer* (US, 2009). On Tsukamoto, see Greg Tuck, 'Sex *with* the city: Urban spaces, sexual encounters and erotic spectacle in Tsukamoto Shinya's *Rokugatsu no Hebi – A Snake of June* (2003)', *Film Studies* 11 (2007), 49–60; on Neveldine & Taylor, see Steven Shaviro, *Post-Cinematic Affect* (Winchester: Zero, 2010), pp. 93–130 and Lorrie Palmer, '*Crank*ed masculinity: Hypermediation in digital action cinema', *Cinema Journal* 51(4) (2012), 1–25.
46. People trafficking is central to a number of post-noirs, including *Dirty Pretty Things* (Frears, UK, 2002), *Lilja 4-ever/Lilya 4-ever* (Moodysson, Sweden/Denmark, 2002), *Eastern Promises* (Cronenberg, US/UK/Canada, 2007), *Mang shan/Blind Mountain* (Li, China, 2007) and *Flickan som lekte med elden/The Girl Who Played with Fire* (Alfredson, Sweden/Denmark/Germany, 2009).

SELECTED BIBLIOGRAPHY OF INTERNATIONAL FILM NOIR

Anderson, Joseph L. and Donald Richie (1982), *The Japanese Film: Art and Industry* (expanded edition), Princeton, NJ: Princeton University Press.
Andrew, Dudley (1995), *Mists of Regret: Culture and Sensibility in Classic French Film*, Princeton, NJ: Princeton University Press.
——.(ed.) (1987), *Breathless*, New Brunswick, NJ: Rutgers University Press.
Austin, Guy (1996), *Contemporary French Cinema: An Introduction*, Manchester: Manchester University Press.
——.(1999), *Claude Chabrol*, Manchester: Manchester University Press.
Babington, Bruce (ed.) (2001), *British Stars and Stardom: From Alma Taylor to Sean Connery*, Manchester: Manchester University Press.
Badley, Linda (2011), *Lars von Trier*, Urbana, IL: University of Illinois Press.
Barr, Charles (ed.) (1986), *All Our Yesterdays: 90 Years of British Cinema*, London: British Film Institute.
Baskett, Michael (2008), *The Attractive Empire: Transnational Film Culture in Imperial Japan*, Honolulu, HI: University of Hawai'i Press.
Bernardi, Joanne (2001), *Writing in Light: The Silent Scenario and the Japanese Pure Film Movement*, Detroit, MI: Wayne State University Press.
Bordwell, David (1988), *Ozu and the Poetics of Cinema*, Princeton, NJ: Princeton University Press.
Bould, Mark, Kathrina Glitre and Greg Tuck (eds) (2010), *Neo-noir*, New York: Wallflower.
Browne, Nick, Paul G. Pickowicz, Vivian Sobchack and Esther Yau (eds) (1994), *New Chinese Cinemas: Forms, Identities, Politics*, Cambridge: Cambridge University Press.
Brunette, Peter (2005), *Wong Kar-wai*, Urbana, IL: University of Illinois Press.
Burch, Noël (1979), *To the Distant Observer: Form and Meaning in the Japanese Cinema*, Berkeley, CA: University of California Press.
Buss, Robin (1994), *French Film Noir*, New York: Marion Boyars.

Cheung, Esther M. K., Gina Marchetti and Tan See-Kam (eds) (2011), *Hong Kong Screenscapes: From the New Wave to the Digital Frontier*, Hong Kong: Hong Kong University Press.
Chibnall, Steve and Robert Murphy (eds) (1999), *British Crime Cinema*, London: Routledge.
Choi, Jinhee (2010), *The South Korean Film Renaissance: Local Hitmakers, Global Provocateurs*, Middletown, CT: Wesleyan University Press.
Conard, Mark T. (ed.) (2007), *The Philosophy of Neo-noir*, Lexington, KT: University Press of Kentucky.
Conway, Kelley (2004), *Chanteuse in the City: The Realist Singer in French Film*, Berkeley, CA: University of California Press.
Devlin, William J. and Shai Biderman (eds) (2011), *The Philosophy of David Lynch*, Lexington, KN: University of Kentucky Press.
Dixon, Wheeler Winston (1997), *The Films of Jean-Luc Godard*, Albany, NY: State University of New York Press.
Doom, Ryan P. (2009), *The Coen Brothers*, Santa Barbara, CA: Praeger.
Durham, Carolyn A. (1998), *Double Takes: Culture and Gender in French Films and their American Remakes*, Hanover, NH: University Press of New England.
Dussere, Erik (2014), *America is Elsewhere: The Noir Tradition in the Age of Consumer Culture*, Oxford: Oxford University Press.
Fay, Jennifer and Justus Nieland (2010), *Film Noir: Hard-Boiled Modernity and the Cultures of Globalization*, New York: Routledge.
Forbes, Jill (1992), *The Cinema in France after the New Wave*, London: British Film Institute.
Forshaw, Barry (2012), *British Crime Film: Subvertng the Social Order*, New York: Palgrave Macmillan.
Frodon, Jean-Michel (1995), *L'Âge moderne du cinéma français: De la Nouvelle Vague à nos jours*, Paris: Flammarion.
Gates, Philippa and Lisa Funnell (2012), *Transnational Asian Identities in Pan-Pacific Cinemas: The Reel Asian Exchange*, New York: Routledge.
Gateward, Frances (ed.) (2007), *Seoul Searching: Culture and Identity in Contemporary Korean Cinema*, Albany, NY: State University of New York Press.
Gerow, Andrew (2010), *Visions of Japanese Modernity: Articulations of Cinema, Nation, and Spectatorship, 1895–1925*, Berkeley, CA: University of California Press.
Giannopoulou, Zina (ed.) (2013), *Mulholland Drive: Philosophers on Film*, New York: Routledge.
Gopalan, Lalitha (2002), *Cinema of Interruptions: Action Genres in Contemporary Indian Cinema*, London: British Film Institute.
Greene, Naomi (1999), *Landscapes of Loss: The National Past in Postwar French Cinema*, Princeton, NJ: Princeton University Press.
Hall, Kenneth E. (2009), *John Woo's The Killer*, Hong Kong: Hong Kong University Press.
Hayward, Susan (1993), *French National Cinema*, London: Routledge.
——.(2004), *Simone Signoret: The Star as Cultural Sign*, New York: Continuum.
——.(2005), *Les Diaboliques*, London: I. B. Tauris.
——.(2010), *Nikita*, London: I. B. Tauris.
Hillier, Jim (ed.) (1985), *Cahiers du cinéma: The 1950s*, Cambridge, MA: Harvard University Press.
Hirsch, Foster (1999), *Detours and Lost Highways: A Map of Neo-Noir*, New York: Limelight Editions.
Hjort, Mette (2005), *Small Nation, Global Cinema: The New Danish Cinema*, Minneapolis, MN: University of Minnesota Press.

Hubert-Lacombe, Patricia (1996), *Le cinéma français dans la guerre froide: 1946–1956*, Paris: L'Harmattan.
Hughes, Alex and James S. Williams (eds) (2001), *Gender and French Cinema*, Oxford: Berg.
Hunt, Leon and Leung Wing-Fai (eds) (2008), *East Asian Cinemas: Exploring Transnational Connections on Film*, New York: I. B. Tauris.
Insdorf, Annette (1995), *François Truffaut*, New York and Cambridge: Cambridge University Press.
Kania, Andrew (ed.) (2009), *Memento: Philosophers on Film*, New York: Routledge.
Keaney, Michael F. (2010), *British Noir Guide*, Jefferson, NC: McFarland.
Keesey, Douglas (2010), *Neo-Noir*, Harpenden: Kamera Books.
Kim, Kyung Hyun (2011), *Virtual Hallyu: Korean Cinema of the Global Era*, Durham, NC: Duke University Press.
Kirihara, Donald (1992), *Patterns of Time: Mizoguchi and the 1930s*, Madison, WI: University of Wisconsin Press.
Kitamura, Hiroshi (2010), *Screening Enlightenment: Hollywood and the Cultural Reconstruction of Defeated Japan*, Ithaca, NY: Cornell University Press.
Kline, T. J. (2010), *Unraveling French Cinema: From L'Atalante to Caché*, Chichester & Malden, MA: Wiley-Blackwell.
Konstantarakos, Myrto (2000), *Spaces in European Cinema*, Exeter & Portland, OR: Intellect.
Lumholdt, Jan (ed.) (2003), *Lars von Trier: Interviews*, Jackson, MS: University of Mississippi Press.
Marchetti, Gina (2007), *Andrew Lau and Alan Mak's Infernal Affairs – The Trilogy*, Hong Kong: Hong Kong University Press.
Marchetti, Gina and Tan See Kam (eds) (2007), *Hong Kong Film, Hollywood and the New Global Cinema*, New York: Routledge.
Marklund, Anders and Mariah Larsson (eds) (2010), *Swedish Film: An Introduction and Reader*, Lund: Nordic Academic Press.
Martin, Richard (1999), *Mean Streets and Raging Bulls: The Legacy of Film Noir in Contemporary American Cinema*, Lanham, MD: Scarecrow Press.
Mazdon, Lucy (2000), *Encore Hollywood: Remaking French Cinema*, London: British Film Institute.
——.(2001), *France on Film: Reflections on Popular French Cinema*, London: Wallflower.
Mazumdar, Ranjani (2007), *Bombay Cinema: An Archive of the City*, Minneapolis, MN: University of Minnesota Press.
Meehan, Paul (2008), *Tech-Noir: The Fusion of Science Fiction and Film Noir*, Jefferson, NC: McFarland.
Mes, Tom (2003), *Agitator: The Cinema of Miike Takashi*, Goldaming: FAB Press.
Mishra, Vijay (2001), *Bollywood Cinema: Temples of Desire*, New York: Routledge.
Miyao, Daisuke (2013), *The Aesthetics of Shadow: Lighting and Japanese Cinema*, Durham, NC: Duke University Press.
Monaco, James (1974), *The New Wave: Truffaut, Godard, Chabrol, Rohmer, Rivette*, New York: Oxford University Press.
Murphy, Robert (1989), *Realism and Tinsel: Cinema and Society in Britain 1939–49*, London: Routledge.
——.(2001), *British Film Noir: Shadows Are My Friends*, New York: I. B. Tauris.
——.(ed.) (2009), *The British Cinema Book*, 3rd edition, London: British Film Institute.
Neale, Steve and Murray Smith (eds) (1998), *Contemporary Hollywood Cinema*, London: Routledge.

Nestingen, Andrew (2013), *The Cinema of Aki Kaurismäki*, New York: Columbia University Press.
Nieland, Justus (2012), *David Lynch*, Urbana, IL: University of Illinois Press.
Nolletti, Arthur Jr and David Desser (eds) (1992), *Reframing Japanese Cinema: Authorship, Genre, History*, Bloomington, IN: Indiana University Press.
Oscherwitz, Dayna (2010), *Past Forward: French Cinema and the Post-Colonial Heritage*, Carbondale, IL: Southern Illinois University Press.
Palmer, R. Barton (2004), *Joel and Ethan Coen*, Urbana, IL: University of Illinois Press.
Park, Jane Chi Hyun (2010), *Yellow Future: Oriental Style in Hollywood Cinema*, Minneapolis, MN: University of Minnesota Press.
Peacock, Steven (2013), *Stieg Larsson's Millennium Trilogy: Interdisciplinary Approaches to Nordic Noir on Page and Screen*, New York: Palgrave Macmillan.
Philippe, Olivier (1996), *Le Film policier français contemporain*, Paris: Cerf.
Phillips, Alastair (2004), *City of Darkness, City of Light: Émigré Filmmakers in Paris 1929–1939*, Amsterdam: Amsterdam University Press.
——.(2009), *Rififi*, London: I. B. Tauris.
Phillips, Alastair and Julian Stringers (eds) (2007), *Japanese Cinema: Texts and Contexts*, London: Routledge.
Powrie, Phil (1997), *French Cinema in the 1980s: Nostalgia and the Crisis of Masculinity*, Oxford: Clarendon.
——.(2001), *Jean-Jacques Beineix*, Manchester & New York: Manchester University Press.
Prakash, Gyan (ed.) (2010), *Noir Urbanisms: Dystopic Images of the Modern City*, Princeton, NJ: Princeton University Press.
Prince, Stephen (1991), *The Warrior's Cinema: The Cinema of Akira Kurosawa*, Princeton, NJ: Princeton University Press.
Rafter, Nicole (2006), *Shots in the Mirror: Crime Films and Society*, New York: Oxford University Press.
Richards, Jeffrey (1997), *Films and British National Identity: From Dickens to* Dad's Army, Manchester: Manchester University Press.
Raghavendra, M. K. (2008), *Seduced by the Familiar: Narration and Meaning in Indian Popular Cinema*, New Delhi: Oxford University Press.
Rolls, Alistair and Deborah Walker (2009), *French and American Noir: Dark Crossings*, New York: Palgrave MacMillan.
San Miguel, Helio (ed.) (2012), *World Film Locations: Mumbai*, New York: Intellect.
Schilling, Mark (2007), *No Borders, No Limits: Nikkastsu Action Cinema*, Godalming: FAB Press.
Schwartz, Ronald (2005), *Neo-noir: The New Film Noir Style from Psycho to Collateral*, Lanham, MD: Scarecrow Press.
Schwartz, Vanessa (2007), *It's So French! Hollywood, Paris, and the Making of Contemporary Film Culture*, Chicago, IL: University of Chicago Press.
Sellier, Geneviève (2008), *Masculine Singular: French New Wave Cinema*, Durham, NC: Duke University Press.
Shin, Chi-Yun and Mark Gallagher (eds) (2014), *East Asian Film Noir*, New York: I. B. Tauris.
Shin, Chi-Yun and Julian Stringer (eds) (2005), *New Korean Cinema*, Edinburgh: Edinburgh University Press.
Sieglohr, Ulrike (ed.) (2001), *Heroines without Heroes: Reconstructing Female and National Identities in European Cinema, 1945–1951*, London: Cassell.
Smith, Carrie Lee and Donna King (eds) (2012), *Men Who Hate Women and Women Who Kick Their Asses: Stieg Larsson's Millennium Trilogy in Feminist Perspective*, Nashville, TN: Vanderbilt University Press.

Soila, Tytti, Astrid Söderbergh Widding and Gunnar Iversen (eds) (1998), *Nordic National Cinemas*, London: Routledge.
Sorrento, Matthew (2013), *The New American Crime Film*, Jefferson, NC: McFarland.
Spicer, Andrew (ed.) (2007), *European Film Noir*, Manchester: Manchester University Press.
Sterritt, David (1999), *The Films of Jean-Luc Godard: Seeing the Invisible*, Cambridge: Cambridge University Press.
Stringer, Julian (2007), *Blazing Passions: Contemporary Hong Kong Cinema*, New York: Wallflower.
Teo, Stephen (1997), *Hong Kong Cinema: The Extra Dimension*, London: British Film Institute.
Vasudevan, Ravi S. (ed.) (2000), *Making Meaning in Indian Cinema*, New Delhi: Oxford University Press.
Vincendeau, Ginnette (2003), *Jean-Pierre Melville: An American in Paris*, London: British Film Institute.
Wada-Marciano, Mitsuyo (2008), *Nippon Modern: Japanese Cinema of the 1920s and 1930s*, Honolulu, HI: University of Hawai'i Press.
Washburn, Dennis and Carole Cavanaugh (eds) (2001), *Word and Image in Japanese Cinema*, New York: Cambridge University Press.
Yoshimoto, Mitsuhiro (2000), *Kurosawa: Film Studies and Japanese Cinema*, Durham, NC: Duke University Press.

SELECTED FILMOGRAPHY OF INTERNATIONAL FILM NOIR

The project of amassing lists of global proto-to-neo-noirs is beyond the scope of this volume. Still, we have essayed to present a wide and varied selection of international films that pertain to the cultures discussed in this work. While these lists are not all inclusive, they nevertheless present some of the finest examples of film noir and films that reveal that noir impulse. For a list of classic films noirs, readers should consult our *Film Noir*, which is a volume in the *Traditions in American Cinema* for Edinburgh University Press.

British Films Noirs

Across the Bridge (Ken Annakin, 1957)
Alias John Preston (David MacDonald, 1955)
All Night Long (Basil Deardon, 1962)
Appointment with Crime (John Harlow, 1946)
Bang! You're Dead (Lance Comfort, 1954)
Beat Girl (Edmond T. Gréville, 1960)
Beautiful Stranger (David Miller, 1954)
Bedelia (Lance Comfort, 1946)
Blackout (Robert S. Baker, 1950)
Blind Date (Joseph Losey, 1959)
The Blue Lamp (Basil Dearden, 1950)
Boys in Brown (Montgomery Tully, 1949)
The Brain Machine (Ken Hughes, 1955)
Brighton Rock (John Boulting, 1947)
Cage of Gold (Basil Dearden, 1950)
Cairo (Wolf Rilla, 1963)
Calling Bulldog Drummond (Victor Saville, 1951)

SELECTED FILMOGRAPHY

Cast a Dark Shadow (Lewis Gilbert, 1955)
Chase a Crooked Shadow (Michael Anderson, 1958)
Cloudburst (Francis Searle, 1951)
The Clouded Yellow (Ralph Thomas, 1950)
Confession (Ken Hughes, 1955)
Contraband (Michael Powell, 1940)
Corridor of Mirrors (Terence Young, 1948)
Cosh Boy (Lewis Gilbert, 1953)
The Criminal (Joseph Losey, 1960)
Crossroads to Crime (Gerry Anderson, 1960)
Daybreak (Compton Bennett, 1948)
Dear Murderer (Arthur Crabtree, 1947)
Desperate Moment (Compton Bennett, 1953)
Don't Talk to Strange Men (Pat Jackson, 1962)
Double Confession (Ken Annakin, 1950)
Dual Alibi (Alfred Travers, 1948)
Dulcimer Street (Sidney Gilliat, 1948)
Escape Route (Seymour Friedman, Peter Graham Scott, 1952)
Face the Music (Terence Fisher, 1954)
Faces in the Dark (David Eady, 1960)
The Fallen Idol (Carol Reed, 1948)
Fanny by Gaslight (Anthony Asquith, 1945)
Five Days (Montgomery Tully, 1954)
Footsteps in the Fog (Arthur Lubin, 1955)
Forbidden (George King, 1949)
Fortune is a Woman (Sidney Gilliat, 1957)
The Frightened City! (John Lemont, 1961)
The Gentle Gunman (Basil Dearden, 1952)
The Good Die Young (Lewis Gilbert, 1954)
Good-Time Girl (David MacDonald, 1948)
Green For Danger (Sidney Gilliat, 1946)
The Green Scarf (George More O'Ferrall, 1954)
Hell Drivers (Cy Endfield, 1957)
Hell is a City (Val Guest, 1960)
Home at Seven (Ralph Richardson, 1952)
Hotel Reserve (Lance Comfort, 1944)
The House Across the Lake (Ken Hughes, 1954)
Hunted (Charles Crichton, 1952)
Hysteria (Freddie Francis, 1965)
I'll Get You for This (Joseph M. Newman, 1951)
Impulse (Cy Endfield, 1954)
The Intimate Stranger (Joseph Losey, 1956)
The Intruder (Guy Hamilton, 1953)
It Always Rains on Sunday (Robert Hamer, 1947)
Joe Macbeth (Ken Hughest, 1955)
Kill Her Gently (Charles Saunders, 1957)
Kill Me Tomorrow (Terence Fisher, 1957)
Lady of Vengeance (Burt Balaban, 1957)
The Limping Man (Cy Endfield, Charles de la Tour, 1953)
The Long Dark Hall (Reginald Beck, Anthony Bushell, 1951)
The Long Haul (Ken Hughes, 1957)
The Long Memory (Robert Hamer, 1953)

247

The Man Between (Carol Reed, 1953)
The Man Upstairs (Don Chaffey, 1961)
The Man Who Watched Trains (Harold Finch, 1952)
Mantrap (Terence Fisher, 1953)
The Mark (Guy Green, 1961)
Mine Own Executioner (Anthony Kimmins, 1947)
Mr. Denning Drives North (Anthony Kimmins, 1952)
Murder by Proxy (Terence Fisher, 1954)
Murder in Reverse (Montgomery Tully, 1945)
Murder without Crime (J. Lee Thompson, 1950)
My Brother's Keeper (Alfred Roome, 1948)
Naked Fury (Charles Saunders, 1959)
The Narrowing Circle (Charles Saunder, 1956)
Night and the City (Jules Dassin, 1950)
The Night Has Eyes (Leslie Arliss, 1942)
Night without Stars (Anthony Pelissier, 1951)
No Orchids for Miss Blandish (St. John Legh Clowes, 1948)
No Road Back (Montgomery Tully, 1957)
Noose (Edmond T. Gréville, 1948)
Nowhere to Go (Seth Holt, 1958)
Obsession (Edward Dmytryk, 1949)
The October Man (Roy Ward Baker, 1947)
Odd Man Out (Carol Reed, 1947)
Paranoiac (Freddie Francis, 1963)
Passport to Shame (Alvin Rakoff, 1958)
Payroll (Sidney Hayers, 1961)
Peeping Tom (Michael Powell, 1960)
A Place to Go (Basil Dearden, 1963)
Pool of London (Basil Dearden, 1951)
Port of Escape (Anthony Young, 1956)
Portrait of a Sinner (Robert Siodmak, 1960)
The Quiet Woman (John Gilling, 1951)
Recoil (John Gilling, 1953)
Rough Shoot (Robert Parrish, 1953)
Sapphire (Basil Dearden, 1959)
Séance on a Wet Afternoon (Bryan Forbes, 1964)
Secret People (Thorold Dickinson, 1952)
The Seventh Veil (Compton Bennett, 1945)
The Shakedown (John Lemont, 1960)
The Small Back Room (Michael Powell, 1949)
The Small Voice (Fergus McDonell, 1949)
The Small World of Sammy Lee (Ken Hughes, 1963)
Soho Incident (Vernon Sewell, 1956)
The Square Ring (Basil Dearden, 1953)
Stolen Face (Terence Fisher, 1952)
Street Corner (Muriel Box, 1953)
Street of Shadows (Richard Vernon, 1953)
Take My Life (Ronald Neame, 1947)
The Unholy Four (Terence Fisher, 1954)
Web of Evidence (Jack Cardiff, 1959)

British Neo-noir

The Big Sleep (Michael Winner, 1978)
The Criminal (Julian Simpson, 1999)
Croupier (Mike Hodges, 1997)
Dance with a Stranger (Mike Newell, 1985)
The Debt Collector (Anthony Neilson, 1999)
The Disappearance of Alice Creed (J. Blakeson, 2009)
Eastern Promises (David Cronenberg, 2007)
Following (Christopher Nolan, 1998)
Fragment of Fear (Richard C. Sarafian, 1970)
Get Carter (Mike Hodges, 1971)
The Hit (Stephen Frears, 1984)
I'll Sleep When I'm Dead (Mike Hodges, 2003)
The Krays (Peter Medak, 1990)
The Long Good Friday (John Mackenzie, 1980)
Mona Lisa (Neil Jordan, 1986)
The Offense (Sidney Lumet, 1972)
Out of Depth (Simon Marshall, 2000)
The Silent Cry (Julian Richards, 2003)
The Squeeze (Michael Apted, 1977)

French noir

Silent Era

Fantômas (Louis Feuillade, serial, 1913)
Judex (Louis Feuillade, serial, 1916)
Les Vampires (Louis Feuillade, serial, 1915)

Pre-war and Occupation

La Bête humaine [*The Human Beast*] (Jean Renoir, 1938)
La Chienne [*The Bitch*] (Jean Renoir, 1931)
Le Corbeau [*The Raven*] (Henri-Georges Clouzot, 1943)
Faubourg-Montmartre (Raymond Bernard, 1931)
Hôtel du Nord (Marcel Carné, 1938)
Le Jour se lève [*Daybreak*] (Marcel Carné, 1939)
Le Mystère de la chambre jaune [*The Mystery of the Yellow Room*] (Marcel L'Herbier, 1930)
La Nuit de carrefour [*Night at the Crossroads*] (Jean Renoir, 1932)
Pépé Le Moko (Julien Duvivier, 1937)
Le Quai des brumes [*Port of Shadows*] (Marcel Carné, 1938)

Postwar

L'Ascenseur pour l'échafaud [*Elevator to the Gallows*] (Louis Malle, 1958)
Bob le flambeur (Jean-Pierre Melville, 1956)
Les Diaboliques [*Diabolique*] (Henri-Georges Clouzot, 1955)
Impasse des deux-anges [*Dilemma of Two Angels*] (Maurcie Tourneur, 1948)
La môme vert-de-gris [*Poison Ivy*] (Bernard Borderie, 1953)
Panique [*Panic*] (Julien Duvivier, 1947)

Quai des Orfèvres (Henri-Georges Clouzot, 1947)
Razzia sur la chnouf [*Raid on the Drug Ring*] (Henri Decoin, 1956)
Du rififi chez les hommes [*Rififi*] (Jules Dassin, 1955)
Le Salaire de la peur [*Wages of Fear*] (Henri-Georges Clouzot, 1953)
Touchez pas au grisbi [*Don't Touch the Loot*] (Jacques Becker, 1954)

New Wave

Alphaville (Jean-Luc Godard, 1965)
À bout de souffle [*Breathless*] (Jean-Luc Godard, 1960)
Bande à part [*Band of Outsiders*] (Jean-Luc Godard, 1964)
Classe tous risques [*The Big Risk*] (Claude Sautet, 1960)
Deux hommes dans Manhattan [*Two Men in Manhattan*] [Jean-Pierre Melville, 1959]
Le Deuxième souffle [*Second Breath*] (Jean-Pierre Melville, 1963)
À double tour [*Web of Passion*] (Claude Chabrol, 1959)
Le Doulos [*Finger Man*] (Jean-Pierre Melville, 1963)
Pierre le fou (Jean-Luc Godard, 1965)
La Piscine [*The Swimming Pool*] (Jacques Deray, 1969)
Plein Soleil [*Purple Noon*] (René Clément, 1960)
Le Samouraï (Jean-Pierre Melville, 1967)
Tirez sur le pianiste [*Shoot the Piano Player*] (François Truffaut, 1960)
Le Trou [*The Hole*] (Jacques Becker, 1960)
Z (Constantin Costa-Gavras, 1969)

Neo-noir

La Balance [*The Narc* or *The Informer*] (Bob Swaim, 1982)
De battre mon cœur s'est arrêté [*The Beat That My Heart Skipped*] (Jacques Audiard, 2005)
Le Cercle rouge [*The Red Circle*] (Jean-Pierre Melville, 1970)
Comptes à rebours [*Countdown*] (Roger Pigaut, 1971)
Coup de Torchon (Bertrand Tavernier, 1981)
Le Cousin (Alain Corneau, 1998)
Détective (Jean-Luc Godard, 1985)
Diva (Jean-Jacques Beineix, 1981)
Garde à vue [*Under Suspicion*] (Claude Miller, 1981)
Un Flic [*A Cop* or *Dirty Money*] (Jean-Pierre Melville, 1971)
Mesrine [*Killer Instinct/Public Enemy No. 1*] (Jean-François Richet, 2008)
Nikita (Luc Besson, 1990)
Le petit lieutenant (Xavier Beauvois, 2005)
Place Vendôme (Nicole Garcia, 1998)
Police (Maurice Pialat, 1985)
Police Python 357 (Alain Corneau, 1976)
Un Prophet (Jacques Audiard, 2009)
Série noire (Alain Corneau, 1979)
Vivement dimanche! [*Confidentially Yours*] (François Truffaut, 1983)
Selected Japanese Films Noirs

Silent Noirs

A Page of Madness or *A Crazy Page* [*Kurutta ippeiji*] (Teinosuke Kinugasa, 1926)
Chuji's Travel Diary [*Chuji tabi nikki*] (Daisuke Ito, 1927)

SELECTED FILMOGRAPHY

Crossroads [*Jujiro*] (Teinosuke Kinugasa, 1928)
Jirokichi the Rat [*Oatsurae Jirokichi Goshi*] (Daisuke Ito, 1931)
Police Officer [*Keisatsukan*] (Tomu Uchida, 1933)
Dragnet Girl [*Hijosen no onna*] (Yasujiro Ozu, 1933)

Early Noirs

Osaka Elegy [*Naniwa Erejii*] (Kenji Mizoguchi, 1936)
Sisters of Gion [*Gion no shimai*] (Kenji Mizoguchi, 1936)

Postwar Noirs

Drunken Angel [*Yoidore tenshi*] (Akira Kurosawa, 1948)
Women of the Night [*Yoru no onnatachi*] (Kenji Mizoguchi, 1948)
Stray Dog [*Nora Inu*] (Akira Kurosawa, 1949)
I Saw the Killer [*Kyatsu o nigasu na*] (Hideo Suzuki, 1956)
Street of Shame [*Akasen chitai*] (Kenji Mizoguchi, 1956)
I am Waiting [*Ore wa matteiru ze*] (Kurahara Kureyoshi, 1957)
Stake Out [*Harikomi*] (Yoshitaro Nomura, 1957)
The Lower Depths [*Donzoko*] (Akira Kurosawa, 1957)
Black River [*Kuroi kawa*] (Masaki Kobayashi, 1957)
The Guy Who Started a Storm [*Arashi o yobu otoko*] (Inoue Umetsuge, 1957)
Endless Desire [*Hateshinaki yokubo*] (Shohei Imamura, 1958)
Red Quay [*Akai hatoba*] (Masuda Toshio, 1958)
Conflagration [*Enjo*] (Kon Ichikawa, 1958)
Rusty Knife [*Sabita knife*] (Masuda Toshio, 1958)

1960s

Take Aim at the Police Van [*Sono gosôsha wo nerae: 'Jûsangô taihisen' yori*] (Suzuki Seijun, 1960)
Afraid to die [*Karakkaze yarô*] (Yasuzo Masumura, 1960)
The Sun's Burial [*Taiyo No Hakaba*] (Nagisa Oshima, 1960)
The Last Gunfight [*Ankokugai no Taiketsu*] (Kihachi Okamoto, 1960)
Kenji [*Tales of a Gunman* cycle] (Hiroshi Noguchi, 1960):
    Ryuji the Gun Slinger [*Kenjû buraichô: Nukiuchi no Ryû*]
    Man in Lightning [*Kenjû buraichô: Denko sekka no otoko*]
    Man With a Hollow Laugh [*Kenjû buraichô: Futeki ni warau otoko*]
    Man Without Tomorrow [*Kenjû buraichô: Asunaki otoko*]
Crimson Pistol [*Kurenai no kenju*] (Yoichi Ushihara, 1961)
Greed in Broad Daylight [*Hakuchuu no Buraikan*] (Kinji Fukasaku, 1961)
Pigs and Battleships [*Buta to gunkan*] (Shohei Imamura, 1961)
Zero Focus [*Zero no shoten*] (Yoshitaro Nomura, 1961)
High and Low [*Tengoku to Jigoku*] (Akira Kurosawa, 1963)
Theater Of Life: Hishakaku [*Jinsei Gekijo – Hishakaku*] (Tadashi Sawashima, 1963)
Youth of the Beast [*Yaju no seishun*] (Seijun Suzuki, 1963)
Cruel Gun Story [*Kneju zankoku monogatari*] (Takum Furukawa, 1964).
Pale Flower [*Kawaita Hana*] (Masahiro Shinoda, 1964)
Abashiri Prison or *Man from Abashiri Jail* [*Abashiri bangaichi*] (Teruo Ishii, 1965)
Tattooed Life [*Irezumi ichidai*] (Seijun Suzuki, 1965)
Brutal Tales of Chivalry [*Showa Zankyoden*] (Kiyoshi Saeki, 1965)
The 893 Gang [*893 Gurentai*] (Sadao Nakajima, 1966)

A Colt is my Passport [*Koruto wa ore no pasupoto*] (Takashi Nomura, 1967)
Slaughter Gun [*Minagoroshi no kenju*] (Yasuharu Hasebe, 1967)
Branded to Kill [*Koroshi no rakuin*] (Seijun Suzuki, 1967)
Big Time Gambling Boss [*Bakuchi-uchi: Socho Tobaku*] (Kosaku Yamashita, 1968)
Man Without a Map or *Ruined Map* [*Moetsukita chizu*] (Hiroshi Teshigawara, 1968)
I, the Executioner [*Minagoroshi no reika*] (Tai Kato, 1968)

Neo-noirs

Shinjuku Mad [*Shinjuku Maddo*] (Koji Wakamatsu, 1970)
Stray Cat Rock: Sex Hunter [*Nora-neko rokku: Sekkusu Hanta*] (Yasuharu Hasebe, 1970)
Cherry Blossom Fire Gang [*Junko intai kinen eiga: Kantô hizakura ikka*] (Masahiro Makino, 1972)
Female Prisoner #701: Scorpion [*Joshuu 701-Go: sasori*] (Shunya Ito, 1972)
Girl Boss: Escape from Reform School [*Sukeban: Kankain dasso*] (Nakajima Sadao, 1973)
Battles Without Honor and Humanity [*Jingi naki tatakai*] (Kinji Fukasaku, 1973)
Graveyard of Honor [*Jingi no hakaba*] (Kinji Fukasaku, 1975)
The Inugami Family [*Inugamike no ichizoku*] (Kon Ichikawa, 1976)
The Man Who Stole the Sun [*Taiyo wo nusunda otoko*] (Kazuhiko Hasegawa, 1979)
The Beast to Die [*Yaju Shisubeshi*] (Toru Murakawa, 1980)
The Yakuza Wives [*Gokudo no onna-tachi*] (Hideo Gosha, 1986)
Violent Cop [*Sono otoko kyobo ni tsuki*] (Takeshi Kitano, 1987)
The Most Terrible Time in My Life [*Waga jinsei saiaku no toki*] (Kaizo Hayashi, 1993)
Gonin [*Gonin*] (Takashi Ishii, 1995)
Shinjuku Triad Society cycle [*Shinjuku kuroshakai*] (Takashi Miike):
  China Mafia War [*Chaina mafia senso*, 1995]
  Rainy Dog [*Gokudo kuroshakai*, 1997]
  Ley Lines [*Nihon kuroshakai*, 1999]
Another Lonely Hitman [*Shin Kanashiku Hitman*] (Rokuro Mochizuki, 1995)
XX cycle:
  Beautiful Beast [*XX: Utsukushiki kemono*] (Toshiharu Ikeda, 1995)
  Beautiful Killing Machine [*XX: Utsukushiki kino*] (Takahito Hara, 1996)
  Beautiful Prey [*XX: Utsukushiki emono*] (Toshiharu Ikeda, 1996)
Onibi – The Fire Within [*Onibi*] (Rokuro Mochizuki, 1995)
The Stairway to the Distant Past [*Harukana jidai no kaidan o*] (Kaizo Hayashi, 1995)
The Trap [*Wana*] (Kaizo Hayashi, 1996)
Bullet Ballet [*Baretto baree*] (Shinya Tsukamoto, 1998)
Serpent's Path [*Hebi no michi*] (Kiyoshi Kurosawa, 1998)
Jubaku: Spellbound [*Kinyû fushoku rettô*] (Masato Harada, 1999)
Film Noir [*Koroshi*] (Mashiro Kobayashi, 2000)
Pistol Opera (Seijun Suzuki, 2001)
Gun Crazy: A Woman from Nowhere (Atushi Muroga, 2002)
A Snake of June [*Rokugatsu no hebi*] (Shinya Tsukamoto, 2002)

Hong Kong New Wave

The Butterfly Murders (Tsui Hark, 1979)
Cops and Robbers (Alex Cheung, 1979)

The Secret (Ann Hui, 1979)
The System (Peter Yung, 1979)
Happenings (Yim Ho, 1980)
Dangerous Encounters of the First Kind (Tsui Hark, 1980)
Man on the Brink (Alex Cheung, 1980)
Love, Massacre (Patrick Tam, 1980)
Long Arm of the Law (Johnny Mak, 1984)

Johnny To Neo-noirs

PTU (2003)
Breaking News (2004)
Election (2005)
Triad Election (2006)
Exiled (2006)
Mad Detective (2007)
Sparrow (2008)
Vengeance (2009)
Life without Principles (2011)
Drug War (2012).

Jingfei pain ('cops and robbers') films

Infernal Affairs trilogy (Andrew Lau [Wai-keung Lau], 2002–3)
One Night in Mongkok (Tung-shing Yee, 2004)
Bystanders (Im Kyung-soo, 2005)
Confession of Pain (Andrew Lau, 2006)
The Detective (Oxide Pang, 2007)
A Love (Kwak Kyung-taek, 2007)
Protégé (Tung-shing Yee, 2007)
Accident (Pou-soi Cheang, 2009)
Breathless (Yang Ik-june, 2009)
Overheard (Felix Chong, Alan Mak, 2009)
Secret (Yoon Jae-gu, 2009)
Shinjuku Incident (Tung-shing Yee, 2009)
Yeouido Island (Song Jung-woo, 2010)
Overheard 2 (Felix Chong, Alan Mak, 2011)
Punished (Wing-cheong Law, 2011)
Nightfall (Chow Hin Yeung Roy, 2012)
Cold War (Lok Man Leung, Kim-ching Luk, 2012)

South Korean neo-noirs

Nowhere to Hide (Lee Myung-se, 1999)
Happy End (Jung Ji-woo, 1999)
Vengeance trilogy (Park Chan-wook)
  Sympathy for Mr Vengeance (2002)
  Oldboy (2003)
  Sympathy for Lady Vengeance (2005)
Bad Guy (Kim Ki-duk, 2001)
Public Enemy (Kang Woo-suk, 2002)
A Tale of Two Sisters (Kim Jee-woon, 2003)

INTERNATIONAL NOIR

Memories of Murder (Bong Joon-ho, 2003).
Hypnotized (Kim In-shik, 2004)
Spider Forest (Song Il-gon, 2004)
A Bittersweet Life (Kin Jee-woon, 2005)
A Dirty Carnival (Ha Yoo, 2006)
Puzzle (Kim Tae-kyung, 2006)
Voice of a Murderer (Park Jin-pyo, 2007)
Black House (Terra Shin, 2007)
Seven Days (Won Shin-yeon, 2007)
The Chaser (Na Hong-jin, 2008)
Handphone (Kim Mi-hyun, 2009)
Mother (Bong Joon-ho, 2009)
No Mercy (Kim Heyong-joon, 2010)
Secret Reunion (Hun Jang, 2010)
Parallel Life (Kweon Ho-young, 2010)
Bedevilled (Jang Chui-soo, 2010)
The Man from Nowhere (Lee Jeong-beom, 2010)
I Saw the Devil (Kim Jee-woon, 2010)
Enemy at the Dead End (Owen Cho, Kim Sang-hwa, 2010)
The Yellow Sea (Na Hong-jin, 2010)
Hindsight (Lee Hyun-seung, 2011)
Silenced (Hwang Dong-hyuk, 2011)
Nameless Gangster (Yun Jong-bin, 2012)
Helpless (Byun Young-joo, 2012)
The Thieves (Choi Dong-hoon, 2012)
Pieta (Kim Ki-duk, 2012)
Confession of Murder (Jeong Beyong-gil, 2012)
New World (Park Hoon-jung, 2013)

Nordic Noir

Angst [Anguish] (Oddvar Bul Tuhus, N, 1976)
Ariel (Aki Kaurismäki, SF, 1988)
Besættelse [Obsession] (Bodil Ipsen, DK, 1944)
Bortreist på ubestemt tid [Away For an Indefinite Period] (Pål Bang Hansen, N, 1974)
Bron [The Bridge] (Måns Mårlind, Hans Rosenfeldt, Nikolaj Scherfig, DK, TV series, 2011–)
Calamari Unioni [Calamari Union] (Aki Kaurismäki, SF, 1985)
Døden er et kjærtegen [Death is a Caress] (Edith Carlmar, N, 1949)
The Element of Crime (Lars von Trier, DK, 1984)
En forbryder [A Criminal] (Arne Weel, DK, 1941)
Europa (Lars von Trier, DK, 1991)
Flammen og citronen [Flame and Citron] (Ole Christian Madsen, DK, 2008)
Flicka och hyacinter [Girl and Hyacinths] (Hasse Ekman, S, 1950)
Forbrydelsen [The Killing] (Søren Sveistrup, DK, TV series, 2007–12)
Hets [Torment] (Alf Sjöberg, S, 1944)
Hodejegerne [Headhunters] (Morten Tyldum, N, 2011)
Insomnia (Erik Skjoldbjærg, N, 1997)
Jeg mødte en morder [I Met a Murderer] (Lau Lauritzen, DK, 1943)
John og Irene [John and Irene] (Asbjørn Andersen, Anker Sørensen, DK, 1949)
Juha (Aki Kaurismäki, SF, 1999)

SELECTED FILMOGRAPHY

Laitakaupungin valot [*Lights in the Dusk*] (Aki Kaurismäki, SF, 2006)
Le Havre (Aki Kaurismäki, SF, 2012)
Män som hatar kvinnor [*The Girl with the Dragon Tattoo*] (Niels Arden Oplev, S, 2009)
Mordets melodi [*Melody of Murder*] (Bodil Ipsen, DK, 1944)
Nattevagten [*Nightwatch*] (Ole Bornedal, DK, 1994)
Olet mennyt vereeni [*You've Gotten Into my Blood*] (Teuvo Tulio, SF, 1956)
Ørnen: En krimi-odyssé [*The Eagle*] (Mai Brøstrøm, Peter Thorsboe, DK, TV series, 2004–6)
Pusher (Nicholas Winding Refn, DK, 1996)
Pusher 2 (Nicholas Winding Refn, DK, 2004)
Pusher 3 (Nicholas Winding Refn, DK, 2005)
Radio tekee murron [*The Radio Breaks In*] (1951, SF, Matti Kassila)
Raid (Tapio Piirainen, SF, 2003)
Rejseholdet [*Unit One*] (Søren Sveistrup, Mai Brøstrøm, Peter Thorsboe, DK, TV series, 2000–4)
Reykjavik-Rotterdam (Baltasar Koramakur, I, 2008),
Rikollinen nainen [*A Criminal Woman*] (Teuvo Tulio, SF, 1952)
Rikos ja rangaistus [*Crime and Punishment*] (Aki Kuarismäki, SF, 1983)
Sellaisena kuin sinä minut halusit [*Just as You Wanted Me*] (Teuvo Tulio, SF, 1944)
Smala Sussie [*Slim Susie*] (Ulf Malmros, S, 2003)
Snabba Cash [*Easy Money*] (Daniel Espinosa, S, 2011)
To mistenklige personer [*Two Suspicious Characters*] (Tancred Ibsen, N, 1950)
Tulitikkutehtaan tyttö [*The Match-Factory Girl*] (Aki Kaurismäki, SF, 1990)
Vares: Yksityisetsivä [*Vares: Private Eye*] (Aleksi Mäkelä, SF, 2004)
Varjoja paratiisissa [*Shadows in Paradise*] (Aki Kaurismäki, SF, 1986)
V2: Jäätynyt enkeli [*V2: Dead Angel*] (Aleksi Mäkelä, SF, 2007)

Neo-noirs (American)

1980s

Black Widow (Bob Rafelson, 1987)
Blood Simple (Joel Coen, 1984)
Blue Velvet (David Lynch, 1985)
Body Heat (Lawrence Kasdan, 1981)
Cop (James B. Harris, 1988)
D.O.A. (Annabel Jankel, Rocky Morton, 1988)
Eyewitness (Peter Yates, 1981)
The First Deadly Sin (Brian G. Hutton, 1980)
Hammett (Wim Wenders, 1982)
House of Games (David Mamet, 1987)
I, the Jury (Richard T. Heffron, 1982)
Manhunter (Michael Mann, 1986)
No Way Out (Roger Donaldson, 1987)
The Postman Always Rings Twice (Bob Rafelson, 1981)
Prince of the City (Sidney Lumet, 1981)
Sea of Love (Harold Becker, 1989)
Thief (Michael Mann, 1981)
To Live and Die in L.A. (William Friedkin, 1985)
Trouble in Mind (Alan Rudolph, 1985)

True Confessions (Ulu Grosbard, 1981)
Union City (Marcus Reichert, 1980)
Year of the Dragon (Michael Cimino, 1985)

1990s

After Dark, My Sweet (James Foley, 1990)
Blood and Wine (Bob Rafelson, 1996)
Bound (The Wachowskis, 1996)
Cape Fear (Martin Scorsese, 1991)
China Moon (John Bailey, 1994)
Dead Again (Kenneth Branagh, 1991)
Deep Cover (Bill Duke, 1992)
Devil in a Blue Dress (Carl Franklin, 1995)
Goodfellas (Martin Scorsese, 1990)
The Grifters (Stephen Frears, 1990)
Hard Eight (Paul Thomas Anderson, 1996)
The Hot Spot (Dennis Hopper, 1990)
The Kill-Off (Maggie Greenwald, 1990)
A Kiss Before Dying (James Dearden, 1991)
L.A. Confidential (Curtis Hanson, 1997)
The Last Seduction (John Dahl, 1994)
Lost Highway (David Lynch, 1997)
Miller's Crossing (Joel Coen, 1990)
Mulholland Falls (Lee Tamahori, 1996)
Night and the City (Irwin Winkler, 1992)
Palmetto (Volker Schlondorff, 1998)
Payback (Brian Helgeland, 1999)
The Public Eye (Howard Franklin, 1992)
Red Rock West (John Dahl, 1993)
Romeo Lies Bleeding (Peter Medak, 1993)
Se7en (David Fincher, 1995)
State of Grace (Phil Joanou, 1990)
Twilight (Robert Benton, 1998)
The Usual Suspects (Bryan Singer, 1995)
White Sands (Roger Donaldson, 1992)

2000s

The Black Dahlia (Brian De Palma, 2006)
Brick (Rian Johnson, 2005)
The Departed (Martin Scorsese, 2006)
Femme Fatale (Brian De Palma, 2002)
Heist (David Mamet, 2001)
Insomnia (Christopher Nolan, 2002)
Kiss Kiss Bang Bang (Shane Black, 2005)
Lonely Hearts (Todd Robinson, 2006)
The Man Who Wasn't There (Joel and Ethan Coen, 2001)
Memento (Christopher Nolan, 2000)
Mulholland Drive (David Lynch, 2001)
The Salton Sea (D. J. Caruso, 2002)
Sin City (Frank Miller, Robert Rodriguez, 2005)

2010s

The Killer Inside Me (Michael Winterbottom, 2010)
Dead Man Down (Niels Arden Oplev, 2013)
Drive (Nicolas Winding Refn, 2011)
The Girl with the Dragon Tattoo (David Fincher, 2011)
Killer Joe (William Friedkin, 2011)
Killing Them Softly (Andrew Dominik, 2012)

Bombay Noir

Aag [*Fire*] (Raj Kapoor, 1948)
Barsaat [*Rain*] (Raj Kapoor, 1949)
Awara [*The Vagabond*] (Raj Kapoor, 1951)
Baazi [*Wager*] (Guru Dutt, 1951)
Taxi Driver (Chetan Anand, 1954)
House No. 44 (M. K. Burman, 1955)
C.I.D. (Raj Khosla, 1956)
Pyaasa [*Thirst*] (Guru Dutt, 1957)
Howrah Bridge (Shakti Samanta, 1958)
Kala Pani [*Black Water*] (Raj Khosla, 1958)
Madhumati (Bimal Roy, 1958)
Post Box 999 (Ravindra Dave, 1958)
Guest House (Ravindra Dave, 1959)
Kaagaz Ke Phool [*Paper Flowers*] (Guru Dutt, 1959)
Bambai Ka Babu [*Gentleman from Bombay*] (Raj Khosla, 1960)
Jaali Note [*Counterfeit Bill*] (Shakti Samantha, 1960)
Kala Bazar [*Black Market*] (Vijay Anand, 1960)
China Town (Shakti Samanta, 1962)

Mumbai Neo-noir

Johny Mera Naam [*My Name is Johnny*] (Vijay Anand, 1970)
Parwana [*Moth*] (Jyoit Swaroop, 1971)
Zanjeer [*Chains*] (Prakash Mehra, 1973)
Deewar [*The Wall*] (Yash Chopra, 1975)
Sholay [*Flames*] (Ramesh Sippy, 1975)
Don (Chandra Barot, 1978)
Nayakan [*Hero*] (Mani Ratnam, 1987)
Parinda [*Bird*] (Vidhu Vinod Chopra, 1989)
Satya (Ram Gopal Varma, 1998)
Company (Ram Gopal Varma, 2002)
Kaante [*Thorns*] (Sanjay Gupta, 2002)
Maqbool [*Macbeth*] (Vishal Bharadwaj, 2004)
D (Ram Gopal Varma, 2005)
Ram Gopal Varma's *Sarkar* (Ram Gopal Varma, 2005)
Omkara [*Othello*] (Vishal Bharawaj, 2006)
Johnny Gaddaar [*Johnny Traitor*] (Sriram Raghavan, 2007)
Sarkar Raj (Ram Gopal Varma, 2008)

INDEX

À bout de souffle (Breathless, 1960), 40–1, 46, 51–3, 73–4, 116, 138, 203, 250
Accident (2009), 138, 253
Adler-Olsen, Jussi, 165
Against All Odds (1984), 203
Aikawa, Sho, 123–4
Aldrich, Robert, 120, 230
Alfredson, Tomas, 240
Algiers, 48
Altman, Rick, 139, 153, 236, 238
Altman, Robert, 199
American Gigolo (1980), 214
Amin, Ash, 217
Anand, Chetan, 186–7, 257
Anand, Dev, 183, 185–7, 191
Anand, Vijay, 187, 191, 257
Anderson, Joseph, L., 110–11, 241
Andrei, Frederic, 78
Andrew, Dudley, 12, 160, 175, 179, 241
Angst (1976), 167, 177, 254
Another Lonely Hitman (Shin Kanashiki Hitman, 1995), 122–3, 128, 252
Anti-Rightist Movement, 5
Appiah, Kwame Anthony, 224, 236, 239
Appointment with Crime (1946), 24, 246
Arcady, Alexandre, 76
Arestup, Niels, 82
Ariel (1988), 172, 177, 254
Aronofsky, Darren, 240
Art of Losing, The (Perder es cuestion de metodo, 2004), 228

Arvas, Paula, 175–7, 180–1
Asano, Tadanobu, 132
Asquith, Anthony, 22, 247
Atlanta, Georgia, 213
Atomic Bomb, 86, 205, 209
Attenborough, Richard, 20, 25
Audiard, Jacques, 83, 250
Audition (1999), 132
Auerbach, Jonathan, 225, 236
Austin, Guy, 83, 241
Awaji, Keiko, 106, 108
Away for an Indefinite Period (Bortreist på ubestemt tid, 1974), 167, 177, 254
Aznavour, Charles, 52–3

Baazi (Wager) (1951), 183, 186–8, 257
Bachchan Films, 189–92
Back to the Future III (1990), 201
Bad Guy (2001), 138, 253
Badham, John, 125
Badley, Linda, 172, 175, 181, 241
Bad Lieutenant: Port of Call New Orleans (2009), 240
Bahr, Ehrhard, 225, 236
Baidao, 142, 144, 148
Baker, Roy Ward, 23, 248
Balance, La (1982), 73–4, 76, 79–81, 250
Bando, Junosuke, 90
Bangkok, 146–7
Bang! You're Dead (1954), 28, 246
Bantu, 2

258

Barbareschi, Luca Giorgio, 227
Barencey, Odette, 4
Baret, François, 83
Barsacq, Leon, 46
Baskett, Michael, 111, 241
Batalov, Alexei, 7
Battle of Algiers, 48
Bauman, Zygmunt, 227, 232, 236, 239
Bean, Sean, 30
Beautiful Beast (*XX: Utsukushiki kemono*, 1995), 125, 252
Beautiful Killing Machine (*XX: Utsukushiki kino*, 1996), 125, 252
Beautiful Prey (*XX: Utsukushiki emono*, 1996), 125, 252
Becker, Étienne, 40
Becker, Jacques, 40, 63, 66, 68–9, 71, 74–5, 84, 177, 250
Bedevilled (2010), 138, 254
Behind the Green Door (1972), 213
Beijing, 5
Beineix, Jean-Jacques, 38, 65, 84, 244, 250
Bell, Melanie, 27, 34
Belle de Jour (1967), 81
Bello, Maria, 11
Belmondo, Jean-Paul, 52, 55, 116
Benjumea, Carlos, 230
Bennett, Compton, 20, 247–8
Benshi, 87, 119
Benson, Leslie, 13
Bergman, Ingmar, 6, 8–9, 13, 160
Bernard, Raymond, 4, 249
Bernardi, Joanne, 87, 110, 241
Berry, Richard, 75
Bertin, Yori, 51
Besson, Luc, 38, 124–5, 250
Beugnet, Martine, 83
Bharadwaj, Vishal, 190, 257
Biesen, Sheri Chinen, 12, 218, 225, 236
Big Doll House, The (1971), 115
Bilginer, Haluk, 229
Birchall, Bridget, 59–60
Bird (*Parinda*, 1989), 190, 192, 257
Bittersweet Life, A (2005), 138, 150, 254
Bizet, Georges, 3
Black Angel (*Kuro no tenshi*, Vol. 1, 1997), 125
Black House (2007), 138–9, 150, 254
Black Market (*Kala Bazar*, 1960), 187, 257
Black River (*Kuroi kawa*, 1957), 107–10, 251
Black Seconds (*Svarte sekunder*, 2002), 168
Black Society Trilogy, 123–4
Black Spring (*Kuroi haru*), 107
Black Swan (2010), 240
Black Water (1958), 187, 257
Blier, Bernard, 43
Blind Corner (1963), 27

Blind Mountain (2007), 240
Blind Shaft (*Mang jing*, 2003), 233–5
Block, Lawrence, 194
Blue Dahlia, The (1946), 67, 158, 178
Blue Lamp, The (1950), 25–7, 246
Bob le flambeur (1956), 59–60, 83–4
Body Double (1984), 213
Body Heat (1981), 34, 194–5, 204, 211, 214, 217, 225, 255
Bogarde, Dirk, 22–3, 25–7
Bogart, Humphrey, 24, 53, 186
Bohringer, Richard, 78
Boileau-Despreaux, Nicolas, 40
Bondebjerg, Ib, 161–2, 180
Bong, Joon-ho, 138, 149, 154, 254
Bonnie and Clyde (1967), 202
Boorman, John, 199
Boozer, Jack, 221–2, 236, 238
Borde, Raymond, 15–16, 31–3, 36, 59
Bordwell, David, 111, 217, 241
Bould, Mark, 31–2, 34–5, 153, 172, 175, 180, 192, 220, 236–8, 241
Boulting, John and Ray, 20, 24, 246
Bound (1996), 226, 256
Boyle, Danny, 226
Branded to Kill (*Koroshi no rakuin*, 1967), 116, 131–4, 252
Brandes, Georg, 162, 178
Breaking News (2004), 137, 253
Breathless (1983), 138, 253
Brent, George, 26
Bride Wore Black, The (*La mariée était en noir*, 1968), 74
Bridge, The (*Bron*, 2011–), 163, 165, 177, 254
Brighton Rock (1947), 24, 27, 246
Broden, Daniel, 160, 175, 179
Broe, Dennis, 225, 236
Brooker, Peter, 195
Brunelin, André-Georges, 40
Brunish, Anne-Marie, 160
Buchholtz, Horst, 28
Budapest, 9
Bullet Ballet (1998), 127, 232, 240, 252
Buñuel, Luis, 81
Burakumin (Village People), 86–7
Burch, Nöel, 110, 241
Burman, M. K., 187, 257
Burnett, Charles, 225
Busan, 151
Buss, Robin, 83, 141, 153, 241
Butler, David, 225, 236
Butterfly Murders, The (1979), 136, 252
Bystanders (2005), 138–9, 253

Cabrera, Dominique, 230
Cacho, Daniel Gimenez, 230

Cain, James M., 80, 159, 194, 201, 204–6, 208–12, 214–18
Caine, Michael, 31
Calamari Union (1985), 172–3, 177, 254
Calef, Noel, 40
Caller, The (Varsleren), 168
Cameron, Ian, 59
Camus, Albert, 42, 206, 209–10
Cannes Festival, 6, 154, 213
Carlmar, Edith, 158–9, 177, 254
Carmen (1875), 3
Carné, Marcel, 67, 114, 158, 178, 249
Carstairs, John Paddy, 20
Case Closed (Meitante Conan/Detective Conan, 1994), 121
Castells, Manuel, 226, 236, 239
Cat People (1982), 213
Cavalcanti, Alberto, 19
Cavanaugh, Carol, 110, 134, 245
Cercle Rouge, Le (The Red Circle) (1970), 40, 42, 55–7, 62, 64, 71, 250
Chabat, Alain, 79–80
Chains (Zanjeer, 1973), 189, 257
Chambers, Marilyn, 217–19
Chanal, Pierre, 158
Chandler, Raymond, 30–1, 159, 175, 179, 194, 203
Chang, Grace, 2–5, 12
Chartier, Jean-Pierre, 222, 236
Chase, James Hadley, 14, 22, 31
Chaser, The (Chugyeogja, 2008), 138–9, 150, 254
Chasseur (The Hunter, 1980), 76
Chaumeton, Étienne, 15–16, 31–3, 36, 59
Cheung, Alex, 136–7, 252–3
Chi, Yingchi, 12
Chibnall, Steve, 18, 29, 31, 33–5, 242
Chihaya, Akiko, 90
China, 2, 5, 6, 12, 34, 48–9, 86, 97, 110, 148, 154, 227, 233, 235
China Town (1962), 187, 257
Chinatown (1974), 34, 137, 142, 145–7, 150, 153–4, 202–3, 230, 239
Chopra, Vidhu Vinod, 190, 257
Chopra, Yash, 189, 257
Christensen, Rune, 161–2, 167, 175–6, 180
Chuji's Travel Diary (Chuji tabi nikki, 1927), 103, 250
C.I.D. (1956), 183, 187, 192, 257
CinemaScope, 120
Citizen Kane (1941), 17, 191
Classe tous risques (1960), 66, 73–4, 250
Classification and Ratings Administration (CARA), 213
Clement, René, 63, 250
Cloudburst (1951), 20, 247

Clouzot, Henri-Georges, 39–40, 60, 63, 73, 249–50
Clouzot, Vera, 44, 47
Clowes, St John Legh, 22, 248
Coen, Joel and Ethan, 133, 194–5, 205–6, 209–11, 218, 221, 226, 237–8, 242, 244, 255–6
Cold War, 2, 5, 9, 13, 20, 38, 138, 224, 253
Cold War (2012), 138, 253
Collier, Joelle, 144–5, 150, 154
Collins, Jim, 201–4, 218
Colt is My Passport, A (Colt wa ore no passport, 1967), 112, 116, 134, 252
Columbia Pictures, 5
Combes, Marcel, 40
Comfort, Lance, 27–8, 246–7
Company (2002), 190, 257
Comptes à rebours (1971), 40, 56, 250
Conard, Mark T., 83, 242
Confession of Murder (2012), 138–9, 254
Confession of Pain (2006), 137, 253
Confidentially Yours (1983), 74
Conflagration (Enjo, 1958), 113, 251
Connelly, Michael, 194
Conrad, Michael, 55
Conway, Kelley, 12, 242
Cooke, Paul, 1, 12
Copjec, Joan, 150, 153–4, 166–8, 171, 176–7, 180
Cops and Robbers (1979), 136, 252
Corman, Roger, 115
Corneau, Alain, 37, 40, 55, 69, 79, 250
Cosh Boy (1952), 27, 34, 247
Costner, Kevin, 201
Cotillard, Marion, 202
Cotten, Joseph, 16–17
Counterfeit Bill (Jaali Note, 1960), 187, 257
Court, Hazel, 27
Cousin, Le (1998), 73, 79, 80–1, 250
Coutard, Raoul, 40, 53
Cranes are Flying, The (Letyat Zhuravli, 1957), 6–7, 13
Crank (2006), 240
Crank 2: High Voltage (2009), 240
Crazed Fruit (Kurutta kajitsu) (1956), 114
Crazy Page, A (Kurutta Ippeiji, 1926), 88, 110, 250
Creekmur, Corey K., 182, 192
Crenna, Richard, 58, 72, 215
Crichton, Charles, 27, 247
Crime and Punishment (Rikos ja rangaistus, 1983), 172, 177–8, 181, 255
Criminal, A (En forbryder, 1941), 162, 177, 254–5
Crimson Pistol (Kurenai no kenju, 1961), 116, 251

Croce, Fernando F., 133
Cronenberg, David, 240, 249
Crossroads (1928), 88, 90–1, 101, 110, 251
Croupier (1998), 226, 249
Cruel Gun Story (*Kenju zankoku monogatari*, 1964), 112, 251

D (2005), 190, 257
Dadaism, 88–9
D'Agostini, Philippe, 40
Dahl, John, 214, 226, 256
Daily Express, 21
Dances With Wolves (1990), 201, 204
Dance With a Stranger (1984), 30, 249
Dancing with Crime (1949), 20
Dangan Runner (1996), 126
Dangerous Encounters of the First Time (1980), 137, 253
Dassin, Jules, 16–17, 40, 51, 60, 71, 73, 105, 248, 250
Dave, Ravindra, 187, 257
Daybreak (1946), 20, 247
Day Break (2006), 232
Dead Men Don't Wear Plaid (1982), 201, 210
Dearden, Basil, 25, 246–8, 256
Death is a Caress (*Dodener et kjaertegen*, 1949), 158–9, 177, 179, 254
Death of a Tightrope Walker, or How Pete Q. Got Wings, The (*Nuorallatanssijan kuolema eli kuinka Pete Q sai siivet*, 1978), 173
Death Spiral (*Kuolemanspiraaldi*), 168
D'Eaubonne, Jean, 46
De battre mon coeur s'est arrêté (2005), 73, 82, 250
Decae, Henri, 40, 51, 53
Decoin, Henri, 40, 250
Dédée d'Anvers (1948), 37
Deep Cover (1992), 225, 256
Deep Throat (1972), 213
De Gaulle, Charles, 41, 54, 59–60
Delacorta, 78
Delair, Suzy, 43
Delon, Alain, 56–8, 70–2
Deneuve, Catherine, 58, 72, 81–2
Denmark, 156, 161, 163–4, 232, 239–40
Deol, Abhay, 230
De Palma, Brian, 191, 213, 256
Departed, The (2006), 11, 256
Desser, David, 111–12, 133, 135, 192, 236, 239, 244
d'Estaing, Valéry Giscard, 54
Detective (1984), 73, 83
Detective, The (2007), 137, 146, 253
Detective 2, The (2011), 137, 253

de Toth, André, 214
Deuxième souffle, Le (1963), 40, 42, 55–6, 60, 62, 64, 68–9, 74, 250
Devil in a Blue Dress (1995), 225, 256
Dewaere, Patrick, 56, 59–60, 79
Diaboliques, Les (1955), 37, 40–1, 43–7, 51, 59–60, 242, 249
Diamond, Yukai, 126
Dickos, Andrew, 83
Dietrichson, Phyllis (Character), 163
Dillinger, John, 202
Dimendberg, Edward, 70, 83, 141, 144, 153–4
Dinerstein, Joel, 225, 237
Dior, Christian, 47
Dirty Carnival, A (2006), 138, 254
Dirty Harry (1971), 119
Dirty Pretty Things (2002), 240
Disney, Walt, 210
Diva (1984), 65, 70, 73, 77–9, 81–3, 250
Dixon, Pierson, 9, 13
Dmytryk, Edward, 17, 19, 178, 248
Dog Day Afternoon (1975), 228
Doll's House, A (1879), 162
Don (1978), 189
Dors, Diana, 21, 26–7, 31, 33
Double Indemnity (1944), 63, 158, 177, 194, 204, 212, 214, 216, 222
Doulos, Les (1963), 40, 42, 55, 57, 62, 64–9, 74, 250
Douy, Max, 46
Dragnet Girl (*Hijosen no onna*, 1933), 91–4, 109, 251
Dressed to Kill (1980), 213
Dreyer, Carl Theodore, 173
Driscoll, Mark, 98, 111
Drive (2002), 126–7
Drive (2011), 240, 257
Drug War (2012), 137, 148, 169, 253
Drunken Angel (*Yoidore tenshi*, 1948), 4, 103–6, 109, 251
Dubois, Marie, 52
Dubro, Alec, 110
Duhamel, Marcel, 60
Duke, Bill, 225, 256
Dullin, Charles, 43
Durgnat, Raymond, 18, 31, 33, 153
Duris, Romain, 82
Dutronc, Jacques, 82
Dutt, Guru, 183, 186, 192, 257
Duvivier, Julien, 114, 158, 249
Dyer, Richard, 12, 221, 225–6, 237, 239

Eagle, The (*Ørnen: En Krimi-odyssé*, TV series, 2004–6), 163, 178, 255
Eastern Promises (2007), 240, 249
Eastwood, Clint, 107, 119, 201

Easy Money (*Snabba Cash*, 2011), 163, 168–71, 178, 212, 255
Eccleston, Christopher, 30
Edison Kinetoscope, 87
Egypt, 9
Eiga (Descriptive Pictures; film), 87, 91, 102, 117, 127, 252
Ekman, Hasse, 160–1, 177, 254
Ekyan, André, 55
Election (2004), 137, 253
Element of Crime, The (*Forbrydelsens element*, 1984), 172–3, 177–8, 181, 254
Enemy at the Dead End (2010), 138, 254
Engelstad, Audun, 158–9, 162, 167, 175–6, 179–80
Eppu Normaali (Rock band), 173
Épuration (TV Movie, 2007), 42, 44
Erickson, Glenn, 18, 32–4
Erickson, Todd, 29, 32, 34
Europa (1994), 172, 177, 254
Evil Dead Trap (*Shiryo no wana*, 1988), 125
Exiled (2006), 137, 253

Fabbri, Jacques, 78
Fabian of the Yard (TV Show, 1954–6), 23, 34
Fabian, Robert, 23, 25, 27, 32, 34
Fairbank, John K., 12
Farewell My Lovely (1975) 30
Farewell to Southern Tosa (*Nangoku Tosa o atoni shite*, 1959), 114
Far From Heaven (2002), 198
Farr, Derek, 19–20
Fatal Attraction (1987), 213–14
Faubourg-Montmartre (1931), 4–5, 249
Fay, Jennifer, 179, 184, 191–2, 221, 225, 227, 238, 242
Female Convict Scorpion: Beast Stable (*Joshuu sasori: Kemono-beya*, 1973), 115
Female Convict 701: Scorpion (*Joshuu 70-1-go: Sasori*, 1972), 115
Field, Simon, 133–4
Fifth Republic, 41
Figgis, Mike, 30
Filmen og det Moderne, 161, 180
Film Noir (*Koroshi*, 2000), 128, 252
Fincher, David, 171, 256–7
Fingers (1978), 82
Finland, 156–8, 164–5
Fiorentino, Linda, 226
Fire (*Aag*, 1948), 185, 257
Fisher, Terence, 26, 247–8
Fistful of Dollars, A (1964), 128
Flame and Citron (*Flammen og citronen*, 2008), 163, 177, 254
Flames (*Sholay*, 1975), 189

Flic, Un (*Dirty Money*, 1972), 40, 42, 55–6, 58, 62, 72, 250
Fools' Gold, 74
Forbes, Bryan, 34, 248
Forbes, Jill, 83, 242
Forbidden (1948), 27, 247
Force of Evil (1948), 228
Forshaw, Barry, 176, 178, 181, 242
Fossum, Karin, 168, 176, 181
Fox, Michael J., 201
France, 15, 24, 38, 41–3, 48–9, 52–4, 59–60, 62, 64–5, 68–9, 72–3, 83–4, 112, 148, 184, 206, 222, 225–6, 232, 239–40, 242–3
Frank, Nino, 166, 180
Franklin, Carl, 225, 256
Frears, Stephen, 240, 249, 256
Frederick, Sarah, 98, 111
French Connection, The (1971), 228
French Impressionism, 89
French Resistance, 38, 42–3, 68
Fresson, Bernard, 81
Friedkin, William, 228, 255 257
Friendship that Started a Storm, The (*Arashi o yobu yujo*), 114
Friis, Danes Agnete, 165
Frow, John, 237–8
Frozen River (2008), 232–3, 235
Fukami, Taizo, 99
Fukuyama, Francis, 224, 237–9
Fuller, Samuel, 63, 199
Fulton County, 213, 218
Furukawa, Takumi, 112, 251
Futurism, 88
Futurist Manifesto (1909), 88

Gabin, Jean, 40, 49, 51, 63
Gallagher, Mark, 133–5, 237, 239, 244
Gallagher, Tag, 220, 226, 237–9
Galt, Rosalind, 1, 12
Gandhi, Indira, 189
Gandolfini, James, 206
Gangster No. 1 (2000), 29
Garcia, Nicole, 81, 82, 250
Gardner, William O., 110
Garnett, Tay, 178, 194, 204, 209
GATT, 1
Geller, Theresa L., 133, 135
Gentleman from Bombay (*Bambai Ka Babu*, 1960), 183, 187, 257
Gerard, Jerry, 213
Gere, Richard, 214
Gerhart, Karen M., 110
German Expressionism, 89–90, 158, 210
Germany, 38, 158, 184, 206, 226–7, 232–3, 239–40
Gerow, Aaron, 110, 133–4, 242

Gershon, Gina, 226
Get Carter (1971), 31, 249
Gibson, Mel, 11
Gilbert, Lewis, 27, 247
Gilda (1946), 4–6, 12
Gilliat, Sidney, 24, 247
Giovanni, José, 40, 68–9
Girl and Hyacinths (*Flicka och hyacinter*, 1950), 160–1, 177, 254
Girl Boss: Escape from Reform School (*Sukeban: Kankain*, 1973), 119, 252
Girl Boss: Guerilla (*Sukeban: Gerira*, 1972), 115, 118–19, 252
Girl Boss: Revenge (*Sukeban*, 1973), 119
Girl on the Bridge, The (1951), 222
Girl who Played with Fire, The (*Flickan som lekte med elden*, 2009), 176, 180, 240
Girl with the Dragon Tattoo, The (*Män son hatar kvinnor*, 2009), 11, 155–6, 171, 176, 178, 180, 239, 255, 257
Girl with the Dragon Tattoo, The (2011), 171, 274
Glass Shield, The (1994), 225
Glazer, Jonathan, 29
Glenn, Pierre William, 40
Glitre, Kathrina, 31–2, 34–5, 153, 172, 175, 180–1, 192, 237–8, 241
Godard, Jean-Luc, 40–1, 52–3, 73–4, 76, 79, 83, 175, 199, 203, 243, 245, 250
Godfather, The (1972), 82, 190
Goku Midnight Eye (1959), 121
Golden Marie (*Casque d'or*, 1954), 174, 177
Goldman, Merle, 12
Goodis, David, 40, 194
Good the Bad and the Ugly, The (1966), 128
Good Time Girl (1948), 26–7, 247
Gopalan, Lalitha, 191–2, 242
Gordon, Andrew, 111
Gorky, Maxim, 106
Gorrara, Claire, 83
Goulet, Andrea, 83
Graebner, William, 205, 218
Grand Pardon, Le (1982), 76
Granger, Stewart, 24
Grant, Barry K., 133, 135, 192, 236–9
Great Britain, 9, 15, 17–19, 22, 26, 30–4, 184, 243
Greene, David, 28
Greene, Graham, 24, 32–3
Greene, Naomi, 83, 242
Greer, Jane, 230
Greville, Edmond T., 20, 246, 248
Griffith, Kenneth, 24
Guest House (1959), 187, 257
Gun Crazy: A Woman from Nowhere (2002), 128, 130, 252

Gun Crazy Episode 4: Requiem for a Bodyguard (2003), 131
Gupta, Sanjay, 190, 257
Guy Who Started a Storm, The (*Arashi o yobu otoko*, 1957), 114, 251
Gyangu Eiga (Gangster Films), 102

Haas, Hugo, 222
Haine, La (1995), 67
Hamlet, 129
Hammett, Dashiell, 106, 128
Handphone (2009), 138, 150, 254
Hanley, Jimmy, 25
Hanson, Helen, 31, 34, 191
Hanzai Eiga (Crime Films), 102
Happenings (1980), 137, 253
Happy End (1998), 138, 148, 151, 253
Hara, Kensaku, 94
Hara, Takahito, 125, 252
Hark, Tsui, 136–7, 153, 252–3
Harlow, John, 24, 246
Harry Potter (Films), 198
Hartnell, William, 24
Harvey, Sylvia, 169–70, 181
Hasebe, Yasuharu, 115–16, 252
Hassan, Kamal, 190
Hathaway, Henry, 212
Havre, Le (2012), 174, 178, 255
Hayashi, Kaizo, 119–20, 133, 135, 252
Hayer, Nicholas, 40
Haymen, David, 226
Haynes, Todd, 198
Hayward, Susan, 36, 59–60, 242
Haywire (2011), 240
Hayworth, Rita, 4, 6, 12
Headhunters (2011), 163, 165, 167, 178, 254
Heat (1995), 190, 255
Hedling, Erik, 176, 180
Heibang (black gang), 141
Heidao (black path), 141–2, 144, 148
Heisenberg Uncertainty Principle, The 207, 209
Helgeland, Brian, 11, 256
Hell of a Woman, A, 79
Helpless (2012), 138–9, 254
Henning, Eva, 160–1, 165, 168, 176, 181
Henry, Gregg, 11
Hero (*Nayakan*, 1987), 190, 192, 257
Herrand, Marcel, 45
Herzog, Werner, 240
He Walked By Night (1948), 8, 73
Highsmith, Patricia, 194
Hill, Peter B. E., 110
Hillis, Ken, 141, 153
Hindsight (2011), 138, 151, 254

263

Hirsch, Foster, 113, 134, 214, 217–19, 242
Hitchcock, Alfred, 81, 198, 214
Hitchens, Dolores, 74, 250
Hjort, Mette, 176, 180, 242
Hodges, Mike, 31, 249
Hokkaido, 113, 128
Hollywood Renaissance, The, 193, 199, 202, 223
Hong Kong, 2, 5–6, 11–13, 136–9, 141–2, 144–6, 148, 152–4, 233, 242–3, 245, 252
Hoskins, Bob, 29
Hotel du Nord (1938), 222, 249
House No. 44 (1955), 187, 257
House of Light, 100–1
Howard, Trevor, 19
Howrah Bridge (1958), 187, 257
Ho, Yim, 137, 253
Hughes, Alex, 83, 243
Hughes, Ken, 22, 25, 27, 246–8
Hui, Ann, 136, 253
Human Beast, The (*La bête humaine*, 1938), 174, 178, 249
Hundred Flowers Campaign, The, 5
Hungarian Revolution, The, 9
Hungary, 9, 13
Hunt, Courtney, 232
Hunt, Leon, 133, 135, 232, 243
Hunted (1952), 27–8, 247
Huntington, Lawrence, 20
Hurt, William, 214
Huston, John, 14, 239
Hyangjin, Lee, 139, 153
Hypnotized (2002), 138–9, 254
Hyytiäinen, Janne, 174

I am Waiting (*Ora wa matteru ze*, 1957), 112, 114, 251
Ibsen, Henrik, 158–9, 162
Ibsen, Tancred, 159, 178, 255
Ichikawa, Kon, 113, 251–2
Ichi the Killer (2001), 132
Ijima, Ayako, 89
Ikeda, Toshiharu, 125, 252
Ikiru (1952), 123, 129, 133, 135
Iles, Timothy, 133
Imamura, Shoehei, 107, 251
I Met a Murderer (*Jeg mødte en morder*, 1943), 162, 178, 254
Impasse des deux-anges (1948), 40–1, 43, 45–6, 249
In a Lonely Place (1950), 113
Indochina, 48–9, 52–3
Indridason, Arnaldur, 165
Infernal Affairs (*Mou gaan dou*, 2002), 11, 137, 243, 253
Inoue, Masao, 89
Inoue, Umetsugu, 114, 251

Insdorf, Annette, 59–60, 243
I Saw the Devil (2010), 138–9, 150, 254
Ishibashi, Ryo, 122, 128
Ishihara, Yujiro, 114–16, 134
Ishii, Takashi, 125, 251–2
Indiana Jones (Films), 198
Insomnia (1997), 163, 167, 178, 254, 256
International, The (2009), 227–9, 239
International Monetary Fund, 227
Itatsu, Yuko, 110
Ito, Shunya, 115, 252
Iversen, Gunnar, 159, 176, 179–80, 237–8, 245
Iwama, Sakurako, 99
Izewska, Teresa, 7

Jameson, Frederic, 79, 83, 195, 201, 217, 223, 226, 237–9
Janczar, Tadeusz, 7
Jansen, Marius R., 110
Japan, 22, 85–135, 240–5, 250
Jarvenhelmi, Maria, 174
Jidai-geki (Period Film), 102, 118
Jingfei pian (cops and robbers), 137
Jinming, Song, 233
Ji-woo, 138, 253
Joe Macbeth (1955), 22, 247
John and Irene (*John og Irene*, 1949), 162, 178, 254
Johnny Traitor (*Johnny Gaddaar*, 2007), 191, 257
Johnson, Edward, 12
Jones, Griffith, 24
Jorholt, Eva, 161–2, 180
Jour se lève, Le (1939), 67, 249
Juha (1999), 174–5, 180, 254
Jurassic Park (1993), 198
Just as You Wanted Me (*Sellaisena kuin sinä minut halusit*, 1944), 158, 178, 255

Kaaberbøl, Lene, 165
Kalatozov, Mikhail, 6–7
Kanal (1956), 6–8, 13
Kaplan, David E., 110
Kapoor, Raj, 185–6, 257
Kasdan, Lawrence, 34, 194, 215–16, 225, 255
Kassila, Matti, 157, 178, 255
Kassovitz, Mathieu, 67
Katsudo shashin (Moving Pictures), 87
Kaurismäki, Aki, 156, 170–8, 181, 244, 254–5
Kawabata, Yasunari, 89, 91, 111
Kawajiri, Yoshiaki, 121
Keaney, Michael F., 15, 18, 25, 27–8, 32–4, 243
Keene, Ann T., 13

INDEX

Keitel, Harvey, 82
Kelly, Richard, 240
Kent, Jean, 26
Kersh, Gerald, 2425
Kharbanda, Kulbhushan, 230
Khosla, Raj, 183, 187, 192, 257
Kikukawa, Rei, 130
Killing, The (1956), 113, 191
Killing, The (*Forbrydelsen*, 2007–12), 163, 165, 177, 232, 254
Kinema Junpo, 88, 113, 132
King, Donna, 177, 181, 244
King, George, 24, 27, 247
Kinugasa, Teinosuke, 88–90, 110, 250–1
Kirihara, Donald, 95, 111, 243
Kismet (1943), 184
Kiss Me Deadly (1955), 230
Kiss of Death (1947/1995), 203
Kiss of Death (*Dodskys*), 158, 203
Kitamura, Hiroshi, 111, 241
Kitano, Takeshi, 119, 252
Klein, Christina, 149–50
Klein, Norman M., 142–5, 147, 153–4
Kline, T. J., 83, 243
Kobayashi, Akira, 114–15
Kobayashi, Masahiro, 128
Kobayashi, Masaki, 107–8, 251–2
Kogure, Michiyo, 101, 104
Koivula, Ilkka, 174
Korda, Alexander, 16
Korea, 86, 98, 111, 133, 136, 138–9, 142, 148–54, 191, 242–4, 252–3
Konstantarakos, Myrto, 83, 243
Kowloon, 5–6
Krays, The (1990), 30, 249
Krokstade, Mia, 160–1, 176, 179
Kruger, Otto, 161
Kubrick, Stanley, 113, 191
Kuga, Yoshiko, 103
Kukic, Dejan, 169
Kulick, Don, 176, 181
Kurahara, Kureyoshi, 112, 251
Kuroi Ame (Black Rain), 86
Kuroi Fune (Black Ships), 85
Kurosawa, Akira, 4, 22, 103–7, 111–12, 118, 123, 128–30, 133, 135, 244–5, 251–2
Kushner, Barak, 97, 111
Kushner, David, 13
Kyo, Machiko, 101
Kyoto, 98–9, 113

Labro, Philippe, 84
Ladd, Alan, 70
Landis, Carole, 20
Lang, Fritz, 173
Lange, Sven, 162

Lapidus, Jean, 169, 176, 181
Larsson, Stieg, 165, 167, 171, 176–7, 179–81, 243–4
L'Ascenseur pour l'échafaud (*Elevator to the gallows*, 1958), 40–1, 49, 51, 249
Last Page, The (1952), 26
Last Seduction, The (1994), 214, 226, 236, 256
Lau, Andrew, 11, 243, 253
Laura (1944), 161, 178
Lawrence, D. H., 212
Le Breton, Auguste, 40
Le Chanois, Jean-Paul, 40
Lee, Nikki J. Y., 182, 191
Lee, Sang-il, 132–3
Lee, Susanna, 83
Lehtolainen, Lola, 165, 168, 175, 181
Leo, Melissa, 232
Léon (*The Professional*, 1994), 124
Leonard, Elmore, 194
Lesou, Pierre, 40, 65–6
Let Him Have It (1991), 30
Leung, Wing-fai, 133, 135, 243
Lewis, Jon, 218
Ley Lines (*Nihon Kuroshakai*, 1999), 123–4, 252
Li, Yang, 233, 240
Life without Principles (2011), 137, 253
Lights in the Dusk (*Laitakaupungin valot*, 2006), 172, 174, 178, 255
Lippit, Seiji M., 111
Liu, Lucy, 11
Lilja 4-ever/Lilja 4-ever (2002), 240
Lloyd, Christopher, 201
London After Dark (TV Show), 23, 32, 34
Lone Star (1996), 232
Long Arm of the Law, The (1984), 137, 253
Long Good Friday, The (1979), 29–30, 249
Long Haul, The (1957), 27, 247
Losey, Joseph, 17, 23, 246–7
Lost Weekend, The (1945), 222
Love, A (2007), 138, 253
Love, Massacre (1980), 137, 253
Lower Depths, The (1957), 106, 251
Lower East Side (New York), 105
Luhr, William, 176, 180
Lumet, Sidney, 228, 249, 255
Lumière Cinematograph, 87
Lynch, David, 221, 237–8, 242, 244, 255–6
Lyne, Adrian, 213
Lyotard, Jean-François, 54, 59, 60, 72, 224, 236–7, 239

Macbeth, 22, 190, 247, 257
MacDonald, David, 26, 246–7
MacFarquhar, Roderick, 12
Machido, Hiroko, 101

Mackenzie, James, 29, 249
Madama Butterfly (1904), 3
Mad Detective (2007), 137, 253
Madhumati (1958), 183, 257
Madoff, Bernie, 171
Maiku Hama Trilogy, 126
Mak, Alan, 11, 243, 253
Mak, Johnny, 137, 253
Mäki, Reijo, 165
Makino, Shozo, 87
Malle, Louis, 40–1, 49, 249
Malmström, Lars, 13
Maltby, Richard, 217
Maltese Falcon, The (1941), 14
Mambo Girl (*Man bo nu lang*, 1957), 2, 6
Manchuria, 86, 98
Manèges (1950), 37
Man from Nowhere, The (2010), 138, 250, 252, 254
Mankell, Henning, 165, 168, 176, 181
Mann, Anthony, 8
Mann, Michael, 190, 202, 255
Man on the Brink (1980), 137, 253
Man on the Run (1949), 19
Man Who Wasn't There, The (2001), 194–5, 204–6, 208–11, 213, 218, 226, 256
Man with a Hollow Laugh (*Kenju buraicho: Futeki ni warau otoko*, 1960), 115, 251
Man without Tomorrow (*Kenju buraicho: Asunaki otoko*, 1960), 115, 251
Maqbool (2004), 190, 257
Marcantonio, Carla, 237, 239
Marinetti, Filippo, 88
Mark, Chi-Kwan, 13
Marran, Christine L., 111
Marseilles, 67–9, 73
Martin, Nina K., 219
Martin, Richard, 199–200, 203–4, 217–19, 243
Martin, Steve, 201
Martinez, Dolores, 118, 129–30, 133, 135
Masuda, Toshio, 112, 114, 116, 251
Match-Factory Girl, The (*Tulitikkutehtaan tyttö*, 1990), 172, 178, 255
Matsuda, Shunsui, 87, 119
Mature, Victor, 27
Mazdon, Lucy, 84, 243
Mazumdar, Ranjani, 183, 192, 243
McArthur, Colin, 55, 59–60
McAuliffe, Hinson, 218
McCann, Sean, 211, 218
McClintock, Alex, 223–4, 237–8
McDermott, Charlie, 232
McDonald, Keiko Iwai, 111
McDormand, Frances, 206
McGuigan, Paul, 29
McLeod, Joan, 40

McMillan, James F., 59–60
McQueen, Steve, 76
Mean Streets (1973), 74
Medak, Peter, 30, 225, 249, 256
Mehra, Prakash, 189, 257
Melody of Murder (*Mordets melodi*, 1944), 162, 178, 255
Melville, Jean-Pierre, 37, 40–1, 46, 58–75, 79, 82–4, 128, 245, 249–50
Memories of Murder (*Salinui chueok*, 2003), 11, 138–9, 149–51, 254
Menegaldo, Gilles, 84
'Merry Widow, The', 3
Mes, Tom, 124, 133, 135
Mesrine (2008), 69, 73, 83, 250
Mifune, Toshiro, 103–5, 129
Miike, Takashi, 123–6, 130, 132–3, 135, 243, 252
Miklitsch, Robert, 12, 179, 225, 237
Millennium Trilogy, 165, 167, 171, 177, 181, 244
Miller, Henry, 212
Miller, Lawrence, 18, 32–3
Miller's Crossing (1990), 226, 256
Miller v. California, 213
Mills, Hayley, 28
Mills, John, 23–4
Mishra, Vijay, 192, 243
Mississippi Mermaid (1969), 74
Miss Julie (1888), 162
Mitchell Brothers, The, 213
Mitchum, Robert, 70, 113
Mitsui, Hideo, 93
Miyao, Daisuke, 90, 110, 113, 116, 131, 133–5, 243
Mizoguchi, Kenji, 94–102, 111–12, 243, 251
Mizukubo, Sumiko, 93
Mochizuki, Rokuro, 122, 124, 252
Moen, Arve, 158–9, 176, 179
Moine, Raphaelle, 237–8
Monroe, Marilyn, 21, 212
Montand, Yves, 55–7, 71
Montazel, Pierre, 40
Montmartre, 4–5, 47, 63–4, 74–5, 249
Moodysson, Lucas, 240
Mori, Toshie, 111
Morocco, 48
Mortal Thoughts (1991), 226
Most Terrible Time in My Life, The (*Waga jinsei saiaku no toki*, 1993), 11, 119–21, 133, 135, 252
Moth (*Parwana*, 1971), 191, 257
Mother (2009), 138, 254
Mrsic, Dragomir, 169
Mueller-Stahl, Armin, 228
Mukokuseki (borderless), 113–14, 121
Munch, Edvard, 158–9

Murder My Sweet (1944), 4, 158, 161, 178, 203, 222
Murnau, F. W., 89
Muroga, Atsushi, 128, 130, 252
Murphet, Julian, 144, 154
Murphy, Robert, 18, 23–4, 26–8, 31–4, 242–3
My Brother's Keeper (1948), 19, 248
My Name is Johnny (*Johnny Mera Naam*, 1970), 191, 257
Myth of Sisyphus, The (1942), 210

Nagase, Masatoshi, 120
Nagata, Mitsuo, 99
Nakadai, Tatsuya, 107
Nakagawa, Yoshie, 89
Nakahira, Ko, 114
Nakajima, Sadao, 119, 251–2
Nakakita, Chieko, 104
Naked City, The (1948), 73, 105–6
Nameless Gangster (2012), 138, 254
Naremore, James, 16, 32–3, 137, 139–42, 153, 156, 160–1, 166, 176, 178–80, 199–200, 217–18
Natsume, Rei, 125
Navketan Studio, 186–7
Neale, Steve, 217, 243
Nehru, Jawaharlal, 187–8
Nesbø, Jo, 165
Nestingen, Andrew, 155, 175–7, 180–1, 244
New Deal (Roosevelt), 211, 218
Newell, Mike, 30, 249
Newley, Anthony, 25
New Look of 1947, 47
Newton, Robert, 19
New World, The (2013), 138, 254
New York, 12–13, 31–3, 59–60, 63, 70, 72, 75, 83–4, 105, 111, 134, 153–4, 175–7, 179–81, 191–2, 213, 217–18, 227–8, 232, 236–8, 241–5
Next Room, The (1995), 226
Niagara (1950), 212
Nicholson, Jack, 141, 146, 203, 225
Nieland, Justus, 179, 184, 191–2, 221, 225, 237–8, 242, 244
Night and the City (1950/1992), 16–18, 24–5, 27, 32–3, 203, 248, 256
Nightfall (2012), 138, 253
Night Moves (1975), 199
Nightwatch (*Nattevagten*, 1994), 163, 178, 255
Nikkatsu Noir, 107, 112–18, 120–3, 129, 131, 133–4
Nogueira, Rui, 68, 84
No Mercy (2010), 138, 254
Nomura, Takashi, 112, 116–17, 251–2

No Orchids for Miss Blandish (1948), 22, 248
Nordisk, 163
Normandy, 67, 72
Norsk Film, 163
Norway, 156, 163–4, 167, 232, 239
Nouvelle Vague (New Wave), 41, 73, 84, 120, 137, 173, 199, 203, 242, 244
Novak, Phillip, 142, 146–7, 153–4
Nowhere to Hide (1999), 138, 253
Nummi, Rami, 157–8, 177, 179

Obsession (*Besættelse*, 1944), 162, 177, 254
Obsession (1949), 19, 248
October Man, The (1947), 23, 248
Odds Against Tomorrow (1959), 9
Ogata, Ken, 128
Ogawa, Yukiko, 90
Oka, Joji, 93
Okamoto, Daisuke, 134–5, 251
Okuru, Fumio, 99
Oldboy (2003), 138, 150, 253
Omkara (2006), 190, 257
Once Upon a Time in the West (1968), 128
One False Move (1992), 225
One Night in Mongkok (2004), 137, 253
Only God Forgives (2013), 240
Oplev, Niels Arden, 155, 171, 178, 239, 255, 257
Orbaugh, Sharalyn, 110
Organization for Economic Cooperation and Development, 227
O'Rowe, Catherine, 31, 34
Osaka Elegy (*Naniwa erejii*, 1936), 94–6, 98, 110–11, 251
Oscherwitz, Dayna, 84, 244
Oslo, 158, 176, 179, 181
Osteen, Mark, 225, 237
Osugi, Ren, 123–4, 127
Othello, 190, 257
Out of the Past (1947), 64, 113, 201, 203, 230
Owen, Clive, 227, 229
Overheard (2009), 138, 253
Overheard 2 (2011), 138, 253
Oxide, Pang, 146, 253
Oyama/Onnagata (Female Impersonators), 87
Ozu, Yasojiro, 91–4, 111–13, 241, 251

Page of Madness, A (*Kurutta Ichipeiji*, 1926), 88–90, 250
Palmer, Lorrie, 237, 240
Palmer, R. Barton, 15, 18–19, 32–3, 144, 153–4, 176, 180, 193, 218, 236–7, 244
Palmer, Tim, 84

Paper Flowers (*Kaagaz Ke Phool*, 1959), 186, 257
Parallel Life (2010), 138, 254
Paris, 12, 32, 34, 37, 45–7, 50–1, 53, 59–60, 63, 67–78, 80–2, 84, 158, 160, 174, 220, 242–5
Paris Commune, 174
Park, Chan-wook, 138, 253
Patrick, Nigil, 24
Payback (1999), 11, 256
Peacock, Steven, 177, 181, 244
Pearson, Lester, 9
Pease, Donald, 141, 153
Pellegrin, Raymond, 55
Pellonpää, Matti, 173
Penn, Arthur, 199, 202
People's Republic of China, 5, 12
Pépé le Moko (1937), 114, 249
Perec, Georges, 79
Perry, Matthew, 85–6
Persson, Magnus, 177, 180
Peterson, Lowell, 15
Petley, Julian, 18, 32–3
Pfeil, Fred, 177, 180
Phillips, Alastair, 12, 59–60, 111, 133–4, 244
Pickup (1951), 222
Pickup on South Street (1953), 63
Pietà (2012), 138–9, 254
Pigalle, 63–4
Pigaut, Roger, 40, 250
Pinto, Jerry, 184, 192
Pistol Opera (2001), 131, 252
Pitfall (1948), 214
Place, Janey, 15, 171, 181
Place Vendôme (1998), 73, 81, 250
Point of No Return, The (1993), 125
Polanski, Roman, 34, 137, 142, 146–7, 150, 202, 230
Polars, 37–8
Politique de Redressement, 42
Police Python 357 (1976), 40, 42, 55, 56, 250
Polonsky, Abraham, 228
Pompidou, Georges, 54
Porter, Gregory, 212, 218
Port of Shadows (*Le Quai des brumes*, 1938), 114, 174, 178, 222, 249
Post Box 999 (1958), 187, 257
Postman Always Rings Twice, The (1946), 80, 113, 158–9, 178, 194, 204, 207, 218, 222, 225
Postman Blues (1997), 126–7
Postmodernism, 74, 140, 172, 195, 202, 224, 236–9
Poujoly, Georges, 51
Powrie, Phil, 38, 59–60, 62, 84, 244

Prakash, Gyan, 189, 192, 244, 257
Preston, Robert, 20
Prince, Stephen, 105, 111
Production Code, 94, 198, 211–12
ProKino (Proletariat Cinema), 94
Prophet, A (2008), 11, 83, 250
Protégé (2007), 137, 253
Psycho (1960), 214
PTU (2003), 137, 253
Public Enemies (2009), 202
Public Enemy (2002), 138–9, 250, 253
Puccini, Giacomo, 3
Punished (2011), 138, 253
Pure Film Movement, The (*jun'eigageki undo*), 87–8, 110, 241
Pusher (1996), 163, 178, 255
Pusher 2 (2004), 163, 178, 255
Pusher 3 (2005), 163, 178, 255
Puzzle (2006), 138, 254

Quai des Orfèvres (1947), 39–41, 43–6, 56, 73, 250
Quick Draw Kid, The (*Hayauchi yaro*, 1961), 117

Rabinowitz, Paula, 141, 153
Radio Breaks In, The (*Radio tekee murron*, 1951), 157–8, 178–9, 255
Rage in Harlem, A (1991), 225
Raghavan, Sriram, 191, 257
Raghavendra, M. K., 187, 192, 244
Raid (2003), 163, 178, 255
Raine, Michael, 134
Rainy Dog (*Gokudo Kuroshakai*, 1997), 123–4, 252
Rajakaruna, R. A., 110
Rambling Guitarist (*Guitar o motta wataridori*, 1959), 114
Rapace, Noomi, 155
Rashomon (1950), 22, 106
Ratnam, Mani, 190, 257
Rayns, Tony, 133–4
Razzia sur la chnouff (*Razzia*, 1955), 40–1
Reagan, Ronald, 30
Realisme Noir, 37, 39, 42
Rear Window (1954), 213
Rebhorn, James, 228
Red Harvest, 106, 128
Red Quay (*Akai hatoba*, 1958), 114, 116, 251
Red Rock West (1993), 226, 256
Redvall, Eva, 177, 180
Reed, Carol, 8, 16, 247–8
Refn, Nicholas Winding, 178, 240, 255, 257
Reggiani, Serge, 55, 65
Règlement de comptes, Un, 68
Reilly, James, 232

Reiner, Carl, 201
Renant, Simone, 43
Renoir, Claude, 40, 47
Renoir, Jean, 158, 178, 249
Reservoir Dogs (1992), 190, 225
Revolver (2005), 240
Rich, Jaime, 134
Richards, Jeffrey, 25, 32, 34, 244
Richardson, Natasha, 30
Richet, Jean-François, 69, 83, 250
Richie, Donald, 110, 241
Rieder, John, 222, 237–8
Rififi (1955), 40–1, 49–51, 59–60, 71, 73, 244, 250
Rigoletto (1851), 2
Ritchie, Guy, 240
Rolls, Alistair, 38, 59, 244
Romeo is Bleeding (1993), 225
Ronet, Maurice, 75
Ronin, 107, 121, 129
Roome, Alfred, 19, 248
Roosevelt, Theodore, 86
Ropars, Marie-Claire, 73
Rosier, Caty, 56
Rotterdam (*Reykjavik-Rotterdam*, 2008), 163, 178, 255
Rouse, James, 222
Roy, Arundhati, 237, 240
Roy, Bimal, 183, 257
Rudolph, Alan, 226, 255
Run Lola Run (*Lola Rennt*, 1998), 126
Russo-Japanese War, The, 86–7
Rusty Knife (*Sabita naifu*, 1958), 112–13, 251
Ryokan (Japanese-style inn), 113
Ryuji the Gun Slinger (*Kenju buraicho: Nukiuchi no Ryu*, 1960), 115, 251

Sabu, 123, 126–7, 132
Sacré Cœur, 63–4
Saint-Germain, 45, 47
Saito, Buichi, 114
Sakaguchi, Ango, 109–10
Sakakibara, Seiyo, 92
Sale Guerre, 48
Salt for Svanetia (*Sol' Svanetii*, 1930), 7
Samanta, Shakti, 187, 257
Samoilova, Tatiana, 7
Samouraï, Le (1967), 40, 62, 67, 69–70, 74, 250
Sanae, Takasugi, 99
Sargent, Joseph, 228
Sarkar (2005), 190, 257
Sarkar Raj (2008), 190, 257
Sartre, Jean-Paul, 42, 52, 206, 211
Sato, Barbara, 111
Satya (1998), 190, 257

Sautet, Claude, 66, 73–4, 250
Sawato, Midori, 119
Sayles, John, 232
Scandal (*Shubun*, 1950), 106
Scarface (1983), 191
Scarlet Gang of Asakusa, 91–2, 111
Scarlet Letter, The (2004), 138–9, 150
Schatz, Thomas, 220
Schepelern, Peter, 172, 177, 180–1
Schilling, Mark, 114–15, 134, 244
Schoonover, Karl, 1, 12
Schrader, Paul, 14, 32, 136–7, 153, 157–8, 177, 179, 199, 213–14
Scorsese, Martin, 11, 62, 74–5, 77, 137, 173, 195, 256
Scott, Ridley, 226
Scruggs, Charles, 141, 153
Searle, Francis, 20, 247
Seberg, Jean, 52
Secessionist Building and its Surroundings (1923), 92
Secret (2009), 138–9, 253
Secret, The (1979), 136
Secret Reunion (2010), 138, 151, 254
Sellier, Genevieve, 84, 244
Selznick, David O., 16
Seoul, 151, 153, 242
Série noire (1979), 37, 39–40, 42, 55–6, 58, 60, 62, 65, 68, 73, 79–80, 194, 250
Serpico (1973), 228
Servais, Jean, 49
Seven Days (2007), 138–9, 254
Seven Days to Noon (1950), 20
Seventh Seal, The (1957), 6, 8–9, 13
Sex Maniacs (*Aiyoku ni kuru chijin*), 98
Sexy Beast (2000), 29
Shadows in Paradise (*Varjoja paratiisissa*, 1986), 172, 178, 255
Shalhoub, Tony, 206
Shallow Grave (1994), 226
Shashin Shosetsu (Photographic Fiction), 98, 111
Shaviro, Steven, 237, 240
Shelley, Barbara, 27
Shiganoya, Benkei, 94, 99
Shiina, Kippei, 123
Shimura, Takashi, 103–4
Shin, Chi-Yun, 133–5, 154, 239
Shinbashi, 87
Shindo, Eitaro, 95, 99
Shinjuku Incident (2009), 137, 253
Shinjuku Triad Society (*Shinjuku Kuroshakai: Chaina Mafia Senso*, 1995), 123–4, 252
Shinko Shashin (New Photography), 92
Shishido, Jo, 113, 115–17, 120, 127, 132, 134

Shop at Sly Corner, The (1946), 24
Shvorin, Alexander, 7
Side Effects (2013), 198
Sidel, Mark, 192
Sidetracked (*Villospar*), 168, 181
Signoret, Simone, 37, 44–5, 56, 59–60, 242
Sijia, Deng, 2–4
Silenced (2011), 138, 254
Silver, Alain, 31–4, 153, 177, 179, 199, 217–18
Silver City (2004), 232
Simonin, Albert, 40
Sinai Peninsula, 9
Singer, Bryan, 190, 256
Singh, Navdeep, 230
Sippy, Ramesh, 189, 192, 257
Sisters of Gion (*Gion no* shimai, 1936), 94, 98, 110, 251
Six Feet Under (*Manorama*, 2007), 230
Sjøberg, Alf, 160, 178, 254
Sjöwall, Maj, 164–5
Slaughter Gun (*Minagoroshi no kenju*, 1963), 116, 252
Slaymaker, Douglas N., 109, 111
Sleeping Tiger, The (1954), 23, 30
Slim Susie (*Smala Sussie*, 2003), 163, 168, 178, 255
Small Sad World of Sammy Lee, The (1963), 25
Smedley, Nick, 217
Smith, Carrie Lee, 177, 181
Smith, Murray, 196, 198, 217, 243
Smith, Simon C., 13
Snake of June, A (*Rokugatsu no hebi*, 2002), 132, 238, 240, 252
Sobchack, Vivian, 67, 84, 143, 168–70, 177, 181, 241
Soderbergh, Steven, 198, 240, 245
Someone to Watch Over Me (1987), 226
Southland Tales (2006), 240
South/Southeast Asia, 86, 184
Sparrow (2008), 137, 253
Spicer, Andrew, 28, 32–4, 59–60, 84, 184, 191–2, 237–9, 245
Spider Forest (2004), 138, 250, 254
Spiral (*Engrenages*, TV series, 2005–), 232
Spivs (2003), 30
Stagecoach (1939), 201
Staiger, Janet, 217
Stairway to the Distant Past, The (*Harukana jidai no kaidan o*, 1995), 120, 252
Star Wars (1977), 76
Steeman, S. A., 40
Stephens, Chuck, 134, 221, 237–8
Stockholm Noir Trilogy, 169
Stokes, Melvyn, 4, 12
Stormy Monday (1989), 29–30

Storper, Michael, 197, 217
Story of a Crime (*Roman om ett brott*), 164
Strange Affair, The (1968), 28
Stranger, The, 210–11
Stray Cat Rock: Delinquent Girl Boss (*Nora-neko rokku: onna bancho*, 1970), 115, 252
Stray Cat Rock: Sex Hunter (*Nora-neko rokku: sex hunter*), 115, 252
Stray Dog (*Nora inu*, 1949), 104, 106, 109, 123, 129, 251
Street of Shame (*Akasen chitai*, 1956), 94, 101–2, 110, 251
Street with Train (1922), 92
Storper, Michael, 197, 217
Strindberg, August, 162, 178
Stringers, Julian, 133–4, 182, 191, 244
Studer, Carl, 57
Sublette, Ned, 12
Suez Canal, 9
Suez Crisis, 9, 13
Sugimoto, Miki, 118–19
Sulik, Boleslaw, 13
Sunset Blvd. (1950), 120, 186
Suomi-filmi, 163
Supreme Commander of Allied Powers (SCAP), 102
Surrealism, 89, 126, 221
Suvakci, Mahmut, 169
Suzuki, Norifumi, 119
Suzuki, Seijun, 107, 112, 116–17, 131–4, 251–2
Svensk Filmindustri, 163
Swaim, Bob, 74, 250
Swaroop, Jyoti, 191, 257
Sweden, 156, 160, 163–4, 169–70, 232, 239–40
Sylvester, William, 28
Sympathy for Lady Vengeance (2005), 138–9, 253
Sympathy for Mr. Vengeance (2002), 138–9, 253

Taguchi, Tomorrowo, 123–4, 126
Taine, Hyppolyte, 178
Taiwan, 78, 87, 123–4, 135
Take Aim at the Police Van (*Sona gososha wo nerae: 'Jusango taihisen' yori*, 1960), 112, 251
Takeshi, Caesar, 124, 132
Taking of Pelham 123, The (1974), 228
Tale of Two Sisters, A (2003), 138, 150, 253
Tam, Patrick, 137, 253
Tanaka, Hiroyuki, 123, 126
Tanaka, Kinuyo, 92, 99
Tanaka, Kogai, 98
Tanaka, Yuki, 111

Tanazaki, Jun'inchiro, 87
Tang, Zhaoyang, 233
Tansman, Alan, 97, 111
Tarantino, Quentin, 29, 126, 190–1, 221, 225, 237–8
Tarkovsky, Andrei, 172–3
Tassone, Aldo, 84
Tattooed Life (Irezumi ichidai, 1965), 117, 251
Taxi Driver (1954), 187, 257
Taxi Driver (1976), 74, 76, 137, 199
Teague, Colin, 30
Telotte, J. P., 15–16, 32–3
Tennessee, 213
Terajima, Susumu, 127, 132
Tetsuo, the Iron Man (1989), 127
Tetzlaff, Ted, 27
Thatcher, Margaret, 29–31
They Made Me a Fugitive (1947), 19, 24
Thieves, The (2012), 138, 151, 254
Thin Man, The (1934), 78
Thirard, Armand, 40
Third Man, The (1949), 8, 16–17
Thirst (Pyaasa, 1957), 186, 257
This Gun for Hire (1942), 69–70, 237
Thompson, Jim, 40, 79–80, 194
Thompson, J. Lee, 21, 28, 31, 35, 248
Thompson, Kristin, 217
Thomsen, Ulrich, 229
Thorns (Kaante, 2002), 190, 257
Thornton, Billy Bob, 205
Thorsen, Nils, 173, 177, 181
Tianlin, Wang, 2
Tierney, Gene, 16
Tiger Bay (1959), 28
Tilly, Jennifer, 226
Timsit, Patrick, 79
Tirez sur le pianiste (Shoot the piano player, 1960), 40–1, 51, 53, 60, 74, 250
Toback, James, 82
To Catch a Thief (1955), 81
Todorov, Tzevtan, 166, 177, 180
To, Johnny, 137, 253
Tokyo, 87–8, 91–2, 96, 103–5, 113–14, 120, 123, 125, 127, 129
Tokyo Asahi Shimbun, 87
Tokyo Fist (1995), 240
Tokyo Twilight (Tokyo boshoku, 1957), 113
Torment (Hets, 1944), 160, 178, 254
To Sleep so as to Dream (Yume miru yoni nemuritai, 1986), 119, 134
Touchez pas au Grisbi (1954), 40–1, 66, 71, 74, 250
Touch of Evil (1958), 14, 113, 153, 199, 22
Tourneur, Jacques, 63–4, 84, 201, 214, 230
Tourneur, Maurice, 40, 45, 249
Tournier, Jean, 40

Towne, Robert, 202
Trap, The (Wana, 1996), 120, 252
Treaty of Portsmouth, The (1905), 86
Triad Election (2006), 137, 253
Trintingant, Marie, 79
Trou, Le (1960), 69, 250
Truffaut, François, 40–1, 48, 52, 59–60, 65, 73–4, 80, 199, 243, 250
Tsuen Wan, 5
Tsukamoto, Shinya, 127, 132, 238, 240, 252
Tsunoda, Tomomi, 99
Tsutsumi, Shin'ichi, 126–7
Tuck, Greg, 31–2, 34–5, 153, 172, 175, 180–1, 192, 221–2, 237–8, 240–1
Tulia, Teuvo, 158, 178, 255
Tunisia, 48, 75
Turner, Kathleen, 214–15
Tuttle, Frank, 69
Twentieth Century-Fox, 16
Two Jakes, The (1990), 203
Two Suspicious Characters (To mistenklige personer, 1950), 159, 178, 255
Tykwer, Tom, 126, 227–8

UFO Scare, 209
Ugetsu Monogatari (The Lust of the White Serpent), 87
Umemura, Yoko, 99
UN Convention on the Rights of the Child, 170
Unforgiven (1991), 201
Unger, Deborah Kerr, 11
United Nations, 9, 13, 227
Unit One (Rejseholdet, TV series, 2000–4), 163, 165, 178, 255
Upham, Misty, 232
Ushihara, Yoichi, 116, 251
Ushinawareta (lost decade), 125
US Immigration Act (1924), 88
US Occupation of Japan, 102–3, 111
Usual Suspects, The (1995), 190, 256

Vaananen Kari, 173
Vagabond, The (Awara, 1951), 185, 257
Vampyr (1932), 158
Vanel, Charles, 44
Varela, Matias, 169
Vares: Private Eye (Vares, 2004), 163, 165, 178, 255
Varma, Ram Gopal, 190, 257
Vasudevan, Ravi, 183, 192, 245
Velvet Hustler (Kurenai no nagareboshi, 1967), 116
Vengeance (2009), 137, 253
Ventura, Lino, 55
Verdi, Giuseppe, 2

Vernet, Marc, 141, 152–4, 177, 180
Vertigo (1958), 214
Vierikko, Vesa, 173
Villain (*Akunin*, 2010), 132
Vincendeau, Ginette, 29, 32, 34, 37, 39, 58–60, 63, 65–6, 84, 222, 238, 245
Vint, Sherryl, 236, 238
Violent Cop (*Sono otoko, kyobo ni tsuki*, 1989), 119, 252
Virdi, Jyotika, 183, 192
Virilio, Paul, 55, 59–60
Voice of a Murderer (2007), 138, 254
Volonte, Gian-Maria, 57
von Trier, Lars, 156, 171–8, 181, 241, 243, 254
V2: Dead Angel (*V2: Jäästynyt enkeli*, 2007), 163, 178, 255

Wachowskis, The, 226
Wada-Marciano, Mitsuyo, 110, 245
Wahlöö, Per, 164–5
Wajda, Andrzej, 6–7, 13
Wakao, Ayako, 101
Walker, Deborah, 38, 59, 244
Wall, The (*Deewar*, 1975), 189, 257
Wallander, Kurt, 165
Wallengren, Ann-Kristin, 176, 178
Wang, Baoqiang, 234
Wang, Shuangbao, 233
Wanted for Murder, 20
Ward, Elisabeth, 153, 199, 217–18
Warner, Jack, 19, 25
Warsaw Uprising, 7
Warshow, Robert, 220
Washburn, Dennis, 110, 134, 245
Watanabe, Fumio, 107
Watari, Tetsuya, 116
Waterloo Road (1945), 24
Watts, Naomi, 227
Webb, Clifton, 161
Weinstock, S. Alexander, 13
Welles, Orson, 14, 16–17, 113, 120, 153, 173, 191, 199, 222
Whistle Down the Wind (1961), 34
Wicked Woman (1953), 222
Widmark, Richard, 16–17
Wiggins-Fernandez, Wilhelmenia, 78
Wilder, Billy, 63, 120, 177, 186, 194, 204, 214
Wild Strawberries (1957), 6
Wild, Wild Rose, The (*Yau mooi gwai ji luen*, 1960), 2–3, 5–6

Williams, James S., 83, 243
Window, The (1949), 27
Wire, The (2002–8, TV series), 232
Wise, Robert, 9
Woll, Josephine, 13
Wollen, Peter, 24, 32, 34
Woman and Eros (*Kvinnen og eros*), 159, 176, 179
Woman in Question, The (1950), 22
Women in Cages (1971), 115
Women in the Night (1948), 94, 99–101, 251
Women of the Night (*Yoru no onnatchi*, 1948), 110–11
World Bank, 227
World Trade Organization, 1, 227
Wottitz, Walter, 40

Yacavone, Peter A., 106, 111
Yakuza, 4, 87, 102–11, 115, 117–19, 122–4, 126–7, 132, 152
Yamada, Isuzu, 94, 99
Yamamoto, Reizaburo, 103, 106
Yi, Lixiang, 233
Yasui, Nakaji, 92
Yellow Balloon, The (1953), 28
Yellow Sea, The (2010), 138, 150, 254
Yeouido Island (2010), 138, 253
Yield to the Night (1956), 21, 26, 30
Yojimbo (1961), 106–7, 128–30
Yokohama, 85, 113, 120
Yokohama, Mike, 120
Yokosuka, 115
Yonekura, Ryoko, 128
York, Michael, 28
Yorozu Choho (Universal Morning Report), 88
Yoshimoto, Mitsuhiro, 111, 245
Youth of the Beast (*Yaju no seishun*, 1963), 116, 251
You've Gotten Into My Blood (*Olet mennyt minun vereeni*, 1956), 158, 178, 255
Yung, Peter, 136, 253

Zedong, Mao, 5
Zemeckis, Robert, 201
Zero Woman: Red Handcuffs (*Zeroka no onna: Akai wappa*, 1974), 119, 125
Zhang, Yang, 3
Zhou, En-lai, 5
Žižek, Slavoj, 148–9, 154
Zola, Émile, 162, 178

EU representative:
Easy Access System Europe
Mustamäe tee 50, 10621 Tallinn, Estonia
Gpsr.requests@easproject.com

www.ingramcontent.com/pod-product-compliance
Lightning Source LLC
Chambersburg PA
CBHW061707300426
44115CB00014B/2597